MW01484712

# T R I P W I R E

A Novel by
Robert Adams

Copyright © 1999 by Robert Adams
All rights reserved

LIBRARY OF CONGRESS CATALOGING IN PUBLICATION DATA
Adams, Robert
Tripwire / by Robert Adams

ISBN 978-0-6151-8337-4
2007

Published by Robert Adams
Edited by Kent R Adams and Robert M Adams
–Set in Times New Roman–
Cover design by Robert Adams

Without limiting the rights under copyright reserved above, no part of this publication may be reproduced, stored in or introduced into a retrieval system, or transmitted, in any form or by any means (electronic, mechanical, photocopying, recording or otherwise), without the prior written permission of the owner of this book.

**To Ed**

*...may he be riding high in the sky*

# A CKNOWLEDGMENTS

As a child, my mom and dad would load my brother and I up several times a year to travel to their hometown of Winfield, a small farming community above St. Louis, Missouri. A vivid memory that I cherish from those visits was at the end of each day when my grandma would sit at her old oaken desk in the dining room and record the day's activities. It was a comfort to me then, knowing that my time with her was important enough to write about. Years later, in that faraway land called Vietnam, it seemed the natural thing to do to pick up my own pen and begin chronicling my daily adventures, both the good and the bad, which I continue to do to this day. In 1997, in the midst of my struggle with PTSD, I decided to pick up my pen in a new light, to write of my tour in Nam and the events thereafter as an attempt to find a solution to my enigma. Thus I was able to glean from the many journals from my past the content of this story. So be assured, the pages of *Tripwire* are certainly, and completely, true.

Throughout *Tripwire* you will see letters that I had sent to my folks from Vietnam which they had saved and returned to me. These letters are recorded verbatim to add insight to the mindset of a 19 year old soldier.

I wish to thank my awesome wife, Donna, for her unwavering support in this and any endeavor I may take on. She has filled my life with so many good things, and I cherish each moment that I am with her. Also I would like to express my deepest appreciation to my older brother and friend, Kent, who took on with zeal the task of editing my book with the eye of the impeccable teacher that he is.

Then there are family and friends who make it all worthwhile. My mom and dad, Virginia and Clifford, my new adoptive parents Frank and Elga, our children, Jenn and Stef, Sunny and Chad, Nicki and Haley, Craig and Tony, and our growing flock of grandchildren– Lexi, Austin, Taylor, Cristina, Bryce, Jake, Josie, and Gabe. And last, but in no way least, to all of my good friends with the Army Corps of Engineers in Rock Island, Illinois, of which there are too many to mention here (except for Karl).

Finally, a special thanks to my good friend Jim Dobson, who has helped me in more ways than he will ever realize. Thank you, Jim.

Robert Adams.
December, 2007

# FOREWORD

✎...*6:29 p.m., Wednesday, May 30, 1984, outside of Oquawka, Illinois...The horizon stretched* in front of me forever. Fourteen miles ahead and still out of sight was my destination, Burlington, Iowa, where a hot shower and dinner waited. Seven miles behind me I'd left the small river town of Oquawka, nestled just above Lock and Dam 18 on the Mississippi River, where I'd been based out of all week. The afternoon was hot for the middle of spring, but that was okay. I'd been looking forward to this run to clear out the cobwebs and reflect on the last couple of weeks. *Got to figure out a way to get off the road,* I thought, pounding through a dust cloud kicked up by a passing truck. *My son's over a year old now, and surveying the river week after week is beginning to take its toll on the home front.* I pulled up beside a fence gate, reaching behind one of the brace posts to grab a plastic water cup I'd stashed on the way to the job site this morning. *This road life is a lot like the missions in The Nam,* I thought, removing the cellophane and gulping down most of the water. *Stand-down on the weekends, then hit the bush again. It's almost like...* –I splashed the rest of the water on my face and tossed the cup down while resuming a steady gait– *...it's almost like I'm trying to recreate my Nam tour.* Ahead of me fields of corn and soy beans were just beginning their short journey toward harvest season. Above the unfolding drama my goal still lay hidden beneath the bobbing blue horizon. *...almost like recreating my Nam tour,* I reflected. *Don't make sense. Why in the world, would I want to do that?...* ✎

# THE TRAIL
## PART I

Thursday, October 22, 1970, Day 1 / 364 days to DEROS
—arrival—

**M**y heart pounds. I swallow hard. Sound explodes. Lights flash. Shouts, curses and a swell of steamy heat push through the opening hatch. My eyes rivet onto a soldier appearing in the opening. Sergeant bars clamp to fatigues starched hard as his face, chiseled black and glistening. An ominous sneer is smeared below eyes narrow and streaked red that rake over us as he bends forward and points a powerful arm into the darkness.

"MOVE OUT!" Legs stiff from the long flight I push into a tangle of GI's and ride the wave to the exit where I find my flight attendant squeezed behind our tormentor. Our eyes meet, and she offers me a last look of hope.

*You said that nothing was going on!…that nothing….* I step outside and her sweet essence withers in an atmosphere reeking jet fuel and some foul thing burnt and rancid. I force a breath, peering into a temporal world of darting shadows and strange sounds until a shout from behind push leaden legs toward earth, and all of the months of agonizing about this moment fall upon me, and my legs tremble as I place my feet upon...

Vietnam.

1

\*       \*       \*

I wrap a clammy hand around one of the iron slats welded over my bus window as we leave Cam Rahn Bay International Airport behind and pull onto a cracked asphalt road. The dingy headlights seem unable to penetrate the thick night as we begin to worm through an endless grind of putting mopeds, ancient bicycles and two-wheeled carts. Beside our convoy rush a throng of little people with dark piercing eyes and thin yellow flesh stretched over high cheekbones and sallow foreheads, the tops of which are covered with thick shocks of shiny, jet-black hair. To my Midwest eyes they resemble the toy china dolls with the bobbing heads you'd throw down a couple bucks for at a carnival back home. And to my Midwest ears their language sounds like nothing more than crows cackling over road kill. Some pause to stare, but most ignore us as the incandescent streetlights cast an eerie hue onto this new and primitive world.

We soon leave Cam Rahn's shantytown behind, and I will my body to relax as the convoy rumbles into open country.

I shoot up as I detect the distant rattle of machine gun fire.

"Bill, you hear that?" I stare into the night until a gust of dusty wind snaps my eyes shut, and I slump back into my seat.

\*       \*       \*

I opened my eyes, squinting into a bright light shining in front of the bus. Bill was asleep, purring softly over the idling diesel engine as a familiar odor I couldn't quite place accompanied a sultry breeze sifting through the window. After a minute we continued, passing through two rows of concertina wire and a towering chain link fence with more wire on top. Bill sat up as the engine shut off and the door opened.

"Form up, men. We ain't got all day!" shouted a pudgy sergeant dealing out orders in front of a World War II vintage barrack.

"You'd think we was in damn Basic again," said a voice from behind as we hurried out the bus.

Gathering into a crude formation, the sergeant began rattling out names, "Adams, Robert M., Barrack 1. Andrews, William R., Barrack 1—" Why he didn't assign all names between A through whatever to a particular barrack was beyond me. But, being at the front of the alphabet I didn't linger on it; at least Bill and I were still together. Searching through the pile of duffel bags,

2

we located ours and, entering our barrack, threw them beside a bunk toward the rear and crashed.

Friday, October 23, 1970, Day 2 / 363 to DEROS
—hide and seek—

"Formation at 0600!" The shout opened my eyes to a stream of sunshine pouring through an open window. I pushed my head from my pillow and swung my legs off the bed, my ears catching a steady drone coming from a group of GI's by the front door. Wiping the sleep out of my eyes I dropped to the floor and approached the source of their curiosity– a large map of South Vietnam. It was painted in bright colors against a glossy white background with bold lines dividing the country into four military regions: the I and II CORP to the north and the III and IV CORP taking the southern half. Running along the coast of the South China Sea were the military installations, their division emblems pinned next to the names. It didn't take long to learn that nobody wanted to end up near the northern border, the DMZ: Demilitarized Zone. Some said it was like getting a death penalty and, for all I knew, it was.

"Pretty big fucking place, huh?" Tom Bartlett, from my AIT platoon, said as he walked up behind me.

"Looks like we're pretty far south. Too bad we can't be stationed here."

"Eleven Bravo? Shit, ain't no action here. Why, I hear this is like an R&R center." –Bartlett's grin widened– "Enjoy it while you can, Adams, and remember, only 364 killing days left to fucking DEROS." The military acronym for "Date of Expected Return from Over Seas", was the day we were all waiting for, even now.

Bill, finally getting his boots on, joined us as we headed out the door.

Outside, the air was cool, contrasting with last evening when we had sweated ourselves to sleep. *Wow!* –beyond the front gate stretched a gleam of turquoise that continued to the horizon– *the ocean!* I found a spot next to Bill and scanned the gravel lane running down the middle of the Replacement Center. A dozen two-story whitewashed barracks sat in rigid formation, indifferent to the explosion of rich green hues drenching their tropical backdrop. The barracks were similar to the ones I had stayed at in Fort Lewis, Washington, except unlike the manicured lawns and painted rocks that lined the walkways in the stateside base, these looked unkempt, reminding me of the dozens of neglected children we had passed on our trip from the airport.

3

"Form up, men!" bellowed a much heavier sergeant than the one that had greeted us upon our arrival. "You ladies already forget how to act like soldiers? Now form up in ranks of four. Dress right...DRESS!" In spite of the cool morning, beads of sweat were forming on the fat sergeant's forehead as we spaced ourselves, wondering where this would lead. He studied his clipboard for a full minute before looking up as if to convey to us that he was, the "Man".

"Gentlemen, welcome to the Republic of South Vietnam. You are currently assigned to the Cam Rahn Bay Replacement Center. This will be your duty station until orders come down for your unit transfer." –he paused to brush some lint off his heavily starched fatigue shirt– "Expect three to five days for your orders to come down. So, gentlemen, *be* patient. Formation is 0700, 1300 and 1800 hours. At these times I will hand out the latest release of shipping orders as they come down from S-1. If your name is called, report to CQ for instruction on deployment to your unit. If your name is not called..." – a smiling pause– "...you will remain in formation to receive detail assignment." A thick drop of sweat slid down his nose, exploding on his clipboard. He smeared it into the paper before clipping off a dozen names. "You men are dismissed. The rest close ranks and count off in groups of eight."

The sergeant dished out details as if passing out lollipops to a bunch of homeless kids– from mopping to KP to painting barracks. After instructing each group where to report, I headed out with seven others for our assigned area, but nearing our destination, members of our group began to drop out, one by one. Within a few minutes only three remained, all, coincidentally, from my platoon at Fort Lewis.

"Why'd everyone split?" Kerry Harwick asked, watching the last guy to drop out disappear behind a nearby barrack.

"Well," I shrugged, "I don't know where *they* went, but it looks better 'n the direction *we're* heading."

"Time to employ some of our 'Escape and Evasion' training?" Bartlett inquired, winking at me. "Just doncha lead the way this time, huh, Adams?" I smiled at our private joke as we began walking toward the shadows beside Barrack 9. Bartlett was one of the unfortunates on my team as I had led them into the dark forested recesses of Fort Lewis' backcountry. Our goal had been simple enough– escape from a simulated POW camp and find our way to our "safety zone", a couple of trucks parked somewhere in the middle of the Washington *State rain forest.* ...

✎...*At dusk they* let us go. Our Company was so pumped with threats of mistreatment if captured by the mock VC, we took off like a hoard of mad turkeys. With a blast of adrenaline I bolted across a clearing in front of the POW compound only to run headlong into a swollen creek– expecting I guess to skim right across the water's surface. Bartlett and the other two on my team had to drag me out of the icy chest-deep water. With no flashlight or compass and freezing our butts off we groped in the dark for four hours before finally spotting a pinpoint of light in the distance. Confident our travail was nearing an end the four of us sped toward the welcoming glow. Almost there, a fierce voice shouted out of the darkness, "HIT THE DIRT, ASSHOLES!" Our hopes vanished as we realized I had led my cold, wet and exhausted band in a huge circle– we were right back *where we started.* ...✑

...*Skirting the barrack,* we found refuge at the USO and spent the remainder of the morning in its Rec Room playing ping-pong and pool. Concentrating on a bank shot, I recalled the words the DI had shouted at us after that failed E&E course. "Men, when you get to Vietnam, Charlie will *not* be so accommodating!" Charlie, what is he really like? As menacing as that DI had claimed, or just another sap like me wanting to get back home? The way he talked, Charlie lived in a rain-soaked hole, ate dirt, drank blood and had only one desire burned into his brain– *KILL*!

Saturday, October 24, 1970, Day 3 / 362 to DEROS
—solace in the sea—

"Come on, Bill, the water's great!" The sensation of a million beads of salty brine was raking away the tremendous stress of the past few days. "Hey! Come on! This is KP...Vietnam style!" When I was a kid, I'd been to the Gulf of Mexico. The memory of that trip came flooding back as I pushed seaward: the salty air, the white sand, the foaming surf and unimaginable size of the water before me. The power of these waves, though *–explosive!*– a mighty engine of eternal motion dissolving away whatever lay in its path. This was fun!

"But I can't swim and you don't know what's out 'dere!" Bill sat by the surf's edge, satisfied with the warm water lapping at his feet.

I pointed a dripping finger towards the mountains beyond the Replacement Center. "Can't be any worse than what's out there!"

"You go ahead!" –he skipped a shell into the surf– "But we better not stay too long! You know we shoulda waited for Bartl–" The cool rush of a wave engulfed Bill's words as I dove beneath it and pulled myself to the silky bottom. The churning waves clouded the water, so I swam blind, running the rippled silica *between my fingers....*

✎....*June, 1963, Cottage Grove, East Moline, Illinois...One more trip should do it,* I thought while hoisting the trimmed trunk of a sumac tree onto a huge forked limb of a massive burr oak tree. Danny and I had spent our first week of summer vacation cutting the tree-like plants growing abundantly in the slough down the street. *Yep, this is gonna be the best summer yet!*

"Hey, Danny, when we get this done, we could sleep in this thing!"

"How 'bout tonight?!" Danny enticed, lashing the log in place. "After dark, let's sneak over here."

I liked his idea– a perfect chance to practice for Africa. It was our plan that, when we turned eighteen, we'd take a canoe down the Mississippi River to New Orleans –the Miss was just a few blocks away– and sneak aboard a freighter heading for Africa. Once near its coast, we'd jump off with our canoe and head for shore to begin a new life, like our hero, "Tarzan of the Apes". But first, we had a lot of planning to do: weapons, canoe, tools, food, clothing– although a loincloth was all we'd need. All had to be bought and stored safely, and secretly, away. It was our chance for true freedom, to live in the untamed heart of *the African Congo....*✐

...*AEEEEEEEE! silently rips* from me as pain slides like a branding iron from neck to tailbone. I struggle to stand, hacking salt water from my lungs as I jerk up my head. Nothing. Looking shoreward, Bill's gangly form sits by the water's edge, picking up and blowing sea froth as you would a dried dandelion. I whip my head around. What looks like some miniature sea-creature from a Jules Verne novel floats a few feet in front of me. I see more nearby. *Maybe I'd better* –I connect the creatures with the pain stabbing my spine– *get* –I begin a furious water sprint toward shore– *outta here!*

Bill looks at me blankly. "Out so–"

"My back!" –I spin and point in one motion– "What do you see?!"

"Nut'n'," he rasps, "just a red streak running down the middle. Looks like some kinda rash." –he peers closer– "What happened out 'dere? Electric eel get cha?"

"I dunno. Some kinda...blobs like...jellyfish! Gotta be! Man, I didn't know they could sting like that...like a thousand bee stings all at once!" –I attempt to massage my back– "That's the last time I'll get in that oversized swimming pool."

"At least till next time," Bill says with a grin. His smile fades as the reverberation of a faraway explosion jerks our heads around. The blast seems to signal that our adventures for the day are at an end, and we head back to our barrack.

Sunday, October 25, 1970, Day 4 / 361 to DEROS
—under the Southern Cross—

It was drizzling. Clouds hung low and gray, pressing our spirits as we huddled in our field jackets at morning formation. *Crazy place, blazing heat yesterday, then this.* Besides my back aching from yesterday's misadventure, my thumb throbbed. The swelling still had not gone down much. Nine days ago I had been playing one on one with Toad, a buddy of mine from home. Jumping for a rebound, I had rammed my right thumb into the ball. "Hey, Blondie," Toad croaked as I doubled-over and squeezed my thumb, "maybe that'll keep ya outta Vietnam."

"I doubt it," I grimaced. "They'd probably ship me over in a wheelchair."

Formation began as usual, the fat E-6 chanting out names as if at a high school graduation. *Never did have a chance.* I tensed my muscles to generate some body heat. *Classified 1A, lottery number 132...not a chance.* The E-6 paused to chew on an unfortunate GI who couldn't keep in a chuckle in response to his buddy's remark. *Why couldn't this war of ended before I graduated? But no way. It just had to get worse after that Tet thing...whatever that was. Shoulda stuck it out in college.* I smiled to myself, conscious of the risk of incurring the wrath of the hard-core E-6. I knew the answer to that. After I had graduated in '68 and in spite of my desire to get into the commercial art field, I wasn't ready for more classroom crap. I thought I'd suffered there enough and needed a big break. *Man, did I ever get one.* –I continued to smile– *Lifting weights and shooting hoops with Alhgren when I*

7

*shoulda been hard at it with the books. Then dropping out after three months. Man, am I stupid.*

"Dismissed!" The fat sergeant went his way and we went ours, easily escaping to the sanctuary of the USO.

The news came at the 1300 formation. Tomorrow morning, Company D-3-3 would transfer to Chu Lai, home of the American Division! Scanning the map, I breathed a sigh of relief. We wouldn't be in the DMZ. Instead, our new home would be near the southern border of the I Corp, fifty miles south of a city called Da Nang.

*Mom and Dad and Kent,*         *Sunday, October 25, 1970, 3:30 pm*

*Greetings from Sunny Vietnam! I've been here 4 days now and we're just waiting around to be shipped off to our unit. We're doing just what we've been doing the past week at Ft. Lewis - <u>nothing</u>. We have 3 formations a day. 7 - 1 - 6 pm to give out shipping orders and then assign details the rest of the day. Well, this is like an advance course on escape and evasion. After we're herded out for a detail, it's our prime objective to escape, <u>then</u> evade. I've been lucky so far where I haven't had a detail yet! I usually hang out at the USO. Pool tables, ping pong, just about everything you need. They've got showers and sinks. So it's not bad at all. We're in the cooling down part of the year now. Dry and humid. Very. But not nearly as bad as I thought. I haven't got my permanent address yet - I'll have it next letter. Me and most of my old Co. D-3-3 will be stationed in Chu Lai (CHEW-LIE) up north a ways. Americal Division. Probably mechanized. Not bad at all. I'm thankful I am still with all my friends. We left Fort Lewis Thurs. morn. 10 am. We were lucky for on our 22 hour flight we were to stop in Hawaii, Wake Islands and Okanowa Islands. In Hawaii it was 78 degrees -beautiful- I didn't imagine how good it looked. We were there an hour so we roamed the airport in our baggy fatigues. I had already read all my books so I looked for another good selections (bought "Sirens of Titan," science fiction, by same author of "Cat's Cradle"). We rode Trans Am Airlines, a very big one, almost like a 747. Wow! We actually got to see 3 movies on board. "Marooned" (I already saw it at Parkway Theater), "On a Clear Day You Can See Forever" (Barbara Stristrand) and some Walt Disney's film– "Boat-Niks" (something like "McHale's Navy"). We were served 3 fantastic meals and a big snack before landing in Cam Rahn Bay. We landed at 8 pm. It was already dark, but really hot. Wake Island was small. 5 X 2 miles. Went down to the beach.*

*Water sure was nice and warm - and coral all over. Got me a couple pieces. Okanowa was dull - nothing much there. Stayed there an hour.*

*We're outside of the city here. South Vietnamese sure are little here. They work around the base a lot. Mountains on one side of us. Almost like Ft. Lewis and a beach you can go swimming in on the other side. Hope I can go water skiing in Chu Lie. Heard you could. Running out of room. Things aren't too bad here at all. So <u>don't</u> worry. All I'm doing now is waiting for a pool table - there's 8 in here! Take it easy. I'll send address in couple of days. Bye for now.*

*Love. Your son, Bob*

# CHU LAI REPLACEMENT CENTER

Monday, October 26, 1970, Day 5 / 360 to DEROS
—99 bottles...—

Vibrating through the Asian sky, the C-130 transport ushered us north. In the guts of the bulky plane, perhaps as an ominous premonition, infrared cast a reddish glow onto ninety-two fresh young faces. There were no windows, so we were left with whatever thoughts we could muster– attempting to talk would have been useless anyway over the roar of the engines. My quiet companions perhaps fantasized of a haven far away from the reality that lay ahead. Closing my eyes, I dozed off, my only escape from the cabalistic world *hidden beneath me....*

✎*....June, 1963, Cottage Grove...Tapping again on* the glass pane, the window opens a few inches. "Be right out," I hear in a whispered hush out of the darkness. A minute passes. About to tap again, the window opens to its full extent. Danny's head appears in the opening, a shock of disheveled brown hair almost hiding his eyes.

"Coast is clear," I say, answering his sideward glances.

Dressed only in cut-offs we scoot across the yard, down the block and across the street to old man Miller's wooded and unkempt property and the site of our new home in the trees. Above our half-naked bodies the moon is waxing and the stars are aglow, adding a surreal ambiance to our mystic safari into the "Dark Continent" of Miller's lot.

Standing like a fortress in the center of the lot is our objective: a massive bur oak tree. Its giant trunk thrusts into the sky before disappearing into a constellation of leaves.

Energized by the midnight adventure, I hook fingers and toes, toughened by our jungle training, into the rough bark and scale to the first branch a dozen feet above the ground. The thick limb shoots out at a steady upward incline where it divides into a huge fork. There, our new home waits! It's a precarious tightrope up the limb, with only the aid of a few small branches to aid in our balance. Danny and I hoped this would prevent an assault on our treehouse by the "River Rats", a surly gang of neighborhood bullies that roamed the small grove.

Stepping onto the platform, I gaze into the moonlit leaves, shimmering in a soft breeze. Near our tree is another burr oak, onto which I had lashed a thick hemp rope onto one of its upper limbs. With it we can swing across, an adrenaline rush I live for. I spot Danny; he inches toward me, staring intently at the dark limb below him. *The night is safe, for my enemy sleeps at night.* The gentle wind massages my sun-browned skin, sending a friendly chill up my torso. *I belong to this wild and dark wilderness. Alone and unseen, I am at peace. ...*✐

*...My eyes squint* into a flood of light spilling into the transport's interior.

"Welcome to Surf City!" –greeting us at the door is a young E-4 specialist with a boyish grin– "Load up in the trucks out hea and we'll take ya on over to the Replacement Centa."

Stepping outside the hatch, I suck in a deep breath. *Not bad.* Several other specialists are standing by the trucks, laughing at a joke, probably at our expense. A quick glance above their laughter reveals an almost desert-like terrain surrounding the remote airport. Looking east, I spot the tops of some military buildings peeking over the airport hangers. I turn my gaze west. Before me an unending range of mountains work their way up and down the coast. At the foot of the mountains lie a brilliant ribbon of lush green, shrouded in a velvet haze of purple.

We board the trucks and soon the Americal Division unveils before me. The China Sea appears first, glimmering on the horizon. Below and pressing against a resort-like seacoast is a vast assemblage of concrete, tin, steel, plywood, paint, rope, wire, sandbags, flags and GI flesh.

The trucks slow as we near a cluster of whitewashed buildings: Division Post Exchange, USO, barbershop and even a bookstore. We turn right and rumble down a shallow hill and past row after row of brightly painted plywood and tin bungalows. Traffic is brisk and more than a few times we feel the icy stares of GI's walking along the shoulder. We're the *FNG*'s –Fucking New Guys– and hold no respect anywhere in the military world.

It was drizzling as we arrived at the Replacement Center, increasing to a steady downpour from an unbroken bank of clouds as we processed in for the rest of the afternoon, a ritual as sacred to the military as Buddha was to the Vietnamese. Forms, records, tests– by six o'clock my head was spinning with paperwork as bad as had several typhoons they said had struck Chu Lai the previous week. Before letting us escape their paper gauntlet, a medic issued us a supply of malaria pills we were supposed to renew each month. One small pill we were to take daily, and another large, orange "horse" pill, as referred to by one of the specialist, we were instructed to take every Monday.

A wet and humid evening was tempered by a pleasant surprise as we arrived at our assigned block of barracks. The missing third of our D-3-3 unit was here; they had shipped out of Oakland instead of Ft. Lewis. Now we were complete! A raucous reunion launched– swapping stories, reviving friendships and general FNG craziness.

Bill and I followed the crowd to the RC's only entertainment spot: a barrack converted into a snack bar. Inside sat several dozen small tables drenched with austere light provided from naked light bulbs threaded from the wooden ceiling. Plywood flaps were propped open over the windows, but gave little relief to the drove of GI's herding into the muggy tenement. The scuffed tile floor, its color now unrecognizable, was covered with a litter of cigarette butts, candy wrappers and sand deposited by new combat boots marching to and from the concession counter.

The place was packed. Wading through the sea of green GI's, I spotted Randy Bradshaw and Augie Gonzales at a corner table, a couple of buddies from my Delta platoon. Augie, a huge, hairy Hispanic from Texas who usually wouldn't hurt a fly, already looked glassy-eyed as he slammed the last of his beer. Randy was Augie's antithesis: well built, of short stature and even shorter temper. He leaned in his chair against the wall while nursing his brew.

11

Augie lowered his bottle. "Bradshaw, check it out."

"Wow! I can't believe it," I exclaimed, grabbing a folding chair, "you guys fly out of Ord?"

"Sure as shit," Randy answered. "Never thought we'd see any of you again." –he tipped another sip– "Bill, you strike it rich in Vegas yet?" Bill lived just northeast of the gambling capital.

"Ya think I'd be *here* if I did?"

Augie pushed himself to his feet. "Let me buy you some beers, man." I nodded in casual agreement; I had never imbibed, being raised a God-fearing Baptist, plus a devoted weightlifter/health nut since the age of thirteen. I watched the big guy make his way through the crowd. *Maybe it's time for some catch up.*

"So," Randy inquired, "how was your leave?"

"Too short," I said, recalling a farewell party, hosted by my friend, Bob Ahlgren. He had modeled it after our favorite movie, *The Wild Bunch*; we'd seen the grisly western seventeen times– sometimes I think to prepare me for Vietnam. "It sure felt weird going home with short hair."

"'Member that wig we almost bought in Seattle?"

I chuckled. "*Only* a hundred and fifty bucks. I swear I almost did it, man, just to–"

"–keep the fucking locals off our backs," Bradshaw finished. "Man, they hated our GI guts. Even my goddamn girlfriend seemed embarrassed to have me around...fucking drag."

Bill leaned back and clasped his fingers behind his head. "My hair was so short my damn horse didn't even recognize me."

Augie was weaving through the crowd with an armload of brown bottles. "What a fucking line." –he plopped the brews on the table– "Two for Andrews, two for Adams, two for Bradshaw," –he gave me a wink– "and *three* for me." He sat down and drained half a bottle.

I took a small swallow and almost gagged. Forcing another sip, I didn't let on: this was a new world and I was willing to try new things.

We spent the next few hours in worlds far from Vietnam. I sat trance-like, sipping my beer, enjoying the diversion of small talk, of places I had never seen but intimately knew as we spun our lives and hopes together– already yearning for the day we would be free from these foreign shores. Too soon, though, the evening dwindled. Augie was slouched in his chair, staring at nothing while dangling a half-empty bottle between thumb and forefinger. Bill and Randy weren't having much luck in getting up a Euchre game. I was working on my sixth beer and feeling pretty good– it didn't taste so bad anymore.

Tuesday, October 27, 1970, Day 6 / 359 to DEROS
—sea of calm—

I forced my eyes open. A dull throbbing radiated from forehead to temple. "Wake up, Bill." –my voice was an octave lower– "Gotta get going."

"Uhhhhhh," was all I heard as Bill turned over on the bunk below me.

*I'll never do that again*, I promised myself as we headed for the RC mess hall. Returning to our barrack after last night's celebration the sidewalk was doing a slow clockwise spin. Trying to follow it, I tumbled off the walk and into the sandy lane.

Though an early morning rain had given us a brief respite, the oppressive air now clamped my fatigues uncomfortably to my skin. I looked at my clown-sized fatigues. *I can't wait to get rid of these things. The new guys…it's bad enough to be here, but to be looked down on because we're new arrivals….* My thoughts trailed off as we entered the bustling building where most of the FNG's were attempting to eat their way out of the previous evening's mistakes. The poorly maintained mess hall was rivaled only by the mess it served: soggy powdered eggs, burnt coffee, cold toast and leathery prunes greeted our reluctant taste buds, made numb after last night's boozing. After washing down the tasteless chow with a carton of orange juice, we dumped our trays at the KP window and headed for the door.

"Now what?" Bill wondered aloud as a private, looking green as the eggs, pushed past us to run behind the building to deposit his breakfast onto the sand. Tuning out the poor GI's retching, I stopped to listen to the surf drumming the shoreline. Beyond the surf stretched an unending multitude of gray swells that heaved to the horizon. Its mesmerizing display of power filled me with a calm and for a few moments, I was home.

"Truck's probably here." –I turned my head inland while rubbing last night's sleep out of my eyes– "Classes start at eight." Our boots clanked down the metal-grated sidewalk as the eternal beat of the waves dissolved in the breeze.

13

*Dear Mom and Dad,*　　　　　　　　　*Saturday, October 31, 1970*

*Hi! I'm up here in Chu Lai right now at another replacement Station on the coast of the China Sea. My unit (Americal) is located on the coast also. While being hot and dry down at Cam Rahn, it's in the middle of the rainy or monsoon season here. The sea has been very rough because of two medium-class typhoons that hit last week (Kate & Joan). It has been raining for 4 days straight - but it stopped today. I've started my review training or schooling. I'm on my 5th day of six. The barracks and food isn't much compared to Cam Rahn but still not that bad. They spray this area with mosquito poison so as yet haven't seen 1 mosquito although cockroaches and rats quite big.*

*Almost whole Co. D-3-3 is here now. Even those who shipped out from Oakland. VanWinkle isn't though. Saw Danny Moore's name on mess hall wall here.*

*Just wanted to say hi. Got a lot more letters to write. Oh, - paid today. Sent $160.00 home! Think that includes savings bond. Kept - $40.00.*

*Write soon and bye now. Love, Bob*

# DELTA COMPANY

Monday, November 2, 1970, Day 12 / 353 to DEROS
—Topp's shop—

T he morning of our eighth day at the Replacement Center was a blessed relief, though seasoned with uneasiness: I was thankful the week of training was over, but I knew the day of reckoning was at hand. The day that I, too, would become fuel for the Vietnam War Machine, to be consumed as had thousands of other American boys who had been pumped into its powerful pistons.

Formation was scheduled for 1400. We spent the morning hours paired with our closest buddies, hoping perhaps that our close proximity would somehow increase our chances of being transferred together. We didn't understand why we had to be separated. We had trained as a unit– why not fight as one? It was the Army way, though, and there wasn't a thing we lowly privates could do to prevent it.

Lunch came and so did a plate of chipped beef and gravy. My hands were cold as my fork as I shoveled its burden of salted leather into my mouth. The fruit cocktail wasn't much better. The syrup had little luck permeating the hard chunks of peaches and pineapple. Today, though, I didn't care, for my mind was having trouble staying afloat in a sea of raw nerves. Bill was silent, as was everyone else. The clank and clatter of steel and glass echoed in the room; I knew I wasn't the only one who dreaded the next few hours.

*Where will I be this time tomorrow?* I swallowed the thought with a mouthful of tepid milk. *On the front lines? Fighting for my life? Watching everyone around me get shot up? Looking down and seeing...and seeing–*

Bill stands up. "Ya ready?"

We retreat to the barrack to await the hour when Uncle Sam will throw our fates into the wind. My comrades lay like corpses in the dark room, save for a few flecks of dingy light filtering through the plywood flaps. I gaze into the darkness, conscious of my breathing. My spit sticks in my throat, just as had that chipped beef. I try to close my eyes, but my eyelids keep popping open, as if the shades are wound too tight. *Help me, God. Protect me, please. Keep me safe. Please, oh God, please watch over me–* I force my eyes shut and stare into my eyelids, seeing starlit apparitions that cruise from one fear to the next. Their culmination pins me to my *4 x 6* ration *of brown wool....*

✎ *...2:46 p.m., Saturday, August 6, 1994, home...Blood and sweat* mix with a thin coating of gun oil as I press the muzzle against my temple. Upstairs, life goes on. My wife and son watch the tube, relaxing after a long day of yard work. The sting of cold steel fades as it absorbs the heat of my skin. *Can't tell a soul what it's like inside of my brain. Rotten week. Going to work like nothing is wrong. If I only KNEW what was wrong! What good did that shrink do...nothing! No matter what I learn about this shit, it don't do no good!* I crack a smile as a movie image from *Joe versus the Volcano* flashes in my head. *"You have a brain cloud, Mr. Banks."* At least he had something with a name he could hold on to, something to pass around like a favorite appetizer at a party. I lower the gun. *I can't do this. I'm not that big of a coward...not yet.* Wiping a smear of blood on my temple, I release the magazine and begin to clean my virgin Glock like it's my newborn, oiling the barrel, spring and slide, pushing the bolt into place till I hear the erotic click as it seats. My head falls forward. A full minute passes.

I snap up and shove the magazine home.

"VIET!" –I chamber a round– "FUCKING!" –I point *the barrel*– "*NAAAAM!*"...✏

...*"FALL OUT!"* I roll off the bunk and join the herd gathering in front of the barracks. Across the road, a dozen trucks sit; their drivers stand like butchers waiting for the slaughter. Taking a place beside Bill, I glance at Augie and Bradshaw; they stare straight ahead, standing "at ease", to await the coming sentence. The ocean breeze has blown aside the rain and with it a few of the wind-whipped clouds, revealing an occasional patch of the endless blue sky. The drumming of the ocean creates an appropriate backdrop to the event at hand and overhead several fretting gulls hover, more interested in snatching up the mess hall debris than in witnessing the coming pronouncement.

"Men," a sergeant major standing in front of one of the trucks begins, "these are your final transfer orders. After you receive your unit assignment, locate and board the truck identified with your brigade and battalion's name and insignia. You will then be transported to your company headquarters for deployment in the field. Good luck, men."

The sergeant calls out our names. Names lovingly bestowed by our mothers as we had lain on her breast, names we carried with pride to baseball practice, to summer camp, to the senior prom. Now– they were all we had.

Bill gets nailed first. "The following personnel are to report to the 196th Brigade, 1st Battalion of the 46th Infantry: Andrews, William R., Bravo Company–" Picking up his duffel bag, Bill's eyes flash at mine. There are no words; his look says it all. He works his way through formation with several others. Finding their truck, they toss their bags inside and climb aboard. The sergeant continues with the next group as Bill's truck pulls away, his form lost in the shadows beneath the faded canvas. *There goes my best friend.* I always seem to migrate toward guys like Bill, guys who don't seek the limelight. Guys who'd rather go fishing than cruise the one-ways: the underdogs of the world. I stare straight ahead. *Maybe I'm one, too.*

"The following personnel are to report to the 198th Brigade, 5th Battalion of the 46th Infantry: Adams, Robert M., Delta Company–" I swing my bag over my shoulder as his words erode into syllabic garbage. Fourteen others climb in behind me and as the truck pulls onto the road, I give a last look at Company D-3-3, now scattering like sand in the wind.

*　　*　　*

"Delta Company! Adams, Robert M., Moreno, Dennis R.! Your new home, guys!"

We threw our duffel bags to the ground and jumped off the tailgate. "We'll see you guys around, huh?" I offered to the remaining four. "At least we're in the same Battalion."

Hoisting our bags over our shoulders, the departing truck left us standing in front of a small one-story plywood and tin bungalow. A thick coat of blue paint covered the building, as if attempting to hide its many flaws. Beside the screen door hung a weathered sign with large red letters: CQ OFFICE - 5/46 BATTALION GROUP, DELTA COMPANY.

Opening the door, a specialist E-4 was sitting behind a gray metal desk. His slight, bony frame resembled that of a Vietnamese as he pecked on an electric typewriter. In the far corner hummed a slate-gray floor fan sitting next to the only other furniture in the room: three upright file cabinets.

The specialist squinted through his wire-rims. "Don't tell me," –he searched his cluttered desktop– "Adams and Moreno? Got your *201*'s this morning."

"That's right," Moreno offered.

"Welcome to Delta Company. I'm Tom Gilespie, Company Clerk. Topp's not here right now. Should be back soon, though. Why don't you take your bags and grab a bed? You'll probably be hooking up tomorrow." –he shuffled more papers, then put his finger to a sallow temple– "Oh, yeah. Got your orders?"

"Hey," I asked, handing him the paper, "I hear the Division's going on stand-down?"

Gilespie raised his pencil-thin eyebrows. "They still feeding you new guys that crock of shit? We ain't going nowhere."

"So, ah," began Moreno, "where is it we'll be going?"

"Not sure. They move around a lot. They were in Ky Tra yesterday. I guess. I'm not sure. Topp will fill you in." As if concluding the subject, Gilespie swung back to his typewriter. "Go grab a bed."

*     *     *

The screen door slammed open. A beanpole of a first sergeant stuck a jaded face into our barrack. "You two come with me," his gritty voice rattled. A freshly lit Lucky Strike dangled between a bulbous blue-veined nose and bony shoulders supporting an M-16 and bandoleer over an unzipped flak jacket. "I'll take you to get your gear." –he brushed a graying temple with a knobby hand– "Jeep's outside." Not waiting for an answer, he turned and let the door smack shut.

Moreno raised an eyebrow. "What's with the 16?"

It was a short trip to the supply shed. I watched Topp from the back seat; his red nose glowed above a paunch that stuck out like he'd swallowed a volleyball, reminding me of a typecast for a *Sad Sack* character. Before the jeep coasted to a stop Topp jumped out, his long legs rushing to the screened door where he glanced both ways before opening.

"Outfit these guys up," Topp barked, shooting bloodhound eyes at an E-5 through the office window. He opened the door and again peered both ways before waving us forward. "Report to CQ when you're done."

"Is that guy for real?" Moreno asked while watching Topp spin out and head toward the CQ.

The E-5 pushed a well-used chrome-shopping cart at me. "A real prick," the E-5 said matter-of-factly. We followed him down an aisle of olive-colored metal shelves stacked high with combat gear. "You're from D-Company. Good outfit. Topp's the only asshole in the bunch. Been paranoid ever since he hassled some Grunts couple months back…threatened to frag his ass…now he thinks everybody's out to kill 'im." –he stopped to throw in two gas masks, rucksacks and four plastic two-quart canteens– "The juice has *fried* his fucking brain." He tossed in several ponchos, poncho liners and two air mattresses.

"Wow," I exclaimed, eyeing the mattresses. "Everybody get these?"

"Got a shit-load of 'em 'bout a month back. We'll pass 'em out till they're gone. Then it's back to good ol' motherfucking earth."

We stuffed our gear into our rucks and the E-5 took us for a short walk to the munitions shed.

"What the fuck is that smell?" Moreno asked.

"What? You mean the shitters? Goddamn, doncha FNG's know nothing? They burn it, man, with kerosene. Can't *even* bury it. Fuck, wait till *you* get

18

that cocksucking detail."

"No way, man."

The E-5 turned a smile. "You wait." –he issued us each an M-16 rifle with six magazines, bandoleer and enough ammo to fill them– "That'll give you something to do rest of today... 'less you get shit-burning detail. Remember, eighteen rounds per magazine, don't want to overload the spring." –he led us out and locked the door behind him– "Got some thirty-round banana clips on order. You can switch 'em out when they get here."

Another cigarette was tucked between Topp's rubbery lips as we opened the CQ door. "Give your weapons and your ammo to Gilespie. He'll lock 'em up for you until you head out. I don't want anyone carrying a weapon here but me." –he paused, taking a long drag with well-practiced jowls– "Tomorrow morning there'll be a chopper at Fat City to take you to your unit. You'll be in Third Platoon." –Topp hacked up some phlegm– "We'll lock your duffel bags in cold storage. Be here by 0700." Without a second glance he turned and whisked out the door.

*The war is killing this guy. Wonder how I'll end up a year from now?*

*    *    *

Straight ahead, the sun dips below the horizon. It is still bright, though– as bright as midday. Staring into the light, the blare of an approaching jet turns my head. Through one of its windows I see my mother's face. She is trying to tell me something, but I can't hear her for the roar of the descending jet. I call out to her, but the jet smothers my voice. The light grows brighter, so bright that the jet fades in its brilliance, along with my mother's image. All that remains is light and–

*SSSSSSSSSSSSSSLAMMMMMMMM!* sends me bouncing off my bed as the explosion's flash scorches the inside of our sleeping quarters. I hold the floor and peer wide-eyed into the blackness as a piercing silence floods the room.

"What was that?!" Moreno is kneeling beside me; the sound of air rasping through his lungs competes with a cricket that has resumed its chirping in the far corner. Somewhere a siren begins to wail.

My hair feels as though I am plugged into an electric socket. "I don't–"

"Get the hell out of there!" I jump up and push open the door. Topp is standing in green skivvies and his oversized flak jacket. His M-16 is glued to his fingers.

Moreno grabs my shoulder and looks through the door. "Topp! What–"

"ROCKETS! Get in that bunker!" Another blast behind Topp transfigures him into a Banshee pointing a bony finger at a bunker placed strategically *between the barracks....*

✎...*2:12 p.m., Monday, May 7, 1972, home...*"*You going to* be gone long?" Mom stood at the door, palms on her hips, fingers pointed behind her like she did when I was a kid and about to do something she didn't approve of.

"No. Just hafta check out one more place."

"Well, remember, dinner's at four. Your dad doesn't like to be kept waiting."

*I am not four years old, Mother.* "Don't worry. I'll be back waaaay before–" A distant boom from a 105 howitzer jerks Mom's head toward the Arsenal Island proving grounds, a large military installation four miles down river.

"I never get used to that noise." –she looks back to see me tucked neatly underneath my car– "What are you doing *under there? Bobby?*"...✎

Tuesday November 3, 1970, Day 13 / 352 to DEROS
—Moreno—

The night passed. The VC had fired more than a dozen rockets on Chu Lai. Getting to bed, I had gazed through the door for a long while before sleep would come, troubled by the fact that Charlie would dare throw bombs at the main base. The morning brought a quick trip to the mess hall, after which we rushed to grab our rucksacks to make it to the CQ before the seven o'clock deadline.

Nearing eight o'clock, Topp rushed into the office.

"Second Platoon got hit this morning. Walked into an ambush. Took three guys out." –Topp stooped over and peered through the screen window before continuing. His hands were shaking– "Your flight's canceled. We'll see if we can get you out first thing tomorrow. Adams, you'll be going to Second now. Moreno, you're still going to Third."

"This ain't real, man," Moreno said as we left the CQ. He gave me a glance, as if looking for support. "I mean, this ain't *nothing* like they said it'd be. Shit. This is beginning to look like a real fucking war."

I took a deep breath and forced myself to slowly exhale. "How 'bout we go down to the beach awhile, get our minds off this while we can. Maybe this is just one big bad dream."

We decided to grab a snack at the Battalion USO, after which we checked out the sandy stretch of paradise beyond a row of guard towers strategically spaced every two hundred meters. We began a slow pace south, following the blue-gray surf where it kissed the shoreline.

"Where you from, man?" Moreno asked.

"Illinois. Ever hear of Rock Island?"

"Just from that Johnny Cash song."

"Well, it's right on the Mississippi River."

Moreno grinned. "I *have* heard of that." –he stooped over to pick up a white fan-shaped shell– "I'm from Western Nebraska. Hay Springs. Know where that's at?"

"Not really."

"It's nowhere. You know, this is the first time I've even seen a fucking ocean." –he brushed the drying sand from inside the shell– "Man, we are as far from home as you can get. But here we are in the middle of a shit-storm, waiting to get our asses blown away."

"We'll get through this somehow." –I didn't sound convincing– "We got to."

"So tell me about your family, Amigo. Uncle Sambo didn't take that away from you, too, did he?"

"He tried to get my older brother, Kent. We went for our physicals together in Chicago."

"What happened?"

"You're not gonna believe this, but Kent had flat feet. Got him a deferment cause of *flat feet*. Man, can you believe that?"

"Shit. Lucky dude."

"Awww, he wouldn't a done no good, anyway. Guy is a bookworm. Straight A's and all that." –I was surprised to hear a hint of pride in my voice– "Sucker is smart, man. Made the Dean's list at WIU." –I hesitated, kicking at some driftwood in my path– "He don't belong here. Woulda killed him."

"*HE* don't belong here? Man, I got me a wife back in the states," –he paused, as if he wasn't sure if he wanted to share the next line, but he pushed on– "and a kid on the way."

21

"Wow, man, what are *you* doing here then?"

"Beats the ever-living *fuck* out of me."

We fell into silence, content to watch the surf play tag with our boots as we hunted for shells.

"So, Adams, where'd you work before you ended up in this man's army?"

"Went to college for a while. Well, a short while. Dropped out after three months and ended up in this dump called McLaughlin's Body Company. Started out emptying trash. Then after six months I got up to forklift operator. Think that's the only good thing that came out of being drafted...leaving that place. Only reason I stuck it out there was to pay for my car."

"Yeah? Whaja have?"

I picked up a flat stone and skipped it in the surf ahead of me. "Brand new Ford *Maverick*. Vermilion. Beautiful. But my parents are selling it now that I'm here."

"Selling it? Why, they think you ain't coming ba–"

*BAAALAAAMMMMMMMM!*

We hit the ground as straight ahead a rocket slams into the beach, whipping up a thick cloud of sand and white smoke.

"Shhhit!" Moreno squeals, raising a sand-mottled face. "Ain't anyfuckingplace safe around here?!"

"No!" I shout, recalling the jellyfish episode at the Cam Rahn Replacement Center. Another round thunders further inland, out of our line-of-sight. "Okay," I announce, "let's head back."

Before leaving the beachfront, Moreno paused; he leaned back and returned the white shell *to its home....*

✎*...9:42 a.m., Tuesday, July 8, 1969, Chicago...Jimi Hendrix strut If 6 Was 9 on the 8-track as I pulled my '70 Ford Maverick* to the curb at the south end of Old Town, a hippie hangout just north of the Chicago Loop. That way we could circle to the far end and back and still have plenty of time to catch the afternoon Cubbies game. Ahlgren and I were sure that this was the year the "CUBS WILL SHINE IN 69", as testified on my car's bumper sticker.

We started up the avenue to investigate the head shops, pretending to be part of the counter culture as we blended with the freaks wandering Old Town. I had never so much as touched a marihuana cigarette, but I didn't mind looking the part and this was *the* spot to purchase the beads, bracelets, headbands, incense, bumper stickers, belts, T-shirts, bell bottoms and fringed jackets to look it.

We combed the dimly lit digs that lined the litter-strewn sidewalk, mesmerized by the musty odor of leather and smooth rush of raspberry and peppermint candles. Inside, the mystic swish of Pink Floyd, The Doors, Led Zeppelin, or Cream wailed messages of confusion and despair as longhaired freaks slouched on over-stuffed easy chairs, half-stoned amidst curls of burning incense while waiting for a sale of their drug paraphernalia. Their attire was universal, adhering to a dress code as stringent as their military counterparts: colorful bandanas wrapped tight around foreheads, beaded leather vests thin from wear, tarnished brass or silver-buckled belts, faded tie-dyed T-shirts and decaying bell bottom hip huggers whose ragged edges all but hid scuffed combat boots or Kurdish sandals. Like gypsies we wandered the numinous shops, hoping to grasp what the meaning of life *was all about....*✎

*Dear Mom and Dad,*                    *Tuesday, November 3, 1970 - 1 p.m.*
*Hello! Well I finally got my orders and my address which is:*
  *PFC Bob Adams, 309-44-5058, D 5/46 198ᵗʰ, APO SF 96374*
*So I guess you can start writing. My Unit (198th) is located on the coast also. Things aren't too bad here at all. One other guy from D-3-3 is here with me too. Dennis Moreno. He's a Mexican from Nebraska, a real nice guy.*

*There isn't much going on at all out in the field. Mostly VC working in small groups of 2 to 4 men. About all they do is set out booby-traps cause their too scared to fight face to face. Right now most deaths are due to carelessness with our own forces. Drugs. Sleeping on guard, etc.*

*I found out that if we want to we can be out of Nam in 8 months or by next June cause we are deactivating. But I'm thinking about extending or staying the full year plus 30 days extra. This way I'll have a lot more money and by Christmas of 71 I'll be out of the Army completely! A 5 1/2 month early out cause they won't have any need for me once back in the states. What do you think I should do?*

*I'll stop now. Don't worry about me. About 3 or 4 of my friends are also in the 198th, so that's pretty good. Hasn't been raining much here for 3 days though a storm is brewing now over China Sea. The food is real good, serve a lot of fried chicken. Write soon and take care. Tell me what Kent is doing. Bye now, Bob*


Wednesday, November 4, 1970, Day 14 / 351 to DEROS
—into the wilderness—

Six o'clock came too soon. I dug myself from of the warmth of my woolen army blanket. Moreno, too, was stirring, stretching his arms to the ceiling to kick in his circulation. I shoved my feet into my boots and stepped outside. *Wonder what Bill's doing right now? Maybe he's already out there. Maybe he's already shot at Charlie, or Charlie's shot at him.*

"Ready," Moreno says.

A surreal aura permeates the warm November morning. The air is almost tangible, as if I can scoop it up and stuff it into my pocket. The buildings, the sky, the trees– everything is too vivid, too intense. As I down a mouthful of powdered eggs, I hear my heart pounding a steady beat, loud enough to cause me to look down to make sure my fatigue shirt isn't noticeably vibrating with its cadence. And my fork. It feels too heavy to hold, as the food is too thick to swallow. Walking back afterward, the ground floats beneath me, making it difficult to tell when my feet are touching the earth and when they are not, as if some unknown entity is propelling them forward against my will. Too soon we reach our barrack; too soon we grab our rucksacks; too soon we arrive at the CQ.

Gilespie is waiting.

Wind-blown clouds move with us as our Jeep speeds through the main glut of Chu Lai. We turn toward the mountains at the PX, then past the airport and to the main gate, turning north onto Highway 1.

In a few minutes we rumble under a colorful sign: An Tan. The village teems as Gilespie snakes around vehicles of every size, shape and propulsion rushing along the pot-holed macadam road. Roadside entrepreneurs press the road's edge with hand carts selling, bartering and squabbling over freshly picked, plucked, caught, or hand-made produce. Almost hidden behind the commotion sit a clutter of unkempt huts and shanties. Some are built of mud brick, others of plywood and tin and still others of what looks like nothing but straw. A scene from the *Three Little Pigs* flashes in my mind, cutting a thin smile. Ancient Vietnamese men, decked in white cotton pajamas, squat on wooden walkways beside darkened doorways. Their reddish lips paint wide toothless grins, gums blackened by some mystic weed they chew while watching their world flow before them. Weaving through the village, the pandemonium of the marketplace seems to hover above us before being swept into the updrafts created by the nearby mountains.

We exit the village. Our road suddenly seems an intrusion upon the lush green rice paddies spreading before us. Every few minutes a military vehicle of some sort passes, but more often the local conveyance peddles, putts, rumbles, whizzes, bangs, or scoots around us. Mammoth black water buffaloes, the John Deere tractors of this third world, dot the countryside like giant raisins as they trudge man-made dikes with sun-darkened boys, feet bare and expertly welding bamboo sticks to guide the beasts. In the boundless paddies beside the dikes stoop women and girls in water up to their shins thinning and weeding the rice. They wear black silk pants, colorful silk blouses and conical straw hats to shade their slender bodies.

At last my eyes take in the unfeigned world of South Vietnam. I recall my first impression of these curious people as I lean back and close my eyes. *These people…maybe they're not so different from me after all.*

My eyes open as Gilespie passes through the stone gates of Fat City: a jumbled collection of shanties bordering the remote military base. He quickly maneuvers through the marketplace, turning down a quiet lane that soon leaves the village behind.

A chill rides up my spine as the site of the "Americal Helicopter Support Base" comes into view. Slapped on the northern flank amidst a silver field of concertina is a collection of hangers and buildings rising out of a crop farmer's nightmare of hard red clay. Stubby dust-covered shrubs fight with the clay that continues on the western flank until fading into an army of deep-green rice plants. Above the paddies stand a line of battle-wearied mountains. Their nearness reveals ragged slopes, worn bare from decades of battering by the armies that had invaded their world.

Gunning through a red dust devil the temperature rises as we drive across the airfield's hot surface. Gilespie pulls up beside an aging gray-green helicopter before jumping out to talk to the pilot. Inside the chopper cabin and looking as bewildered as Moreno and me, sit seven FNG's.

"That'll be the colonel," Gilespie says, returning. He points toward an approaching jeep. "He's gonna escort you to your assigned platoons. This is your lucky day, boys, ain't everybody gets to hitch a ride on the colonel's bird."

"Good morning, men!" snaps the colonel as he jumps out of the jeep. His suntanned, deeply-lined face looks as rugged as the near-by mountains. A nametag above his angled fatigue shirt pocket reads, "HARDING". "It's good to have you aboard!" Not knowing whether to salute or shake hands, we just nod our heads. Colonel Harding takes a dog-eared map out of his canvas briefcase as Gilespie indicates to which platoons we are assigned.

Gilespie jumps into his jeep. "See you at stand-down!"

Colonel Harding motions us to board. The pilot fires the ignition. I squeeze beside an M-60 machine-gunner; he peers out of the doorless cabin with hands locked onto the stock of his well-oiled gun. The rotors push the long blades, gaining speed as the turbine revs up. The blades soon drown all other noise as the colonel takes a seat opposite the pilot and places a headset over his ears.

With a surge of power the chopper scoops forward, head down, tail up to gain momentum. At the edge of the strip it banks toward the wall of mountains. This is my first chopper ride– one more contingency Basic or AIT hadn't prepared me for. The closest parallel I can come up with is the Tilt-a-Whirl ride at Star-Lite Park and I can only summon my lungs to catch half-breaths as the chopper climbs to just below the clouds. A combination of gale force winds blasting through our cabin and a deafening chopping noise makes rational thought impossible. Before reaching the first line of hills, the chopper banks south, parallel to the toe of the mountains.

I find my breath as the chopper levels off and regain my composure enough to take on my first macroscopic view of the flourishing landscape of Vietnam. Far below, a network of rice paddies nestle between islands of palm and bamboo, forming odd geometric patterns that look like the scattered fragments of a gigantic jigsaw puzzle. Beyond the gunner's helmet, the sun illuminates the distant coastline with its pristine white beaches. To the west, an endless Stygian jungle glares at me with foreboding eye.

My weight hits zero as the chopper drops into a string of small hills nestled between the rice fields and the first mountain ridgeline. Just feet above the ground we swoop over a grassy hill and hover in the middle of a small glade overtaken by elephant grass. The spinning blades create a mini cyclone, matting the grass to the ground as if some invisible force had decided to take a brief respite. In the flattened grass, blue smoke churns in gyrating currents.

Colonel Harding motions to me with a pointed finger followed by a thumbs up. I grab my gear. Moreno taps me on the arm and holds out his hand. I seize it and give him a firm shake. I turn and pause on the edge of the steel floor. The battle cry "The quick or the dead!" branded into me for the last five months flash in my mind as I brace for a jolt and jump.

The chopper lurches forward and disappears over a thick grove of trees on the far side of the clearing. I crouch with my 16, rucksack and more than my share of anxiety as the song of the rustling grass swallows the bray of the departing chopper. In the brief instant before my rational mind jolts me to my present context, the sweet musty scent of the earth whispers around me: no sign of violence here, no impoverishment, no cruelty, no hatred, no apathy. Just an unblemished patch of green offering to man what God had always intended– peace and hope.

I look through the chopper's dissipating heat waves and discern what had been here all along– five GI's, crouching on the perimeter of the clearing, their weapons at the ready.

# MISSION ONE

Wednesday, November 4, 1970, Day 14 / 351 to DEROS
—2nd Platoon—

One of the soldiers motions me to approach. "I'm Nelson Burch." –he offers a meaty hand– "You'll be in my squad." –his sky blue eyes glint a friendly twinkle from beneath a prominent brow ridge– "This here's Ski, Wad, Fritts and Yoss."

I deal out a cold hand, praying my voice won't shake. Their faded, mud-encrusted fatigues contrast against my shiny green clown outfit. I feel my face redden.

Nelson removes his fringed bush hat to reveal a shock of matted corn-silk hair. "Let's head back." –he backhands a sweaty forehead– "Adams, follow Yoss. Remember. Five-meter spread. No noise."

Nelson carries an M-16 with an M-79 grenade launcher attached beneath, nicknamed "over-under". It's wedged under his right arm as he moves with eyes glued more to the ground than ahead. Yoss falls in behind him. His fatigues hang on a skeletal frame as he points his rifle into the brush that he scrutinizes with dark, rat-like eyes. A nod from Wad's sun-bronzed face tells me to proceed. He sports an M-60 machine gun with ease as he turns a glance at Fritts, who looks wearied under his burden of 60 ammo draped around rounded shoulders.

With legs unsteady, I begin to pick through the brush. It's slow going, but it's time I need to calm the stream of air rushing through my lungs. After a few minutes, though, something unexpected happens. I relax. My cold hands recover their natural warmth. My mind begins to click off the rules of survival that were until a few minutes ago a jumble of theories and speculations. It makes sense now. *This* is where I belong. These teenage men will risk their lives for me and I know I will do the same for them. It's us against them– simple-basic-true.

We left the thicket of shrub trees and entered an open field of grass on the side of a long sloping hill. Now clear of cover, Nelson moved with more deliberation. In a strange way he reminded me of my Aunt Mary. Maybe it was his eyes, hiding shyly in deep sockets. Or maybe it was the way he carried his big-boned frame, plodding sloth-like, not unlike an old lady strolling to the corner grocery store to buy some milk and eggs. Whatever it was, I instinctively trusted him.

At the far end of the grassy field we entered another grove of short bushy trees. The cool shade, though relieving my eyes, hindered my vision until a growing light told me we were nearing its edge. Emerging, a panoramic view of lush rice fields and the distant white coastline burst before me. Sitting on the edge of the vista and almost buried beneath a wealth of swaying elephant grass was a circle of tent-like structures forming a perimeter thirty meters in diameter.

"Hey, Adams," Yoss asked in a strange eastern accent, "could I get your poncho?" –he sounded like he had a clothespin clamped over an out-ofproportioned nose that appeared glued between his eyes– "Our hootch needs a back wall. Helps keep out the draft at night."

I tossed him my poncho and continued after Nelson. He stopped outside of a tent in the center of the perimeter, constructed of several plastic ponchos snapped together and supported by hand-cut poles. A PRC-25 radio leaned against the front support pole at the entrance. Just inside, two sets of combat boots moved restlessly.

"Hey, LT," –Nelson cupped his hands to light a cigarette– "new guy's here."

The lieutenant, a black man supporting a generous six-foot frame, smiled as he stood. "Am I glad to see you!" –he held out his hand– "We're kind of short-handed after yesterday. I'm Lieutenant Owens, but I'll answer to L-T. This is Sergeant Branson."

"Hi ya, fella," –Sergeant Branson grabbed my hand– "call me Buffalo." He also was black, easily outweighing LT by fifty pounds. The sergeant's nickname aptly fit him.

I offered my hand. "I'm PFC Adams."

"You can drop the rank." –LT turned to Nelson– "Adams the only guy we getting?"

"Looks like it," Nelson said, blowing out a stream of blue smoke.

"Shit, still leaves us two short. Have to cut another position. Tell Blondie to hook up with Nichols' squad. Then get Adams briefed on our SOP." –LT looked at me– "Just do what Burch says and he'll keep your shit together. We'll be here the rest of the day, so that should give you time to get squared away."

Nelson approached a tent facing the southwest side of the perimeter. Two GI's were there, one sitting cross-legged and nursing a cigarette while watching his partner stir up some chow.

"What's up?" the sitting man said, peering at us with eyes as blue as thunderbolts. "We getting our men?"

"Nope," said Nelson, "least not today. This here's Adams. He'll be in my squad. LT wants you to move over with Nichols tonight. Might get some more guys tomorrow."

"Hi, Adams. Call me Blondie." –he swung his cigarette toward the other guy– "That's Pane." –Pane offered a smile, extending a lean hand while

Blondie sucked in a long drag and stared at Nelson– "Why the fuck don't *we* get him? We're the motherfucking squad that's short."

Nelson's square jaw stiffened as the twinkle deserted his eyes. "You know I lost a guy yesterday, too. Anyway, it's only for a day or two. Then you can get back to your normal squad."

"Goddamnit." –Blondie's forehead flushed, accentuating his nearly white eyebrows– "Now we gotta move all this shit." –twisting his cigarette into the dirt, his scarecrow straight hair rustled on his scalp like new wheat in a spring breeze– "Okay, Pane, let's get packing."

Pane darted hawk-like eyes at the half-warmed turkey loaf. "What about my motherfucking C's?"

"Why doncha give 'em to LT? He's the one spooning you shit."

"Not even." Pane forked a slice of turkey into his mouth. His hawk eyes fit a beak-like nose and narrow cheeks that whittled down to a point at the chin.

Nelson left them to their grumbling. We arrived at our site and I dropped my rucksack and sat down by one of two tents sitting side-by-side and angled toward each other, forming a shallow 'V'.

"You can bunk with Yoss and me." –he eyed my ruck– "What you got in there? Looks a little light." –he pushed my poncho liner aside– "Where's your C's? And your 16 ammo's still boxed up. You don't need this." –he threw my gas mask on the ground– "No machete? No frags, C-4...man, didn't they give you nothing?"

"Hey, I didn't have a chance to load my ammo. Topp made us lock it up and the guy in supply just gave me the M-16."

Nelson took his hat off, shaking his head. "That lazy asshole. And that Topp is a bastard. You got to learn this right now, Adams, he don't give a shit for *nobody* but his own sorry ass. He knew you wouldn't have time to load your magazines." –he sat back and took a deep breath– "Okay," –he grabbed a box of ammo– "first things first. Let's load your mags. Then we'll see 'bout getting you some *C*'s."

I felt like an idiot. *I was walking with no ammo in my 16? What if some VC had jumped out of a bush? Yell, BANG! BANG! BANG! at him?*

Yoss helped Nelson and me load my magazines, after which Nelson took me around to panhandle whatever C-rations we could muster. The GI's were more than glad to get rid of some of their meals, like the canned eggs, or the ham and beans, which they referred to as ham and motherfucks. But they were better than nothing and I had a chance to meet the platoon members. Besides Nelson and Blondie, the third squad leader was a backwoods character that went by the name "Hillbilly". His icy blue eyes flashed as he gave me a wiry handshake along with a cackling "Howdy," revealing some poor dental care with a chipped tooth punched into the right side of his smile. I liked him right off. He reminded me of that Festus Hagan character from the *Gunsmoke* TV western.

Sergeant E-5 Mark Nichols ruled the last squad. The moment his dark eyes pierced mine, I knew I wanted nothing to do with him.

Our medic was a black guy with a friendly disposition: Deno Belton. But we could call him Doc. Nelson told me not to be fooled by the fact that he was a Conscientious Objector– Doc was the bravest guy there. The other names were thrown at me too quickly to retain them all and only a few of their names clicked as I headed to my position. A guy called Retchin was a monster of a man, his arms as big as my legs. Another, Spanky, appeared to have American Indian blood in him. Harvey, slouching over a bent deck of cards, looked like the laziest man alive. And a Mexican guy called Ramos came off as arrogant and hot-tempered, but maybe I didn't catch him at the right time. The rest held their own mysteries, but I knew soon a personality would hook up with each of them.

By the time we returned, I had a respectable number of C-rations, at least enough to get me through a couple days. I took out a P-38 can opener Nelson had given me·and opened a can of beefsteak.

"Hey, Yoss? What do ya use to heat this stuff?"

Yoss looked like a half-drowned rat as he concentrated on writing a letter. "Look in my ruck," Yoss began in his nasal pitch. "There's a bar of C-4 in there. Just tear off a hunk and roll it into a ball. Then put it in the stove and light it."

"You light the C-4?"

"Don't worry. As long as you don't smash it, it'll just burn. Just don't step on it or nothing."

I found the clay-like, almond-colored plastic explosive wrapped in green cellophane and tore off a small chunk. Rolling it into a ball I placed it in the makeshift stove, an empty C-ration can minus both ends with a dozen holes punched in its side. Using Yoss' lighter, I stretched out my arm and put a flame to it. Immediately a smokeless, blue flame encompassed the ball. Like a miniature sun, the hungry flame turned yellow as it licked the orb.

"Wow, cool," I said as I placed the can on the stove with its bent lid. "So, Yoss, where you from?"

"I was born in the Bronx. I grew up in the Bronx and I *hope* to die in the Bronx," Yoss recited as if a line from a movie.

"Man, how'd you get stuck in the Infantry? You're a long ways from New York City."

"Same as you, and most everyone else here." –he glanced across the camp– "'Cept LT, Buffalo and of course, Nichols."

"I didn't like his looks."

"Neither does anyone else, 'cept his sidekick, Nick. He worships him. Here," –Yoss tossed me his towel– "use this to take the can off." –removing the can, I found a dying marble-sized ember of soft blue energy– "Nichols 'bout got us all killed yesterday. Moved out without scouting ahead."

"I hear somebody mention my favorite asshole?" –Wad ducked to allow his well-proportioned six-foot frame to exit the hootch. His sun-bleached hair gleamed in the late afternoon sun– "He ever jumps in front of my sites, they'll hafta scoop him up with a goddamn spoon."

"So what happened?" I asked as I dug into the steaming can.

Yoss put his pen down. His curled hair was the color of overheated coffee, contrasting against his pale, freckled skin. He seemed an aberration from this warring bunch.

"Yesterday morning we were in Ky Tra Valley. We'd just hooked up and outside this stand of trees we were ambushed." –Yoss pulled himself out of the hootch, sat up and drew his legs to his chest– "By the time we knew what hit us, they were gone. Had us scoped out real good." –Yoss looked at Wad– "Hit Schermerhorn first. He was in our squad. Good man. Then Decker, Retchin's AG–"

"AG?"

"Assistant Machine Gunner. Deck took a round in the hip and Red, Blondie's blooper-man, got it in the guts."

I diverted my gaze beyond Yoss, taking in the turquoise haze fringing the distant coastline. The glistening beachfront seemed to mock at the horrors waiting just a few miles from its guarded sanctuary.

Yoss slowly exhaled. "Anyway, we backed into our NDP, Night Defense Position," he explained, "and we scooted out the other side while LT called in a dust-off and arty. Red was hurt'n' bad by the time the dust-off got to us. Then we CE'ed out–"

"Combat Extraction," Wad interjected.

"Anyway, we set up here last night." –Yoss sucked in a breath– "Jeez, I'm glad to get out of there. Huh, Wad?"

"Wada patrol!" Harvey lumbered toward us with a half-dozen canteens. A lethargic southern drawl aptly fit a mop of limp brown hair and smooth lanky frame. "Ya guys need any?"

"Fucking *A*, we do." Ski's sea-green eyes were almost hidden beneath a shock of rumpled, caramel-colored bangs as he leaned out of the hootch and tossed a two-quarter at Harvey.

"Well, fuck you, too, ya lazy cocksucka." –Harvey turned up a stringy mustache– "Tomorra it's ya mudafuck'n' turn."

"Fuck, wait till stand-down. *I'll* show you how to drink and I don't *even* mean water."

"I'll drink ya young ass unda the taba *enytime*, Ski-bo."

"We'll see about that." Ski threw himself back into the hootch, crossing his dusty boots as he switched back to sleep mode.

Stringing the canteens onto a length of nylon parachute cord, Harv joined the rest of his squad heading out the south side of the perimeter.

"Yoss, what do we do with these?" I held up my empty c-ration can.

"Open the other end then smash it flat and throw it out far's you can." –he thumbed his hand toward the grass beyond the hootch– "If you just toss it a little ways, the mongoose fuck with us all night and it's easy to mistake 'em for sappers." –Yoss picked up his pen– "Why don't you get your bed squared away? Night comes pretty quick around here."

"So where ya from?" Wad asked.

I took my air mattress out of my ruck. "Illinois, on the Mississippi."

"No shit?" –Wad flashed a smile– "Damn, I'm right below you, in Missouri."

"Yeah? Most of my relatives live right above St. Louis, in Winfield. My dad moved to Illinois before World War II to look for work."

"I'm not too far from St. Louie." –he ran his fingers through his close-cropped oyster-white hair– "Ever hear of Scott City? It's about a hundred miles south of there."

"Nope. What's it close to?"

"Cape Girardeau...Jackson...Chars–"

"Hey, I've heard of Jackson," I said, unscrewing the air-mattress tube. "My Uncle Leo used to live there. Small world, huh?"

"I thought so till they sent me to the armpit of Southeast Asia. Where'd ya take Basic?"

"Fort Lewis, Washington," I grunted between breaths. "After Basic...didn't even get a leave. Sent us...right across the parade field to...start AIT."

"That sucks. Sent you one helluva long ways, man. I didn't even hafta leave my home state, sent me to Lenardwood. Weekends I'd get to drive home. It was great."

"Yeah? I got to Seattle once," –I thumbed the air hole– "took a ride up the Space Needle. Was no fun dealing with the locals, though."

"Wad, you ready?" Fritts was dealing out a ragged deck of cards onto a mud-stained towel. His russet-colored hair was even more crinkled than Yoss'. It fit his pudgy face, not yet hardened by life's tribulations– it reminded me of any one of the red glowing faces on the flight from Cam Rahn to Chu Lai.

I finished inflating my mattress and stuffed it in the corner of the hootch. *This ain't so bad,* I thought as I stretched onto it. With a full belly and a long awaited sense of belonging, I drifted into *a dreamless sleep....*

✎ *...Tuesday, July 18, 1972, Lock and Dam 25, Missouri..."Just like Huck Finn,* huh?"

Derwin flipped back a strand of straw blond hair as we poled through the backwater channel on our homemade raft. "Still wanna go to the pool?"

"Sure, if Nikki'll give us a ride." –I briskly speared my pole into the muddy water– "Think Rochelle will be there?"

"You like her, huh?"

"I guess. Who wouldn't?"

"She'll be there cause I think she likes you, too."

"Yeah?"

"That's what Michele said."

34

"When?"

"After church Sunday."

Suddenly I tired of our Mark Twain adventure. "Wanna head back?"

"What about our cookout?"

I looked to shore where our driftwood fire was fast dwindling into a pile of red-hot coals.

"Don't worry, Bob. We got plenty of time."

My cousin was right. No sense wasting a gorgeous day thinking about girls. After all, this was important stuff we were doing, building an official Mississippi driftwood raft like our predecessors and exploring the backwaters near my second home of Winfield, Missouri. Most of my relatives had grown up here: Mom, Dad, both of my grandparents and an assortment of aunts, uncles and cousins.

"How much longer you figure you'll be down here?"

"Long as Grandma lets me stay with her."

"She ain't gonna kick you out."

"I know," I laughed. "Hopefully till I start college."

"Wish you could live here."

"Don't think I haven't thought about it."

Derwin was my favorite cousin. Six years my junior, he was just getting started on life's adventures. He stuck to me like glue, knocking on Grandma Wheeler's door before the sun had a chance to stretch, barely giving me time to scarf down breakfast, then saying goodnight long after daylight petered out over the blue country horizon. It was a great summer –a dream summer– a summer with The Nam *finally behind me. ...*✎

...*"Adams." I jerked* up my head, for a moment not realizing where I was. Nelson was squatting on his haunches looking into the hootch. "Yoss and I are gonna set out our M-A. You and Ski watch our position." –he glanced over the tent at the western treeline, now shrouded in shadow– "It'll be dark soon." Crawling outside, Nelson and Yoss were heading out the north side of the NDP. A small canvas bag was slung over Nelson's shoulder.

"Okay, Ski, I give up. What's an M-A?"

Ski was digging through his C-rations. A stub of a cigarette burned under his hooked Polish nose. "There's a lotta shit they don't teach us back in the World." –he flipped a C to the ground– "That's one of them." –Ski looked up as if to scrutinize Nelson and Yoss as they disappeared into the shadows–

35

"You and I would call it a booby-trap. But you know as well as I that they're outlawed by the Geneva Convention. So, the Army gets around it by calling it a 'Mechanical Ambush', M-A, for short." –he tossed another can by his feet— "Don't mean nothing." –he smiled– "Long as Uncle Sammy calls it something else, it's cool." –he reached into his ruck and pulled out a third can and tossed it to me– "Let's get some chow, dude."

By the time Nelson and Yoss returned, Ski and I were scraping out the last of our C's. Ski tossed his flattened can in the brush outside our hootch.

"Shit, Ski," Nelson flared, "throw your cans out further."

"I like listening to the furry little critters at night. Gives me something to do."

"Yeah? Then you can take *my* shift tonight." –Nelson grabbed a couple of C's out of his ruck– "Oh, yeah, Adams, take one of your dog tags and thread it onto your bootlace here like mine."

"What for?"

"It's Company Regs. But other than that it serves two purposes: you don't sound like you're wearing cowbells and in case, you know, something happens–"

"Oh, come on," Fritts spat, "don't sugar coat it. It's so if you get your ass blown away they'll know what parts go in what bag."

"Okay," Nelson said, opening a can of sliced pork. "Anyway, you go through a pair of boots every month or so, so don't forget to transfer your tag over." –he touched his lighter to the C-4– "Tomorrow I'll show you how to hook up an MA."

"Ski was just telling me about those. How many of 'em you put out a night?"

"Depends. Any trail leading to our NDP hasta have one. Then the main trail. So usually two or three." –Nelson checked his watch– "Since we got six tonight, guard won't be so bad."

"No shit," Wad said, "it'll be nice to cut a few more Z's."

The western treeline was now hidden in darkness, though the distant beaches still held to its golden hues. "First watch starts at eight," –Nelson speared a peach slice and stuffed it in his mouth– "last ends at six. Since there's six of us now, that's, what, an hour forty each?"

"You always *were* the mathematician," Ski interjected.

Nelson threw him a sideward glance. "We rotate shifts every night, so nobody gets screwed on the last one. Tonight, Adams, you take first watch since it's your first night. Yoss gets second. Then me. I'll wake Ski so they can finish up from their hootch." –he paused to drink the syrup out of his can– "There's three rules to remember on guard duty. One: if we get any unfriendly fire, yell out 'incoming', and I mean loud enough for the whole damn NDP to hear. Two: if you think there's a gook out there, yell 'outgoing' before throwing a grenade or opening up."

"What's the third?"

Ski grinned at Nelson. "You hear any of us snoring, kick his ass."

"*I* can't help it if I snore." –Nelson smiled, eyes twinkling– "But Ski's right, VC are attracted to noise like leeches to a hot crotch."

Ski pulled a Winston out of his C-ration pack. "You smoke?"

"Tried it in AIT. Got so sick I turned green."

"How 'bout saving me your Winston's then?"

"I'm a Salem's man, Bob," Nelson said.

"No problem. Yoss?"

Yoss was returning from taking a leak. "Can't stand the shit."

"Yeah," Ski said, "you're a good little Jewish boy."

"Fuck you," Yoss said matter-of-factly as he sat down and leaned back on his elbows. "You Wisconsin farmers will put anything in your mouths."

I smiled, catching Nelson's eye. "They fight like this all the time?"

"Sometimes I swear I was their mama." –Nelson leaned over and nudged my arm– "They just won't admit they like each other."

*     *     *

I lean against my rucksack, searching for a comfortable position with my now locked and loaded M-16 firmly grasped in my hands as the last rays of light fade into the South China Sea. In its wake, a sobering stillness ripples across the coastal plains and wash over us. The night wastes no time in engulfing the landscape, leaving us a lone island in the abyss of the Vietnam night. The stars shimmer in the heavens with a special brilliance. Not a cloud interferes with their ballet across the equatorial sky.

Everyone but Ski has settled down; he finishes a cigarette, cradling it in his palm to hide its glowing tip. I now understand why the tents, or hootches, as they tagged them, are angled toward each other. At night it is necessary to see the other hootch front, otherwise there could be a potential danger when trying to alert the other half of the squad.

A faint rustling interrupts my skyward gaze. I lean forward, careful not to make any noise and stare into the obscure brush. Straining to discern the source of the noise, I slide my thumb several times over the safety lever on my 16 to make sure I can quickly release it should the need arise. I hold my breath. Ten seconds. The grass moves again, accompanied by a tinny rattle that could only be that of a C-ration can. I exhale. *Probably a mongoose. No wonder Nelson chewed Ski out.*

I turn and squint into the hootches. Ski has retired. The rhythmic sound of my comrades' breathing reminds me of my responsibility and their trust in this FNG. I am alone. I am a thin wall of defense sitting between the hostile forces beyond and the continuing existence of Second Platoon, Company D, of the 198th Brigade. Not only are these brave men depending on me, but so also their mothers, their fathers and all who love and care for them.

Thursday, November 5, 1970, Day 15 / 350 to DEROS
—man in black—

The aromatic aroma of coffee brewing coaxed my eyes open; Nelson and Ski were stirring up breakfast. I propped my hands behind my head and gazed outside. The morning breeze had resumed where it had left off the day before as the sun, already well above the horizon, faded in and out as an occasional gray cloud drifted across the *wild November sky....*

✎*....June 1961...*"*Last call for* breakfast!" I jumped out of my sleeping bag and checked the sky through the screen door of the sun-faded canvas tent. It was as blue as a robin's egg! I hastily threw on my cut-offs, thongs and a brand-new Grand Ol' Opry T-shirt and hurried outside. The aroma of flapjacks and thick country bacon sizzling on the iron skillet was all that kept me from the rush of white water pulsating through the slick boulders strewn throughout Deep Creek, just a stone's throw from our campsite. Mom was flipping pancakes onto paper plates as I joined my brother, who was already munching on a juicy slice of bacon. I grabbed a seat in front of a plateful of the golden disks and covered it with a generous dosage of Aunt Jemima maple syrup. The wheat cakes sucked up the golden succulence like a sponge that made each bite a taste of heavenly sweetness. Dad, already

38

finished with breakfast, was busy fixing the fishing poles for the day's adventure on the rapids, set deep within the bowels of the Great Smoky *Mountains of Tennessee....*✐

               *...I pulled myself* out of the hootch and stretched to my full height. "What's for breakfast?"

Nelson handed me a packet of instant coffee. "Grab your cup and make yourself some Java."

."Think I'll try a can of those eggs. I sure got enough of 'em yesterday."

Ski picked up his can of boned chicken and eyed me with a grin. "You ever eat that shit?"

"No, but how can they screw up eggs?"

"Take a whiff."

I took my P-38, punctured the lid and held the can to my nose as a soft belch of pungent air escaped from the slit. I jerked the can away. "Man, smells like sulfur or something."

Ski laughed. "You know they're fucking leftovers from the Korean War?"

"Here," Nelson offered, "have some fruit cocktail."

Bleary-eyed, Yoss crawled from his slumber. "We hooking up this morning?"

"Soon as LT gives the word," Nelson answered.

"Hope it's the RP," Ski said. "Mamasan souvenir bookoo boom-boom, huh, Yoss?" Yoss ignored Ski as he headed for his morning leak.

I wiped off my P-38. "So what's the RP?"

Ski pointed his spoon toward the rice fields stretching toward Chu Lai. "That, my friend, is the RP. Short for Rocket Pocket. It's where the short rounds end up when the dinks rocket Chu Lai. Good thing is, it's the *safest* fucking place in our AO." –Ski blew out a neat smoke ring– "*And* there's bookoo villes to check out."

"C'mon, Yoss," Nelson said, "let's unhook the MA before you get started on chow."

I sat back to enjoy breakfast. Across the perimeter LT and Buffalo were moving from one position to another as the camp went through its morning ritual. The occasional clank of a canteen cup or the rattle of an M-16 being readied for the day created a whispering discord that drifted on the cool morning's patchy breeze.

"Hey, men, how ya doing this morning?"

"Sure as hell beats Ky Tra," Ski answered. "We heading for the RP?"

"In that direction. We'll hook up at 1000 hours. Hillbilly will take point. You guys can have drag. So how was your first night in the bush, Adams?"

"Not bad, LT."

"Nelson told me you were shorted on your gear. I'm going to talk to Topp about this when we get back. I don't want none of my men less than a hundred percent."

"Gimme *two* minutes with that jack-off," Buffalo growled.

LT chuckled. "See you guys at 1000."

\*　　\*　　\*

"How y'all a doing this fine morn'n'?" Hillbilly removed his faded boony hat, revealing a Nordic crown running in tawny waves– as yellow as freshly churned butter. He toted his ruck with ease, wearing only a sleeveless olivine T-shirt above his belt; not an ounce of fat covered his six-foot frame.

"We're a head'n' for the motherfuck'n' rear 'n' hot chow," he twanged as he continued out the perimeter and established a slow pace heading into the valley below. Spanky, squat, athletic and carrying a 16, followed Hillbilly. His dark, ruddy face gave us a smile as he passed. He was walking what Ski had called *slack*, staying just an arm's length behind the pointman. Bromlow, a short-legged beefy character who reminded me of Randy Bradshaw from my D-3-3 unit, followed, carrying a 16. Langley, hollow-chested and bony, allowed ten-meters to pass before falling in behind Bromlow. Retchin came next. Carrying the awesome 60, he was by far the platoon's biggest man, sporting a chocolate-colored boxcar mustache as thick as his six-two frame. Chadborne, his new AG, followed close behind, big-boned and scowling.

By the time our squad was ready to fall in, Hillbilly was a hundred meters out. Wad and Fritts fell in ahead of Nelson. He in turn signaled me to fall in behind him. Yoss came behind me and Ski took "drag", the last man in line.

A mass of dark clouds was building above the grassy hilltops to the west, generating erratic gusts that helped cover our movements through the dry brush. It was a gentle sloping walk to the smaller hills bordering the verdant flats of the lush rice paddies. Emaciated trees, elephant grass and hilly slopes and saddles hid most of the platoon from view. Occasionally, though, I would make a rise and get a glimpse of the long line of Grunts, stretched in a thin line like one of those connect-the-dots pictures I played as a child. I now understood the advantage of stringing out the platoon in such a fashion. An ambush would only take out a small number of us, unless, of course, they caught us from above as we were crossing a valley.

Thirty minutes into the hump, Nelson turned toward me and held up his palm, then spiraled a finger and pointed at me. Correctly interpreting his signing, I signaled Yoss to stop. Yoss and Nelson sat down to rest, using their rucks as backrests. I tossed my ruck down and sat beside it, grasping my legs as I tucked them up to my chest. Within five minutes the signal moved down the line to hook up again. I learned that this happened a lot during the course of a hump, which translated into little ground covered on most days. Sometimes LT needed to check his grid map to make sure we were heading for the correct checkpoints. Other times the point man would see something he didn't like. Or maybe LT just thought we needed a break for water and a smoke.

Approaching one-thirty, we entered a dense thicket of scrawny trees atop one of the larger hills. A hodgepodge of mottled clouds filled the sky, silencing the morning breeze, which resulted in a rank of sweaty brows filing into the shelter.

"We'll set up here." –LT wiped the sweat off his forehead, gazing at the lustrous fields of green that encompassed the Rocket Pocket– "If the rain holds off, Nelson, we'll take your squad to check out our AO."

LT, Buffalo and Charles Tucker, our radio-telephone operator "RTO", found a suitable site in the center of the stand. In turn the squad leaders established their positions around them. Our squad, being the last into the new NDP, chose a position by the incoming trail.

Nelson dropped his ruck. "Let's get this hootch up. I'm starved."

Yoss picked a spot next to where Wad, Fritts and Ski had claimed, and after booting off the sticks and rocks, spread his poncho onto it. Nelson, picking out a couple of small trees, expertly macheted a roof support pole about seven feet long and two end poles, three and a-half feet long. After trimming the rough knobs from the end poles, he pounded them into the ground with his entrenching tool on the opposite sides of Yoss' floor poncho. Nelson had me help him secure the roof pole to the end poles with some nylon bootlaces as Yoss cut four corner stakes and drove them in at the corners of his poncho. After securing the roof pole, Nelson pulled out two ponchos he already had snapped together, threw them over the roof pole and began snapping their ends to the floor poncho. Yoss, meanwhile, using bootlaces that were already attached to the floor's corner grommets, secured the roof corners to the corner stakes. Nelson then cut a cross-pole about five feet in length and he and Yoss placed it on top of and perpendicular to the center of the roof pole. Attaching to their ends the cords that closed off the roof ponchos' hooded sections, they drew them up to the cross-pole, which provided more headroom inside. Nelson finished by using my poncho to close off the rear of the hootch, leaving the entrance open and facing the outside of the perimeter.

Within ten minutes from cutting the first pole, we were pulling lunch out of our rucks.

*     *     *

"Let's get this shit on the road," Tucker said, hoisting his bulky radio equipment onto his back. It was hard not to like Tucker right off. With a tangle of ebony wool over a honed face, he wore a happy-go-lucky expression as he rolled off his words in an easy going, don't give a damn, kind of way.

"Keep your black ass patient a minute," Doc said.

"Now, Doc, you *know* I love this shit and I know *you* love it, too, man."

"Yeah, *right* I do. This is my *dream come true*, vacationing in sunny Vietnam, patching up your scraggly asses whenever they get in the way of some VC bullet." It was obvious Doc was a class guy. Unlike his fellow Grunts, his fatigue pants were clean and bloused, his face scrubbed and his hair trimmed under a carefully molded boony hat.

At 1300 hours eight Grunts and a rookie headed out of the northwest side of the perimeter. Nelson took point, with Yoss tagging his heels on slack. LT fell in next to guide Nelson with his ever-present grid map, with Tuck following for quick access to the radio. Wad and Fritts ruled the middle with heavy gun support. Doc came next, while Ski and me guarded the rear. Our spread was less than this morning's hump, I guessed to increase our reaction time in case of trouble. It was nice to travel light, carrying only pertinent weapons, ammo and water. A couple of the guys were carrying small Kodak Instamatic cameras in makeshift cases attached to their web belts, an idea I intended to implement after I got my own camera.

The clearing skies kicked up crisp gusts of wind that curled about our patrol as we wound down the hill on the side facing the Rocket Pocket, the rustling brush again covering the occasional clank or rattle while we plowed through the waist-high grass. Several hundred meters took us into a forest of immature palm trees bordering the shallow ridge like a hula skirt as far as I could see. Beneath the umbrella of fan-shaped leaves, a kaleidoscope of soft light flickered through the hissing canopy as I scanned left and right, thankful for the shield of trees that kept the dry wind sailing over our heads. Nelson led us along the darting matted floor for half-an-hour before taking us toward the far side of the bald ridgeline and by the time we neared an area stippled with stands of napalm-scarred trees, we were ready for a break.

Tuck got on the radio. "Charlie Papa, Charlie Papa, Echo Foxtrot. Break."

*"Gotcha, Echo Foxtrot. How me? Break."*

"Same same, Charlie Papa. Arrived checkpoint Victor Tango 1. Break."

*"Roger, Echo Foxtrot. Copy. Arrived checkpoint Victor Tango 1. Out."*

Tuck swung the pack to the ground and clicked the phone into the unit. "Shit, LT, this mother gets heavy. Then carrying this 16, ammo, 'n' everything else, what's a man to do?"

"How 'bout not complaining so loud," Wad spoke up. "You're gonna wake goddamn Charlie up."

"Let goddamn Charlie wake up." –Tuck gestured with his 16– "I'll shove this right up his skinny little ass."

"Ten minutes," LT said as the laughter died.

*     *     *

We haven't moved a hundred meters when movement inside the treeline catches my eye. I stare at the point and spot it again. It's a man, dressed in black.

"LT," I half-whisper, half-yell through the wind. "LT, wait up."

"What's up, Adams?"

"There," –I point– "in the treeline. I think I saw a VC."

"Open up where you last saw him."

I hesitate.

"Now, Adams, do it!"

I raise my 16 while switching off the safety and pop one, two, three rounds. The percussion rips the air.

"Let it go!" LT yells, pointing his rifle toward the trees.

I switch to full auto and spray the trees with a swath of deadly fire.

"Give 'im shit, Adams!" Tuck yelps as the cartridges steam through the foliage.

LT stares at the treeline for ten seconds. "Good job, Adams." I pull another magazine out of my bandoleer, shove it into the housing and chamber a round.

LT pauses for a last look. "Next time don't wait to tell me. Just open up. We can always talk about it later. Okay, let's move out. Everybody keep their eyes peeled like Adams here."

Nelson gives me a wink. "Way to go. You must have eyes like a hawk. They coulda been setting us up for an ambush."

As he turns back, I smile. My days as a FNG are over. I am, a Grunt.

\*     \*     \*

Nelson dug through his ruck, pulling out a canvas bag containing the Mechanical Ambush. "Ready?"

"Busy day, huh?" I was cleaning the remnants of dinner out of my canteen cup with some water we had just humped from a water patrol.

"Some days you get all the shit." —Nelson picked up his over-under and pointed at some thorny bushes hugging the trail fifty meters from our position— "We'll set it up down there."

"Okay," Nelson said as we arrived at the MA site, "this time just watch to get a handle on it. This can get hairy real quick if you're not careful." —he placed the canvas bag on the ground— "First, find a place where the trail's the narrowest so there ain't much chance of him spotting it. This here's good." —he kneeled and took out a length of wire wrapped around a popsicle stick— "This is the tripwire." Tied to the end of the wire was a cut-off section of plastic spoon with only the eating portion and an inch of the handle remaining. A small hole was drilled into the end of the handle, onto which the wire was connected.

Nelson took out a hand-sharpened eight-penny nail and a common wooden clothespin with wire wrapped around it. "This doohickey connects it all together." He unrolled the wires. One of the wires had a blasting cap attached to its end. Its opposite end was spliced: one splice held a metal eyelet; the other was attached to one of two thumbtacks pressed into the jaws of the clothespin. The other thumbtack secured another wire ending with another metal eyelet. A hole had been drilled into the middle of the clothespin.

"Take the clothespin, and with the jaws facing the trail, push the nail through the hole to secure it to the trunk of this bush. Keep it a foot or so in from the trail. You don't want to go any lower than knee height, else a mongoose or other varmint might trip it."

Nelson picked up the plastic spoon. "Now squeeze the clothespin apart and slide the spoon between the thumbtacks like so, not too far, so it'll slip out real easy. Then stretch the wire across the trail and tie it to a bush on the other side. Keep it the same height as the spoon and tight." –Nelson took a six-volt battery out of the bag– "Take the wing nuts off and put the eyelets on; it don't matter which goes on which. Tighten them down good." –Nelson leaned back on his heels– "Got that so far?"

"I think so. Who thought this up, anyway?"

"No idea." –he took off his hat to wipe his brow– "It's been passed down from unit to unit, Grunt to Grunt, for I don't know how long. Now that we got the tripwire in place, take some brush and camouflage it best you can, especially where the plastic spoon is." We took a few minutes to gather some brush and conceal the ends of the wires.

"Now comes the tricky part." He took out the claymore mine, a curved rectangular OD green fiberglass casing ten inches long, six inches high and an inch and a half thick. Printed in relief on the arched front were the words, "FRONT TOWARD ENEMY". On the claymore's top was a peep sight and a detonator well which was meant to receive a blasting cap. At the mine's base were two scissor-type legs that folded down to secure it in the ground.

"Placement of this is pretty critical." –he backed several feet from the tripwire– "You gotta make sure it's far enough from the wire so he'll get the full effect of this fucker, but not too far so as not to get a clean kill. You know there's a thousand steel BB's encased in a pound of C-4 in here. So," –he stuck the mine on the side of the trail five feet from the tripwire– "assuming this dink don't have no idea we're right down the trail, he'll probably be moving at a pretty good clip...this should do just fine. Point it right at the middle of the tripwire and up thirty degrees. Keep the angle a little low and it should pretty much cut him clean in half."

He picked up the wire securing the blasting cap. "This is the ignition wire to the whole thing." –Nelson moved in back of the mine– "Get behind me." –I backed up as he kneeled– "First, lay the firing wire flat like this and make sure it's hid good. Once it's hot, you don't *even* mess in front of it again. The next part you do real careful-like. Take the blasting cap and...carefully...push it into the detonator well at the top of the mine." –Nelson let out a breath– "I hate that part. It's got a shorting plug so static electricity won't trigger it, but, damn, still makes me shit bricks. Last, take the camouflaged bandoleer and place it over the top of the claymore to keep out the dirt. Then put some brush in front of it to break up its outline."

He stood and stretched. "Soon as the gook trips it, the spoon flips out and the thumbtacks hit, completing the circuit. Then no more gook. Pretty good alarm system, huh? Just make sure it's hidden good, else Charlie might see it and turn it back on us."

"You can't always be this careful," Nelson said while heading back. "Sometimes you can't see too good, or it might be raining. Do the best you can, that's all."

*      *      *

"Hey, Adams. You're up." Fritts was squatting in front of the hootch, his form black against the night sky.

I crawled outside. "Wow, pretty night."

"Yeah," Fritts whispered, untying his boots. "Sometimes it's bright enough to write a letter."

"I believe it."

"Well, night." Fritts crawled over to his hootch and placed his boots at the end of his bed before sliding onto his mattress.

I placed my 16 on my lap. *What a day,* I thought, as I checked the luminescent hands on my watch. *Nine-forty...guard duty till eleven-twenty. Hope I can get used to this night shift work. Kinda like working third shift at McLaughlin's.* I pulled my boots on, gazing with half-opened eyes at the wealth of elephant grass swaying quietly in a wash of soft blue moonlight.

*My first contact today...just like that. Wonder if I hit the guy? Man, he could be lying out there right now with my bullet in him, and I don't even know it. Too weird.* I stared down the trail toward the bushes holding the MA. *There could be VC heading down our trail right now, looking for us. That would mean that I'd be the first guy....* I unconsciously thumbed my safety, feeling the hair rise on the nape of my neck. *Hope that MA works.* I looked at the waxing moon, having completed a third of its journey across the night sky. A faint breeze rustled the leaves above me. *This is only day two. How can anybody get out of here without getting blown away sooner or later? Well,* I thought, checking my watch again in the moonlight, *guess the best way to get out of here in one piece is to work on surviving day number three and not worry about day four, day five, or day three hundred....*

Friday, November 6, 1970, Day 16 / 349 to DEROS
—re-supply—

"Hey, Adams." Hillbilly's whiskered jaw clenched as he swung his ruck over his shoulders. "I hear ya kicked that gook's ass yesterday."

"Wasn't that big a deal."

"Bullshit. Enytime ya get a crack at ol' Charlie it's a big deal." –he checked the safety on his 16– "Ya kin be in my squad *enytime*."

Shortly after rising, Nelson and I had dismantled the MA. The hairy part had been disconnecting the blasting cap. After that– piece of cake.

"Damn," –LT handed Tuck the phone– "they canceled our rendezvous with Third Platoon." –he looked around; most already had their rucks on– "Third Platoon took mortar fire this morning. They want us to check it out. Nichols, Buffalo will take you and Hillbilly's squad out at 1000 hours. You'll hook up with a patrol from First to help beef up your number. I've already got the checkpoints. Plus I got a re-supply scheduled for 1600, so, Nelson, be ready to take your men out by 1530. Buffalo should be back by then for your radio support." LT dropped his ruck and pulled out his poncho, the signal to re-establish our positions.

"Nichols probably got a hard-on thinking 'bout that patrol," Ski said as he dumped his ruck. "Right the fuck up his alley." –he pulled out his poncho and tossed it to Fritts– "I'll see if I can find those poles again, then it's R&R for the rest of the day."

"Most of it, anyway," said Nelson, taking out his ponchos. "Least we don't hafta cut no LZ this time."

"Then this is it?" I asked Nelson as we began to rebuild the hootch. "We just sit around all day?"

"Don't complain. We take every one of these days we can get. Just don't let on to LT that you're too disappointed."

After setting up the hootch, Nelson and I settled in as Ski and Yoss joined Wad and Fritts in a game of Spades. I ended up taking a nap that extended into early afternoon. When I awoke, Nelson was still asleep. Few others were stirring in the camp. "Can't believe how tired I was," I commented to Yoss as I crawled outside. Yoss was busy writing another letter. "Man, Yoss, you sure write a lotta letters," I said as I took a dog-eared paperback out of my ruck.

He didn't look up. "Got a lot of cousins," was all he offered. Deciding not to pursue it, I leaned back for a couple more chapters before lunch.

*    *    *

Nelson swung his bandoleer over his shoulder. "Let's get going. LZ's two hundred meters out."

We moved out in single file. Tuck fell in toward the front and Ski took drag while I fell in ahead of him. The blending of the soft afternoon breeze and a rapid succession of clouds lent to a cool afternoon and after the long repose my legs nearly sprung me down the trail. In less than ten minutes we were forming a thirty-meter wide semi-circle atop a small knoll.

"My air mattress better be here," Wad said as he peered at the northern horizon.

"No shit," Fritts replied, "I am fucking *sick* of listening to your damn complaining all night."

"A month ago we didn't even *know* what an air mattress was," interjected Nelson. "Now you spoiled little boys can't live without it."

The rhythmic thumping of the re-supply bird corked the talk. Tuck got on the horn. "Alpha Bravo 2, Echo Foxtrot, how copy? Break."

*"Gotcha fine, Echo Foxtrot. Alpha Bravo 2 request smoke. Break."*

Nelson pulled the pin on a smoke canister and threw it into the center of the semi-circle.

"Alpha Bravo 2. Smoke is popped. Smoke is popped. Break."

*"Roger, Echo Foxtrot, we have one red smoke on the ground. Break."*

"Affirmative, Alpha Bravo 2, one red smoke. You are clear for landing."

Nelson walked to the center of the semi-circle and held his 16 over his head with both arms to provide the chopper a target to guide in on. The chopper, still several hundred feet up, adjusted its vector while dropping toward our LZ.

*CRACK! CRACK! CRACK!* jerks our heads left. Everybody hits the ground except Nelson, who runs to grab the phone out of Tuck's hand.

"Hot LZ! Pull out! Pull out!" Nelson shouts into the unit as he falls to one elbow. Immediately the chopper leans port and swoops toward the Rocket Pocket.

I find my breath, surprised I had hit the ground so fast without thinking. We continue to lie in the tall grass as the smoke hisses, *"Hey, VC, some juicy*

*GI tidbits over here!"* As if reading our minds, Nelson signals us to back away from the dissipating cloud.

"Anybody see where the shots came from?" Nelson puffs while crouching in an area of tall brush seventy-five meters away.

"They was shooting at the bird, man," Tuck answers. "Could be anyfuckingwhere."

A bead of sweat slides down Nelson's sideburn. "Let's get back and let LT know what's going on."

Within ten minutes two Huey Gunships cackle in low profile across the RP below our camp.

"Here they fucking come!" Ski shouts, looking up from his simmering can of beefsteak. "Now, ain't that a *beeeeautiful* sight."

LT is on the horn, making sure the pilots are aware of our position as they hug the first line of hills before zooming directly overhead. A faint odor of jet fuel settles on us as I watch them disappear over the next hill, their blapping quickly dissipating in the steady breeze rising from the RP.

"You *know* those fucking gooks didi'ed soon as they squeezed off that first clip," Blondie declares from across the perimeter.

"Fuck'n' *A*, they ran, " Nichols shoots back. They *always* run. "Wish just fucking once they'd face us in the open."

"Like some kinda wild west shoot-out, 'eh, Nichols?" Hillbilly interjects.

Blondie was right. The gun-ships found no trace of VC activity and summarily withdrew to Fat City. We settled in as the receding light isolated our positions into solitary castles of defense. Wad, first on guard, leaned against his ruck and placed Ski's 16 on his lap. I laid my head down and fixed my eyes on the poncho roof, glad that this thin plastic veil offered, at least in my mind, some degree of safety from whatever may be out there. As my eyes closed, I wondered why, after this relatively easy day, I was so tired. But before I could conjure up an answer, I was fast asleep.

Saturday, November 7, 1970, Day 17 / 348 to DEROS
—'ug yuice—

We'd been lucky for the past couple of days, but as our sweaty ranks entered an area flourishing with palm and bamboo, the boiling skies told me our luck wouldn't carry us through the evening. A hot and sticky five-hour hump had taken its toll on my rookie legs and with gratefulness I dropped my ruck and sat down hard beside it.

Third Platoon's campsite held a dozen hootches hugging the rice fields of the RP, nestled on a loamy, almost bare, forest floor. That, along with the fermenting vegetation in the water soaked fields, filled my nostrils with a not unpleasant sweet, musty odor. Enjoying a generous drink of water, my ears tuned in to the unnatural silence beneath the wealth of large palm trees; only the mosquitoes whining above the quiet conversations of the Grunts or a heavy drop of dew spattering onto the hootch-tops were discernable.

"Yoss," I asked, looking in the trees, "where's all the birds at? Ain't seen a one yet."

Yoss was digging out some crackers. "Gone. Shelling's scared 'em probably to Cambodia by now."

"You're kidding. A jungle with no birds?"

"Yep. Only things left are mongoose, lizards, snakes and tigers."

"Tigers?"

He plopped one of the crackers into his mouth. "Haben't deen one yet, but dey're out 'dere."

"What about these critters?" I asked, brushing three mosquitoes off my arm.

Yoss stuffed in another cracker. "You ain't gob no 'ug yuice yet?" He pulled a small oily green bottle out of his cargo pocket.

I squirted a small amount in my hand. "Man, this stuff stinks."

"It's the GI's numba one friend. See those leeches?" He pointed at what looked like slender gray worms three-quarters of an inch long stealing toward us.

"Land leeches. They're attracted to body heat. Here, let me show ya how to keep 'em off." –he squirted a thin ring around each of his boots, ankle high– "They won't go past that line. They ain't so bad where we'd been last couple days. Too dry or something. If you find one on you, squirt it and–"

"Fuck, boys," Hillbilly announced as he returned from Third Platoon's Command Post, "no hot chow tonight. We got ourselves anotha motha-*fuck'n'* night in the boonies."

"That's right, men," LT continued. "CE's been canceled. Some trouble down in the 196th's AO switched priorities on us. Hang out while we figure where we're going to set up."

"Adams?"

I squinted at a figure approaching in the half-light beneath the thick foliage. "Moreno! I forgot about you being in Third Platoon. How ya doing, man?"

"Fan-fucking-tastic," he said, shaking my hand. "'Cept for those mortars the other night, it ain't been that bad. See any gooks yet?"

"Got me a shot at one the other day on this patrol."

"No shit? Blow his ass away?"

"I dunno, man. Hey, when'd ya get the M-79?"

Moreno held up the stubby grenade launcher. "Dudes call it a blooper. Shit. Soon as I stepped off the chopper, they took my 16 and gave me this fucking hunk of metal."

I glanced at Yoss. "Hey, Yoss, this here's Dennis Moreno. We came out together."

"Hey, Yoss, how ya–"

"Listen up!" LT announced from the CP. "We're going to set up along the face of the RP. Those two positions will move over to form up to your ends. Hillbilly, you take the south end, and Nelson, the north."

"Hey," Moreno asked, "after you get set up, wanna play some cards?"

"Sure. What's your game?"

"Ain't nothing but Spades around here."

I swung my ruck over my shoulder. "Euchre's my game, but I'm willing to learn."

The coming of dusk signaled it was time to get back to my squad. It had been good to see Moreno again. But it wasn't the same as being with my squad members. I guessed Moreno sensed it, too. After only a few short days, that bond had already exceeded that of any I had known with D-3-3 or even the bubblegum friendships back home.

*Dear Mom & Dad,*                                                    *Sat. Nov 7, 1970*

*Hello! How's everybody in your part of the world? Have you received your Xmas present yet? Sure am gonna hate to turn 20 Nov 25. Oh well.*

*Since I last wrote, Monday or Tuesday?, I finished that six day schooling they give all of us replacements. They then trucked me and about 14 others to our new unit at the 198th Brigade. It is located just a little north of the Chu Lai Replacement Center, on the coast also. The facilities are maybe a little bit better. At least it's closer to the main PX & a short walk from the USO. I am in D Company again & in 2nd Platoon. About 3 days ago they took me & 8 others to the airstrip to be flown in by helicopter to the different Platoon locations out in the mountains. We must be about 15 miles from our main base. The ride on the chopper was really exciting & somewhat scary. Especially when descending. All 4 Platoons are fairly close together. They dropped me in this field and from there we humped about half a mile to the edge of a hill where there was a small base camp. We didn't do to much at all & had lots of free time. Instead of digging foxholes and wearing steel pots & all we build tents every night out of our plastic ponchoes & sleep on air mattressess. And we just wear something like a green cowboy hat called booney hats. So it isn't bad at all. We didn't do a thing yesterday except go to get some resupplies a chopper was bringing in but some VC fired at it. We were supposed to have gone in today on stand-down, or a 3 day rest period. But of course the choppers were delayed somehow & now we have to stay another night. 14 choppers were going to pick up our whole company. We must get about 10 hrs. sleep a night with about a 2 hr. guard a piece. You don't have to worry cause this is a real good outfit I'm in. Everybody really works together. There's 25 in our Platoon.*

*Well, sure hope our pick-up makes it tomorrow. The weather's held up real good. Although it'll probably rain tonight a little.*

*I found out that I already had my required overseas shots in AIT.*

*There are 3 others from AIT from my Platoon in D-3-3 here in the 198th. Although there in Co. A, B, & C. So we're really split up.*

*Right now I'm with 3rd Plt. At the original camp of 1st Plt. 1st & the mortar Plts. are across the valley from us.*

*Can't think of much else to write so will stop now. Take care & write.*

*Love, Your son, Bob*

The thickening clouds sped the descent of nightfall, and as Ski assumed first watch, the sky let loose with a torrent of rain that sent him diving for his hootch. He cursed the rain as he positioned himself on the end of his mattress, resigning himself to a miserable watch. I, though, found comfort in the steady pounding on my plastic guardian that drowned out any suspicious sounds that would've otherwise pricked my ears. And knowing I was warm and dry, while Charlie must be hiding on a night like this, instilled a feeling of peace. All that remained was this miracle of nature, and as nature took its course, I closed my eyes on my fourth day in the bush.

# STAND-DOWN ONE

Sunday, November 8, 1970, Day 18 / 347 to DEROS
—evening in paradise—

A wide, toothy grin spread across Blondie's sun-lit face. "Birds are *inbound!* Let's get this cluster-fuck in the air!" Second and Third Platoons' waited in a swirling haze of purple smoke on the edge of a dry rice paddy as three UH-1C Gunship *Hogs,* each outfitted with a pair of *60*'s and two twenty-four round rocket launchers clicked toward us in single-file. Blasting past us, the choppers split to provide cover for nine UH-1D slicks following close behind. The slate-gray bird's powerful turbines slamming the tropical air were a beautiful combination of sight and sound, not only because they were sending us to the rear, but also because these high-tech feats of engineering took total dominance over the terrain: they were the Grunt's security blanket in the sky.

The sun had already begun its flawless descent toward the mountains behind us. After two delays, due to an emergency extraction of the 196th, we had finally gotten word of incoming birds shortly after five. Another group of choppers was simultaneously picking up the other platoons several klicks to our north.

"Keep with your squads!" LT shouts over the thunderous peel of air being shred apart by nine eggbeaters alighting in two staggered rows. Hunching over, I follow my squad through the deafening whirlwinds to a chopper on the far row.

"Sit here on the edge!" Ski shouts. "Just lean the fuck back and enjoy the ride! But keep your ruck on! Keeps ya from sliding out!"

"Sliding out?!"

My breath leaves me as the chopper lifts and tilts forward to gain momentum. I reach behind me to grab onto something– all there is are the backs of Ski's and Yoss' rucks. *If I go, they go with me!* I promise myself as the chopper clears the trees and begins a sharp turn back toward the RP.

"See!" Ski shouts into my ear as the ground rushes by three hundred feet below. "Centrifugal force keeps us locked in...cool, huh!" It was cool. *Is this living or what? Where else can you carry a loaded machine-gun, pee anywhere in your backyard and get a free chopper ride?* As the birds level off far above the maze of rice fields, Yoss pulls out his Instamatic and clicks some shots at the sun-drenched China Sea, now bathed in a palette of crimson and golden hues that would make any landscape artist drool.

I stare into the soft blanket of green beneath my feet and savor the relief of surviving my first mission. How these other guys, who've been through who-knows-what, must be feeling about getting another stab at doing what everybody else takes for granted. *Wonder how long a guy can go with a few days of R&R followed by three weeks in the bush? Uncle Sam says twelve months,* I think as Ski nudges me, *so guess I'll take his word for it.*

"They beat us in!" Ski shouts, pointing to the airstrip. More than a dozen steel birds are on the airstrip a thousand feet below. Their rotors still spin while dozens of Grunts from First and the Mortar Platoons exit toward a row of trucks parked beside the field.

Our choppers bank left, then right to line up on the airstrip. Nearing the ground, the pilots seem to slow their fall by pulling back the choppers' noses, as if reining in a horse, to set down softly behind the others. I jump into the nearest truck filling with Grunts. The truck full, it leaves the base behind as I relax against my ruck and watch the sun bow to the mountains, whose shadow soon engulfs us in its race for the horizon.

In a few minutes we begin to chug through Fat City's marketplace. The village is teaming with the yellow masses as they rush to finish their business before curfew. My head turns as one of the guys in the truck cab ahead cranks up *Satisfaction* on his portable tape deck and holds it on top of the cab roof. Taking it as a queue, several Grunts begin to pump their weapons overhead while others twirl their belts of 60 ammo like a lasso as they compete for attention in tempo with the Stones cult hit. The celebration escalates. GI's throw out shouts and leftover cans of C's and chocolate bars that lure the locals to the edge of the road. The enamored spectators shout "Numba One! Numba One!" showing their black or white teeth and waving their arms like cheering a Fourth of July Parade.

"Look at that! They fucking love us!" Ski shouts, bobbing a 16 overhead in one hand and machete in the other.

"At least when it's still light out!" Wad yells, pointing his M-60 high into the air. I watch Blondie, in the truck ahead of us, attempting to impersonate a hula dancer. *What have I got myself into?*

*     *     *

"Stand-down your weapons, men!" Topp's hands shook as he positioned himself outside the Armory; he looked like an over-ripe tomato ready to pop. "Let's get this done, men! Then you can grab a bunk, get cleaned up and get some hot chow!"

I pulled in on the last of the trucks as night settled into a clear and cool *Jewel of Southeast Asia* Vietnam evening. The ebullient sounds of shouts and laughter from the relieved GI's danced in my ears as I jumped from the truck bed and willed my internal clock to slow to a crawl; I was determined to savor every minute of this stand-down. Many of the Grunts were pounding down the dirt lane toward the EM Club or to the Mess Hall, already brimming with hungry GI's as most had given priority to their craving for "real food" before cleaning their grimy bodies.

I handed my 16 and bandoleer over and followed my squad to claim a bunk in one of two barracks assigned to Second Platoon. Next, it was to the showers. Nelson, Wad and Fritts, though, headed for the Mess Hall.

"Let's clean this shit off," Ski said, stripping to his shorts.

"Fucking *A*," Yoss answered.

I hurried to where a truck had dumped a large pile of clean fatigues on the ground in front of the shower area. Sorting through the mound, I unearthed the most faded, beat up uniform I could find. *These! Even has an Americal patch!* I ripped off my clothes and tossed them into the truck. *For three miserable weeks I had to endure that greasy, putrid, green, brand-X FNG clown suit. No more! These have probably seen a lotta action. Most likely been in that Ky-Tra Valley I've heard about.*

The shower area sat on a slab of concrete, on top of which was a single, whitewashed concrete block wall enclosed within a screened-in, wood-framed structure to keep out the nasties. I carefully placed my clean fatigues on one of the still-dry benches, found an available shower and turned it on. After being in the bush for only one week, the warm water cascading over me was heaven.

Shaving afterwards, I gazed beyond my reflection and into the Vietnam night, my mind lulled by the soothing song of the crickets as a cool evening breeze caressed my face. I felt reborn. I– was– there! After months of training, preparing, praying and crying, my first mission was behind me. And I survived! Tonight I was no longer an insecure wet-behind-the-ears kid of nineteen. I *was– a man. ...*

✎*...Saturday, October 14, 1972...My hand brushed* against her arm, sending a shiver up my spine as I watched a rash of goose-pimples wash over her forearm. *She feels it, too.* Beyond Sheryl's perfumed hair, McGinnis' Melon Market came into view. The open-air market was displaying its October bounty of Halloween fare: sheaves of corn lashed teepee-like amidst mountains of bright orange pumpkins nestled in reefs of yellow straw, black kegs of homemade cider stacked in pyramids along the side of a rustic red barn door, and guarding the market's perimeter, a platoon of smiling scarecrows.

"Wanna stop for a snack?" Art threw out as he swerved into the parking lot, kicking up a cloud of white dust.

"*Don't!*" Sue scolded.

"Susan, you're cruis'n' for a bruis'n'," Art sang to the melody of the Buckingham's hit song.

"Arthur Gerald Davis," Sheryl began in a motherly voice, "*you're* the one cruising for a bruising."

"Yes, ma'am."

The October sun warmed my shirt as I escorted my date through the maze of pumpkin rows, her sensual perfume wafting over the country air as I walked as near as I dared– I hadn't even gotten up the nerve to hold her hand yet. She was the one, though. I had known it from that first day at Blackhawk College. I had sat there like a Rodin, entranced as she chatted with her girlfriends in the student union, unable to take my eyes *off of her....*✐

..."*You starting a* mustache?" Yoss jerked me out of my euphoria as he scrubbed his ivories.

"Yep. Tried to grow one in AIT, but had to shave it off. DI said each hair had to be exactly the same length." I rubbed my hand over my clean-shaven cheek and stared into the mirror. "This one ain't coming off...never."

"Chow, anybody?" Ski said while pulling on his fatigues.

Yoss spit out a mouth full of toothpaste. "Mind if I put my clothes on first?"

"I'll meet you guys over there. I gotta eat, man." Ski slammed the screened-in door with his bootlaces still untied.

"How long's Ski been here?"

Yoss spit. "Two weeks longer than me. I've been in country almost two months now."

"How about Nelson?"

"Not much longer than us. Three months or so." –Yoss pulled a clean T-shirt over his head– "Nichols, Settle and Doc's got the most time in-country. The rest of them average, oh, four, maybe five months. Newest guy before you was Fritts. Been here three weeks."

"And he's already Wad's assistant gunner?"

"Don't take long to figure out where you belong out there."

"Ready?" I paused in front of the mirror to reposition the boony hat crowning my new seasoned look. *Not bad.*

We found Nelson stooped over at the bottom of the wooden steps leading to the Mess Hall.

"Ate too fast," he rasped, "ain't used to real chow yet." –he wiped bile from his mouth with a dirty shirtsleeve– "Man, that eggnog *is* good, though. Guess I shouldn't a drank that third one."

"Ski in there?"

"Nah, he skied to the EM Club."

We found a table by one of the windows and sat down with trays brimming with thick steaming slices of roast beef, dressing, mashed potatoes covered with brown gravy, carrots and peas combo, buttered rolls and several cartons of eggnog.

"We get to eat like this all the time?" I asked Yoss while wolfing down a generous scoop of potatoes.

"They always feed us like this the first day in, then it's pretty much what everybody else eats. But it ain't bad." We downed a second helping and staggered through most of our third, forgetting Nelson's departing warning not to stuff ourselves. As our stomachs stretched, the din that had greeted us upon our arrival shrank; most of the GI's had headed for the showers or the beer hall.

I stood up. "Want to roll on over to the EM Club?"

"Why not."

The EM Club was located two blocks south of our company area, sharing a front row seat along the beach with several palm trees leaning toward the sea as if yearning for a closer look. From a distance, the inviting glow of yellow streaming from the windows seemed to mesh with the hullabaloo of inebriated Grunts and the throbbing bass of CCR's *Green River*.

We turned off the sandy lane and followed a worn path that led to the entrance, the wooden building looking much like the snack hootch at the Replacement Center, its large screened-in windows propped open, the flaps appearing as the jaws of so many dogs panting to cool themselves. The similarities ended as I pushed open the screen door. Above an ornately crescent-shaped mahogany bar hung a gilded-framed mirror, vibrating from two giant speakers sitting on either side. My eyes followed an assortment of rock posters: Stones, Beatles, Doors, Iron Butterfly, Cream. They lined the walls, almost obscured by cigarette smoke twisting into half-a-dozen ceiling fans, reminding me of the smoke grenade Hillbilly had popped to bring in the birds just a few hours earlier. The fans spun their pleasure onto several dozen small round tables below, each harboring a small band of rag-torn Grunts quaffing their brews.

"Over here!" Ski shouts. We work our way through the rabble of grunts to where Ski, Retchin and Harvey sit at a table cluttered with cigarette butts and beer bottles. "Barkee! Another round here!"

"How the fuck are *you*!" Retchin bellows. He grabs my hand, holding it in a powerful grip while scrutinizing me through thick glasses. "*Who* the fuck are you?"

"He's slightly wasted!" Ski yells, glassy-eyed. He hands the barkee a ten dollar MPC with Chief Hollow Horn Bear staring back from the military payment certificate. "Ain't you, you cocksucking faggot!"

"No fuck'n' more 'n you!" –Retchin continues to eye me with a glassy stare– "You that new guy who blew away that fucking dink?"

"That's me," I answer and already regretting my suggestion to come here, but maybe Retchin is just letting off some steam. After all, he did lose his Assistant Gunner a few days ago.

"Well, let me shake your hand. That was fuck'n' great!"

"You already shook his hand once." –Ski smashes a cigarette stub into an overflowing ashtray– "Man, are you in love with this guy?"

"GIMME 'NOTHER FUCK'N' BEER!" Retchin thunders. He jerks his hand from mine and flips Ski the bird. "You fuck'n' candy-ass motherfucks know I can drink any fuck'n' one of you cocksuck'n' fuckheads under this fuck'n' table and I'm..." –he empties three quarters of the bottle– "...GOING TO SHOW YOU DOGSHITS HOW!"

Harv grins. "Hey, dude, if ya got something on your fuck'n' mind just come out 'n' say it."

Retchin peers at Harv over his dark plastic-framed glasses. "I told you I fu...I tol' yo'...." –Retchin's eyes go white, his neck limp as his head bobs forward. He jerks his head up– "Fuck. My gut. Where'd ja...put...fuck'n' door?"

"You jas foller me and I'll sho ya." –Harv helps Retchin up and points him in the right direction– "Straight ahead thare, big feller." –Retchin leans forward, squinting through the smoke– "See it thare? It's right the fuck in front of you!"

"Fucker neva could handle the juish," Harv comments as Retchin pushes through the door.

"Think he'll make it?" Yoss asks.

Ski squeezes a last drag on his cigarette. "Not a fucking chance in hell. But what the fuck, we'll pick him up on the way back."

I sip my beer and survey the beer hall. Only a few are from our platoon. Blondie, Chadborne and Spanky are at the next table matching us beer for beer. Nichols and his cohort are sulking at a corner table across the room.

"Where's Hillbilly and the others?"

Harv and Ski look at each other.

"Adams..." –Ski leans forward and motions me toward him with his index finger– "...first thing you gotta learn, there's two kindsa people in this here country of Viet-*fucking*-Nam."

Ski points a finger at himself and then at Harv. "We...we is the juicers. Them guys out there..." –he points into the night– "...*they's* the fuck'n' Heads." –Ski leans in closer; the bitter scent of alcohol is strong on his breath– "You gotta decide, man. Whachu gonna be? A juicer, or a head?"

"I'll, ah...I'll think about it, Ski." I lean back and force a full swallow of beer.

"You do that, Mr. Adams. You think about that." –he jerks fish-bowl eyes at Yoss– "You're a fucking juicer!"

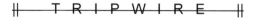

"Fucking *A*, Ski, I'm a juicer!"

\*　　\*　　\*

"Yoss?" Nearly an hour had passed before I could make a graceful exit and I was surprised Yoss decided to leave the same time as me. "What guys in our platoon smoke grass?"

"'Eh, Hillbilly's their leader. Call themselves the 'Second Platoon Heads'." –he looked toward the sea as it patted the shore– "They're probably hard at it right this minute."

"How do they get it in the middle of a military base?"

"It ain't hard. They buy it from the kids by the perimeter fence."

"The kids sell it?"

Tuesday, November 10, 1970, Day 20 / 345 to DEROS
—badge of honor—

"All right!" Nelson exclaimed as the six-by pulled over. "Wish it was this easy to hitch a ride in West Virginny."

"Where you guys head'n'?" the driver asked, shifting into second.

"PX!" Nelson shouted into the cab. "Where else would a fucking Grunt be going," he whispered to Yoss and me. The truck whined up the hill, accompanied by a stiff wind and a platoon of gray clouds blowing from the sea and lowering the temperature enough to make our ride to the Post Exchange an uncomfortable one.

The PX was bustling as we entered the aluminum-framed doors of the department-like store. Dozens of GI's wandered the aisles, wearing clean, starched fatigues, polished boots and green military baseball caps with their unit patches neatly stitched onto the fronts. As I admired an aisle stuffed with the latest stereo sets, a GI stopped short as he spotted me. I shrugged it off, but as I picked out several candles in another aisle, two more GI's stopped to stare at my boots before moving on, shaking their heads. *Ok, what'd I do? I took a shower last night and I know I don't look like no FNG no more.*

I joined Yoss and Nelson at the stationery aisle, picked up some writing paraphernalia and headed for the checkout counter.

"Nelson?" I asked as we crunched through the white limestone parking lot. "What was going on in there? Why were we treated like scum or something?"

"Get used to it. That's all." –Nelson stuck his thumb out– "See your boots? That's the first thing they look at. If they're all scuffed up, you're tagged a fucking Grunt." –a deuce and a-half pulled over– "I don't think it's that they don't like us," he said as we climbed into the bed, "they just give us a wide berth. Either they're jealous we don't have to follow their spit-shined and polished bullshit rules, or else they're scared we'll blow their shit away." –he paused– "Just...just think of your unpolished boots...as a badge of honor." Nodding, I pulled up my collar as the truck gained speed on the hill.

*     *     *

"Man, I forgot to get that camera!" I exclaimed as I entered our hootch. I threw my bag on my bed and plopped down beside it. The wind had picked up since we'd left the PX, howling now through the screened-in window. "What's up today?"

Nelson sat cross-legged on the bed next to mine opening a can of Fritos corn curls. "Supposed to go to some kinda meeting around two or three. Re-orientation or some bull-shit." He offered me some corn curls and I scooped up a handful.

Yoss was busy loading film into his camera. "How about a picture, Adams, to send to your girlfriend?"

"Sure. Could I get two, so I can send one to my parents?" I sat up and crossed my legs, trying to look cool as the camera clicked.

"Now get some of me. Just aim and press this button."

Ramos stuck his head into the door at the far end of the hootch. "Hey, guys, mail call."

There was a letter from my parents and Grandma Birkhead, plus one from Ahlgren, Toad, Greek, Linda, Dwight Baudendistel and Penny Powel. Before leaving, LT announced that all three men who were wounded in the ambush, including Red, were going to recover, but they were sending them back to the World for extended care. "Company Reorientation Class will be at the Mess Hall at 1500," LT said before departing.

"Fucking bullshit class," Retchin commented as we left the CQ. He looked pretty good considering what he had gone through last night. At breakfast, Blondie had told us that Ski and Harv found him on the beach singing *Puff the Magic Dragon* while attempting to build a sandcastle, but the surf kept washing it away.

After reading and re-reading my letters, I joined my squad and headed for the Mess Hall. It only took a minute to realize this was as big of a joke as the "Jungle Training Class" I had to endure at the Replacement Center. Discussed were various philosophies of jungle warfare, tactics, logistical support and so forth. That part wasn't so bad, but then they brought in a male nurse from the local aid station to talk about field foot care, followed by the dangers of venereal diseases. The catcalls during this session got so out of hand that the poor guy gave up. He left the podium with a departing insult— calling us a bunch of government mules that almost started a riot. Topp, the unfortunate MC, tried to quell the rabble. "Now, men! This man has volunteered his time to instruct you on these important topics!" —his lower lip quivered enough to make him sound as if he were talking through a fan— "Let's give him the respect that is his due!"

"Send that two-bit red-necked peckerwood to the mothafuck'n' bush," Hillbilly quipped, "then we'll give 'im the respect he deserves!"

"Now you men had better control your behavior..." —Topp unconsciously reached for the M-16 he usually kept slung over his shoulder, forgetting he had left it at the CQ— "...or I'll be forced to call in the MP's!"

"What *they* a gonna do, Topp," Hillbilly shot back, "send us to the Nam?" A huge roar erupted.

"Okay, okay, okay, men! Settle down!" —Topp waved his arms for silence— "Tomorrow night, I've got an Australian floorshow at 1900 hours at the Brigade USO! And tonight!" —he paused for effect— "We're trucking in two pallets each of beer and soda!" —Topp rubbed his hands together, pushing up on his toes as he emphasized the beer— "They'll be available at CQ by 1800 hours!" The hoots turned to cheers, and Topp, pleased in placating his adversaries, couldn't resist holding his hands high as if he'd just announced his candidacy for President. We tramped out, applauding our *good old boy*— Topp.

Wednesday, November 11, 1970, Day 21 / 344 to DEROS,
—lucky dude—

At six a.m. Company-D was dead silent. Last evening, Topp, after dropping off the beer and soda, skied off to who knows where, not daring to show his face during the Grunt's sacred revelry. It was an even crazier night than the previous one; the beer gushed as freely as an overflowing mountain stream in the middle of a monsoon cloudburst.

Yoss had only consumed a couple beers and I stuck to drinking soda since I'd lost my taste for the fermented brew. We braved the brunt of the alcoholic storm in the relative safety of our hootch, where an occasional drunk would meander off course to stagger through one end and trip out the door at the other. Nelson stumbled in around two a.m. He purred from one bed to the next before curling up on his own.

Yoss and I enjoyed a quiet breakfast, followed by a stroll along the beachfront. Afterward I decided to see if I could locate the whereabouts of Private First Class William R. Andrews.

*　　　*　　　*

"Excuse me," I said as I entered the 196th CQ office. "I was wondering if I could get some information on one of your guys?" The office was empty except for the company clerk, leaning back in a gray swivel chair with hands locked behind his head.

"Sure. Waddya need?"

"I'm trying to locate a guy from my old AIT unit. Name's Bill Andrews."

"How long's he been in country?"

"Three weeks."

The clerk opened a file cabinet and pulled out the company manifest. "Know what company he's in?"

"Sorry, man, I forgot."

"No problem." –he skimmed through a manila folder– "Huh." He ran through the folder again.

"Something wrong?"

"Not sure." –he pulled out a faded green binder– "He doesn't seem to be on the active...wait, here it is. Andrews, William R., formerly of Bravo–"

"Formerly?" I stammered as a shot of adrenaline pulsed through me.

"Now I remember. Talk about luck. Dude got himself a case of pneumonia. Sent him back to the World. Gave him a general discharge at that. Lives in a place called...Pie-oh-chee, Nevada. Where the fuck is that?"

"It's Pee'-och," I corrected, exhaling my tension. "It's close to Las Vegas. He always talked about getting a job there some day."

"Well, hey, maybe now the dude'll get that chance."

\*     \*     \*

"...a house, in New Orleans...they ca–all, the Ri–sing Sun...". Blondie sloshed part of his umpteenth beer on the floor as he and Retchin belted out the words to The Animals' hit song. They finally gave up as the Australian band, The Imperials, began the second stanza. Huge Bose speakers framed the ends of the low makeshift stage as the amateurish group cranked out a deafening metallic reverberation that quite effectively hid the occasional miscued note.

I was sitting with Nelson and Yoss, sipping a Coke. Yoss was taking flicks what seemed like every minute.

"Shit, Yoss," Ski shouted from behind, "why doncha just use a movie camera?!"

"Because I don't *have* a fucking movie camera!" Yoss shouted back. Before Ski could react, Yoss turned and flashed a shot in Ski's face. "There's one for your girlfriend!"

"EAT ME!" Ski cried, still smiling so as not to let everyone know Yoss had just gotten the best of him. "Better watch it, or I'll cram that camera right up your Jew-ish ass!"

"Children!" –Nelson turned Yoss back toward the front– "Behave yourselves! Let's not disturb these nice people here trying to entertain us!" The embarrassed dual quieted down as the Imperials went into their grand finale with *We gotta get out of this place*, again by The Animals. The company of Grunts let out a whooping hand-clapping cheer as the musicians exuberantly dove into the chorus, for they knew this was what every GI lived for. Even I got into the spirit, holding my drink high while laughing at Blondie's continued attempt to perfect the hula, and hoping that this wouldn't be the last thing that *I* ever did.

# MISSION TWO

Thursday, November 12, 1970, Day 22 / 343 to DEROS
—Rocket Pocket blues—

Jeez, loueez, Adams, what you got in there?" Yoss huffed as he helped Ski hoist the ruck onto my back.

"Everything I forgot last time. And a case of C's."

Ski's green eyes widened. "A *whole* case of C's? You are fucking crazy!"

I leaned forward to find my center of gravity. "Don't feel...so bad." I wasn't borrowing anything this time. Along with the C's, I had an entrenching tool, machete, smoke grenades, frags, MA bag, two sticks of C-4, a one-quart and two two-quart canteen, poncho and liner and an M-60 ammo can to keep my growing library and stationery dry.

My platoon filled two trucks, now twenty-eight men strong, having picked up two guys yesterday to fill in Blondie's squad: Terry Mocko and Ed Bethards. Mocko was a runty guy that reminded me of that goofy caricature, Alfred E. Newman, of *Mad* Magazine fame. By contrast, Bethards was tall and slender –a squared-away looking fellow– though he had yet to crack a smile. Quite a contrast: Bethards, somber as a rock, and Mocko, his lips locked into a bizarre smile as if the victim of a cruel joke by some mad scientist. *New guys. You never know what you're going to get.*

*　　*　　*

LT thumped the cab roof. "This is it!" How he figured this was our drop-off point was beyond me; the landscape was unchanged since splitting with First Platoon fifteen minutes ago. To our west, an unending line of mountains flanked a maze of dikes and rice fields stretching to their sodden feet. Monotonous gray clouds crawled overhead as a stiff breeze slapped at us, unimpeded by an expansive coastal flat that dwarfed our trucks.

"Hook up." –LT jumped to the ground– "First checkpoint is two klicks. We'll hump this dike far as we can. Tuck, radio CP we're heading out."

Hillbilly moved cautiously down the exposed pathway as the danger of toe-poppers, pungy stakes and tripwires were ever on his trained mind. Ten minutes down the trail and I began to understand why Ski had looked at me the way he had this morning. The farther I went, the farther the heavy ruck hunched me over. If it wasn't for my years of weight training I doubted I would've made it to our first break; our platoon had taken a number of unforeseen detours as Hillbilly and LT had sought to decipher the rice puzzle.

LT called a halt and I gratefully sank to the ground. "How much farther, Yoss?"

"We're 'bout halfway there. These humps ain't much fun, huh?"

I threw a handful of water on my face. "Gotta get rid of some of these C's, man."

"You'll get your chance sooner than you think."

"Yeah?" Too tired to pursue it, I leaned against my ruck and pulled my hat *over my eyes....*

✎...*August, 1964, home...*"*How mucha want?*"

"Fifty," Danny said, lying down on the bench.

"Wanna go for sixty-five?"

"No way. I'm stick'n' with fifty."

I added two tens to the bar and pulled the weight to Danny's awaiting hands as he lay prone on the bench. "Okay, try for six." Danny hefted the weight easily for three repetitions, slowing through four and five, straining at six. "Push! You can do it!"

"Take it!" I grabbed the weight and swung it to the basement floor.

"That was good. My turn. I'm going *for seventy-five.*"...✎

*...I arrived at* our NDP exhausted, but in better shape than the first half of the hump. *Maybe my muscles are remembering seven years of lifting weights,* I thought as I swung my ruck around to my knee before lowering it softly to the ground.

"We'll set up here tonight," LT called out from his position, set amidst an island of bamboo surrounded by a large rice paddy. "We'll move again tomorrow and try to find a better NDP...this is too exposed for my comfort. Blondie, be ready to take your squad out for recon in one hour." He got on the horn while the rest of us began constructing our hootches, most of us longing for a few hours sleep to recover from last night's carousing.

66

Blondie's squad muddled out at two with LT, Doc and Tuck, hoping I'm sure for a short and trouble-free patrol. The remaining Grunts took to their three R's: reading, writing and resting. I got off a couple more letters to the Greek, one of my high school buddies and Dwight Baudendistel, a friend of mine from Basic.

The first time I had met Dwight was at the Induction Center in Chicago. After being sworn in, he started up a conversation that soon led to his favorite subject: God. He was a new convert to Christianity and when he discovered that I too was of the faith, well, he smothered me with attention as he discussed God this and God that and God, God, God! God! God! His church had prayed that when he entered the service God would provide for him a Christian friend– and I was the victim! By the time we had boarded the plane that evening to head out for Seattle, I was in earnest prayer, too– praying that Dwight would stop badgering me like a Labrador puppy enamored with his new owner.

It wasn't that I didn't like the guy. I just wasn't as intense toward my beliefs as he– maybe more seasoned. I trusted Christ for my salvation and even prayed to him every day, but I didn't care to talk about it every waking second. After Basic, Dwight headed for the east coast to be a Chaplain's Assistant while I ended up in Nam. He never did stop writing, though, his letters always chock full of Bible verses and words of hope and always a tract or two to hand out. I never did, though.

Friday, November 13, 1970, Day 23 / 342 to DEROS
—bookoo souvenea—

Closing in on our second NDP of the mission, the flat monotony of rice fields and dikes began to give way to forested hills and meandering streams that bordered the first ridge of mountains. I was sure we were nearing a village. The paths we now traversed were bordered by colorful shrubs and flowers and were wide and well-worn with years, if not centuries, of use. Every few minutes a Vietnamese woman would pass, giving us a curious stare, or a water buffalo, laden with bundles of sticks or gardening tools, would all but block our path as a village boy prodded it along.

LT turned and held up his hand. "Break!" –he looked irritated– "Get your MPC's ready!" he snuffed while watching a group of women approach toting makeshift cardboard baskets fitted with leather harnesses around slender brown necks.

"You buy fom numba one soda gil!" one of the young women commanded Yoss and me as she walked toward us. Her lithe frame was attired all in silk, flowing black below her waist and burgundy above, and her voice was fragile as a lotus pedal– yet strong, like its stalk. "I got bookoo souvenea, bookoo pop, you buy!" Her smile lit up her dark eyes as she held up several plastic beaded necklaces and colorful headbands.

"I buy one soda," Yoss said, taking a buffalo dollar out of his wallet.

She looked at me while brushing a strand of shiny black hair from her eyes. "You buy two pop."

"Okay." –I handed her a twenty-five cent certificate– "I'll take two."

"You no give enuf money, GI. You give me dolla'. Pop Fefty cen'."

"Fifty cents?" I queried to Yoss. "It's only a dime back home."

The soda girl looked at me with indignation. "You dinky-dau. Back home you no got Soda Gi'l to sell you pop. I sell you pop fefty cen'."

"Okay, okay." –I handed her a dollar– "How much for the headband?"

"Numba one headband," she pronounced, proudly displaying the brightly-colored yellow memento with the word    V * I * E * T * N * A * M  embroidered boldly across the front. "Two dolla'. You buy. You fend buy."

"I'll take one..." –I dug out the money– "...and one of those beads, too. How 'bout you, Yoss, you buy?"

"Just the pop," Yoss said, opening his soda.

"You make me bookoo happy, GI. You numba one." She pocketed my money and began to work her way toward the front of our platoon.

I popped open the Coke and took a gulp. "Fifty cents for a warm can of pop? I can't believe it."

I stashed my goods into my ammo can as LT signaled to move out. "See you tomowo!" one of the soda girls shouted as they started back. "You buy bookoo more souvenea!" We turned from their waving farewell and dug into the last leg of our hump, up a steep hill, my ruck feeling fifty pounds heavier as I leaned into the steep slope. At the top of the highest of a group of four hills we entered a small open glade; LT decided that it would be a perfect site to establish a base camp for the next several days. As part of our mission, we were to set out several listening posts to scout for any sign of VC using the ville for support. At the same time we were to attempt to better relations with some much needed medical care– a tricky act to juggle.

"Hear Nichols ain't *even* going close to the ville this time," Ski said while securing his end of the hootch's roof pole.

"I sure as fuck hope not," Nelson answered. "Don't need no strong-arm tactics like that again."

"Yeah?" I said as I began tying down one of the roof corners. "What happened?"

"He got carried away 'inspecting' one of villager's homes. Just about blew away one of the mamasans. He thought she was hoarding rice for the VC, ends up all she was doing was getting it ready to take into Fat City to sell."

"That wasn't for positive," Yoss broke in. "We weren't sure what she was going to do with it."

"Maybe so, but Nichols had no reason to knock her down and stick his 16 in her face. Place coulda exploded any second. No telling what woulda happened."

"Well," I said, "I just hope it don't happen during my tour. I don't need it."

Nelson sat down hard on the grass by the hootch entrance. "Neither do I, Adams, neither do I."

Saturday, November 14, 1970, Day 24 / 341 to DEROS
—the ville—

"This is part of the Division's pacification program," LT began as we gathered around him, "so be friendly, be generous, but *also*...be cautious. Move slowly through the ville and be on the lookout for any suspicious signs of VC involvement. This village has historically been friendly, so keep it on the sly. You may like to bring along some C's or smokes to offer in case you're invited into their homes, but always have someone with you. If you suspect something, don't do anything stupid. Send someone to get me and I'll check it out with you. I want no compromising on this. Also, I don't want anybody but those assisting Doc to put down your weapons for even a second. You never know what to expect in these places. Just remember we're their guest and they have the right to be treated with respect."

Now understanding what Yoss was talking about during the mission's first break, I took a minute to unload half of my C's into my fatigue jacket. Nichols' squad stayed to hold down the fort; the rest of us headed down the hill.

Halting us at the open village gate, LT, Buffalo and Doc Belton continued inside, asking an old woman where they might find the village honcho. She pointed to an attractive white stucco building. It was a beautiful home by anyone's standard. A caramel-colored tile roof crowned the two-story dwelling and its upper balcony was adorned with rich geometric designs that overlooked a brushed and groomed brick courtyard. A gaunt old man with a wisp of white hair on his sun-browned head and dressed entirely in white, answered the door and invited them inside.

The village was in full swing, taking on the tasks necessary to subsist in this non-mechanized, non-electrical, rural culture: clothes had to be washed, food harvested and prepared, water hauled, homes cleaned, animals fed– and all by the sweat of the brow. I was surprised at the beauty of their homes, gleaming like pearls against the tropical background and a wealth of exotic flowers and shrubs flourishing at their foundations that would have made my mom green with envy. Also surprising were the soda girls. So brazen in their selling frenzy yesterday, now hid in the shadows. *Probably knows ol' Mamasan is eyeballing 'em, just like back home,* I thought with some amusement.

"Everything's cool," Doc said as he returned. "How about Hillbilly's squad volunteering to help me set up an aid station by the honcho's home."

"Enything you want, Doc." –Hillbilly looked at the rest of his squad– "We are *at yer* command, right, boys?"

"Just don't make me give no shots, Doc," Langley remarked. "You know I hate that shit."

Doc put his arm around Langley. "Don't worry. If I get a stubborn kid who don't want me to inoculate him..." –he patted Langley's 16– "...you shoot him."

With the Aid Station set up, LT dismissed the rest of us to begin our investigation. Blondie took his men across the courtyard while Nelson directed Ski, Wad and Fritts to split with us to make better time. Everybody appeared genuinely happy as we crossed the courtyard. The old ladies would stop, bow and offer good-natured smiles with blackened teeth. Several small boys soon tagged behind us, hoping for a handout.

"What's with all these black teeth," I asked Nelson, recalling the cheering throng of spectators in Fat City.

"Betel nut," Nelson said, tossing a Tropical Hershey Bar to one of the boys. "Got some kind of narcotic in it. They mash the seeds into a paste and smear it onto a betel leaf, then roll it up and chew it like tobacco. Turns their teeth and gums black and their lips red and eventually rots out their mouth." – Nelson's candy bar lured more kids to follow– "The younger Vietnamese ain't using it much, though. Don't want to look like their grandparents, I guess."

At the end of the courtyard, we joined back up with Ski's group.

"See anything?" Nelson asked while holding off several kids trying to grab onto his last candy bar.

"Hell, no," Wad replied. "Not one VC bunker yet."

Ski caught the eye of one of the soda girls that had raided our platoon yesterday. "Hey, Mamasan, you see VC?"

A look of fury clouded the young woman's face. "I no mamasan! I no see VC! VC numba ten! You caca dau VC, I be *bookoo* happy!"

"See," Ski said, looking pleased with himself, "no VC here. Hey, Adams, gimme a couple cans of your C's."

"Gonna do a little trading?"

He nodded. "Mamasan," –he held up cans of peaches and fruit cocktail– "you trade for hooch?"

"I tell yo' I no mamasan." –her thin features softened– "I take fo' hooch." –she jerked her head back– "I ga numba one banana wine. Be back, tee-tee." She disappeared into the shadow of a nearby door and soon returned carrying several green bottles, each branded with a shiny foil label.

The transaction completed, we began circling back on opposite sides. Before we made it past two homes, though, an older man and his wife flagged us toward their home.

"Chop chop," the man offered, emulating eating with his hand. "You come chop chop. Ona ah house, pease?"

"Sure," Nelson answered. "We honor your house."

Shadowy images from the outside glare followed me inside, hindering my vision as we passed several rooms that lay in darkness. We entered a large central room where a single kerosene lantern strained to cast its pale light into the murky corners. Dead center of the room was a stone chimney, exposed on all four sides. At its base sat a fire pit where several blackened cast-iron pots emitted mysterious odors unfamiliar to my American nose. Adding to the foreign milieu, a cluster of incense sticks released their perfumed aroma from a recessed shelf in the far wall where a tarnished bronze Buddha sat smiling behind the rising curls of white smoke.

The couple motioned us with nodding smiles to take a seat on some straw mats encircling a low table sitting under the lantern and near the chimney stove. We laid our weapons on our laps as the woman handed each of us an elaborate hand-painted porcelain bowl, along with engraved ivory chopsticks. Motioning Nelson to hold out his bowl, she ladled out a portion from one of the pots. He took a large bite of the mixture of greens, meats, noodles and spices and smiling, stated it was "Number one food."

I was determined to appear as pleased as Nelson no matter how it tasted. It wasn't bad, spicy, but tasty.

The couple appeared delighted, often bowing as we made eye contact and my incompetence at the art of chopsticks added to their entertainment. *This better not be poisoned,* I thought as the woman filled our bowls with a similar concoction. Nelson and Yoss didn't seem concerned, though, so I concentrated on enjoying my first visit with a genuine Vietnamese couple. Finishing our servings, she produced a platter that looked like white onion slices but tasted like sweet licorice; it wasn't bad, either.

Nelson stood and bowed in thanks for the meal. Yoss and I did likewise.

"Would you like some of my canned food?" I asked before leaving their dwelling.

"Oh, no, no, no wan, only if gif', one can…numba one."

Nelson stepped over and picked out a can of peaches. "This gift for you." –he placed the can in the woman's hands, along with an extra P-38 he had in his pocket– "You have number one house. We like very much."

\*       \*       \*

We found Blondie's squad standing at the end of the courtyard, opposite where Doc was removing a wart from an old man's foot.

"Got your fill of this place yet?" Blondie asked Nelson.

"Our stomachs have, anyway. That's right, you don't much care for Vietnamese cooking."

"Fuck no. Monkey brains, boiled weeds. Don't see how nobody can stomach that dink shit." –he eyed Mocko– "This guy, though, he'd eat the ass off a water buffalo if you'd let 'im."

"Hey, the shit's good, man," Mocko answered, trying to impress everyone. His crooked smile slurred his speech as he spit his words at Blondie. "Even fucking Hippie liked it."

"Hippie?"

"Bethards," Blondie said, picking up one of the necklaces hanging around the new guy's neck. "Look at the crazy fuck. Ran one of those fucking soda girls out of business yesterday. Beads, bracelets, head bands. What's this war coming to?"

Hippie pulled the string of beads away. "Makes me feel at home, man. Like I'm in Frisco again."

"You mean San Francisco?" Blondie retorted. "Fuck, gimme Kentucky any fuc-king day."

"Hey, what am I going to do with the rest of these C's?" I held up the remaining cans in my fatigue jacket.

"Gimme those," Pane said. "I see somebody who needs 'em."

Pane took my C's and walked up to a hunched-over papasan toting a gourd full of water across the courtyard. Bowing, Pane placed the cans into the arms of the old man and quickly backed away. "If my guess is right," Pane said as he returned, "this should prove interesting."

Before the old man drew three steps, a small boy who had witnessed the transaction let out a whoop that drew half-a-dozen other boys. Like a pack of wolves the boys tore at the old mans arms, grabbing his C's and running off before the old man knew what had hit him. Strangely, though, he didn't appear upset. He hobbled away, happy that at least most of his water wasn't spilled.

"Survival of the fittest," Pane laughed, "how ya gonna act."

*       *       *

"Cannonball!" Fritts yelled as he crashed into the water, dousing our naked torsos as we sunned ourselves on several granite boulders. Our squad had been assigned water detail, so before heading back to our NDP, we thought we'd take advantage of the warm November day for a little R&R. A couple of the village boys had led us to this patch of paradise where the water

73

ran clean and deep through a series of time-polished boulders strewn along the *fast running stream. ...*

✎*...June, 1961, Deep Creek State Park, Tennessee...*"*Last one in* is...WOOOOH!"

"Is a what?!" my brother shouted as he inched into the icy water.

"Co-ho-hod!" I sputtered as the water climbed over my goose-bumped stomach.

Kent followed me to the deepest part of the dammed-off pool, waiting for a minute to acclimate before diving in, only to come up seconds later looking like a cherry popsicle.

Mom, who had just finished cleaning up breakfast, came down to sit on the bank and watch us swim and Dad fish, who was just upstream trying his luck at some trout. "Is that water too cold?" Mom asked, swishing her fingers through the water. "Don't stay in much longer!"

"Awww, Mom!" we answered with shaking voices, "It *ain't that bad!*"...✐

...*"I can better* that!" Wad declared as he climbed onto a boulder atop the one Fritts had jumped off. "Watch this!" He jumped spread eagle into the air, letting out a wild-eyed holler before pulling in his legs and hitting the water.

"You funny, GI! What you name?" the older of the two asked as Wad pulled himself onto the rock beside the boys.

"Wad, my name is Wad. What's your name?"

"You have bookoo funny name, Wod. My name Khiem."

"Time?" Wad answered, "I think your name is funny, too."

"You dinky dau, Wod. Khiem numba one name."

"Okay, guys," Nelson said as he wiped his body down with his towel, "it's time we get back."

"We go, too! We help fight VC!"

"You can come up for awhile, but soon as it starts to get dark, you go back ville, bic?"

"We bic, GI. You big honcho?"

"Me *B-I-I-I-I-I-G* honcho!" Nelson exclaimed, snarling at the kids while clenching his fists.

Reaching our camp, our two boys weren't the only visitors. Half-a-dozen other villagers, mostly from the troop of soda girls who had greeted us

74

yesterday, were busy bartering their way into securing more of our MPC's. Ski, Yoss and I passed out the canteens to their owners before sitting down by our hootch after what seemed in retrospect a long and tiring day.

"Ain't over yet, boys," Nelson said as if reading our minds as he returned from the CP. "We got ourselves LP duty tonight."

It was two more hours before the villagers headed back home. "Damn pacification program," LT sputtered as the last of the villagers disappeared in the trees with a stern warning not to stray outside their ville tonight or there would be bookoo trouble. "This war is turning into a damn carnival."

Ski uncorked one of his bottles of banana wine and passed it around. I volunteered a swig, surprised at how sweet and mellow it tasted. "Can't be much alcohol in here," I commented as I passed it over to Nelson.

"That's why LT turns an eye to it," Ski said, measuring Nelson's swallow. "More like soda pop than anything."

We headed out of camp just before night tapped us on the shoulder. Wad waited for us to clear the perimeter before setting out an MA on the trail that led to the camp; he, Fritts and Ski would have to fill in for our shifts tonight, making it a long night for all of us. Before leaving, Nelson had briefed me on the strategy of a listening post: find a spot where you're well concealed but can catch sight of any VC that may be coming down the trail, set out several MA's and keep your ears open. Guard shifts would be same as at the NDP– only longer.

Reaching the bottom of the hill, Nelson led us back toward our swimming area as darkness covered us. He pulled off the trail before reaching the stream, wanting to avoid its intrusive babbling and secured a spot near several large boulders that offered an opportune view in both directions. We stuck two claymores beside the trail, pushed in the blasting caps and wrapped the firing wires around a small stick staked near the base of the mines that would prevent us from inadvertently pulling them over. We then unstrung the wires back to our position. This time, we wouldn't use tripwires to set it off. Instead, we'd use a small detonating device nicknamed a "clacker", so named because of the clicking sound when the handles were squeezed together to create the electric spark. With one facing down the trail and one up, our SOP was simple: anybody moving on the trail would get perforated with a thousand steel BB's. It would also provide some pretty strong evidence that our friendly little ville wasn't only friendly to us GI's. We would see.

\*        \*        \*

The moon played peek-a-boo with the clouds as I stretched myself awake for midnight watch. I squinted down the trail. *What do I do if a whole regiment shows up? I don't have a radio and I couldn't talk on it anyway without revealing our position.* I remembered LT telling me to shoot first and ask questions later, but I decided if anything happened, I'd wake Nelson.

I try to relax, but my heart is pumping and my hands are clammy as the minutes creep by. An hour passes. I force my hands from my 16. Nelson has sunk into a purring snore. I bump him to interrupt his rhythm. Grunting, he turns further onto his side.

The second hour finds me practicing at reaching for the two clackers to insure I won't give away our position with an unrehearsed movement. Another hour. I fight to keep my eyes from blurring. I stare at the trail– right, left. The quasi darkness creates ghostly images that prick my skin as my imagination transforms them into skulking VC floating *up the trail.*...

✐*...4:55 p.m., Tuesday, June 11, 1974, Fort Aterbury, Indiana... Why ain't they falling?* I stab for an answer as I stand behind the 60, mounted in the back of the jeep. *I know I'm nailing you...DIE!* The 60 eats the ammo like hungry piranha as I spray hundreds of blanks into the horde of 101st Airborne Rangers advancing toward where a handful of green Weekend Warriors and I are meant to defend. *Just like my dreams!* They do not fall. Instead they laugh as they continue their steady march toward my FNG's *and me.* "*DI I I I I I I E!*"...✐

# WIRE IN THE SHADOWS
## PART II

Sunday, November 15, 1970, Day 25 / 340 to DEROS
—no man's land—

"Hold hand still!"

"Hurry, please, chopper be here soon."

"You finganail lok *bery* bad. Need *muk* wok." Molly took my other hand, briskly smoothing off my thumbnail's rough edges with her emery file.

In a few short days I'd fallen for these gentle people with their childlike ways, surviving off the land and whatever nation's army happened to be in the area. You had to admire them. All they wanted was to be left alone and the last thing they needed was for the bullies up north telling them how to do what they'd been doing quite well for thousands of years.

Doc had given the village a clean bill of health and our unfruitful Listening Posts led LT to also give the hamlet his stamp of approval as a friendly, cooperating, VC-free community. With our mission of pacification done, we were waiting to be flown to our next mission in Ky Tra Valley.

Half of the village came to see us off in a fallow bean field several hundred meters outside their gate. I think even LT enjoyed the attention. They were no longer trying to take our MPC's, but instead talked of things friends usually talk of: like asking us what food we eat in "Amerka", how long until we return, or if we miss our mama and papasan back home.

A little after ten we spot a staggered row of choppers coming at us. LT motioned for the villagers to congregate on the side of the field as Pane popped a red smoke and threw it into the center of the LZ.

79

Nichols stood at the far end with his 16 held high to guide in the squadron of slate-gray "slicks", nicknamed thus because of their stripped-down, combat-ready "slick" appearance. They touched ground and we swarmed aboard. I found a place beside Wad on the butt-polished corrugated edge of the cabin floor, feeling confident this time with the much heavier ruck anchoring me in. Beside me the door gunner gripped his M-60, suspended on a thick bungee cord instead of being mounted to the floor.

Four slicks jump into the air and arc around the village to gain altitude. My contented glow, accrued from the past few days, begins to fade as the villagers, still watching us, become wavering dots in a sea of green. That, along with the cooling winds rushing through the cabin, triggers a small but noticeable stab of fear in my chest now that I am about to take another jaunt into virgin territory.

"Binh Son!" shouts Wad, pointing toward a cluster of glittering metal roofs along Highway 1, almost hidden in the expansive landscape.

Above his finger the highway stretches to the muddy horizon, where a growing network of roads reminds me of my brother's ant farm, that is, until a torrential flood from some unknown source deluged it. Looking toward the northern end of Chu Lai's scythe-shaped shoreline I spot a sheen of blue saltwater pushing into the coast and harboring several dozen ships. "Didn't know that was there!"

"Truong Giang Bay! Can learn a lot up here!"

The knot in my stomach tightens as our choppers bank west; before me lies an endless chain of mountains that seamlessly mesh into the slate-gray sky at the horizon. Hurdling the first towering ridge fencing the Rocket Pocket we enter into an ancient world of twisting streams and whitewater rivers that coil and thunder through a vine-matted maze of writhing ravines and canyons.

My stomach lurches as the choppers dive toward a long, wide valley. The door gunner, wearing a harness to prevent him from falling, meticulously scans below. The chopper wastes no time with fancy maneuvers, dropping abruptly onto a thick mat of sawgrass at the edge of a steep, brush-infested mountain.

"Follow me!" Wad shouts. I jump into a gale of wind and blowing water and follow Wad to just beyond the spinning blades. The cold sting of stagnant water filling my boots clears my mind as we train our guns at the treeline until the choppers pick up and escape the valley. The platoon makes for dry ground and Nichols, taking point, begins to cut toward our first checkpoint. This isn't anything like I had envisioned: jumping out of choppers near some VC stronghold and rushing in for the kill. Instead, when we aren't standing still, we inch forward like caterpillars on a frosty night. My squad pulls up the rear, so it is a frustrating hour before I take my first step onto the mountain.

*     *     *

Two hours into the climb a dark plaster of sinister-looking clouds loomed above as we stopped to gulp down a snack and cool our throats with a ration of water before continuing to move up the steep, muddy slope. I couldn't believe the thickness of the tangled underbrush; I could've jumped on top of it anywhere and not come close to touching the ground.

At four p.m., Nichols' took his last swing of the machete on this mountain from hell to reveal a mountaintop covered with a tangle of matted growth battling for dominance with an army of stunted trees.

"Better get this up quick," Nelson said as we found a position on the far side of the NDP, "sky don't look for shit."

As Yoss drove in the last stake and Nelson tied off the last cord, our misery turned into relief. Now assured of a warm and dry night, we turned to our "numba one" priority– food.

"Fuck," Ski said, taking out a can of beefsteak, "eating mamasan's rice and drinking her hooch, I forgot how low on C's I was."

"You're not alone," –Nelson pulled out his last can of meat– "shoulda got that damn re-supply *before* we took off."

"Jeez, I never woulda made it then," Yoss declared.

"We hump like this everyday?" I asked Nelson.

"Usually not this high up. Mountain was a mother, huh, Wad?"

Wad dramatically rubbed his right shoulder. "*You* try carrying that 60 straight up."

"And guess what, boys," Fritts interjected. "When we leave this shit-hole, we'll hafta cut a brand new trail."

"Dinks mighta booby-trapped it," Nelson said, answering my questioning look.

*     *     *

Halfway through my guard a torrent of raindrops begin to explode around me. Bolting inside the hootch, I stare in awe as they fall like paratroopers

81

blitzkrieging an enemy bastion. They quickly form into pools and begin to flow toward me. I grab my canteen cup and scrape a trench to stop them before they can flood our stronghold. Their front line falls in, only to have their comrades swarm over them, filling the trough and threatening to engulf us. Desperate to stop their assault, I jerk up the edge of the hootch floor and bulldoze mud underneath to form a dike. The wall holds. I breathe a sigh of relief while washing off the mud in their watery grave, realizing again I am that thin wall of defense sitting between the hostile forces beyond and the continuing existence of Second Platoon, Company D, of the 198th.

Monday, November 16, 1970, Day 26 / 339 to DEROS<br>—rain, rain, go away—

The steady drumming on the hootch lulled my sense of time as my eyes opened on the top of Mount Hell, crowning the northern flank of the massive Ky Tra Valley. I peered over the top of my poncho liner; it was pea soup mixed with a hard, steady rain. Pulling up my shirtsleeve I noted the time. *Nine-thirty already? Shouldn't we a left by now?* I rose to one elbow, thankful for the comfort of my air mattress and the warmth of my liner.

Nelson ducked inside the hootch. Water dripped from his shirt and hat as he stretched onto his mattress. "LT says we ain't going no place 'til this rain ends." –he toweled his face– "That's the good news. The bad news is…no re-supply 'til this clears up."

"Better clear up soon then," Wad said from the other hootch, looking outside at his soaked rucksack, now almost devoid of C's.

"All I can say is we'd better start conserving our food. Hard telling when this shit will break up."

"Welcome to monsoon," Yoss said as he crossed his arms over his face.

*     *     *

"Two cans of meat, three cans of fruit…" –Nelson flicked his cigarette stub into the rain– "…and four tins of peanut butter. Shit, guess that'll get us through today, anyway."

Yoss heated a can of turkey loaf and divided it three ways, which came out to only one slice per man. Rationing the fruit cocktail was worse– only three spoonfuls each.

Afternoon set in. Unlike the friendly purr of raindrops that had soothed my soul on the last night of my first mission, the steady pounding on the hootch increased to a mind-numbing roar as the heavens belted us with what I supposed marked the official beginning of monsoon season. My dike at the hootch's entrance was still holding, the water merrily gushing alongside it. The thick fog of clouds, rain and steam rising from the warm vegetation, coupled with the uncut brush surrounding our hootches, left us as isolated as if it were night. *Perfect opportunity for Charlie,* I thought as I squinted into the miasma. I couldn't begin to guess what we would do if some VC did happen up the trail. Our MA might get a couple of them, but no doubt it would be a logistical nightmare.

I opened my ammo can and pulled out *The Sirens of Titan* by Kirk Vonnegut, Jr. to escape into its pages for the rest of the afternoon. Every now and then I'd have to scoot my mattress over from the side of the hootch, else the water would siphon in where it touched the tent wall, resulting in an ever increasing dampening of clothing, blanket and spirits. Yoss was dodging an occasional drip from the crosspole while penning another of his unending stream of letters. Nelson, sitting cross-legged, was enjoying his one and only peanut butter tin, spooning it out with some slightly damp crackers from his scant cache of snacks. Next door, Fritts and Wad were embroiled in a game of spades. Ski lay next to them chain-smoking, his head propped on his elbows gazing blankly at a black-stripped gecko checking out our rucks.

Our Last Supper came and went all too quickly, my meager allotment unable to appease my fuel-deprived body. Darkness, or shall I say the absence of all light, enveloped our camp like a premonition of gloom before the hour hand inside my scratched and damp watch-face had reached the bottom of the dial. This unholy blackness was unlike any I had yet to experience, my closest comparison being a night compass course in the middle of the Washington Rain Forest during AIT. But at least, then, I could occasionally see the stars as they glittered near the tops of the mammoth trees that ruled that part of the earth.

\*      \*      \*

A shove on my shoulder. I jerk up, for a moment fearing I had lost my vision. I hear Nelson's whisper. He hands me his lighter and instructs me to use it to read my watch, but to do so underneath my poncho liner. I almost laugh. It would cause it to glow like a lighthouse beacon.

83

I try to find a comfortable spot out of the rain at the end of my mattress. *This sure ain't like the campouts back home.* Memories flood in...*a cheery fire, roasting hot dogs and smores that melt in your mouth. Closing my eyes, secure in knowing Mom and Dad are there to protect me. Dreaming of...*

...*"Be a good* boy, Bobby...take care of Ginny," echoes in my twelve-year-old brain as the coffin-lid slams shut on Grandpa. He went crazy in the end– yell'n' and holler'n' and scar'n' me plum through as I tried not to listen from the kitchen, sipping on a glass of milk, holding an oatmeal cookie so tight it broke in half. But Mama says that's what happens when you get the die-a beeties.

But Grandpa's gone now, gonna bury him on the hill by his church. I climb into the back seat with my brother. He just sits there, not even teasing me.

Mom looks at me from the front seat. Her face is different somehow. I squint hard at her, but it don't do no good. Her face gets all dark and cloudy, like I'm looking through a dirty window. Then she's on that jet again. I call to her, but she can't hear me over the jet's roar. She stares back at me, a tear falling *from her eye....*

...*A drop of* water smacks the side of my cheek and jerks open my eyes. *Damn it! How long have I been asleep?* I reach into the dark and splash rainwater on my face.

Tuesday, November 17, 1970, Day 27 / 338 to DEROS
—isle of hunger—

Day 3. I stick my head out of my poncho liner and stare into the rain. My stomach crawls with hunger pangs as again Nelson ducks into the hootch and stretches onto his mattress.

"Ceiling's still too low. No fucking re-supply. LT says hang on one goddamn more day."

Ski is next-door, his poncho liner draped over his head as he lights a Winston. "Three more..." –he stares into his cigarette pack– "...when they're gone, I'm humping to Chu-fucking-Lai for re-supply myself."

"What we got for C's?" Nelson asks.

"Nothing, less you count two packs of gum."

"That counts. Adams?"

"I'm cleaned out. Shouldn't a gave so much away at the ville."

"Fuck, you didn't know, nobody did." –Nelson holds up two coffee packets– "At least I got these. Yoss, fire up that stove and break out the gum. We got ourselves a meal to prepare."

Yoss looks outside. "Where we getting water for the coffee?"

*     *     *

It's a funny thing about hunger. Salvador Dali must have starved himself before painting *The Persistence of Memory.* The scene of wilted clocks draped lifelessly over the landscape parallels how time slows down until the second hand is just too tuckered out to make one more swing around the block. In those ebbing moments thrust between the seconds, existence becomes excruciatingly vivid as the shadow of the subconscious is stripped away. Every hot exhalation is subject to minute scrutiny; every nerve screams from the epidermis, begging for someone to numb its torment. Toes feel big as cannons as they scrape the inside of my boot. Fingertips become so sensitive that I can only stare in wonder as they peel my eyes from my book, feeling as if they are holding the weight of the world instead of pulp and cardboard. Sleep, then, is the only escape as your stomach gnaws in fitful anguish.

Morning melded into afternoon and afternoon into night, for the interminable rain had temporarily canceled the evening– to be scheduled again at a later time. *Shall we gather at the river,* a gospel song I had heard almost every Sunday as a child played over and over in my head as I lay in my black world. My mind too tired to sleep, my body too rested to rest again– *"...the beautiful, the beautiful ri–ver. Shall we gather at the ri–ver, that flows by the throne of God."* Somewhere far away a drum began a soft cadence.

"People marching and singing, coming down the street," Angel said, looking cautiously through the dusty window down the hard-packed dirt avenue. "They're going to pass by the horses."

"We'll join them!" Pike joked as he helped load the sacks of silver into their saddlebags.

"The Temperance Union?" Dutch clucked at the prospect of a band of outlaws joining a parade full of teetotalers.

Angel pauses as a glint of steel diverts his gaze to the rooftop across the street. "Rifles! One...no three!" Pike quickly walks over and follows Angel's stare. "Maybe more...there, on the roof."

"Son of a bitch." –Pike turns back to the vault– "Lyle, Dutch," he says, motioning them to quickly finish loading up.

"What are they, bounty hunters?" Lyle asks as he stuffs the last of his sacks into his saddlebag.

"Hell, I wouldn't know."

Pike motions two of his bunch toward the windows facing the street. "Buck, with Abe."

"I kill 'em now?" CL asks as he waves a 12-gauge at two young clerks and an elderly lady patron he has cornered in the small office.

"No. Hold them here long as you can till after the shooting starts."

"I'll hold 'em till *hell* freezes over or *you* say different," young CL wheezes with a crazed look in his eyes.

Pike pauses disconcertingly. The saddlebags full, he nods to Dutch, who shoves the office administrator at him. "When I get him out," –he pushes the old man's face against a glass pane on the door– "blast 'em. We'll make a run for it."

"CL, give me that shotgun," Buck says, holstering his 44.

Pike squeezes the arm of the frightened manager, waiting for the right moment as the parade of zealots near the front of the San Rafael's Wells Fargo Administration building. The steady beat of Pike's heart transposes the drumming cadence of the band, now increasing in tempo and soon drowning out all but the blare of the trumpets and the marchers as they fervently sing their battle cry, "*...the beautiful, the beautiful ri–ver...*" As the beat reaches a crescendo, Pike slams open the door and shoves the old man across the wooden porch where he crashes onto the dusty street below. Immediately, a scourge of squalid-looking bounty hunters rise from their concealment on the rooftop across the street and blasts the old man as he tries to escape behind the shocked members of the South Texas Temperance Union. Pike holds up his revolver. "*LET'S GO!!*"

"What?" I say half out loud, looking around me, but seeing nothing.

"You okay, Adams?" a voice whispers. "Go back to sleep."

*Sleep,* I think as my heart still beats in cadence to my dream.

# WIRE IN THE SHADOWS

Wednesday, November 18, 1970, Day 28 / 337 to DEROS
—shit and shrapnel—

Day 4. I scramble outside to pull my ruck within reach. My fingers claw through the ruck, searching.... "Hey!"

"Where the fuck did that come from?" Nelson blurts, seduced by the can's sensuous curves and unopened rims.

"On the side pouch. Musta threw it in there before going to that ville." Chipped beef and potatoes are second on the list as a Grunt's most hated meals, next to ham and eggs. Deemed "shit and shrapnel", the name nails its flavor pretty close.

"Yoss—"

"Way ahead of you," Yoss breaks in. As we worship each rationed bite, no one could have convinced us that our small portion was any less savory than the finest cuisine at a royal banquet in Buckingham Palace.

Thursday, November 19, 1970, Day 29 / 336 to DEROS
—serenity—

Day 5. Morning: I lay burrowed in my liner.

Afternoon: rain assailed our mountain.

Evening: I lay beneath my blanket. *Why get up? Maybe tomorrow the sky will clear. Maybe tomorrow the golden food chopper will save our miserable souls. Like that night, just last week?* Doing guard beneath a gorgeous moon, the silvery grass swaying in a warm breeze. The mongoose feasting on our leftovers: turkey, peaches, chocolate bars, peanut butter oozing with flavor. That eggnog on my first stand-down, dressing, roast beef, brown succulent gravy. It's not fair. All of that food sitting there– and we're here. What did we do? *We did our duty and now we're starving to death? For what?*

Night: I sat up. I had no idea what time it was. Somebody was doing guard, I guessed. *Need to take a walk, gotta stretch my legs.* After laying for four days my legs cramped without much effort, tightening so I'd have to massage them to get them to relax. I'd given up taking my boots off two days ago, opting for the warmth the boots provided.

Strangely, my stomach was no longer expressing its outrage. *Had it given up? Is this what happens in the beginning stages of starvation? If it is, it ain't so*

87

*bad.* I crossed my lymphatic legs and gazed with whomever I was gazing with into *the blackness beyond....*

✎ *....June, 1963, Cottage Grove...Danny and I* lay on the rough sumac treehouse and watched the moon shadows prance about us.

"This is the life, huh?" –Danny sat up and took a small brown paper bag out of a makeshift knapsack– "Thought I'd bring us a snack." He pulled out two peanut butter and strawberry jam sandwiches.

"Wow, Danny, thanks!" –I took a big bite– "Wanna swing over to the next tree after we're done?"

"Show." –he smacked the peanut butter in his mouth– "Shoulda brought some wada."

I massaged the bottom of my feet against the logs. "You know, when we get to Africa, we can do this every night. No more school, no more rules...."

"...and no mo' bullies," Danny said, swallowing a big bite.

"Right. No more bullies. 'Member the time they threw your bike off the dock? Think we should set a trap to get back at 'em."

"Like what?"

"Remember when I caught that rabbit with that snare Lester taught me how to make? Why not try it on those guys?"

"Yeah. We could lure one of 'em into the slough and then, *BAM*! We got 'em."

"All right..." –I wiped my mouth with the back of my hand– "...I got a feeling this is gonna be the best summer yet."

Standing, I unlatch the rope. Balancing for a moment on the edge, I lift my feet and sail through the air with all the freedom the *night can offer....* ✐

Friday, November 20, 1970, Day 30 / 335 to DEROS
—panic on the deck—

The rain still fell on Mount Hell as the morning of our sixth day broke. LT had had it– we were getting off this mountain while we still had the strength. At least down there we could forage for food should the cloud ceiling continue to block our re-supply. Blondie's squad was to take the task of cutting trail. Hillbilly's came next and then ours. This time, Nichols would cover the rear.

\*       \*       \*

I fought to regain my footing after sliding a full ten feet into Yoss, who was trying to right himself. The combination of boots and water had obliterated the shallow-rooted vines and brush, transforming the trail into a muddy water slide. LT passed word down the line to check the safeties on our *16*'s, for with all the sliding and falling, he didn't want anybody's weapon to discharge into somebody's back. Mocko, Ramos and Hippie were trading off cutting trail every few minutes and I know that more than one of us thanked his lucky stars that it wasn't him up front.

Before we got a quarter of the way down, we ran into another obstacle. The runoff had cut a thunderous channel of mud-churned froth across our path. With no way to cross, we were forced to follow its course.

One good thing it did provide– cover. We could scream at the top of our lungs and the guy in front of us could barely hear us. Plus it made our going easier, for as the twisting contours guided the channel down the mountain's face, it eased our straight-line plummet. The tradeoff, though– time. Two o'clock came and went and still the bottom was nowhere in sight.

Just past five, the rain began to subside. *Blondie's gotta be close to the bottom by now.* I glanced at the darkening sky. *Another hour and we're–*

*RRRRRRRRRRRRRIIIIIIIIIIIIIIIIIP*!

I smash into the mud. Blasts of automatic gunfire resonate into the valley for ten seconds– then silence.

Several muffled whoops from GI's gear down my heart. Word shoots up the line that Blondie's squad had surprised a small patrol of VC walking along a trail at the base *of Mount Hell. ...*

✎*...10:01 p.m., Friday, July 4, 1975, Soule Bowl, East Moline, Illinois...Peggy held up* both hands like someone'd just yelled, "*Stick 'em up!*" "Look! That one took off sideways!" A shower of sparks hit the chain-link fence as the fireworks canister burst with a hollow *POP*!– sending purple and red sparklies across the faded grass of the football field.

"That was unusual," commented Peggy's straight-laced husband, Bill. More boomers followed the accident, exploding in the sky overhead, popping like a battery of quad-fifties mowing down a wall of sequoias. I released Sheryl's hand and cupped my ears as my chest unconsciously tightened. *What am I doing here?*

More big sprayers lit up the sky– some whistled, some ripped, some boomed, igniting the sky with a dazzling rainbow of color that stuck in my eyes for a few moments before fading to white shadow.

"Whoa!" Peggy shrieked as one of the fireworks exploded prematurely just fifty feet over the crazies lighting them.

"What *is* it with these this year?" Sheryl exclaimed.

"Maybe the humidity," Bill scientifically shot back.

Another popper shot my head down low; I had had enough.

Two more pre-maturerers rocket just above the field, sending a fire shower into the bleachers close to the display. An ambulance drives onto the field. I'm not sure why– I'm halfway to the exit, don't know and don't care if my spouse is following. She is. So are Bill and Peggy. Another low round. The crowd scatters. The show ends. Lights. Shouts. Curses. Sirens pealing. Red lights flickering. Then black. Walking up Nineteenth Street hill for home. Trees taunt me beside the road. Muffled voices float along the shoulder. I duck at the oncoming headlights. I feel the pain *in my eyes...*✎

*...Regaining my feet,* I continue to where the mountain gives up its reign. The gathering platoon stands over two VC. One grimaces while Doc tries to stop a gush of blood pouring from his thigh. The other lies silent on his stomach with his hands lashed behind him. On the side of the trail, two waxy bodies are riddled with gaping bloody holes. LT is on the horn calling in a chopper. The rain has reduced to drizzle and the clouds are again visible– just in time to cart away our prize.

"Shoulda told 'em to throw a couple cases of C's on that bird, LT," huffs Blondie as he spots Nichols. "Hey, Nichols! I beat cha to this un'!"

Blondie is pumped. Even my hunger pangs are lost in the excitement as he repeats his story.

"Ol' Ramos saw 'em first. Told Mocko to get on his ass and he opened on rock and roll. Then Hippie and I came up and while Ramos was reloading, we finished 'em off. Christ, think even Mocko got off a few." –Mocko only smiles crazier than usual– "The only dink we missed fell on his face and put his hands behind his head...well-trained bastard, huh?"

"Hillbilly," LT says with a wave of his arm, "take your squad up the trail a ways in case any more gooks happen our way. Nelson, you do likewise that way. Soon as the chopper comes, we'll move half a klick and set up...don't *even* want to be near this spot tonight."

Within twenty minutes we detect the clatter of inbound choppers. Another minute reveals two of them flying just below the ceiling of clouds. One drops to hover thirty meters off the trail while Doc and Blondie assist the wounded man over; Wright and Pane escort the other prisoner. The second bird, a gunship, scans the terrain to provide cover should the need arise. In less than a minute it is over.

"Looky what the tooth fairy brought!" Blondie exclaims. He throws two cases of C's to the ground. "Boys musta read my mind." Ramos rips open the boxes, revealing two-dozen beautiful boxes filled with everything a starving Grunt could want.

"Squads grab six boxes each," LT calls out.

We head east along the dink trail; LT follows close behind Blondie and Pane. We still can't hurry. At every rock, stick, or C-ration lid, Blondie carefully steps over it and points it out to Pane, who in turn points it out to LT and so on till it reaches drag. Mount Hell falls behind us as we enter into a series of rolling hills and valleys. LT finds his spot, twenty meters off the trail and with the brush sparse, our hootches are soon built.

"What's wrong with this picture?" Nelson says, peering overhead. "The fucking rain's stopped."

"Another thing about to stop..." –Ski rips open a box and pulls out a cigarette pack– "...is *my nicotine fit.*"...

✎...*8:26 a.m., Monday, October 13, 1975, Silvis, Illinois...*"Okay, take the end of this tape to that lath over there."

"Right," I said, eyeballing a florescent orange stick nearly hidden in the dense brush.

"Hold it, hold it." Mary frowned, glancing up from her field book. She sounded frustrated. "No, no. You don't walk *around* the brush. You have to pull it straight *to* the point to get a good distance."

"Riiiiiight." I walked back to the starting point and picked up a machete. *Remember this, Nelson? Amigo? Man, wonder what you're doing right now?* I began to tediously chop through the weeds. *Looks like I've ended up right back where I started. Shoulda finished college. Shoulda took the right courses so I coulda got my Associates Degree. But nooooooo, take all art classes...the fun stuff. Stupid idiot. Too anxious to get that job at Twenty-First Century Advertising.*

A sharp tug on the steel tape stopped me mid swing. "You're off line! Move left a step!"

*Who is this anyway? A girl surveyor? And with an attitude at that. Twenty-First Century Advertising. What a joke that was. Not in business two months before going bankrupt. Man, if only...damn brush, cut! ...it'd taken off. I'd be right there on the ground floor. Big times, here I come. Instead, here I am supporting a wife and kid for a whopping four bucks an hour.* I smiled to myself. *Well, at least it beats the twenty-five cents an hour I was doing it for in The Nam....*✎

Saturday, November 21, 1970, Day 31 / 334 to DEROS
—sunshine and coconuts—

"Checkpoint ahead," LT softly passed up to the pointman. Blondie veered into a small grove of banana trees and we dumped our rucks off our sweaty backs.

"It's almost out." Langley grinned up at the clouds, now thinning to the point to where some blue was breaking through. He had bet Retchin two packs of Marlboro that we'd see the sun before noon. It was 11:43.

"Fuck..." –Retchin looked from his watch to the brightening glow– "...you'd better hide behind that fuck'n' cloud till I say."

Taking our first break of the morning, I sat down to check out my feet. The last time my boots were off was on Mount Hell, five days ago. I pulled one off, peeled the damp sock away and...*what...is...that?! Looks like a big, white, shriveled up prune!* I inspected my sole; it was as deeply wrinkled as an eroded cornfield after a spring drenching. Freeing my other foot, I located a can of foot powder in one of my side pouches, popped the lid open and shook the can. Nothing came out. I stuck my finger in and brought out a thick glob of chalky goo. *What a joke. What good is jungle foot powder if it don't work in the jungle?*

Massaging my feet, I felt an odd sensation wash over me. My eyes squinted from an unnatural glow that had begun to radiate onto my feet, hands and even the ground.

"Fuck!" Retchin growled. It was 11:54.

\*  \*  \*

My stomach was complaining again as we approached our Delta Company's Command Post, strategically positioned in the center of its three satellite platoons to provide mortar fire support. In the past hour, the terrain before us had opened considerably. Thick, toothy saw-grass hugged the VC trail that wove through a labyrinth of rolling hills, cut by dozens of serpentine streams running toward the grass soup plains of Ky Tra's main valley floor. Entering the CP's perimeter, it was fortifying an almost bare, muddy knoll. Two 60mm mortar tubes sat in the camp's center, angled to the sky. A slow-running stream meandered beside the camp, but what caught my eye were seven cases of C's stacked by the LT's hootch.

"We're just staying long enough to get our checkpoints," LT announced. "Grab four meals each. We'll be getting another re-supply tomorrow."

"Heard that before," Ski mumbled behind me.

"Hey, looky..." –Yoss bent over besides the dwindling stack of C's– "...catch, Adams."

I turned over the green oblong shell. "Coconut?" I took my machete and split it apart enough to pull it open with my hands. Tucked inside was the coconut seed I was familiar with. Careful not to spill the juice, I broke it open and poured the watery milk into Yoss' waiting canteen cup.

"Yewh, still green," Yoss said with puckered lips.

I pried some of the meat from the shell and divided it among us, also giving a piece to Nelson, who was already chomping away on some cold ham.

"Bullshit bomber," Nelson said, pointing overhead with his spoon at a lone plane droning far above the valley floor.

"What?"

"They fly around dropping *Chieu Hoi* leaflets," Yoss answered.

Nelson bit into his chunk of coconut. "It's just some propaganda bullshit Higher-Higher uses to get the gooks to surrender. Promise 'em a warm bed and shit if they turn themselves in."

"Does it work?"

"Fuck. They come in for a week or so to get fattened up, then sky up again."

"Sounds like a plan, huh, Adams?" Ski added. "Our side gives these gooks more R&R than us sorry-ass Grunts."

We were in and out of the CP in twenty minutes. It was hardly enough time to cool down, but LT wanted to make an early camp, thinking we deserved it after the tribulations of Mount Hell. It was okay with me; my body was dragging from the morning hump. They say an army moves on its stomach? I believed it now.

LT located a decent spot a klick and a-half southeast of the CP. It was a good Night Defense Position, just off the main trail, flat, with not a whole lot of clearing to do– and dry. I macheted a stout roof pole and a couple of shorter ones for the end supports of our hootch, eager to dig into my cache of food.

The hootch done and the MA set out, I took a few moments just to gaze at the beautiful cans of C's, sitting neat and pretty in their cardboard abode. Each meal came with its own mini four-pack of cigarettes, so after tossing them into my ammo can, I broke open a can of chicken and noodles and prepared dinner. I didn't know food could taste so good, though reflecting that if served this same meal back in the World I would have pushed it aside, giving it a revolting gag in the process. Necessity does indeed change your attitude on things.

Finished with the feast, I smashed my empty cans and tossed them well away from the hootch. I was ready for a new project. After a week of rain, my M-16 magazines were begging for a brushing and oil bath. So taking out an old toothbrush and silicone lubricant that I had stored in one of my side pouches, I stripped them down and gave them a thorough cleaning. That done, I decided to keep right on going, breaking down my 16 to give it a good going over as drilled into me time and time again during my infantry training.

"No more 'n one guy cleaning his 16 at a time," Nelson reminded Yoss who had also begun to peer into the dirty chamber of his weapon.

"Be done in a minute," I told Yoss as I reinserted a shiny firing pin into the bolt assembly. As Yoss began to tear into his 16, I took off my boots to air out my feet. Although they didn't look as bad as this morning, they were still wrinkled enough to make the Ancient Mariner shudder at the sight.

Sunday, November 22, 1970, Day 32 / 333 to DEROS
—blood and rice—

For the first time this mission, the morning broke clear and warm. I sat cross-legged in front of my hootch, sipping on a hot cup of coffee while staring with glassy-eyed contentment at some turkey broth bubbling in my C-rat can like the colorful mud pots of Yellowstone.

"Be ready to hook up in thirty minutes," Buffalo advised as he approached our position. "We're humping back to the CP. Might be staying there tonight."

Breaking down was starting to become one of those things I didn't have to think about. And with my equipment dried out, the load was considerably lighter. I draped my fatigue shirt over the top of my ruck to let it air out and by nine-thirty we were standing with our NDP hooked on our backs and ready to move out. Nelson, taking point, made his way to the main trail. The day was warming up nicely and I was enjoying a fresh surge of energy as we began to hump the wide trail.

"Dinks!" Yoss half-shouts, half-whispers to Nelson as we see three VC walking straight at us thirty meters ahead. Each carries a sack on one shoulder and an AK on the other. Spotting us, they drop their sacks and begin to dive into the brush as we switch to full auto and let fly with volleys of fire that rips the morning air. Twigs snapping and dirt flying we empty our magazines and reload. Wad joins us; his 60 sings its song of destruction. Behind us, Mocko and Hippie let their adrenaline get the best of them; they begin to fire past us.

"Watch it!" I shout, ducking as the *sheeennnn*! of a 16 round whizzes by my right ear.

Nelson motions us to cease-fire. "They lit out, guys!"

Wad lowers his 60. "We get any?"

"Let's find out," I say. We approach with caution to the point where they disappeared.

"How many you see?" LT asks from behind.

"Three," Yoss answers. "They were carrying sacks of something."

"Here's a sack." Nelson leans over the bag. Rice is trickling to the ground from a small tear.

I point at a bush a few feet from the sack. "Blood." –Suddenly queasy, I spot two sandal-clad feet– "There's one of 'em." I feel the blood rush from my head; half of his face is missing.

LT slowly walks in to check him out. He looks into the trees. "We're not going on no wild-goose chase to find the others."

"Valley's crawling with gooks," Wad says. "Getting so a guy can't take a leisurely stroll no more."

"Word is from Higher-Higher that this has become a major supply route over the last couple months."

"You know what that means…" –Buffalo kicks at a stick lying on the trail– "…booby-traps."

Monday, November 23, 1970, Day 33 / 332 to DEROS<br>—toe popper—

*Mon. Nov 23rd, 70*                                        *10 AM Hot*

*Dear Mom & Dad,*

*Hello! Today, I mean yesterday I finally received your letters, two of them. Also I received a letter from Dwight. Sorry it's been so long since I've written last but it's really been raining a lot the past week & a half & anyway the chopper can't come out to pick up our mail when it's raining.*

*I'm out on my 2nd mission now. Stand-down lasted 4 days & had a lot of time to relax & had all the free pop I wanted.*

*Thursday, the 12th of Nov, we left Chu Lai by truck & followed highway 1 a little ways south. The 12th thru the 15th we stayed just a klick (1,000 meters) off the highway in what is called the "Rocket Pocket", (an area out side the friendly villages where not much goes on). It was a lot of fun there cause nothing ever happens there. Went swimming & got real good tan in this river at the bottom of this hill our N.D.P. (night defensive position) was on. Every day just about everybody in the nearby ville visited us. Mostly women & children, since men were in RVN army. It was a wonderful experience learning to talk with them. They came selling sovenirs, beads, bracelets, pop, just about everything. Learned how to eat with chop sticks & made a lot of good friends. They're always seem happy & glad to help us out.*

*The 16th our company flew out of the Rocket Pocket on choppers & went to (Key Traw) valley, for our next mission. I am still here & will leave the 26th, so won't get your package till then.*

*That's when the rain started, the night of the 16th just as we were finishing making our hootches on top of a large mountain. We stayed there five days & couldn't move cause of rain. Sure was uncomfortable, cramped up in that tent. - The 20th we started down the mountain & made it to the bottom by night, took so long cause very slippery & kinda steep in places. Followed a creek most of the way down. I kinda enjoyed it. Then the 21st we made it to my present position where I am at this time. It's the Company's command post where they have the mortors locateded. We Went about 2 klicks from here so we could sweep the valley looking for VC. Found a couple but no trouble. Nothing to worry about here cause they travel in groups of 2 or 3 & always run when they see us. And a fire fight lasts only 5 min. or less. About once every 2 months VC fire maybe 2-3 rounds. While we sound like an arsenal. So I can't emphasize enough how safe it really is over here so man, don't worry. From what I hear about the world I think its saver over here. And while everybody's freezing back home I'm getting a good tan.*

*Anyway we got here yesterday, back to the command post, that is and got resupplied, food mail and nothing to do till we go in for re-train, classes for 3 days. After that we'll probably go back to the Rocket Pocket.*

*Thanks so much for that present, what ever it is. And I do have a "re-supply" list I would like you to fill & send. Then I'll answer all your questions. Here's what I could use' of course, that watch. Food!! That bone handle pocket knife of mine. Maypo cereal for breakfast, I kinda miss this most & I can heat it with these heat tabs & small stove we got out in field. & - instant oatmeal (without raisens) packages. About a dozen a month. - instant milk - for the small boxes of "suger crisp" I would love to eat (& have sent). Instant nutriment or Ovaltine - how about if maybe you could get ahold of some small tupperware containers for maypo milk, ect. About 4 containers I could put in this empty M-60 ammo box, (like the one you have for papers) & 2 books. The 'Naked Ape', I didn't read it yet. And another of your choice. {I read books out here all the time. That's all I need for now. Hope you can send it!*

*By the way. Dwight told me in his letter that he'll probably get pernament party & he's decided the Lord wants him to go into the ministry, full time! Still can't understand why he say I'm his very best Christian friend....*

✎*...4:18 p.m., Tuesday, August 3, 1976, Home...Sheryl* glared at me, speaking in a bare whisper. "You did what?"

"I threw the albums out. Hey, are we gonna take this seriously or not?"

"You didn't throw out my Chicago album?"

My face lost some of its evangelical fervor. "I thought you–"

"*YOU DIDN'T!*"...

✎*...7:46 p.m., Saturday, June 5, 1976, Wharton Field House, Moline, Illinois...I placed my* bible in Sheryl's lap as The Lundstrums' Family Gospel Band launched into their invitational hymn *Just As I Am*. It was my queue. As instructed, I paused for a few moments before approaching the front of the stadium with my fellow counselors to encourage the lost to take their first step toward a life-changing decision for Jesus. The weeklong Crusade was now in full swing, harvesting dozens of souls each night as the family of gospel singers played their guitars and shook their tambourines to an addicting repertoire of *country gospel melodies....*

✏️ *...6:56 p.m., Sunday, August 8, 1976, First Baptist Church, East Moline, Illinois...My Bible burned* in my hand as the study group chatted about trivialities– they were so blind. Even Sheryl seemed to take a nonchalant attitude to the world's most important quest: to spread the gospel of Jesus Christ to the Four Corners of the earth. It seemed only Warren Lauritzen and Wayne Kettering appreciated my conviction to the Word, the three of us *trading* verses like prize fighters vying for the championship belt. Since the Lundstrum Crusade, I was on track. I now knew how it all fit together. No more screwing around. No more throwing away what little time was left. *And time IS short,* I thought as I jabbed Wayne with a Phillipians 3:14, he countering with a well-placed 4:13. Just yesterday Warren had heard that by 1984 it would all be over– lock, *stock and barrel....*

✏️ *...August 3, 1976, home...*"Yes, I *did,* Sheryl. The albums went out with this morning's garbage. It probably wouldn't hurt, either, if we got rid of the TV."

"No, Robert. The TV stays."

"Okay, but we'll only use it for religious programming, like on Sunday and stuff."

"Why is it that *whenever* you get something through that thick skull of yours you have *to go berserk?!*"...✏️

*...About seeing the ocean, after the sun came up it was partly cloudy. Looked as if it were a toy swimming pool with dry ice as clouds. Saw several ocean liners - sure small - hard to imagine there can be so much water*

*Had one pay day in Chu Lai - Oct 30 - E-2 pay - 160 saved - 37.50 - bond - & 44.00 spending - will be paided next - Nov. 30 when being paid I just tell how much I want sent home and they send check & bond.*

*I will not extend if you don't want me too. Be good to work in army till summer of '72' so will not spend all my money.*

*198th base camp back in rear is right on China Sea - 100 ft. swimming, PX, U.S.O., real close, modern.*

*Believe me, Danny Moore has it real good if he lives in bunker as radio operator - doesn't do much at all.*

*Last line of my address?*

*APO SF 96374 – Good enough*

*Hope Kent's okay now. Got more letters to write. Take care, God bless. Love, Your Son, –Bob–*

A glob of sweat fell from my brow and smeared my signature. Overhead, thick gray clouds whisked across the sky, occasionally sparing me from the sun as it heated my fatigues like a sauna. From my point of view, this was a bad set up. The entire knob had been cleared, leaving the CP totally exposed. At least we wouldn't be here long– plans were to hook up and head for a new NDP several klicks to the west.

Going on two, Ski took a big swig from his canteen, dumping some more on his flushed face. "Let's hook the fuck up," he whispered under his breath. Ten more minutes brought LT; he and the CP's LT were finally finished going over some last minute changes.

"Hillbilly..." –LT stuffed his map into his shirt– "...move out."

"Thought you'd never fuck'n' ask, LT." –Hillbilly picked up his ruck– "Spanky, keep yer eyes peeled. Got a feel'n' ol' Charlie's been a prowl'n' last night like a shitload of coons."

Leaving the CP behind, Hillbilly led us into the remote jungle northwest of Ky Tra Valley. It was a long hump, Spanky spotted two VC, but by the time he raised his weapon they'd disappeared, probably dropping into a hole or tunnel. As twilight and a mass of sinister-looking clouds closed in, Hillbilly detected three possible booby-traps that he cautioned us to avoid.

Nelson briefed me on the most typical mine the gooks set out: the toe popper, an ingeniously simple device. Charlie would drive a nail through a four-inch long board. Digging a shallow hole in the trail, he would place the board in the hole with the nail facing up. A short length of hollowed out bamboo would be placed over the nail and secured with small rocks. Barrel and firing pin in place, he would load a cartridge into the top of the hollowed bamboo with the tip just beneath the surface. Its location would be marked with a C-ration lid, cigarette butt, candy wrapper, or sticks and pebbles so Charlie would be aware of its location. If someone stepped on it, his weight would drive the cartridge onto the nail, shooting the cartridge through the foot and into the body.

Making camp just before nightfall, Yoss and I set out the MA. It was drizzling, producing wet hands and cold spirits as we spent twice the time finding the right bush, securing the tripwire across our macheted trail and hooking the mine to its electric heart. By the time we returned dusk had given way to night. The hidden moon was no help in dispelling the gloomy evening. But it was probably for the best, for if we couldn't see the VC, they *couldn't see us.*...

✎...*July, 1962, Cottage Grove...Lester stood back,* admiring his work. Everyone called him Lester, even though he was older than Dad. "Welp, there ya go, Bobby."

"Looks great!"

"Not only that, but it's a guaranteed ta work." –he paused, sending a stream of tobacco near the base of the young willow that bent to the snare's will– "Caught me many a rabbit with that un'. Some possum, too. Even a coon once. See, he'll just *snatch* hold of that lettuce and...*BAM*!" –he emphasized the action with a slap against his bibs– "The noose'll grab his neck and string 'im up like a donkey. You just feed this thing just before dark, 'n' then check it first light. You'll get 'im. You just see if you don't get 'im." –he looked into the evening's dusty sky– "Welp, better be a getting ya back *to ya folks.*"...✐

Tuesday, November 24, 1970, Day 34 / 331 to DEROS
—bad water, bad luck—

✎...*August, 1954...Mama say old* lady, her dead. That what Mama say. Everybody at church got thuits on. Everybody look at her in shiny box. Her face have cracks. They all white. Her got *big* red lip. She wear *pretty* white dress. Mama say we got go look. I no want look, Mama. Her SCARY!

HER GET UP! Her get up in box! Her HAPPY! Her got BIG smile! Old man run down by me. Him jump out window. That FUNNY! Her look at ME! Her SCARY! MAMA, MAMA! HER BIG RED MOUTH GET *ME! MAMA, MAMA!*...

✐...*August, 1954...I look in* room. It dark. Something all on floor. I no know what. It dark. Room go round me. I want go, but I no can go. I look on floor. I no want look, but I no can stop. Big pile babies on floor. Babies no move. Babies white and squishy. Blue hot dog things on them. Hot dog things wiggle. Red wormeys things in them. I see curly things. I pick up. They white. They slippery. They cold. They soft like baby soft. My arm white. My feet red. Tummy no feel good. Room all got white bone stuff. I WANT GO! *I WANT GOOOOOOOO!...* ✐

*...THWAMMMMMMMMMMMM!*

I hug the air mattress, the next instant grabbing my 16 and doing a 180 to face the enigma beyond our hootch.

"What?" Ski wheezes.

Nelson whispers, "MA blew. Maybe the main trail."

"Whadowedo?" I stammer.

"Nothing. It'll be light in an hour. If nothing happens in the next fifteen minutes, get some sleep."

*Sleep?* Waves of fear crash over nerves pricked to an erection. I can't stop staring into the night, expecting any second for a troop of madly grinning NVA to stroll merrily into our camp and blast us to shreds. *Wonder if everybody's scared as me? Not Hillbilly, or Nichols. Pane says it don't mean nothing. Maybe it don't, but I plan to get back to the World. I don't wanna die here. Gotta stop thinkin' 'bout dying. Gotta stop thinkin' 'bout dying, or I just might!...*

✎ *...11:50 p.m., Tuesday, June 4, 1980, Ottumwa, Iowa...The loud bang* of a car backfiring in the motel parking lot jolts my body. *What was that?* I stare at the ceiling. *It was like my heart jumped out of place.* A thick drop of fear begins to slide down my throat. *My heart definitely did something, like I never....* I feel the urge to lunge out of bed. But to where? There's no place to go. I turn towards the red glow. *11:51, the night is just beginning. If anything happens....* Amplified through my pillow, I hear my heart as if– for the first time. Stroke– stroKE– strOKE– stROKE– sTROKE– STROKE! I sit up to escape the awful sound. *I'm just one beat away from dying. Just one beat and....* No! No! No! it's okay! It was just a stupid car. Get to sleep. Larry and I gotta lotta work tomorrow. I force my eyes to close. An hour passes; I stare into *the dark ceiling....* ✐

\*      \*      \*

*...I hit the* ground as somebody up front cuts loose with a 16. *How can I dodge bullets for* –two leeches sprint for my hand– *everything in this damn country wants my blood!* The sight of the dead gook we stepped over leaving camp this morning slams into my head– twisted red and sawed in half by our MA. *At least we got some of theirs last night.* Glancing up, I noticed a rectangular sheet of paper stuck in the leaves. *One of those leaflets,* I thought as I inspected it. It was fresh and crisp like a new dollar bill. Confident it wasn't booby-trapped, I carefully picked it out of the bush and turned it over. Printed boldly on the front right was a crest-shaped design with what looked like a goose flying next to a ball of fire with the words "CHIEU HOI" written above it. The rest was Vietnamese gobbledygook, no doubt trying to convince the poor sap to turn himself in.

"Nichols' got one!" passed down the line like the guy'd just pulled in a large-mouth bass. I made my feet, relieved a major skirmish was not at hand.

Continuing, the trail left the cover of trees, skirting around a watery marsh to our right and a grassy field to our left. Beside the narrow path and partially in the water lay the carcass of the slain VC, staring with blithe unconcern into the sun. *Or is this a VC?* I thought as I passed the bloodied corpse, being careful not to brush against him. *If he is, he's unusually large...almost plump.* Within the hour we were pulling off our rucks at the CP and not too soon. For the last half of the hump I had felt like a fistful of scorpions were crammed into my intestinal tract trying to sting their way out. Nelson, too, looked ill as he grabbed his T-paper and E-tool and hurried into the brush.

"Gotta take a dump," I informed whoever might be listening. Returning, I didn't feel much better. My legs were shaky, my gut still ached and my throat was sore.

By one o'clock, a third of the platoon was complaining of stomach cramps, or the *burn 'n' trots,* so aptly described by Hillbilly.

Filling our canteens for the hump out, we watched Third Platoon trudge in from the northeast. Their deteriorating appearance mirrored our own: clothes ashen with dried mud, eyes streaked red from the stress of long stints guarding against the unending threat of death. The intermingling of Grunts was not ebullient as when we had hooked up with them in the Rocket Pocket. We just conjured up a smile or a wave, not ready for prolonged interaction. That would wait till stand-down.

"Got any smokes?"

I produced a pack of Winston's and tossed it to Ski.

"Thanks. You hear that was a fucking Chinaman Nichols blew away this morning?"

"Hope there ain't more of 'em," Nelson said. "Hear they're fierce fucking fighters."

"Hell," –Ski blew out a lungful of smoke– "*that* one ain't gonna be fierce no more. Damn." he said, searching his ruck's side compartment. "I'm out of shit paper."

"Here, Ski." –Yoss tossed him some of his– "Just don't lose all your brains. You might need 'em when you get back to the World."

Ski headed for the brush. "If I wasn't in so much pain...."

"What do you think's going on?" I asked Nelson, who himself was getting ready to head for the bushes.

"Probably this damn creek water," Nelson mused, "don't taste for shit."

"Hey, guys," Wad said, coming back from the LT's hootch. "Bad news. Guy from Third stepped on a toe popper. Fucker was dead before the dust-off could get him out."

"Damn. I knew this was gonna happen sooner or later," Nelson said. "Using the same fucking trails, we're asking for shit like this."

"Fucking *A*, it is," Wad replied. "Every gook within fifty miles must know we're *here by now*."...

✐...*12:51 p.m., Monday, October 6, 1980, LeClaire, Iowa...I stand and* wait by the back door of Tri-State Arial Engineering after returning from a brisk lunchtime walk. I don't dare go inside. *Please, relax!* I tell my thudding heart. Thump, thump-thump. Thump, thump-thump. *What is going on? I'm just out for a walk and.... Ever since that motel....*✐

Wednesday, November 25, 1970, Day 35 / 330 to DEROS
—birthday blues—

✐....*July, 1962, Cottage Grove...Oh, wow! It* worked! The soft glow of dawn was just beginning to shimmer over the eastern sky, illuminating the dewdrops that clung to the small willows in the slough off of Seventh Street. I bent over and warily touched the dead rabbit. *Stiff...and cold. But it worked! I actually caught me a rabbit! Just like Lester said!*

Gingerly picking up the carcass, I released the willow from its burden, though it didn't snap back as when I'd lost my grip on the noose last night. Now it just bent over like old man Miller. I struggled to pull off the noose; it was firmly dug into the neck. *Stupid thing won't come off,* I thought, staring into the *rabbit's frosty eye....✐*

   *...The bloated body* of the Chinaman lay by the trail as I warily approached, his eyes frosted over as he continued his upward stare. The hot sun had nearly doubled its body mass since yesterday, reminding me of a dead sow I had once spotted in a farmer's hog lot. I carefully stepped around him and continued on, thankful for the pain that was slowly snaking through my lower abdominal tract as we humped again towards the CP; it helped me to keep my concentration on the trail. I was now avoiding every stick, pebble and thorn that lay in my path.

   We made the CP by ten thirty. Like the sudden rush from an explosion, half the platoon dropped their rucks and scrambled for the bushes– LT included. The CP, too, was full of sick Grunts. When LT returned from his bush, he handed out halozone tablets and an extra supply of T-paper.

   "Everybody use these tablets in your water supply for the rest of the mission," LT said. "I know they make the water taste like shit, but do it anyway, unless you want to boil your water first."

   We set up our hootches by the creek, hoping to do as little as possible for the rest of the afternoon.

   "Why the fuck ain't *you* sick, Yoss?" Ski inquired as he lay on his bed and cradled his stomach.

   "I'm from the Bronx, Ski. Our stomachs are made of cast iron."

   Ski gripped his stomach as he got up to head for the bushes. "Damn asshole's so sore I can hardly walk."

   I crawled from the hootch. *What a way to spend my twentieth birthday, with a bunch of sore assholes.* With that, I rose to look for an empty bush.

Thanksgiving Day, Thursday, November 26, 1970, Day 36 / 329 to DEROS
—cold chow, hot wine—

   *✎....July, 1962, home...I scrunched my* nose. "I gotta do what?" Dad held his laughter as he shook his head and looked at the pile of rabbit fur lying at my feet.

"That isn't a chicken, Bobby. The *skin* has to come off, too."

"You mean you gotta *cut* it?"

"How else would you get the skin off? Then after you skin it, you have to gut it."

"How?"

"Lay it on its back, *start* at the tail and cut it up to its neck. After you scrape out its guts, throw them in this bucket. Look, I have to change the oil." –he dropped a pair of pliers at my feet– "Use those to pull off the skin," He said, starting toward his car. "You caught it, you clean it."

I turned the rabbit on its back, picked up my pocketknife and held my breath as I pushed the blade slowly into the abdomen. The slit released a stench that shot me *to my feet.* ....✐

...*Our camp lay* under an ashen blanket of fog as a thin sheet of drizzle spread over our camp of anemic-looking men. Last night had been a long night of GI's slithering to the nearest bush, no longer bothering to dig a cat hole. The resulting stench would've made any Missouri hog farmer proud. After rising, LT ordered the waste to be covered to at least prevent the odor from giving our position away.

It was Thanksgiving Day and it had been declared a day of rest, though probably more out of necessity than to celebrate our country's founders breaking bread with the locals.

Late morning, Third Platoon came in; they didn't look much better than us. They were to grab a quick meal and return to their NDP so First Platoon would get an opportunity to feast on some real chow, the idea being not to put all of the GI's in one pot, a big no-no in the Grunt's Book of Life.

The sky was beginning to clear as a chopper flew in at one o'clock, dropping off a full-scale Thanksgiving dinner complete with paper plates, cups and plastic-ware. Spread before us were canisters full of roast turkey, dressing, mashed potatoes and gravy, yams, green beans, cranberries and eggnog. They even delivered a dozen bottles of red wine. All in all it began to look like an old-fashioned country picnic. The only problem was the canisters had been sitting at the airfield for several hours before a chopper had received clearance to deliver the cargo, so everything that was suppose to be hot was cold and everything that was supposed to be cold was hot. But, being Grunts, in spite of the cold eats and hot drinks we filled our plates to the brim and wolfed down as much as our stomachs would allow. Those not afflicted had a grand time; the rest of us shoveled it in anyway.

Before Third departed, I got in a few words with Moreno, asking him about a bandage on his left hand. He said he'd cut it on his blooper during a brief firefight yesterday. I thought about asking about the guy that got blown away, but I knew in the end there was nothing to say. Maybe it was like Pane said– it really *don't* mean nothing. A thousand wars had been fought before and a thousand wars would be fought again. But this was our war and this was our time. It didn't matter how or why somebody got it. It's just that they did is all that mattered. And as for their friends and family, their loved one would forever be lost, caused by the insanity of some unknown enemy in some unknown land over some unknown reason.

But the sun was shining through the clouds now, throwing its hope on the world. The sun never gave up.

Friday, November 27, 1970, Day 37 / 328 to DEROS
—last chopper out—

*Thank God!* A muffled thumping echoing off the distance hills told me that a warm bed was only a few hours away. I wiped off my watch face, fogged over from a steady light rain: five-thirty. The CP had flown out at one and Third had headed for stand-down at two-thirty. We'd been waiting on the edge of a small, water-filled paddy of dense sawgrass since three o'clock and I was beginning to wonder if the rain or the dark might delay an extraction until morning.

"Ain't no stopping us now," Ski muttered under his breath as LT popped a red smoke and tossed it on the edge of the field.

Four choppers floated in smooth and pretty and gathered us up like a mother hen cackling to her young. I leaned back on my ruck and closed my eyes on the trip to the airstrip, the rain continuing as we loaded into the trucks and rode through the streets of Fat City, An Tan and into Chu Lai. Our spirits dampened, we slid off the trucks and checked our weapons into the armory without comment.

This time, the longest line was to the showers. To be clean. As I removed my filthy clothes, I had no other thoughts other than to bathe, to eat and to sleep. And that's just *what I did.* ...

✎...*2:11 p.m., Thursday, May 20, 1971, Day 210 / 155 to DEROS, Chu Lai...*"SECOND GEAR! SECOND GEAR!" Captain Watson's frustrated shouts over the grind of gears and the hot engine caused me to let up on the gas. "DON'T!" –he grabbed the gearshift– "STEP ON THE CLUTCH!" I did as he threw it into second and told me to ease the clutch back. I let it out too fast and almost killed the engine for the third time. "Okay. GIVE IT GAS, THEN SHIFT TO THIRD!" My face was flushed from concentrating on my first driving lesson– though the captain's looked redder– much redder. He was determined to teach me the art of driving a stick shift. After all, I was to be his personal driver.

The past few weeks had been a mixed bag of new experiences since starting my new job with Headquarters, Band and Support Company. We were located on a small peninsula that jutted its dark and jagged cliff into the sea at the northern end of Chu Lai's scythe-shaped shoreline. At night, the pounding surf would lull me to sleep, and I slept as solid as those rocks, secure in knowing this was my new home and would most likely be until my time here was at an end.

My new life as a *REMF*, or "Rear Echelon Mother-Fucker", as Hillbilly used to call them, was beginning to fit me as well as a faded pair of jungle boots. The only hard part was getting used to wearing my stiff, polished jungle boots and starched fatigues. I mean, I was glad to get out of the bush, but still, I wanted to reap the prestige that went with being a Grunt. The typing part wasn't a problem; I could already type faster that the two other clerks in my office: John Anderson and Brian Dudley. We worked from six to six, seven days a week, which generated unending complaints from my fellow lackeys, but then, they'd never spent a mission in the bush where six to six would've been a luxury. Indeed, we had all evening to enjoy: go on a run, swim in the cove just below the company chapel, take a long walk along the sandy surf, watch a movie in the Day Room, or deal into a hand of spades. I was walking on air, still pinching myself to make sure I wouldn't wake up dodging lead in the middle of a firefight or plowing through a mucky rice paddy with a hundred plus pound ruck.

Every three or four days I'd pull guard in one of three tower bunkers that protected the small peninsula. It was a beautiful vista from any of the towers as they sat teetered at the edge of the rocky ledge overlooking the turquoise China Sea. And knowing Charlie was far away scraping at the bottom of some

C-rat can– maybe even the one I'd thrown off Firebase Professional– made the view all the better. Sometimes I'd take my camera to get some great time-exposure shots; just two days ago I got a shot of a gecko feeding on some scraps that my bunkermate had set on the blast wall. They'd even bring us a midnight snack, usually leftover cold beef sandwiches on stale bread that most of the guys would toss to the mongoose. I, though, would snarf them up– anything tasted better than C's.

One of the guys, Lyle Ransom, who bunked in the next hootch over, hailed from my hometown, growing up just a couple of miles from my house. It blew me away when he said he was from East Moline. Since then we'd become good friends. I shared his love of rock and roll– and dew. He had painted his hootch walls entirely black, with black lights and psychedelic posters and he had a huge stereo system that I was surprised had fit through his door. In a way he had replaced Hillbilly, though Lyle lacked his philosophical wit. Of short stature and eyeglasses thick as a coke-bottle, he was the butt of our compatriots' heckling. But he was from my hometown and as such under my protective wing.

Another guy, Terry Hinds, played the coronet in the company band and also served as Chaplain's Assistant. Within a week he had me on the road, working me up to running a full mile. Considering my months of humping in the bush, I was surprised at my lack of endurance and I was sure that I would drop from heat stroke as I struggled to keep up with Terry in the scorching heat. All in all they were a great bunch of guys, and, I thought as I negotiated the captain's jeep down the hill toward my new paradise, maybe I can hang on here until DEROS, a thought that soothed my mind like an aged three-day old bottle *of banana wine....*✎

# STAND-DOWN TWO

Saturday, November 28, 1970, Day 38 / 327 to DEROS
—fudge and Phileas Fogg—

**K**eep this gawdamn line a mov'n'!" Hillbilly razzed from the back. "Ma ass is a pucker'n' like a bugler at a homecom'n' parade!"

The Aid Station was handing out pills for our intestinal ailment and most of the company was lined up, hoping for a cure for their weeklong affliction. I was up front with Blondie. In a few minutes the medic was asking how I felt and if I was allergic to penicillin, then handed me a bottle of white pills I was supposed to take three times daily until they were gone.

Returning to our barrack, Yoss was on his bed, reading from several stacks of letters he was sandwiched between. Only he and three others from our platoon had escaped the ailment.

"Bookoo mail, huh, Yoss?" I asked, throwing several packages and letters I had gathered at the CQ on a bed beside him.

"The more you write, the more you get," Yoss commented dryly, opening another letter.

I tore open the larger package. "All right! Food!" I hoped to get a rise out of Yoss– instead I got a bored glance. On top was an assortment of fudge, cookies and other sweets wrapped in foil. Buried below were small boxes of cereal. I set the package aside and opened the smaller package.

I tried again. "Books! All right again!" I pulled out six paperbacks: *Dick Tracy, Christy, The Last Movie, Around the World in Eighty Days, Getting Straight* and *The Hawaiians.*

Leaning back on my pillow, I opened a belated birthday card from my folks as the Grunts filtered into the hootch. Topp had canceled today's classes to give us time to recuperate, so we settled in for a dozen visits to a dozen specks of America that we each called home. As we lay treasuring our offerings, our abode became our sanctioned refuge and except for the occasional whine from a disgruntled seagull, all was well within our ephemeral nest of tranquility.

Sunday, November 29, 1970, Day 39 / 326 to DEROS
—Sundance—

*Sun. Nov 29 – 70*                                               *5 P.M.*
*Hello,*

*Here I am in the rear again taking it easy and everythings just great! Didn't think we were gonna leave yesterday cause of a light rain, but surprisingly they came anyway. Its the greatest feeling leaving on those birds for hot chow, clean clothes, cold pop, beds and just taken it easy. About the monsoon, it really doesn't rain that much at all -3 days then stops for a week or so. Wow, I really got voo-koo (many) letters and your packages also! Your packages were really super & thank's so muh for them. And the books -wow- I really appreciate them. Reading "Dick Tracy" right now. I was wondering if for Christmas you could possibly get me an instamatic Kodak camera. & film. Lot's of us have n' I could take really tough pictures. Can develop them at the main PX. Would really appreciate. Oh, that present I got ya, it isn't sent from here but from Chicago, Illinois. So should be in good shape.*

*Tomorrow I get paid. Broke right now. Will save most of it. & the BDE. After 198th on address means - Brigade.*

*About your referring me as to being, "on the hill" and, "didn't think the army did this anymore." It is very common over here, & the safest. Setting up on a hill & staying there a couple days. Gives ya plenty time to write & read. Don't do much else. You see, about all we do is be flown in, Company size, split into platoons and find a hill to set up on and that's about it. We move a couple times in the two weeks were out, & then the company, 4 platoons, join together to be flown out again. Very simple - and safe. And about digging foholes & surprise attacks - no way - Your con't sleep n foxholes- there to impractacal - and it would take half the night digging one. And theres no way hey, the V.C. can't sneak up onus without us hearing them. And if it's anything the V.C. fear, it's a GI. Camp. Cause they know what will happen if we even hear a noise near a camp. 4th of July! Mortor rounds. Artillary. Birds fly out with there 'mini' guns. (6000 rounds a minite!! - a bullet covers every 6: the entire perimeter of a football field in less than a minute!!) and charlie knows all of this. And with his one little 30 round magazine & rusty old rifle and mybe 2 or 3 mortor rockets he had to hump all the way from Hanio!! He's not even going to mess with us. And we're fighting Viet cong - not N.V.A. VC. Are just poorly armed farmers in groups of maybe 2 or 3. Everybody over here thinks all this is such a joke fighting these people. There's nothing to it. It almost like rabbit hunting. They say they ought to hire people who enjoy killing for a living. Sorry I kinda got cared away but your worring me about your worrying over me for no reason so please don't worry. If it wasn't for the nonotonous C-rations I think I'd really enjoy myself - beats being back in the states where everythings 'spit & polish". Found out our next missin is on the ridges on the other side of key-traw valley where nothing even goes on. It's more or less a 'rest' station. Oh. - another - 'moral' booster. No one has ever been injured, kelled (by V.C.) or captured inour company for about 2 yrs. A colonal told us. So I'm in a real good outfit.*

*'Standing gaurd' is done in the hooch sitting & we split it up so it lasts only a couple hours - it's dull.*

*I've never been closer to God as I am now. I find myself praying to him ofter before I go anywhere I ask him to watch over us & after I always thank him. I know he's really right here. And Dwight sends me lots of 'moral' boosters - tracks.*

*Calling Home? - $12.00 for 3 minites. Wow! I'll try it sometime.*

*Hope Kent's a success and we had a super thanksgiving dinner out in the field. - fantastic!! Gotta go - there a movie waiting.*

*THANKS FOR THE BIRTHDAY CARD!      Love, Your Son, –Bob–*

This morning I'd arisen like a newborn colt, raring to get on with life, because for the first time in nearly three weeks I wasn't either wet, starving or in anguish. As evening rushed in, so had a beautiful cloudless sky as the China Sea pushed a cool breeze over Chu Lai. Topp provided his usual offering of free beer and soda to appease our band of disgruntled Grunts– and as an added treat, a movie at the battalion USO. M*A*S*H was the last movie I'd seen while on a weekend leave in Seattle and as the lights dimmed and the hoot and hollering from the teenage warriors quelled, I realized that this was another great flick that Ahlgren and I had seen just last year.

For the first time since entering this strange new world, *Butch Cassidy and the Sundance Kid* carried my mind beyond the invisible boundaries of Southeast Asia and sent me hurling through a time portal to where the single action six-shooter reigned. 1969 had introduced a new breed of cinematic directors such as Sam Peckinpah, John Schlesinger and George Hill and their ability to paint the screen with bold brushstrokes of vivid reality captured my imagination like no other medium. For a brief while I rode with Butch, the Kid and Miss Etta Place as they wined and dined their way to Bolivia. I shared in their disappointment as the departing train left them standing in the middle of a decrepit railroad station that a disillusioned Sundance described as "...probably the garden spot of all of Bolivia." Butch's dream of fortune and fame in this unchallenged land seemed bleak, but then, as they gradually accrued the local language and customs, their luck in preying on the naive third-world banks began to turn.

As in most westerns, though, the good guys eventually caught up with the bad guys and by the time Butch and Sundance were fighting for their lives against the Bolivian army, my muscles tensed and my breath quickened. For unlike that green adolescent in the summer of 1969, I now felt a connection to the duo's circumstances as they are surrounded and unable to escape their adversaries. In the end, as the harsh lights and the caterwauling from my comrades met the movie's end, I returned to the shores of Vietnam to continue my own *battle of survival....*

✎*...8:12 a.m., Saturday, July 17, 1971, Day 268 / 97 to DEROS, Sydney, Australia...I shoot a* glance over my shoulder as I duck down a narrow alley. *He's still following me, well, follow this!* Kicking into a sprint, I clear the alley and round the main avenue leading out of Sydney's King's Cross District. The man deserts the chase as I leave him far behind. Slowing to a walk, I continue down the long slope toward Hyde Park, which borders the heart of downtown Sydney. *Man, that place is crawling with fags and whores! Lyle you stupid...putting me into in the middle of the biggest red light district in Australia. And I haven't even seen him since I got here. Probably tripping on acid...shoulda known better. Sure wish I coulda come here with Pat and Ski.*

The clearing sky buoyed my spirits as I turned north on Palmer and headed for the forested parkway in the Royal Botanic Gardens that skirted Sydney Harbor. Just beyond– the futuristic conundrum that formed the nearly completed Opera House. Every morning I'd check it out, appearing as an odd collection of bone-white shells jutting into the harbor, and then again on my evening trek back to my lair on top of the hill.

So far I'd done some shopping, going crazy in a leather shop whose suede scents took me back to the streets of Chicago's Old Town. I had purchased a pair of alligator boots and a fancy shiny black leather coat. It was my third day of R&R and I was already into my fourth roll on my new 35mm Yashica, punching out flicks of the city's bounty of pristine architecture and a gamut of parks that sprinkled the inner city with splashes of forest green. The modern capital offered an endless supply of activity and as I searched for more tantalizing artifacts around each street corner, no longer regretting my decision not to hook up with a farm family in the Australian Outback, part of a military housing program for visiting American soldiers– after all, I thought I'd already spent enough time in the bush in the last year.

It was a lonely trek, though, drifting to and fro in this sea of humanity. I longed to share with them a few words as they blended their thick buttery accents, but I knew they wanted nothing to do with me, an American GI. They would look right through me as though I was made of the recycled newsletters they'd give a curious scan before tossing them into one of the wire baskets that studiously guarded every corner. Thus I wandered the city like a wind-blown eucalyptus leaf in the land of the Kuala Bear and Kangaroo, my only comfort the solitary voice *of my mind....*✏

Monday, November 30, 1970, Day 40 / 325 to DEROS<br>—zeroing in on the dew—

"Ready on the left!" The E-6 paused, looking sternly up and down the row of Grunts lying in the prone position. "Ready on the right!" –another timed pause– "Commence firing!" The military always seemed to have no problem in conjuring a way to take all the fun out of anything. Eighteen of us had taken up Topp's offer this morning that anyone wanting to zero their weapons could skip today's classes and eighteen of us now regretted our decisions. A Basic Training E-6 type was running the show, treating us like first-week rookies. But since I was here instead of there, I figured I might as well swallow my pride and lock my sights as best I could– hard telling when the next opportunity would arise. Squinting to ward off the blowing dust, I squeezed off my third round to complete the shot group and waited for *His Royal Majesty's* supreme edit to cease fire. Peering through a pair of binoculars, my second shot group looked better than the first, which had been

113

way off the cross-hairs. I turned the adjusting screw a half-turn and lowered my sights *one more notch. ...*

✎ *...9:21 a.m., Tuesday, July, 20, 1971, Day 271 / 94 to DEROS, Sydney...Tomorrow is it,* I thought as I began my final walkabout in the mazes of downtown Sydney. Yesterday I'd hitched a ride to the mammoth Taronga Zoo, crossing the harbor on a hydrofoil, floating high as it sailed over the rough waters kicked up by a strong northwesterly wind blowing across Port Jackson. As everything in the capital city, the zoo was immaculate. Even the inmates seemed to cooperate in its upkeep, from the immense African elephant cleaning up its heap of straw, to the clan of Koala making tidy their forest of eucalyptus trees as they munched on its succulent leaves. *Just like being in bush country,* I thought as I watched scores of kangaroo hopping in the generous grassland enclosure– AND with a soda shop *on every corner. ...* ✎

*...By the fifth* volley my shots were right on target. Confident my 16 was sufficiently zeroed, I summoned *His Highness,* handing him my magazine and revealing my weapon's empty chamber. He squinted with his binos through the dust to scrutinize my shot group before nodding his head to indicate that I could join the other "completies", waiting by the trucks.

"What a crock of shit," a skinny guy that I recognized from First Platoon muttered as he shielded his face against the dust whipping around the trucks. "Betcha we'll never see *his* ass in the bush."

"Just once like to see that peckerwood tromping through a paddy up to his neck," Tuck added. "I'd laugh my black ass off!"

We pulled into our compound as evening settled in, the wind having tapered to a gentle breeze that swept over us from the westerly mountains. Topp was waiting for us impatiently by the armory, probably anxious to join his buddies for poker and shots. Hoping for a chance to rest my strained eyes I returned to my barrack and collapsed on my bed, my wind-burnt face stinging as it rubbed against the *rough woolen blanket. ...*

✎ *...3:13 p.m., Thursday, June 19, 1980, south of Geneseo, Illinois...I hit the* ground as the crack of a bullet whizzes over me. "GET DOWN!" I shout at Larry, who seems oblivious to the danger. Laying the level and tripod on the dirt, I peek over a clump of corn fodder to see a

114

woman walking toward the front of her yard. She's about a quarter-mile away and carrying a small caliber rifle. "Probably a 22."

"Now what?" Larry asks from where he lay in a shallow furrow that doesn't quite hide his paunch.

*PLAP!* "Gotta white flag?" Three more cracks scatter in the air. She screams something and clips off two more shots. "We'll just wait 'er out. She's gotta run out of ammo sooner or later."

"What's she so pissed at, anyway?"

"Just some crazy farmer's wife I guess who don't like our looks." –I take a quick scan at the plat– "This *ain't* her land, right?"

"Not according to Albright. This is all supposed to be John Deere property. Said they was gonna use it for a proving ground or something."

"I bet she thinks we're Deere people. Can't say I blame her. I wouldn't want a bunch of equipment stirring up dust right next door."

"Okay, then. Why doncha go tell her that we don't work for Deere?"

*PLAP! PLAP!* "Why don't you go?"

"Cause she'll probably shoot first and ask questions later, that's why."

I raise my head as she squeezes off another shot. "She ain't even aiming at us...firing high." I look at our Jeep *Cherokee*, sitting two-hundred feet away on the opposite side of a barbed-wire fence. I turn my gaze to the unimpeded stretch of tilled dirt that ends at her front lawn. "Maybe, this *is her land.*"...

✏...*9:36 a.m., Sydney...*"*Save the earth* pamphlet, sir?" A honey wheat haired young Aussie woman with faded patched jeans and a colorful tie-dyed smock stuffed it into my hand before I could answer.

Rounding the corner, pedestrians were feeding a nearby trashcan with the recycling fodder from the hippie lady. *That's all I need,* I thought as I was about to throw it into the can's mouth. I hesitated as I spotted a picture of a toilet on the brown paper. *What's this?* I scanned the page for a clue as to its presence.

**Ten ways to save the planet:**

1. **Recycle** – your cans, glass and paper to put them back into the cycle of life for others to enjoy.

2. **Organic farming** – free the earth from the chemical assault being waged by big business corporate farms.

3. **Plant a brick** – and save ten gallons of water a day by placing a brick in your loo.

*A brick? Why would anybody want to...?* I looked up, catching my reflection in a storefront window. The glossy black leather jacket, fancy boots and tight jeans suddenly made me feel like a caterpillar stuck in its silken yoke, eager to be free. I looked at the pamphlet. *Maybe, this is it. Maybe, this is what's been missing. Doing something to help this planet...not take away from it.* I began to walk slowly, no longer aware of the bright colors begging behind the polished glass or the towering modern architecture that ruled the avenue. *Maybe, that girl knows more than all these people. Maybe, she's had a vision of doing things a different way, a better way....* ✏

...*"Hey, boys,"* –Hillbilly stuck his head through the screen door– "we're a gonna do us a fling down at ma hootch tonight. Enybody interested yer a welcome ta join us." Not waiting for an answer, he continued to the next barrack.

I raised my head, kneading my eyes. "What's that about?"

"Damn pot party," Nelson answered. "Don't let 'im corrupt you, Adams...ain't worth it."

*Nelson's probably right,* I thought as I lay my head back down. *But it'd be pretty cool. Imagine me, smoking grass. Innocent little Bobby, the guy who can't even say a cuss word without turning red.*

I gave it five minutes, then, coyly sitting up to stretch, I stretched my way *out the door....*

✏...*6:22 p.m., Wednesday, August 18, 1971, Day 300 / 65 to DEROS, HHC & Band Company...I sat on* the john, considering the thin white stick that strange black dude had handed me after chow. *Do I really want to do this?* I turned it over in my fingers, as if the paper wrapping would clue me as to its contents. *Who knows what's in this thing? Don't even know the dude. But, what's the worst that could happen? Okay, what about the other night? Smoking the weed in Lyle's hootch while snipping on that brownie like an ant. Then Anderson, on the way to my room, lips moving but I don't hear nothing, like he's messing with me. Then his "What's happening..." hitting my ears AFTER he's gone. Opening my locker 'n' slamming it shut with the mute turned on again. Hearing it slam AFTER lying down. So what could be worse? Anyway, doesn't The Nam demand it?*

I peak through a crack in the outhouse door. *Still clear.* I snap my lighter and the end of the stick glows as I suck in the flame. *Now, let's see what this is all about. Probably just dew anyway.* Two deep draughts sting my lungs. *Man, this is strong stuff. Maybe...* –a light-headed buzz– *...man, this works quick!* Another drag. *This don't EVEN feel right.* Three more long drag sends a wormy fear crawling under my skin. *Feel...weird...get...outta...here.*

I toss the burning stub down the commode and open the door. *Don't need that crap.* A wave of dizziness almost takes me to the ground as I hold the door. *What's going on?* My room is halfway up the side of the shallow hill, but it seems like a mile. *Gotta get to my room. Gotta lay down.* I walk up the steps in what seems like slow motion, trying to act normal as I pass a nameless soldier. Reaching the screen door, I navigate the narrow plywood hallway, grab my door and collapse on my bed. *Okay, get...get...get....* My mind snatches the thought and throws it into the blender that is pureeing a thousand other thoughts that are quickly turning into cold gray soup. I stare at the yellow ceiling above my bed, desperate to grab onto a solid thought, to thread back the reel of my mind that is fast spinning out the window and toward the sea. *A reel, a reel, a wheel, wheel wheel wheel. Yes I'm a wheel. What I am is a wheel. A giant pinwheel! See it spin, it always comes back! See it see it see it. Yes! I see it spinning! Wow! It spins everything I've seen! It spins everything I've been! See it spin to Riverside, the water so cold, but it spins right back, the BIG wheel of life, that BIG PINWHEEL that cuts like a knife! It spins my green coat and I hate it! The zipper I can't zip, I can't zip zip zzzzzzzzip it! NO! I can't fix it! It spins the old lady that's trying to waste me, so I slice her and I dice her as she drags me away. It spins to the trees where Tarzan I see. He's so high in the trees where I swing like a bee, but they sting and they cling and they won't go away– HEY! They will not STOP! Until I scream COP! It spins me a beer on a hot Friday night with a basketball game and a girl out of sight who sits on her throne and glows like a queen cause her halo's so bright that I'm sure she's a dream. The monkeys they hide, the monkey's they're five, the monkeys they jive as they hang by their tails and hum their sad wails, from a black tree of gloom, they tap with their nails and bong on my nogg'n' they bong and they bong until my head's it's a sogg'n'. They will not let go, they will not say whoa, so on and on and on they go. Over and over and over and PLEASE! PLEASE do hold on! PLEASE don't let go! PLEASE don't go sailing and PLEASE do go slow!*

*Keep the wheel tight! Keep it in sight! Hold it and hold it with all of my might! But it spins and it spins and it spins out of sight, it's spinning so fast I fear I might take flight! NOW! Snatch out the bum with the stringy gray hair. Yeah HIM, who's star'n' through my bus window snare. NOW! Home I do go and what do I see? The bum from afar– he's a look'n' at me! He acts like he's rak'n', but I know he's a fak'n', though Mom she don't know, to Mom he's aglow. SHIT! He's a rak'n', while Mom cooks the bacon, the bacon to feed, to feed the poor tramp, to feed the poor tramp, to make him a champ. She says he's a man, who just needs some WORK, but I KNOW he does not. I know he's a SOT! For soon he'll be cooking, my body in HELL! Can't anyone TELL?! The man he's a DEMON! He'll laugh when I'm SCREAM'N' and body's a STEAM'N'!...✎*

...*"Adams, my man,"* Hillbilly said as I opened the door. "Come on in and have yerself a toke and a Coke, in eny which way order ya want."

"I just thought, you know, I'd give it a try."

Hillbilly handed me the weed, packaged in a thin sheet of zig-zag paper clamped in the jaws of a small blue and red- feathered roach clip.

"Jis' give 'er a nice long draw and hold it in fer a spell to let it soak in. Then blow it back out, man. That's all."

I sucked in the acrid smoke like I was about to swim the length of the Riverside swimming pool underwater. A harsh, burning sensation filled my lungs, but unlike that cigarette that I had tried behind the bushes in AIT, this didn't make me sick. In fact– it felt good.

The joint didn't make it back. Pane, taking the remaining stub out of the clip, had the honor of swallowing its remnants, a tradition no doubt passed down from generation to generation in the weed smoking communities of the world.

Hillbilly lit another as he expertly wove a tightly-knit bond from our small coterie who dared flaunt authority.

"Here's to the Second Platoon Heads..." –Hillbilly held up his Coke can– "...ta hell with the Juicers!"

Hoisting our cans, we took a swig– then *passed the twig*....

✎...*8:11 p.m., Friday, July 11, 1980, Trenton, Missouri...*"*Good evening, gentlemen.* My name is Holly. I'll be your waitress this evening. May I start you off with a cocktail from the lounge?"

Larry studiously placed his blue linen napkin on his lap. "Whatcha got on tap, Holly?"

"*Heineken–*"

"That's far enough, pretty lady. A frosty mug of ice-cold Heineken, please."

"Very good. And you, sir?"

A frosty mug of ice-cold Heineken sounded great. "I'll just have a Pepsi."

"All right! Why don't you take a minute to look over the menu while I bring your drinks."

"Why doncha drink, Bob?" Larry asked as the waitress brisked away.

"I dunno," I lied. "Just don't, I guess."

"Ahhhh, there's nothing like an ice cold brew to wash the dust down after a long day of running levels. Well," he said, taking a quick sip of water, "I've got to use the little boy's room. Be right back."

This was our third full week of working the desolate hill country in north-central Missouri, which also meant three weeks of eating in the same dismal dives off of I-35. Due for a change, we had driven forty miles to find a restaurant suitable for a couple of hard working guys and the White Horse Inn in Trenton seemed just the ticket.

I studied a painting hanging above the small candlelit table in the posh dining room. *The Night Watch, by Rembrandt*, I thought, recalling the trivia I had gleaned from an Art History course during my short-lived college career. *Man, those were the days. We used to get so drunk.... Like our whole wedding party getting wasted the night before...and now.... Man, that Lundstrum Crusade seems like a lifetime ago. What's happened to me, stuck out here in the middle of nowhere, so far from my family, my friends...my God. Well, at least I made crew chief.*

I looked over to a nearby table where a couple were enjoying after-dinner drinks. *Man, a beer sure would taste good right about now...been so long. How's a guy to act?* I observed another foursome enjoying intimate conversation over cocktails. *What harm could one beer do?* I scanned the room. *Where's that waitress?*

"What's this?" Larry said, returning from the restroom.

"Yours looked so good, Larry, I just couldn't resist."

"Well," Larry said, picking up his frosted *golden mug. "Cheers!"*...✐

✐...*8:15 a.m., Sunday, August 29, 1971, Day 311 / 54 to DEROS, HHC & Band...Thirty feet above* the swaying surface sparkles in the sun. Below, a golden array of light shimmering along a rock wall dances in my eyes. I stroke to the sandy bottom and grab onto a small object. *Cool shell,* I think as I brush it off. I look up and stare into the sea bottom's western horizon. A shiver slides up my spine as I gaze into the expanse of midnight blue and contemplate the rumor floating around the peninsula that sharks regularly feed near an offshore island. My lungs, nearly empty now, dispel any more imaginings of man-eaters as I push off the seafloor and propel my body upward.

Breaking the surface, I stroke to the nearby rock ledge and in one motion pull myself onto its flat surface and stretch catlike onto my back. I was as brown as nutmeg now, having spent most afternoons swimming in the small cove nestled below our unit's flagstone chapel. Whenever I pulled guard duty, they would give me the next afternoon off– and I'd been pulling a lot of guard duty lately. I would offer my services to anyone who cared to duck out– for a nominal twenty-dollar fee, of course. Captain Watson would always assign an extra guy for guard each night, the idea being to let the sharpest looking soldier escape the tedious chore. A few of us tried to make "the man" every time– especially me. I'd get all spiffed up, donning starched fatigues and spit-shined boots, cleaning my 16 till it shone and running over my general orders time after time till I knew them forwards and backwards. Most times I'd make the man, then turn around and offer my services to another poor soul wanting to duck out– for another twenty dollar fee, of course. It was a great moneymaking scheme, plus I got the following afternoon off. Besides, I didn't mind sleeping on the hard cots in the bunker– it sure *beat the bush.*...✐

# MISSION THREE

Tuesday, December 1, 1970, Day 41 / 324 to DEROS
—jewel in the clouds—

*This should work just fine.* I dumped the contents of my M-60 ammo can onto the bed. Pulling up the larger M-16 ammo can, I placed my growing collection of books, stationery, cigarettes, wallet, playing cards and an assortment of souvenirs. "Much better," I muttered to myself as I lifted the can to test its weight.

"You're crazy, Adams!" Ski said, throwing his ruck onto his bed. "That other can was bad enough, but now you're gonna carry *that* big fucker?"

"Long as *I* don't complain, don't worry about it," I said, flipping the lid down and locking it.

Ski stared at me a second longer before turning to Nelson. "So where the fuck we going this time?"

"Guess."

"Oh, fucking great. Land of milk and honey here we fucking come." Ski started stuffing his poncho liner into his ruck.

"Trucks will be here in thirty minutes," Nelson said. "Gotta be at the armory in ten, so let's get moving."

\*       \*       \*

Peering between my feet, a familiar sight came into view. *Ky Tra, here we come.* I glanced at Wad, who was checking the belt on his 60. *God, please get me through this one, and please watch over us....* My prayer drifted off as the smoky peak of Mount Hell came into view, and my gut contracted as I recalled that weeklong trial by starvation and water. The cloudy smoke ring around the mountain also reminded me of last night's adventure; I felt a little guilty for succumbing to the temptation, but not as much as I thought. After all, I didn't even get a buzz out of it– nothing. Hillbilly had said something about it taking a couple times before a high kicks in, and then the world could do you no wrong. I wonder...? *...and please God,* I mouthed, *keep the rain* *away, at least not like last time. And please watch over Mom and Dad, Kent, Linda and everybody else back home. And forgive me my sins. In Jesus name, amen.* My conscience clear, I awaited my fate below.

\*     \*     \*

"Shit!" Wad grumbled as he plunged into knee-deep water at the edge of the chopper. "Just once I'd like to start a mission with dry feet."

The helicopters leaned into their ascension as we goose-stepped to the edge of the ancient paddy. "Got four klicks to cover," LT said as we formed into our humping mode. Blondie's squad took point, following the edge of the paddy for a short distance before cutting southeast, gradually gaining altitude as we humped into the interior of Ky Tra's back country. This time we were on the opposite end of the long valley; Mount Hell was just a ghostly image through the thick tropical air.

God was sending us all kinds of sunshine as we entered our fifth hour, sapping our energy like a sponge. For the past three and a-half hours we'd been ascending a long ridgeline, following a narrow path that now looked more like an animal trail than VC. But Blondie wasn't taking any chances, so the going was slow, hot and exhausting, and by four o'clock we straggled in on one of the many outcroppings jutting from the main section of ridge. High above the valley floor, the view from the NDP was nothing less than spectacular. And in spite of my depleted condition, I couldn't help but admire the ring of mountaintops peeking through the mist like lustrous emeralds on both sides of the ridge. The terrain was sparsely vegetated, which made for an easy set up, as we were yearning for a hot meal and rest. And the best news– no threat of rain. God indeed was making good on my request.

After setting up, Nelson and Yoss headed to set out the MA while I pulled out a can of beefsteak and pineapple slices. With a full belly, I lay my head on the edge of my air mattress and delved into chapter three *of Dick Tracy....*

✎ *...10:04 a.m., Tuesday, September 28, 1971, Day 341 / 84 to extended DEROS...I could still* see the lighthouse a thousand feet down the highway. Below me, my 10-speed was barely distinguishable now as its blue frame faded into the black and gray rubble at the bottom of the steep slope. Beyond my bike, past the highway and the charred shoreline, the ocean stretched to infinity; only a gray shadow-like silhouette of a steamer near the horizon marred its untarnished surface.

Scrutinizing the narrow ridge above me, I guessed that I was nearing the top, for the slope was getting steeper, and slipperier. I was determined to go as far as I could. After all, I owed it to myself– right? *This is soooo cool,* I thought as I continued to mule my way up on all fours, carefully planting my feet firmly into the black cinder-like surface; a slip would mean a two-hundred-foot slide to the bottom of the trough. *A heavy rain could just wash this whole thing away,* I thought as I studied the eroded ridges that spiked the black mountain from head to toe.

My foot slips and I freeze in spread eagle. It isn't much more than an arm's length across now and I wonder if it's wise to continue. I turn and sit on my butt to contemplate the situation, swiping my sweaty brow with a blue tie-dyed T-shirt I'd purchased last evening. Below me, my bike is gone, as is the highway. Just the red cap of the lighthouse and a thin slice of the shoreline visible. Leaning back on my elbows it's nothing but mountain and ocean. *Magnificent! Wish I had a pen and paper with me. What a place to write! But I got my camera.* I snap off several shots of the panoramic view. To my right, the oxbow shoreline leads to Waikiki's emerald oceanfront, where salty white breakers collapse far from *the opalescent beachfront.* ....✑

Wednesday, December 2, 1970, Day 42 / 323 to DEROS
—petrified wood—

"Waddya see?"

I shaded my eyes as I scanned 360 degrees from one of the few climbable trees in the area. "Nothing but trees and more trees. Looks like good a place as any."

Ramos toweled his pillowy, olive-colored face. His spaniel eyes darted again at the brush line. "Okay, Adams, come on down and we'll get to work." *Why does he have to say my name when it's obvious he's talking to me? I mean, who else is up in a tree?*

The morning had been a cruel hump up some of the craggier inclines of this mammoth ridgeline, which seemed to go on forever until finally surrendering to the sea's invincibility. We got a glimpse of one lonely VC on the trail ahead of us right before pulling into tonight's NDP, but he had scurried away before Blondie or Ramos had a chance to open up. Now Ramos was our reluctant leader as Pane, Wright, Spurlin, Fritts and I were assigned the duty of clearing an LZ for an afternoon re-supply. And it appeared to be no easy task, for as we had gained higher ground, the landscape mimicked more and more the tangle of thick stubby brush and stunted trees reminiscent of Mount Hell.

"Unfuckingbelievable!" Spurlin whined. He took another swat against a six-inch trunk with little effect. "Must be petrified wood, else my machete's dull as fuck."

Fritts hacked at his own Rock of Gibraltar. "Why don't we just blow 'em?"

Ramos stopped to catch his breath like a man who needed to lose a few pounds. "LT says...we can't afford to give our position away, especially since...there ain't no way out of here but a day's hump to the paddies."

"Shoulda humped in some Chieu Hoi's to do our shit work," Pane declared, "'stead of pacifying the fuck out of 'em back in the rear."

Spurlin plopped down as his tree finally yielded. "I need a fucking break."

The LZ had to be a minimum of thirty-meters in diameter to safely bring in a chopper, so we hacked, chopped and slashed for two and a-half hours, finally finishing by five thirty. I'd been exhausted many times, but my body reached a new plateau of weariness as we dragged ourselves into camp. Collapsing by my hootch, I dumped half a canteen cup of water on my parched face, praying LT wouldn't pick me for re-supply duty.

LT approached our hootch, looking agitated. "The re-supply's canceled. Maybe get it tomorrow."

"You mean that LZ...."

"Sorry, Adams, but sometimes the shit just don't play out."

"That's just great," I exhaled as LT headed for *the next position....*

✎*...10:44 a.m., Hawaii...In a controlled* slide I scooted down the black cinders and made my way back to the foot of the old volcano, ready now to continue my quest in circumnavigating the island paradise. *Now that's something I can tell my grandchildren about someday,* I thought as I mounted my bike and looked at the summit of the volcanic crater hundreds of feet above me. *Who'd ever thought when I woke up this morning I'd be climbing Diamond Head....*✎

# WIRE IN THE SHADOWS

"Stupid bastards," Hillbilly said after listening in on LT's conversation with the CP. "Them ass-wipes couldn't wade across ma niece's kiddy pool without drown'n'."

Word of yet another Third Platoon casualty spread quickly through our platoon. Cochise, nicknamed thus because of his Apache Indian ancestry, had stepped on a toe popper. It was bad enough that he would probably lose a leg. And worse, the cartridge had been from one of our own M-*16*'s. Hillbilly's fierce Scottish temper surfaced as he ranted about how inept their point men were and how an Irish Setter could do a better job of pointing than they could. I thought of Moreno and his misfortune of being transferred to a platoon that evidently didn't have its "shit" together. Between Hillbilly, Nelson, Blondie and Nichols I wouldn't hesitate to wager that we had the best pointmen in the Company, if not the whole Battalion. *Should make that a special MOS,* I reflected, *11 Bravo 1A, or something like that.* Anyway, they deserved a medal for the stress they put themselves under every humping day out here.

The muffled thump of an incoming bird diverted our attention to our present circumstances. We had hooked up this morning to move to another position further up the ridgeline. But first we were to pick up a re-supply at LZ Sweat, nicknamed thus to pay tribute to the five of us who had donated more than our share of sweat clearing it. I popped a blue smoke and underhanded it to the center of the clearing while Tuck got on the horn and asked for a color ID. Within seconds the chopper seemed to materialize above the trees with a blast of air, blowing a collage of dust, brush and smoke over us while touching down gently onto the fallen canopy. Surprisingly, the pilot shut down the engines, a rare occurrence in the bush, and after the turbines whined to a halt, the gunner announced that hot chow was on board, their way of apologizing for yesterdays aborted mission.

"*All right, fly-boys!*" Retchin bellowed, his mouth already beginning to salivate. "Somebody's watching the fuck out for us!"

Three canisters of fresh, hot food were opened, paper plates passed around, and after piling on the chow, we sat down to a feast that more than made up for the "Thanksgiving-Day Massacre" from last mission. We made quick work of the cuisine, and with contented bellies we bade farewell to the chopper crew, who had taken the opportunity to grab an uninterrupted meal themselves. I often wondered if I'd rather be one of those guys flying in the birds instead of humping it down here on terra firma. Wouldn't be bad duty until you hit a hot LZ, then...I don't know. I heard door gunners didn't last too long out here; they either retired six feet under or went crazy from the stress.

*     *     *

"We know there's VC activity in the area," LT began as Nichols' and our squad gathered round him at our newly assembled NDP. "Unfortunately, Third Platoon proved that this morning. We'll scout the trail heading up the ridgeline to see if we can get the jump on some of them. Nichols, take point the first half and Nelson, you lead coming back. Let's get a couple other guys on point for awhile, too. It's about time we start training some backups, don't want to end up like Third Platoon."

Ski let me take drag as we headed up the ridge, which soon leveled off since we had reached a plateau that dominated the middle portion of Ky Tra's southern backbone. The patrol's purpose was easy enough: see a dink; you shoot 'im. Okay, I could handle that and for the first half I enjoyed walking drag, which was more like walking backwards than forwards. It was the drag man's responsibility to make sure no dinks sneaked up behind us. That wasn't a problem, although it was awkward catching the signals that occasionally passed down the line.

Two hours out and not a VC in sight, so LT gave the signal for a short break before heading back. I pulled a small bag out of my cargo pocket, full of chocolate chip cookies left over from my care package from home. Polishing off half of them, I crossed my arms behind my head and leaned against a tree. "Who ya think's gonna walk point heading back?" I asked Ski.

"Not me," he answered matter-of-factly. "I don't walk point."

"How 'bout Yoss?"

"Done it, and he didn't do too good. Gets spooked too easy, know what I mean? Then Wad's got the 60, 'n' Fritts is his AG." –Ski paused– "Hell, Adams, that just leaves you, huh?"

"How about it?" Nelson asked, overhearing Ski.

A line from *The Wild Bunch* popped into my head. *"Why not,"* I answered more as a statement than a question. The break over, everybody did a 180, placing me in point position. Nelson switched places with Ski and we took off. *How hard can it be, just look for booby-traps.* But after fifty meters I found myself looking ahead more than on the trail as Nelson warned me of a cigarette butt just ahead of me. The responsibility fell on me point blank at the thought of missing the potential booby-trap. Nelson explained everybody behind me was too busy looking to the left and to the right to keep an eye on the trail; this was my *sole* responsibility. Don't worry about what's up ahead; that was the slackman's job. So I began again, directing all of my attention to the ground in front of me. Since we had just covered the same ground a few hours earlier, the going was bearable, but if this was virgin territory, the burden would indeed have been great.

Before I knew it we were back, the task of scrutinizing every anomaly causing me to lose track of time. I had spotted a dozen objects that could've been booby-traps, pointing them out to Nelson so he could relay the word back. Mentally drained, I slumped onto my air mattress and closed my eyes. Maybe I'd do point in a pinch, but on a full-time basis? No way, Jose.

Monday, December 7, 1970, Day 47 / 318 to DEROS
—Mount Hell ditto—

I lay on my mattress, staring at the droplets as they fell from a loose thread on the edge of the hootch. My stomach was playing a familiar song learned so well several weeks ago on Mt. Hell as I counted off the drops. *Here we go again.* The last three days could've played as one: hook up, move along the ridge, set up, cut an LZ. Then the rain would come, which meant no re-supply. Another washout seemed imminent.

Not one encounter with Mr. Charlie, though. *He's probably down in the valley now that we're up here, waiting to come back up soon as we leave.* And, if all the VC were in the valley, then all of the leeches must have migrated to our camp. Three of the rubbery little monsters were clinging to me as my eyes opened this morning. Fat with my blood, they clung to my calf and ankles for dear life until a stream of bug juice dropped them to the hootch floor with my stolen blood coagulating in their bellies. At lunch I had to squirt a circle of bug juice around me just to prepare my C's– felt like I was performing some kind of satanic ritual. Between the leeches, the rain and my gnawing gut, I was ready to get off this ridge– and word was, tomorrow we'd be *doing just that....*

✎...*5:38 p.m., Tuesday, July 29, 1980, Lamoni, Iowa...I rolled up* my window to the Jeep *Cherokee*, Larry getting the other. "Could be a bad one," he said, an ominous glint from an approaching storm reflecting off his eye as he slammed the door shut. I followed his stare to an ugly snarl of clouds west of Lamoni, one of a half-dozen small farm towns littering I-34 in south central Iowa, just a stone's throw from the Missouri border. Larry Owens and I were holed up in a cracker-box motel just off the interstate, an even mile east of town.

Keying the door, we went inside to kick off the day's dust from running levels on a nameless stretch of gravel northwest of town. They all looked the same: chalky-white and narrow, with an endless plume of heat waves in the scope and choking hot as we ran elevations along the hilly corn-country, ticking off enough horizontal and vertical control for an aerial mapping flyover due soon as the summer vegetation left the landscape.

We were beat, ready for a hot meal and a cool drink at Lamoni's Cattlemen's Club soon as we showered. I started to wash up while Larry lounged on his bed, staring through the door he'd left open to let out the stale air.

"Dead silent out there, Bob."

I peeked out of the bathroom. "What's going on?" Through the partially opened drapes I watched as several people gathered on the far side of the motel parking lot.

Larry threw his legs to the floor. "Let's check it out."

I threw my towel over my shoulder and followed Larry out the door. Stopping near the small group, our eyes followed their western gaze to a massive front that was enveloping the small town of Lamoni. It looked like a witch's cauldron brewing above the stand of one-story flats. To the east, the sky still glowed a deep indigo, its brilliance unable to penetrate the dense mesh of boiling dark clouds pushing through the atmosphere from the west.

"Never seen clouds that low," I told Larry as we continued to a narrow strip of dead grass bordering the highway.

"Like pea soup," Larry exhaled, his voice resonating in the still air.

"Twister weather," a grizzled truck driver-type croaked from behind us. A plug of chewing tobacco puffed out the right side of his lean, leathered cheek. Two other spectators, a heavy-set mother in calico with her pre-teen child tucked close to her bosom took a step back at his words. The thought of a twister sent a familiar chill through my bones. *Hope this don't turn into another Typhoon Hester....*

✏ *...10:52 a.m., Friday, October 23, 1971, Day 367 / 58 to extended DEROS, Chu Lai, Vietnam...This is crazy,* I thought as I pecked away on my electric Underwood. Outside, a steady spray of rain and seawater pelted our frail office building, teetering at the edge of a narrow rock peninsula. *But if nobody else ain't moving...I'm not either!*

All morning it'd been getting worse. And with news we were the bull's-eye for a major typhoon didn't seem to upset my compadres one little bit. John was leaning into his typewriter, searching for keys to finish up Warrant Officer O'Malley's latest mess hall inspection report. Captain Watson seemed oblivious to nature's fury as he sat stoically in his gray swivel chair, scanning a stack of weapon status reports that had just come over from S-3.

The window flaps rattled as I looked down on the mess hall that hugged the side of the rocky slope below me. Past the mess hall the hill dipped to a shallow grade that leveled off to a small field where the band members would practice their marching. Beyond that sat the CQ office and rec room, with our living quarters, four rows of white-washed plywood hootches, clustered on the far slope that led to the mainland.

*Eleven o'clock. Said the eye was due around one? Least nothing ain't blown away yet.*

Warrant Officer O'Malley picked up his baseball cap and rolled his chair back. "I don't know about you fine gentlemen, but I, am going to take an early lunch." He squinted out the window at a tuff of ragweed laying flat in the steady gale. "Captain," he said, scratching his gray temple, "don't you think it prudent to dismiss these guys? Getting pretty nasty out there."

Captain Watson looked up from the paper mountain, craning his neck to view outside his window. "You might be right, why don't–" A metallic warbling snapped his head toward the mess hall just in time to see a section of the corrugated roof peel back like an orange skin. It spiraled through the air before collapsing with a loud clap onto the ground beyond the entrance.

The captain quickly stood up. "I suggest you men head straight for your barrack, or better yet, one *of the bunkers."...*

✏ *...5:49 p.m., Lamoni...The little girl,* snuggled in her mommy's skirt, pointed at the black edge of the cold front as it crawled silently toward us. Between us and Lamoni there was nothing to impede our view of the developing drama, just a dusty bean field across the highway that stretched to the town's edge.

Now nearly overhead, all understood that the approaching storm demanded nothing less than our complete attention. The atmosphere degraded. The cloud's emerald-black, marbled body spun in slow conflicting circles, as if embroiled in the midst of a power struggle. Twilight descended as it moved over us, the streetlights popping on along the highway from town like a row of falling dominoes. Glancing back, the mother had taken her child back another step. The truck driver had spit out his chaw as if he'd lost his taste for the weed as he stared at a world turning sour.

Our attention was drawn to the bean field across the highway. A tiny dust devil rose from the ground three hundred yards distance and to our right. It appeared harmless, just out for an afternoon lark as it performed a ballet through the rain-starved field while overhead, the hulking mass had come to a decision– this was where it would concoct its sinister recipe. The front's eddies began to slowly merge while below, the dust devil pranced, insignificant to the spectacle unfolding above. As if drawn by a magnet, I stepped onto the highway's shoulder, wanting to be closer to this bizarre sideshow that nature granted a lucky few. The heat from the blacktop doused a chill that had begun to chug through my limbs.

Not a whisper, but an occasional hunger pang rumbling deep within the monsters bowels, in sharp contrast with the electric crackle of grasshoppers frying on a bug zapper suspended from the motel overhang behind us. The mother pulled her daughter closer to her as the dust devil began to move slowly toward us. To my amazement, the cloud's gyrations began to coordinate with the dust devil, which was growing as it fed on the *ground beneath it....*

✎ *...1:18 p.m., Chu Lai...An ominous silence* prompted me to step outside my barrack. "Wow!" I shouted to Lyle, who was peering out of the door the next barrack over. "Where's the typhoon?"

"Must be in the eye," he answered, squinting at the sky through coke-bottle lens.

"Let me grab my camera." I disappeared inside, returning seconds later with Yashica in hand, checking the film-advance. "Let's go."

"Shit! Check it out, man," Lyle exclaimed as we passed the rec room. The mess hall roof was gone but for a few shards clinging to the edges. Plywood window flaps were torn and hanging in disarray and a few of the wall panels were missing. *So much for O'Malley's mess hall inspection report*, I mused. "Hey, let's get a bite to eat." Entering, the sun shone through the topless building, shimmering off the drenched black and white-checkered tile floor.

"Everything's soaked," Lyle said, squeezing a glob of bread lying on the counter.

Picking up two glasses, I pointed one of them toward the chocolate milk dispenser. "That ain't."

With a full stomach we headed up the hill toward my office at the edge of the rocky finger. Ripped sandbags, sections of corrugated roofing and plywood debris littered the narrow gravel road as we joined a dozen other gawkers engaged in their own sightseeing tour. My office building, totally exposed to the brunt of the typhoon, was surprisingly unharmed.

"Just my luck, the one building I *wanted* to blow away's in perfect shape." Some of the other buildings weren't as fortunate, dismantled as if a giant finger had flicked their southern side. I clicked off several shots of the typhoon's ravaging as a thick cluster of wild gray clouds began moving in from the southeast.

"It's gett'n' close!" one of the gawkers yelled as he and his friends hurried down the hill.

"Maybe we should be getting back, too," Lyle said, biting into a granny smith he'd scarfed on the way out of the mess hall.

"Just a couple more flicks." I aimed at a roofless tower bunker with Lyle in the foreground. Spinning around, I clicked a shot of the panoramic Chu Lai coastline as it horseshoed to the south, towards my old infantry unit. "Okay, let's get outta here!" Walking briskly, the wind increased at an alarming rate, and by the time we reached the rec room the tin roofs were humming the typhoon's song.

"You going to your room or the bunker?!" Lyle shouts over the gale.

"I'm holing up in my room!" I answer, remembering the half-foot of water I had spotted on the bunker floor on the way over.

The wall of the eye is on top of me as I shut my plywood door, locking myself into the small yellow room. I am blind to the outside, having secured the window flap before lunch. The force of the typhoon's backside is much more powerful, the stilted floor lurching as the wind pushes from beneath.

My light bulb pops off.

*I shoulda went to the bunker*! I hug the bed. *What if this thing takes off! What if, this is it! God, why in hell did I have to go and extend my tour just to get killed in a typhoon!*

The world howls. Something heavy bounces off my roof, sending shudders of fear through tensed muscles. Another thud sends me underneath the bed and into darkness as sound takes over, cold arms *clench rigid body.* ...

✏ *...6:02 p.m., Lamoni...Am I watching the birth of...?* my thought dissolves as the dust devil stops. It ceases its childish dancing to assume a new posture: that of an awakening dragon stretching to its full girth. It spins faster, feeding, growing: twenty feet, thirty, then before my eyes a snake-like vortex appears out of the cloud above it, angrily writhing at the devil's zenith, working out its vectors for the great conjunction. A hundred feet– *God, it's so close!*

Now the devil is powerful enough to make its move, to consume not only the ground but the sky above. It begins to pull the black snake in: first a thin ribbon of smoky-green. Then it becomes one with the monster. It thrusts the massive cloud into its orifice and slams it into the earth with an explosive spray of dirt and beans. Its base mushrooms as it inhales the ground. Debris, hundreds of feet from the epicenter rise in the air to join this cataclysmic display of nature's power. The force gorgonizes me, like teetering at the brink of a precipice, draining strength from limbs weak from fear, daring me to defy death and plunge into space and into immortality. I cannot resist. I must join with the creature, as is everything else in this surreal world. I step toward it. Another. Above the roar of the spinning giant I hear a screech from behind. Another hideous cry. That of a human. My forgotten towel falls as I turn my head. The mother and child are gone. So is the trucker. Larry is halfway to our room, screaming at me. Twenty degrees drop in a few seconds, the blast of cold like a slap in the face; I will my body to stop. But still, eyes glue hypnotic to this emerald beam of destruction.

I must go. I must leave now. I force myself to back up. I turn away, grinding my towel into the oily road rock. But yet, my eyes cannot leave. I am one with the twister, no, my twister, my sordid affair with this orgasmic realm of wonder. Envious eyes watching as the twisting spike rapes the world, mocking life in all its frailty.

Then an avalanche of volcanic sound pulsates through my body as the newborn viper abandons me and leaps at the interstate. Leaps over it. Devours it. I dive through my door with a blast of wind and hail slamming it shut, I skittering like a mouse *beneath my bed. ...*✐

Tuesday, December 8, 1970, Day 48 / 317 to DEROS
—white water—

The rain dripped off my boony hat as I leaned over to adjust my new home of plastic, tin and steel. Humping in the steady downpour kept us cool and silent as it fell straight to earth as watery missiles dominating our jungle world. The platoon had stopped for a break, for what reason I didn't know, and I dropped to the earth for a few minutes to rest. Without delay a herd of leeches sprinted toward me, hoping for an easy meal on my American blood. *No way I'm parting with one drop today,* I thought as I pushed myself back to my feet to lean against a nearby tree.

At four fifteen we found Third Platoon buried in a sea of head-high sawgrass a hundred meters from a nameless river that cut through the middle of Ky Tra Valley. The camp was silent; the GI's peered wolf-like from their dark recesses, waiting for God to get around to repairing the tear in the sky that was inundating their world.

LT's intention was to pick up our stockpile of C's, supplies and mail that had been re-routed to Third at a break in the rain this morning and continue across the stream to establish a camp on the other side. Not wanting to linger in the downpour, we stuffed our provisions into our rucks and faded into the wet brush as silently as we had appeared. The grass grew thicker and the rain grew louder as our pointman pushed against the wall of grass. The line stopped; Hillbilly motioned LT forward. The otherwise shallow, meandering stream was now a monstrous swell of muddy gray *thrashing before us. ...*

✐*...11:42 a.m., Saturday, August 9, 1980, Niobrara, South Dakota...The sun was* hot on my back. Hotter than usual, I thought as our Swamp Fox strained against the strong Niobrara current, just a mile in from the mouth of the Missouri River. The last two days had been the same. The aquaduck's worn bubble tires weren't deep enough to make any headway as the Swamp Fox was just able to keep even with the river's strong current. It'd been a good idea anyway– would've beat humping the levels through the water.

"We're never gonna make it back!" I shouted over the jerry-rigged engine to Larry, who was parked on a floatation cushion beside me. Yesterday the muffler had busted, so an enterprising gas jockey had had the brilliant idea of wiring a tin can around it. Worked pretty good, till just after lunch when another hole busted through below the can.

Larry cupped his hands. "Let's ditch this bucket of bolts and walk back to the truck!"

Nodding, I turn the amphibious vehicle to port, it smoothly yielding as the current begins to slide us downstream. I look up at the sun, now high over the trees to my front. *Why is my back still hot?* Glancing behind me, a streak of white fear sweeps through my chest. "FIRE!" Larry's eyes widen as he jerks his head toward dirty orange flames licking at the engine block.

"Head for shore!" he yelps while I maneuver the buggy across the strong current. He grabs his floatation cushion and poises as if to take the plunge. "Don't jump! We're almost there!" The entire rear of the craft is engulfed in flames as the fire swiftly leaps to the blue fiberglass shell. As the aquaduck slides close to the bank's edge, I know it's now or never, for just downstream is a thicket of brush leaning over the water that will make a shore jump impossible. "NOW!" Larry dives, landing with a heavy thud. I'm right on his tail, grabbing the bow line as I leap, thinking I can secure the burning rig to a huge cottonwood that stands ten feet from the water's edge.

"Can't hold it!" I shout as the current pulls the nylon line through hot fingers. The flaming dragon slips downstream, banging into the brush and twisting along the bank before hanging up on a willow hanging over the water fifty feet down the shoreline.

"Think it'll blow?!"

Larry is hiding behind the cottonwood. "If the fire gets to that gas tank before the water does it sure as hell will!"

I step behind the tree with Larry as an old familiar feeling spreads through my limbs. *Just like Nam, blowing those trees. Waiting was the worse…always the wait!*

A billowing cloud of black smoke rises from where the Swamp Fox is caught in its death throes, the fiberglass sizzling as it feeds the hungry blaze. Several loud pops tell us that the flame is devouring the tires. Larry says that with the tires gone maybe it will sink before the gas tank goes. It does: in a cloud of blue and gray smoke. The rushing water soon obscures any trace of the disaster, save for some charred willow branches where it had gone under.

Larry stepped to the water's edge and stared at the spot where the craft had disappeared. "Now what the hell was *that* all about?"

I didn't have to think about it– I knew. "It was that tin can. Overheated the muffler. I'd bet on it."

"So, Bob, what else could go wrong?"

"With a week like we've had so far, I don't wanna guess." Just yesterday our floating bathtub on wheels had run out of gas as we were fighting the current trying to get back to the truck. Without a radio, we were without communication, so we had no choice but to let the river have its way with us. It soon took our small craft to the mighty Missouri, rocking in the brisk seas as we rounded the corner, heading I supposed *for St. Louie....*

✏ *...4:17 p.m., Friday, August 8, 1980, confluence of the Niobrara and the Missouri Rivers...Larry darts a* nervous glance port, then starboard, gripping the wheel tightly as the boat bobs in the rough waves. "I can't swim. I hope you know that."

"Keep the cushion close," I say as I scan the shoreline ahead of me. "We'll get outta this." *But how?* The boat swiftly moves downstream from a stiff northwest wind. *Won't have much time to make a move.* Just ahead are remnants of what was a year ago a sleepy river town until the Army Corps of Engineers moved the whole city into corrugated metal domiciles on top of the bluff as a conclusion to their three-year flood protection plan. Beyond that, the fertile Missouri River bottomland melded into the expansive Lewis and Clark Lake which extended as far as Yankton, more than thirty miles down river.

"Look!" I shout. "There's a truck up there!" I point at a black pickup a half-mile down the shoreline. A boat trailer was hooked behind it. "Must be a boat ramp!" Quickly, I formulate a plan. Reaching behind the seat, I pick up a length of line we used to secure the ATV to the trailer. "This is gonna hafta be quick!" I fasten the line to the end of the bowline. "Wish me luck!" Tying a quick loop at the end of the line, I slip it onto my shoulder and dive toward the Missouri shoreline. The current is strong as I breaststroke diagonally downstream, hoping to negotiate the three-hundred feet to shore before passing the boat ramp. Fifty feet out a sharp tug snaps my body as I reach the limit of the line's length. Sliding the loop to my right hand, I switch to a sidestroke and dig in with all I have, pulling the wounded vessel on while Larry sings out with cupped hands, "Stroke! Stroke! Stroke!" Seeing the ramp coming up fast, I shift to overdrive and force my arms and my legs to pump harder, hoping to reach the shore on the upstream side of the ramp. Seventy-five feet from shore, now fifty, now thirty. My limbs burn in the chilly river. *God, this is living!* I think as my feet touch *the sandy bottom. ...*✐

*...Within a few* minutes we were standing in the middle of Third's NDP wondering what to do next. The rain made the decision– stay with Third. LT advised that we build our shelters between the others to form a tight ring, thus doubling our firepower. Never having set up in a pouring rain, I hoped it would be my last. Finding adequate support poles in the river valley was next to impossible. The corner stakes wouldn't hold, sliding out of the muck like so many greased pigs, so we had to scrounge for longer stakes and greater patience. An hour passed. Now our only objective on this earth was to get the hootches up to escape the cold stinging water darts some vindictive god was throwing at us. Fortunately the rainy clatter covered the noisy mixture of cursing and construction, the racket dissipating harmlessly into the atmosphere.

Thursday, December 10, 1970, Day 50 / 315 to DEROS
—Art 101—

*Merry Christmas! Mom & Dad & Kent,*

*Soon it will be that time again and sure wish I could be there! But xmas should be a different and exciting experience over here. If I'm in the field on Christmas Eve they usually decorate a chopper all up with lights & streamers ect. & they bring packages & goodies to us guys out here. Then xmas day they bring a huge dinner out to us.*

*This mission is just about over. We go into the rear for a 3 or 4 day re-train the 15th. And we've just been sitting around this camp for 3 days now, the rain is stopping us from crossing the river a 100 yards from here, so we probably won't have to cross it. We don't do a thing here so plenty time to write & read.*

*Since I have so much free time out here I thought I might as well be getting an education out here. I know that to perfect the human body, proportion, ect. is the first main goal of an artist. He can best determine his*

136

*progress by improving the naturism or exactness of his drawing so he has a bases on which he can judge his progress. If I could perfect this it would give me a solid foundation for expanding my talent, ec. animals, cartooning, charactorising. Any way I was wondering if you could send me material from my art course relating to the human body. Like the names and muscles of the body and most important parts on the chapter pertaining to people. Also send a couple HB pencils and gum eraser & sketching paper. You can fold the paper in half since I'll problably have to hold it anyway to get in my 12" high X 8 X 6" ammo can.*

*We're due to go in the 15th instead of the 25th, like I thought before.*

*I've found out several items that you might be interested in knowing. Anyone who came to Nam in May - 70 or later has only a 10 month tour.*

*Also after February 71, those out in the field. Me. will go on permanent stand-down, or stay in the rear till they find somewhere to put us. As far as I know this is true. So, the're finally making progress out here.*

*Well, I'll write soon, Hope your getting my letters by now. Oh, I mainly write to Linda S. (#1), Bob Ahlgren (#2 - Griff), Penny Powell (#3). (Toad) Greg Burke (#4). Jim Kapalis #5 (Greek), & Jones (#6). & Grandma's. Thought it may come in handy sometime. So take care and enjoy Christmas & vacation to the fullest. Hope Kent makes it home for holidays. Has Dave Jones got home yet to work at J.D. again? Ahlgren, Augie Rangel, Burke & Kapalis should be home for holidays also. By for now –*

*Your son in Nam, Bob*

*P.S. Rain finally letting up here at 2:30 P.M.*

Saturday, December 12, 1970, Day 52 / 313 to DEROS
—fly like an eagle—

The morning of our twelfth day in Ky Tra Valley ushered in clear and sunny. We emerged from our tents like butterflies escaping their cocoons, stretching towards the glowing orb to dry our stiff and cramped bodies after four days of steady downpour. Leeches had all but overrun the NDP, sucking us dry as the drenched conditions diluted the powerful agent, DEET, found in the bug juice that normally deterred the bloodsuckers. Fortunately, this time we had a good supply of food, which eliminated half the misery we had experienced on Mount Hell. I was able to get caught up on a slew of letters. With each precious sheet I would carefully guard it from the ever-present moisture that threatened to destroy my only link with the civilized world. So between defending my hootch from leeches, writing, eating and pulling long stints of lonely, pitch-black guard duty, I had managed better than last mission.

We split with Third Platoon. LT wanted to gain higher ground and set up at the first opportunity, for word was we might take advantage of the clearing skies to conduct a series of eagle flights. Nelson explained these were fast-paced search-and-destroy missions of short duration, spending most of the time in the air looking for possible sites of enemy activity. Once sighted, the birds would swoop down, drop us off to kill and burn whatever needed killing and burning before continuing to the next site. Compared to the past few days, I was ready for a little excitement.

*       *       *

"Birds are in-bound." –Tuck's words clicked my pulse up a notch– "ETA, ten minutes."

"Everybody make sure you're locked and loaded," LT advised. "When we hit the ground, stay low till the birds clear. Watch my lead, men. Nichols, take the first bird. Have some frags ready in case we find a hut or tunnel complex. The remainder of Nichols' squad secure the LZ. The rest of us will sweep the area in fan formation with five meter spread. See anything, call it out loud and open up. Don't worry, you'll get plenty of back up. Soon as the job's done, I'll give the signal to return to the pick-up zone. Tuck, keep your radio hot. And no smoking or unnecessary talking. The idea is to get in and out quick as we can."

My pulse clicks up another notch as I spy three choppers charging at us. A quick landing and my squad boards the second chopper in line, along with Doc and Buffalo. The birds lift, and the girth of the stream comes into full view, its rolling whitecaps bullying against each other in their push toward the sea.

Jumping over Ky Tra's rugged backbone, the choppers turn west; ahead lay a tumultuous ocean of mountainous ridgelines stretching to the horizon. Far below, a Loach helicopter scouts ahead, and across another ridgeline a row of choppers mirrors ours as they glide on the thermals. *One of our other platoons*, I think, and again, more choppers behind them: Gunships.

A frisson rises in my groin as our chopper banks and dives into a narrow valley bellowing with heat waves. We drop into the front yard of a small thatched hut that is hiding beneath several banana trees.

"Frag it!"

Nichols pulls the pin while running to the opening. "Fire in the hole!" He hits dirt as the frag rips the air.

"Search the area!" cries LT. "Watch for booby-traps!"

The drone of a thousand mosquitoes hum in the motionless air as I sandwich between Ski and Nelson and head to the left of the hut while Hillbilly takes his squad to the right. The crickets silence as we advance into a sunlit area strewn with weeds and stunted trees.

"Stay off the trails," Nelson warns, pointing to one leading away from the hut. We soon reach the edge of an impenetrable wall of braided vines, brush and trees. Without extensive cutting, our search here is over.

"Let's head back," –Nelson removes his hat to swipe a layer of sweat– "no use–"

*RIPPP RIPPP RIPPP RIPPPPPPP!*

I duck, flick off the safety and peer over the sights.

"Head for the hut!" Nelson hollers.

*BAMMMMMMMMM!*

*Grenade.* I round the hut and almost slam into Buffalo, kneeling on the far side with 16 pointing into the air.

"Okay!" Hillbilly shouts from a distance. "Got ourselves a gook!"

Hillbilly comes into view, looking as calm as if he were returning from an afternoon walk in the park.

"*Ran* like a turkey," Hillbilly gobbles at LT. "Didn't git nar too far, though. Had a slight run-in with some GI ordnance."

"Just see the one?"

"Roger that. Thought he'd found himse'f a good hid'n' place by that thicket ova yonda. But not near good 'nough."

"Good job, Hillbilly. Everybody in the field to destroy the crops, then we'll get the hell out of here."

Tugging on what looks like sweet potatoes, I notice smoke coming from the hut. LT exits. Nichols is setting fire to the hut's exterior.

Tuck calls down the birds. The choppers rise, and the hut explodes into a ball of sooty yellow flame. *We just ended a guy's life.* I stare at the flames licking at some green bananas as a hot cloud of black smoke passes through our cabin. Its pungent, moldy stench infuses into an odor that will forever remain in my memory.

My sweat quickly evaporated as a stiff breeze whisked through the cabin. The chopper continued southwest and ten minutes of flight time brought us to a similar search-and-destroy mission. This time we were following up on the aftermath of a previous platoon's work to make sure Charlie hadn't returned. We rechecked the charred remains of the hootch, this time a much larger one that was unnervingly exposed to the sky and sitting near an expansive and irrigated rice paddy. "Either they're dumb as a stump or they got balls of steel," Ski commented upon viewing the rice field. The same acrid smoke lingered in the air as before, smelling like a combination of urine soaked-straw and buffalo dung.

A metallic object caught my eye in front of the hootch. Not thinking I stooped over and picked it up, realizing later that it well might have been booby-trapped. Turning over the blackened circular piece of metal, I observed that it was a Vietnamese coin about the size of a half-dollar, though much thinner. In its center was a hole about a quarter-inch in diameter. *Souvenir,* I mused as I claimed it as official spoils of war and pocketed it.

The field was too large to destroy by hand, so LT made a note to include it as an area to drop a load of foo gas, a burning agent, which they did occasionally as the situation warranted. Finding no more VC, the choppers picked up its cargo and veered north for two more drop-offs, but we found nothing of significance. First Platoon, though, found the remains of a recently deserted NVA hospital with part of the clean-up crew still at the site. Two of the three managed to escape, but they wounded the third and carted him off to a nearby chopper for what I was sure to be a pleasant evening of interrogation at two-thousand feet.

It took nearly forty-five minutes to return to our NDP and combined with the previous three and a-half hours, my head was throbbing like a brass band as we scooted in on our final leg. At the last drop I had noticed that my ears were humming some unfamiliar tunes, and as the chopper left us at the base of our NDP hill, its thumping continued to replay in my head long after they exited the valley.

Sunday, December 13, 1970, Day 53 / 312 to DEROS
—huh?—

"What?"

"I said, got any smokes?"

"Don't know any jokes, Ski. Why?"

"Fuck, Nelson, tell Adams to stop fucking with me."

"Adams, what's the problem?"

"Ken barely hear ya, man, tink ma hearings shot from yesterday. When I talk, sounds like a echo."

"JUST TAKE IT EASY, SEE IF IT GETS BETTER TODAY. WE'RE HOOKING UP IN AN HOUR, OKAY?"

"Okay." I started to hum softly, which sounded like I was shouting into the indoor cistern in my Grandma's house back in Missouri. *Hey, this is kind of cool. Like my own private microphone.* The clatter of breaking down camp was muffled through my infected eardrums and looking up, the leaves were silently swaying in the morning breeze.

At nine, we made another attempt to cross the river. Plowing through the thick growth of sawgrass that dominated the river plain, my head resonated with a high-pitched ringing that would sometime swell, sometime fade to a barely discernible tone. Reaching our old NDP site near the river, I dumped my ruck and sat down hard beside it as a light rain started to fall.

"ANY BETTER?" Nelson asked as he watched Blondie head out with his squad to check out the condition of the river.

I shook my head. "Not yet. Maybe after a night's rest, huh?"

Blondie returned with unsurprising news. The river, though having gone down a little, was still too deep to cross. LT shook his head, for he had orders to cross the river and establish a base to work reconnaissance patrols over the next several days. Our superiors never seemed to consider that things such as a river might exist to thwart their well thought out plans on their little paper maps back in their air-conditioned offices.

Monday, December 14, 1970, Day 54 / 311 to DEROS
— "...a real fucking war" —

"Fucking Third did it again," Wad said, ducking out of the rain.

"Don't tell me," Nelson broke in, "booby-trap?"

"Got two poor fuckers."

Ski was having little luck lighting a damp cigarette. "When?"

"Twenty minutes ago. One guy got shrapnel in his leg and face, but the other wasn't so lucky. Guess he was trying to help when he hit another one. Blew a hole in his chest big enough to drive in a truck. Fuck, who woulda thought there'd be two right next to each other?"

"They give a name of the guy who got killed?" I asked.

"Yeah... Moreno."

Tuesday, December 15, 1970, Day 55 / 310 to DEROS
—AG Adams—

Again the water raged before us; LT was determined to cross.

I raised my head at the sound of approaching choppers.

"About fucking time," Ski said, standing up.

Strapping a case of C's from a belated re-supply to the top of my ruck, yesterday's news was sapping my nerve; reality was sinking in. "*...Blew a hole in his chest big enough to drive in a truck...*" Wad's words haunted me as I heaved the dead weight over my shoulders... *I'm next.*

I leaned into a stiff wind and waded toward the LZ, mired in over two feet of water salted by the recent rains. Our chopper hovered above the surface as Wad, Fritts, Nelson, Tuck and Buffalo crawled on board, but a strong gust pushed the bird out of reach for the rest of us.

The chopper drops again. Ski and Yoss climb on. I try to step onto the skid, but a crosswind pushes the chopper toward me, pressing me into the water. Struggling to regain my feet, my top-heavy ruck causes me to move like a wounded pigeon. The slick lowers and I see my chance. Yoss and Ski stretch out their hands to drag me aboard.

*POP! POP! POP! POP! POP!*

"Get on!" shrieks the door gunner as VC lead smears the chopper wall, just missing him. His 60 hammers and I heave myself out of the paddy and balance on the skid.

"Come on!" Ski shouts. He swings my ruck toward the middle of the crammed cabin as the chopper begins an awkward port spin out of the paddy. I try to push inside, but I can't budge. With half my butt hanging in the wind, the rice soup thrashes fifty feet below. My nails claw the steel floor. My

142

dangling legs go numb. My breath stops in my chest, and a thick muzzle of fear smothers a scream rising in my throat. Three hundred feet and climbing. I thrust my hands to grab onto something, anything, but my bulky ruck prevents me from finding an anchor.

A sharp tug from behind slides my butt into the cabin. A quick glance catches Buffalo's grin. *Why didn't I fall out?* I collapse against my ruck as the chopper levels off just below the clouds. *Centrifugal force must have kept me inside. Fear CAN'T get any worse than that!* The air blows through my wet clothes, cooling body and soul while the jungle terrain appears surreal as a daydream.

The choppers position themselves for another assault into the valley. *Not back down there!* The birds dive, sending a roller coaster shudder up my spine. I check my 16 and jam my thumb over the safety. *We're insane!*

The northern side of the river is a carbon copy of the south: a field of reeds and grass that dominate to the edge of the double-canopy jungle. The birds hug the northern treeline, trying to put as much distance as they can between them and the hot LZ.

*POP! POP! POP! POP! POP!*

The muffled cracks spur the door gunner to slam his trigger-finger against his hammer, his ammo can belching its cache of steel-jacketed ammo as the 60 rains hot lead into the trees below.

My breathing trickles to a crawl. *Charlie might be taking a bead on me right now and there ain't a thing in this world I can do about it! Land, land, LAND THIS THING!* The pilot stalls out the turbines and plummets the last fifty feet.

Still ten feet off the ground, the gunner flags his arm for us to get out. We do and I crash hard. The weight of the ruck pushes my face deep into the muddy bottom. *My God, I'm gonna die with my face in the mud!* I jerk out of the water and suck in a large breath. Crawling to the nearest bush, I sweep it around me like a *toddler's favorite blanket....*

✎ *...5:31 p.m., Wednesday, December 3, 1980, home...No! Not Butchy! He was only 28!*

"His mom says the funeral's Saturday. But you don't want to go to that. Too depressing." –Dad paused– "Still want to go to the Circa tonight? Should be a good one."

"Yeah, sure, okay, Dad. Pick me up, what, around five?"

"Okay, see you then." He hung up, leaving me holding the empty phone. *What did he say it was? Aneurysm of the brain? Just dropped over like a sack of potatoes, right* where *he was working, no warning, no nothing. He was my best friend when we were kids, next to Danny, of course. And now…gone. Life is so unpredictable.…*✐

...*"Call the damn* bird back!" Buffalo shouts to LT. They set Fritts onto the ground next to Doc. "Fritts twisted his ankle!"

"Shit." LT grimaces. "Tuck, on the horn! Everyone form a perimeter! Wad, Retchin, take a position there! And there!"

It starts to drizzle, stinging my face. I pull out of my ruck and crawl to the outside with the rest of the Grunts.

"Wad!" Fritts shouts. "What about my 60 ammo?!"

"Shit, LT, that's right. He's my AG."

"Okay," LT asks, "need a volunteer to take his ammo."

"I'll do it." Fritts removes a barrel bag and three two-hundred round belts of ammo from his ruck. I haul them to Wad's position.

"Thanks, Bob." –Wad eyeballs the terrain– "We'll make a good team, huh?"

The sound of the returning chopper jerks Wad's head up. "This could get hairy." –he repositions his 60– "Anything can happen when a slick comes to the same place twice."

Courting the edge of the treeline on the far side of the valley, the bird makes a wide swing across the river and hugs the field so close he appears to be skiing across the grassy surface.

"Now!" LT commands. Nelson and Yoss pull Fritts up and hobble him into the water and toward the approaching bird. The chopper plops onto the marsh and they load Fritts on, pushing his ruck and 16 on behind him. Fritts gives a feeble wave as the chopper banks starboard and we breathe a *sigh of relief.…*

✎*…9:08 a.m., Thursday, May 21, 1981, Dr. Bull's office, Silvis, Illinois…"Any history of* heart disease in your family?"

The phrase "heart disease" burns through my chest like a white-hot branding iron. "Not that I know of."

"Okay, let's hook you up." The suction cups sap my color as the machine records all of my inner bleeps. Within a minute, he removes the thin EKG strip and lays it on his desk. I stare at it as if it's an ivory serpent that will strike me dead if I dare go too near.

"I wish my heart was as healthy as yours, Bob. All you're experiencing are premature ventricular contractions. PVC's for short. It's nothing *to worry about.*"...✐

...*"Hook up,"* LT ordered. "Got two klicks to cover and not much daylight left."

I secured two of the belts onto the back of my rucksack. "How about a hand," I asked Wad and Langley after an unsuccessful attempt at lifting my ruck.

"You're a glutton for punishment," Langley said, straining on his half of the ruck until the straps were secured over my shoulders. I leaned over to take the weight off my shoulders so I could adjust my towel to prevent the straps from rubbing them raw. *You got to be kidding!* I grabbed the third belt of 60 ammo and secured it over my shoulder. *This must weigh a hundred and twenty pounds!* Adding to the weight of my ruck, case of C's and 600 rounds of ammo, big globs of rain splattered onto us as we began our evening trek into the remote *Ky Tra bush.*...

✎...*7:53 a.m., Thursday, June 17, 1981, Milan, Illinois*..."How far you say you run a week?"

I slid the tripod from the back of the survey truck. "Forty miles."

"Hales! You hear that! Got some competition! This guy's running forty miles a week! Jeez, Adams, why you run so much?"

"Feels good, I guess."

"Feels good? Shit. Running don't feel good."

"Maybe I'll getcha running someday, Dave."

"Me? Run? Fuck! I'll never run."

"Never say never."

"Whadawe got here Halesey, a Jamesey Bondsey guy? Never say never...."

I didn't say anything else. After getting laid off from Tri-State Aerial Engineering, it'd been a long cold winter. But at least the lay-off got me some time to think and with the coming of spring I decided to take up where I'd left off during my last days in Vietnam– running. It made me feel good about myself again. And that was something that'd been missing for quite some time now. I was just glad to get a permanent job. Peddling papers all winter had trashed my van and I was way overdue for some financial security. *Who woulda thought I'd be working in the Army again, and for the Corps of Engineers, of all things. Hope they're not as stupid as they were on that Firebase Professional.* I smiled, watching as Dave set up the field book. *I'm an artist, man, not a surveyor. But at least for now I'm stuck in the survey mode, happy for the bucks at least.…* ✐

    *…Step on a crack and you'll break your mother's…BACK!* thundered through my exhausted mind like the booby-trap that had swept my friend away yesterday. *Step on a crack and Moreno will get…WHACKED!* I couldn't erase the image my mind conjured of Moreno– his face superimposed onto the face of the dead Chinaman, staring into the sun. *The trail, man, the trail. Focus! Less than two months and Moreno is history, just like that. BLAM! Just…like…that. He said we'd get blown away. Remember that? He predicted his own death. Well, one down.… Man, God, I'm only twenty! Think! The trail! Look at it! Wad pointing down, yeah, a cigarette butt. Point it out to Ski. Man…don't screw up…don't EVEN screw up!*

Physically, Ski wasn't doing much better than I, his case of C's pressing him lower and lower to the earth as we followed the well-used trail. *What irony, Ski humping Yoss' evening dinner* –I chuckled to myself– *I wonder if he realizes what he's doing? How could Moreno be so stupid, man! How could he?* A knot in my shoulder wrenched me back to the trail. *Use the pain. Use it! Where is that stupid NDP? Gotta get off my feet. Feels like half the war is going on inside of my gut.*

A blanket of darkness begins to spread across the valley. LT signals the platoon to a halt. Ahead is a wide stream to cross. He motions Nichols to take his squad across. Midstream, Nichols crouches and lets loose with a full clip. The rest of his squad follows suit as I spot four VC racing up the slippery bank fifty meters downstream. Two VC fall, another staggers. The fourth jumps into the brush, popping off several wild shots that fall wide.

Nichols rushes for the opposite shore and slaps in another magazine before cutting the staggering VC in half. He gives LT the thumbs up.

"It's too dark to follow," LT says. "Tuck, give me the hook. The rest of you get across."

146

A steady rain begins to pelt us as LT calls an artillery strike. I follow Wad to the other side and crawl up the greasy bank. Struggling to rise, my knees fold, sending me sprawling down the slope. Clawing back up, I make the top and roll onto my back, gasping for air. Somebody grabs my shoulder strap and pulls. It's Wad. In the dim light I see a smile that gives me the strength to rise. Stooping over to steady the burden, I follow his heels as LT guides us into a mess of shrubs twenty meters from the creek.

We drop our rucks, pull out our ponchos and wrap them around us as the last remnants of light fade away. Over the clatter of raindrops I hear the muffled pounding of artillery echo in the valley. I am grateful for the distant thumping; somebody is watching out for us. The last muted explosion closes a curtain of silence, leaving only the steady beat of the rain. Giving a last thought to my dead friend, Moreno, I dip my head beneath my blanket and *slide into oblivion....*

✎ *...11:53 a.m., Friday, June 26, 1981, Moline Public Hospital, Moline, Illinois...Room 356...this is it.* –I swallowed hard– *What will I say?* Wayne's eye found me as I pushed open the heavy hospital door. "Bob!" His bed was propped up as he lay in a wrinkled, blue-striped hospital gown. Art Davis, my friend and Wayne's brother-in-law, was sitting in a chair at the foot of the bed. On the far wall hung one of Art's posters, "Get Well Soon, Wayne, We Love You!" Art was taking it hard.

I closed the door. *What do I say?* "How's it going?" *God, I hardly recognize him.*

"Great, man! I'm just great. So, how's your new job going? Keeps you out of town a lot, huh?"

"It sure does." How *can he sound so happy? Maybe now that he's a Christian....* "Sorry I couldn't...."

A nurse cracked open the door and peeked in. "It's almost lunch time, Mr. Kettering," –she spoke briskly– "are we going to have to spoon feed you to get you to eat something this time?"

"*I'll* try, I'll *try*, okay?" Wayne answered with a chuckle. "She gives me a hard time, doesn't she?"

"Sounds like it," I answered uneasily.

"You guys try to get him to eat something, okay?"

"We'll stuff it down him if we have to," Art answered as she closed the door.

147

"Hey, Bob," Wayne said. "Did I tell you about my trip out west before I got sick? It was a blast! Took my bike to the Tetons, slept under the stars–"

I couldn't pay attention, although I nodded at the right places and grunted occasionally. I couldn't help but think I was staring death in the face– slow motion death. Least in the Nam you went quick. BAM! No time to think. No time to pray. It just happened. But this...his face is so thin, like some of those old men that chewed the beetle-nut. And his arms. Those weren't Wayne's arms. Too thin. Too pale. Man, this guy was strong as a horse. And what's this he does when he belches? Like his gut is turning inside out. My God– my friend is dying.

Wayne rambled on, relishing his last shot at a good time he'd ever get on this earth. "...even then I knew something was wrong, but I had to go out there, one more time, you know?" His eyes were dry. There were no tears. He was ready and he knew it.

"Can I go getcha something to eat, Wayne? I can only imagine how bad this hospital food is."

"At least all *you* hafta do is imagine it." –he smiled– "Sure, if you don't mind."

"No problem, man. So, what'll it be? Burger and fries? Chinese? Pizza?"

Wayne thought a minute. "How abooooout, Dairy Cream."

"You name it."

"Cherry slushy. Yeah, that's what I want, a cherry slushy. Man, I can't remember the last time I had one of those."

"All right, a cherry slushy it is. I'll be back before you know it."

I sucked in a deep breath as I walked down the hall. *Man, felt like I've just humped through Dragon Valley buck-naked. Why does this have to happen to a guy like that? Why? Guess God sees things different. Sees the big picture. Wonder if that's why he got converted the way he did? Even back then God knew what was going on. He knew Wayne needed that miracle....*

✏ *...11:41 p.m., Friday, August 30, 1974, outside Elkader, Iowa...God! I'm witnessing a miracle!* A myriad of locust and crickets joined the frog's cantata by the Turkey River shoreline, just a stone's throw from where we were camped in preparation for a canoe trip as soon as the sun cracked the horizon. *First of all, how did he ever find us? Said he just started to drive and ended up here? And why now? Could this have something to do with the miracle God showed me this morning? I'd bet my life on it!* Wayne Kettering bowed his head, his face hidden in the shadows from the light of the campfire's dying embers. "Okay, Wayne," I began, "just follow me. God, I know I'm a sinner." –he repeated my words– "I know that without you there is no hope." *I can't believe this! He's asking Jesus to come into his life! It's a miracle! It's gotta be!...*

✏ *...9:17 a.m., Friday, August 30, 1974...Art backs up* on the open field and lets it fly. "Too wide, man!" I shout as the Frisbee sails high and arcs toward the treeline. It weaves through the trees for fifty feet before firmly lodging forty feet up in the fork of a spindly locust tree. "Great! Now what?" I say as Art approaches.

Art shrugs and starts to pull apart the barbwire to cross over. "Wait a second." –I lean over the fence and yank out of the ground a long, dried stalk of horseweed– "Remember the story of David and Goliath?" –Art doesn't answer– "David said, 'With this stone, I shall slay the giant that dares defile God's people,' or something like that." –I snap off the branches from the main stem– "And with this spear, I'm gonna do to that Frisbee what David did to that giant." I flake the dirt off the pointed spear-like root.

"One shot?" Art laughs, squinting through the canopy of limbs, vines and leaves to the orange speck where the Frisbee sits high above. "Yeah, right."

Not sure why I was digging myself into this hole of embarrassment, I feel I must continue. "What I do now," –I raise the spear– "I do in the name of the Lord and as a sign of something great that will reveal itself yet today." Again, Art doesn't answer, staring at me like I'm crazy. But why not? I think I am too.

The spear is clean and straight– well, almost straight. I don't flinch, although I know I should– it's an impossible shot. Bracing my feet I eye the orange speck. "Stand back and watch the power of the Lord," I say as I stretch the spear behind me. Steadying it for a second, I thrust it into the sky. The spear sails high– too high, I think– but then it moves as if guided by some unseen hand. *God!* I mouth as the spear weaves through a plethora of obstacles and hits the orange orb square in the center. The saucer leaves the limb and drifts on the breeze, floating not only to the ground, but to the very edge of the fence line. Art leans over and picks it up. He stares at it as if to insure himself that it's real.

"This is a sign. A sign that something great *will happen today.*"...✎

Wednesday, December 16, 1970, Day 56 / 309 to DEROS
—sunshine on Settle—

*Mom & Dad,*                                                    *12/16/70*

*Guess you'll be getting this letter on about Christmas day. Received your letter dated Dec. 9th yesterday, along with letters from Jones, Art Davis II, & first bill on you present I got you. Did you get it anyway? So Art says he may be going to Nam. He say's he really nervous & from his letter I can believe it. Good thing he's not going out in the field. He didn't even say much about his wife, Sue. Although he wants me to send him some souvieniers off some dead V.C. Got a letter from Kent too, Guess he's doing okay.*

*So I guess you finally started to receive my letters, would you please tell me what letters you received from me last when you write me? It helps me to keep track. I won't get your package till I get into rear. There afraid of damaging them sending them out on choppers. Right now were going in the 18th. At a real good camp right now. Sunny & nice, just waiting around for the 18th. Would you believe I haven't had a hot meal or milk in 16 days! So it really makes you appreciate food. We do heat our C-rations though. Our re-train area in the rear is supposed to be real nice this time. Flush toilets, recreation rooms, ect.*

*Last couple days. Kinda bad. No food. Hungry. & humping a 120 lbs. Ruck sack. Sore muscles now. Choppers, 4, came in to pick us up and take us across this river 3 days ago. Had to get on chopper in a rice paddy with mud up to shins & I was carring 120 lbs. So really was hard walking. Then chopper almost lands on top of me, so fell trying to move in mud & got all muddy & wet. And the 120 M.P.H. wind the blades make didn't help. Then fell in mud again getting off bird on other side, that ruck was just to heavy. Then it was dark before we could get to our camp & had to sleep in rain & all wet. Next day we came here & everythings fine now. My friend Wad is the M-60 machinge gunner here. So yesterday volunteered to be his assistant gunner. All I do is help feed & hook up ammo into his gun. This way I won't have to walk point. Though I'll have to carry 600 rounds of 60 ammo. But that's okay.*

*Your Xmas card really looks great & I'll tell you when I'll call you at USO near our company area. It would've to be about 9 or 10 AM here Sunday.- & 11 or 12 PM Saturday night there.*

*I don't know about that cease fire. & 3th Plt. Is always running into booby-traps. Cause they don't have a good point man & they do stupid things like booby-trapping the V.C. they kill & V.C. don't like GI's messing with there dead. So they get revenge. Don't mess with V.C. & they won't mess with you.*

*Well, I got voo-koo letters to write. So Merry Christmas again & God Bless. Your son, Bob*

"Roger, Charlie Papa. Echo Foxtrot, out." –LT hung up the phone and smiled– "Settle! Front and center! Guess what?! You got a rear job!"

"HOOOOEEEE!" Hillbilly raved. "'Bout time somebody in this sorry-ass platoon got a break. Way ta go, Settle!"

"How soon I go in, LT?"

"Soon as the first bird comes. Tomorrow or the day after."

"Didn't think I'd ever get a rear job, but with sixty days and counting, I ain't complaining!"

Doug Settle was our senior Grunt, even ahead of Nichols. Maybe this was a sign of a change in the wind for us field guys: a year ago the average Grunt wouldn't have had a prayer of getting out of the bush until his DEROS.

A sense of peace settled over me as a cheery afternoon sun evaporated yesterday's ordeal of rain, fatigue and hunger. Pulling out my trusty ammo can, I decided to catch up on my letter writing. Most of the guys made do with a plastic bag to hold their writing supplies, but between the rain and humidity, their paper treasures usually ended up as a wad of wet pulp. Opening the can's watertight lid, my journal, assorted books and writing paraphernalia were crisp and dry, waiting to begin another page home on my favorite blue stationery with the Americal Insignia printed in colorful detail in each of its corners and perhaps later continuing *The Adventures of Sherlock Holmes*. It was indeed a well-vested burden and one in which my aching back could not, and would not, deny me.

Thursday, December 17, 1970, Day 57 / 308 to DEROS
—waiting—

*Great!* I tapped on the watch face and attempted to wind the spring. The glass was fogged so that I could barely discern the Roman numerals, the second hand stuck on "IX". I took it off and tossed it on my poncho liner.

Continuing my audit, I poked my finger through a quarter-sized hole in my right boot, my little toe peeking out like a contented worm in a Granny Smith. "Put down a pair of boots on the next RS, would ya, Nelson? Size 9. These are shot."

"Anything else, guys? Gotta get this to LT."

"How 'bout a watch?"

"Ah, GI, no can do. They luxury to poor, homeless Grunt."

"Okay," I mimicked, "then how GI tell time for guard?"

"Higher-Higher say, that your poblem."

Though our CE was scheduled for tomorrow, LT opted to stay put. Perhaps nearly three weeks in the field had softened his drive to sniff out the elusive VC. We were all ready for a break: shower, bed, cold beer and hot food, sleeping with four walls and a ceiling.

As for Settle, his stint was over: no more searching out the enemy in the blackness of a thankless guard duty and wondering if the night would hold for him some eternal significance. And if Settle's future was just beginning, ours was still on hold. Marriage, children, career, fishing trips and Fourth of Julys, graduations and anniversaries, retirement and contentment from a life well-lived. Milestones we could only imagine as we turned longing eyes homeward, praying to one day be free from our ensnarled web of war where the black widow of death silently watched from the shadows, awaiting its chance to sink its fangs into our flesh. And until our Freedom Bird would at last carry us home, we dared not move too quickly or move too slowly, aching for that day that we knew fondly, oh so fondly, as DEROS.

Friday, December 18, 1970, Day 58 / 307 to DEROS
—Freedom Bird—

The morning sailed in on clear blue skies. A quick no-hassle morning water patrol went off without a hitch, carried out by ours and Hillbilly's squad. After returning the canteens, there was nothing more to do but wait for our CE and as Blondie said, "To the rear and cold fucking beer."

We were slated for a four o'clock extraction and the afternoon drug into a lengthy bout of letter writing and conversation under the hot sun. Most of the talk in our squad came from Ski as he spun exaggerated stories about the "good life" in his home state of Wisconsin– mostly to irk Yoss. Yoss' chin was hard, though, as he counter-jabbed a flurry of monolithic comebacks,

comebacks he'd picked up while doing time on the streets during the endless hot summers in his Bronx jungle. But Ski never learned and with hook-up time nearing, he was still at it when a call came in over the horn. A call before an extraction was never a good omen and this one was no different. The CE had been canceled until tomorrow. And worse, another set of eagle flights were on for three-thirty.

Constrained cursing drifted throughout the camp. We were ready to go in and we let LT know it. LT acknowledged the complaints, saying he'd see what he could do. After all, we were next on the list to go in and the thought of more eagle flights set my infected ear to throbbing.

As if our cursing had somehow reached the ears of Higher-Higher, another call came within five minutes to notify us that the eagle flights were canceled.

"Colonel musta got his star in the nick a time ta save our sorry asses," Hillbilly announced. "Now what about that extraction, LT?"

Before LT could get another word out the radio interrupted again, saying they were sending out a bird for a re-supply.

"Why?" LT asked. "We're going in tomorrow."

"*Battalion says you do,*" was his only reply.

"Bullshit fucking rear!" LT said, slamming down the phone. "I swear it's run by fucking guinea pigs!"

It was a rare sight to see LT's anger flare, but being the career man he was, he didn't call them on it. It was five-fifteen when we heard a single chopper clear the northeast ridge, prompting Harv to toss an orange smoke in a brushy field just outside the NDP.

The chopper set down softly onto the grass and the co-pilot jumped out and asked Blondie who his CO was. Pointing the way, Blondie's squad began unloading the supplies while the co-pilot approached LT.

"Got a Spec-4 Settle here?" the co-pilot inquired. "I'm to take him back with me, something about orientation for his new MOS."

Turning a smile he waved toward Settle's position. "Settle, your Freedom Bird's here!"

"And another thing," the co-pilot continued, "Battalion sent hot chow; I guess it's their way of apologizing for the screw up. Just bring the canisters back on tomorrow's CE."

Settle was stuffing his gear into his ruck and carrying on with his compatriots as they surrounded him to pass out congratulations and best wishes. Lifting his ruck onto his shoulder, his eyes sparkled with a new light– the light of hope. And with that glowing aura, he warmly imparted to us the wish that we'd all come out of there real soon, to get on with the job of living that was our due.

# STAND-DOWN THREE

Saturday, December 19, 1970, Day 59 / 306 to DEROS
—cots and concrete—

Wind whips through my blond hair as gray clouds threaten to douse our receptacles of redemption. But I don't care. Tonight let it rain as it has never rained before, for I'll be safe from its ranting– laying warm and cozy without the dread of guard duty or the threat of enemy's eyes to disturb my insouciant slumber.

My shackles from the monotony of the last three weeks fall as a sliver of silver bursts before me, crowning Chu Lai like a bangle of diamonds sparkling against a shimmer of whitecaps gliding slowly shoreward. Below my swaying feet I watch the ancient forge of humanity replace my new world of green jungle flora, twisting streams and the stench of sweating Grunts. *This is all right,* I think, as my bird sinks to the tarmac. *There just ain't no limits!* I jump off the steel deck, pull the ruck over my shoulder and climb onto the nearest truckbed. *Just gotta hang on...climb over the rough spots, and keep going.*

A cold, dark evening of wind and thunder greeted us as we pulled into an unfamiliar complex not far off of Highway 1. Topp was nowhere to be seen. LT assisted us in stowing our ordinance in a freshly cured concrete blocked building. Opposite the armory were eight sandbagged bunkers, each guarding a pristine gray-blocked barrack. Two much longer buildings framed the eastern and western ends of the new compound. The structures stood like alien monoliths in the middle of the desert-like terrain with not a tree, bush, or weed to push through the alkaline sand that ruled the fringes of Chu Lai.

Before the rain came, a pickup truck dumped an offering of Christmas letters and packages. Five packages came my way along with several letters, and with the blessed burden secured in my arms, I found my way to the barrack assigned to Second Platoon.

The concrete barrack was split into four rooms with two hallways crisscrossing the middle. I opened a plywood door, stepped inside, and stopped. I recalled a few days ago when I had yearned for four walls and a ceiling, but this was like a prison– with a window. I sat my ruck beside one of six canvas-covered cots and looked through the lone window, reminding me of what a prisoner might stare through as his existence eroded into meaningless moments of time.

But I had the Christmas packages! Priceless treasures from home, ripe for the taking. Just looking at them was satisfying enough, put together by hands that cared and chose with loving concern. Concern for me.

Ten seconds was enough. I tore open a package from my Grandma Wheeler. Chocolate-chip cookies, hard candies, pecans, almond and brazil nuts, homemade peanut brittle. The second package, from Grandma Birkhead, was also crammed with sweets. The last three were from Mom and Dad. Two of them were stuffed with food basics I'd requested just about every time I wrote: Maypo cereal, Kool Aid, Bouillon Cubes, instant milk packets, small boxes of Frosted Flakes, Sugar Pops, Sugar Crisp and a package of Fig Newton's. Truly, "food of the gods".

The last package brought out the kid in me– Christmas gifts! Wrapped in shiny bright paper of midnight blue, canary yellow and Christmas green. Adorned with silver bells and golden horns, colorful green wreaths, laughing Santas, flying reindeer and waxy red candles crowned with glowing yellow flames.

I ripped into the top gift. *My dad's hunting knife!* He had made it while serving in the South Pacific during World War II. I slid it from its sturdy black leather sheath and wrapped my hand around the handle, constructed of thick fiberglass rings that supported a quarter-inch thick, eight-inch long steel blade. I strapped the monster on my ammo belt. *Wait till the guys see this!*

I barely noticed my squad-mates entering the room. Outside, a hot meal and shower beckoned, but those peripherals seemed unimportant. Instead, our souls were nourished with the gifts and letters from cherished ones. For a short time, *we were home....*

155

✎...*8:56 a.m., Saturday, July 30, 1983, Davenport, Iowa...*"Come on, Davy!"

"Fuck you, Adams!"

"Davy!" I chortle as I run backward in front of him, which isn't hard since his pace is barely hitting ten minute miles. "We're almost there, man!" In spite of the early hour the air is hot and sticky as we pass the five-mile marker in the Midwest jewel of running events, the renowned Quad City Bix 7. Dave had been training since early spring, along with Chris Haley, Steve Slaght and me, and now it was time to test his mettle. Till now his farthest run had been in Canton, Missouri, where he had passed the one-hour mark. "Looky here, Davy!" I had huffed as I held my watch in front of his face. "And you said you'd never run!"

"Need some water?"

"Yeah, Bear, get me some."

I grab a cup at a water station and pass it to him. Taking a quick gulp, he throws the rest on his flushed face.

"Only a mile and a-half left, man! You can do it!"

By now we're near the back of the pack, this year nearly six thousand strong, the city's largest running event yet. Haley, who'd just turned forty, is way ahead as he is going all out for the event, having even invited Dave and me over last evening for a pre-race spaghetti dinner. I'm running as a bandit, an unofficial entrant, and unconcerned about time because I'm obligated to jump out of the race before hitting the finish line anyway. A self-proclaimed purist, I didn't care for these staged events where all that mattered were splits, form and style. Back in April I'd run my first marathon– alone. No water, no cheering crowds, no banners and photographers at the finish line. Just legs, guts and a hell of a lotta air.

We turn onto Brady Street and head for the final mile, marked by the point where the street drops as it meets the top of the Mississippi Valley bluff. At its base it's a sharp left and a sprint for the finish line. "This is it, Davy! This is what we've *been training for!*"... ✎

# WIRE IN THE SHADOWS

Monday, December 21, 1970, Day 61 / 304 to DEROS
—white boxers—

Ski twisted my arm to get a better look at the new watch my folks had tucked in a small package beneath the knife. "Hey, watch it!" I shouted over the whine of the truck's engine. We were riding in the back of a six-by, being chauffeured to the PX. They couldn't keep us stranded on that desert island of sand forever. After the PX run, we'd be taking in a few classes at our old unit area.

"Nice! Think they'd send me one, too?"

I winked at Yoss. "Not a chance, they try to have nothing to do with Wisconsiners."

"Adams! Buddy! Not you, too. We Midwesterners got to stick together, man."

The trucks rumbled into the PX parking lot and stopped in a cloud of white dust.

"You got thirty minutes to get your shit," the driver announced, "then I'm heading for HQ. Don't be late."

As thirty-five Grunts entered through the spotless glass and aluminum doors of the modern PX building, an air of tension spread throughout the store. Filtering through the aisles, some of us took full advantage of our fearful persona, hooting at a neat row of army caps here, guffawing at a stack of white boxer shorts there. It *was* fun– knowing that our presence instilled fear in some and even terror in others. I couldn't help strutting just a little as I picked out a toothbrush, a can of Planters peanuts, several small paraffin candles and a deck of cards and headed for the cashier. I fell in at the end of a long line and as I waited, a boisterous Grunt from First Platoon bullied his way in front of several "office" types. As I watched them back off, I knew it wasn't right and I knew how we had gotten our shady reputation. My head a little lower, I reached the checkout counter and quickly paid for my merchandise.

Tuesday, December 22, 1970, Day 62 / 303 to DEROS
—Dear John—

With a catered lunch behind us, a series of afternoon classes threatened to ruin the remainder of our day, being conducted in our desert outpost. I settled

157

on my cot to catch up on my reading; eight more letters had arrived at this morning's mail call. And finally one from Linda! I was beginning to wonder what was going on with her. I ripped open the envelope and consumed the first paragraph. By the third, though, I crumpled the paper and tossed it across the room. *Fred Schultz? I can't believe it. Fred Schultz? What's wrong with her, anyway? Same old story...just thought it'd never happen to me. But why not me? I'm probably never coming back, anyway. Why shouldn't she look out for number one? Who cares, anyway? Fred Schultz? Sounds like one of those stupid characters in "Hogan's Heroes".* "Hey, Yoss, guess what? My girl just dumped me."

Yoss was lying on his back sifting through his mountain of mail. "How long did you know her?"

"About a year. It just stinks she waited till I'm halfway 'round the world. Now she's dating some guy called Schultz."

"Sergeant Schultz?" Ski popped, who'd been feigning sleep in the opposite corner. Ski surprised me by taking a more serious tone. "Forget about the bitch, Adams. It ain't worth it...believe me."

"You're right, Ski." I tore open the next letter. "When's class start?"

"1500 on the fucking nose." Ski turned toward the wall and curled back up into a ball.

*     *     *

*Hurry up, man...let's get out of here!* The instructor droned on about tactical strategies utilizing air support in mountainous terrain or some such nonsense. His discourse was sprinkled with military acronyms, gibberish to the everyday field infantryman. As the snickering increased, so did the level of redness in Topp's face, who had decided to join us– at least during daylight hours.

Another cramp clamped its claws onto my lower intestines like a vice grip, causing my thighs to flex and draw up toward my abdomen. *Gotta get outta here, man!* "...strategic deployment in a THA, or tactical helicopter assault, the combat soldier must utilize..." A loud ringing in my head cut off the E-7's voice. I pressed my hands against my ears and the pitch fell an octave as a surge of nausea pushed some foul-tasting bile into my mouth. *Gotta get outta here! NOW!*

"I'll be in my barrack," I whispered to Nelson. "don't feel so hot."

158

Halfway to the barrack my gut contracted like an iron accordion and my lunch took the nearest exit to the outside world. At the same time, what felt like liquid fire running through my lower tract told me I'd better head for the can– quick! By the time I waddled to my cot it was all I could do to curl up in the fetal position, bury myself under my poncho liner and hang on for the ride. Chills came next, shaking and convulsing my flushed body, now burning with fever. My left ear ached as it had never before.

Wednesday, December 23, 1970, Day 63 / 302 to DEROS
—lightning from God—

Sleeping long and hard, the morning's light brought me back to the world of the living. Sometime after midnight my system finally took a turn for the better, the pain in my ear subsiding and my gut no longer erupting with the regularity of Old Faithful. I raised my hand to my forehead and felt that it was now cool and moist, although the rash I had developed yesterday still dotted my chest and stomach, for which I had no explanation. During a morning shower, I discovered that my left ear was caked with a weird crusty substance, but I was able to wash most of it out from a supply of Q-Tips I used for cleaning my 16. I still felt weak, but hungry– a good omen.

After chow, Topp hit us with news that eagle flights were a go for late morning. But as the morning unfolded, an incoming thunderstorm canceled Topp's plans and I breathed a sigh of relief as I slinked back into hibernation. The storm quickly rumbled through and in less than an hour a rumor of a noon CA angrily spread through our barrack, for we had been told that we'd be in the rear for five days this time. I wasn't sure if I'd be strong enough to take on the daily grind of bush humping again and prayed it wouldn't be so.

As noon neared, so did another ominous bank of thunderclouds. I watched from my door as they pulled themselves along the mountainous terrain until hovering black and menacing above us. The lunch truck pulled into our compound as a quiver full of lightning bolts began to smash around us. *Thank you, God!* I thought as LT announced that the CA had been canceled.

# MISSION FOUR

Christmas Eve, Thursday, December 24, 1970, Day 64 / 301 to DEROS
—FNG LT—

We were loading our gear as LT approached with another officer. LT looked tense as he nodded to the man standing beside him. "Men, this is Lieutenant Hunter."

Much shorter than his counterpart, Lieutenant Hunter tipped the pudgy side of the scales.

LT readjusted his stance. "He's your new LT. Two days ago, I received transfer orders to Cam Rahn Bay. So, my time here is over." –he relaxed, swinging his hands to his front– "It's been a pleasure serving in the best damn platoon in the best Company in this Battalion and I know you'll give Lieutenant Hunter the same respect you've given me. Thank you, men." –LT Owens turned to salute our new LT– "Good luck, Lieutenant."

Returning his salute, LT Hunter turned to address us. His dark eyes peered like tiny eight balls through a pair of wire-rimmed glasses.

"Good morning, men, I'm looking forward to serving with you. All I ask is that if you do the best job you can, you'll find that I'm the easiest guy in the world to get along with." A stocky frame supported a layer of milky white skin that I swore had never seen the slightest hint of a tan. He removed his hat to reveal jet-black hair, cropped close as the stub of a mustache below an ample nose. "We'll just continue to do things the way Lieutenant Owens has been doing them until I get the feel for your procedures. I'll be counting on you to help me get up to speed. So, that's all for now, men. Thank you. A truck will be here to pick us up in thirty minutes."

We spent the next few minutes bidding farewell to LT. A few handshakes, a pat or two on the back and he got in an awaiting jeep. He gave us the peace sign for his farewell offering as the driver spun the wheels in the soft sand, and *he was gone....*

*✎...5:11 p.m., Thursday, March 15, 1984, Washington D.C....I slowed as* I approached the sprawling monument halfway through my "dream-run" around the Capitol City. I was in town for a land surveying conference, held at the Washington Hilton, a dozen blocks northwest of the White House. I'd sneaked out early, ducking into a restroom to change into my blue nylon running suit. *So this is it,* I thought as I hooked my hands behind my head to catch my breath while passing the endless rows of names etched into the black marble. *Wish I could remember Hippie's name.* I ran through my usual litany, hoping one day to nail down his name: *Method, Hester, Fester, Dedman, Tom, Tim, Jed, Sed, Med. Damn! I can't remember. But at least I know Moreno's. There's a year. Okay...1966, 1967....* I moved towards the center of the black marble V, passing dozens of silent memorials: wreaths, letters and even a faded pair of jungle boots. I recalled my own supple pair of boots I'd forgotten to take with me when my Freedom Bird landed in Seattle– even ran back onto the tarmac trying to flag down the 727 as it taxied away. *Man, I miss those boots.*

I stopped near the center of the V. *Here it is...1970. Man this list is huge...take me all day to scope it out.* Squinting toward the top of the black monolith, I began to scan the rows *of sacred names....✎*

*      *      *

*...LT Hunter stopped* to scrutinize the rolling topography, typical of the foothills that bordered the Rocket Pocket before checking his grid map for the hundredth time.

A big drop of sweat slid down his face. "This looks like it," he grunted.

A short hump to the top found a knob of barren terrain where we built our shelters *to await Christmas....*

*✎...5:24 p.m., March 15, 1984, Washington D.C....I give up. No way can I find Moreno, Anyway, it's getting late, gonna be a long run back.* My body was stiff as I pushed into a slow jog, swinging my arms and twisting my head to work out the kinks. Within a few minutes though, I was warming up nicely as the activity in the Mall lured me to take a last look before turning toward the White House.

Adrenaline picks up my pace as twilight closes in. *What is this, Night of the Living Dead?* What had earlier been a quiet street just north of the White House was now teaming with vagrants who seemed to be– coming out of the sewers. A landmark I'd noted on the way out told me it is one mile to the Washington Hilton. I quicken my pace as one of the greasy nomads chuckles at me, swinging his bottle as I run by. *Who are these weirdoes?* Sucking it in, I step up to seven-minute miles as the streetlights pop on behind me like mortar rounds walking up the avenue. Ahead, the sidewalk is littered with disheveled men, staking out claims as they set up their cardboard tents. *Just like setting up a hootch in this concrete jungle, though I know I'd rather sleep in the ones we had in the Nam.* Glancing to my left, I dodge a dirty bottle as it rolls toward my path, escaping a drunk's open hand. He leans against the brick wall to absorb its heat, his head back and his eyes rolling up white above tobacco-stained mouth. *Just like the old men with their Betel nut.*

*There it is!* The welcome sight of the Hilton kicks me into a sprint. *I will NEVER do that again!* I think as I pull up in front of the luxurious hotel. I look back at the unfolding evening ritual and wonder if any of these wandering tribesmen might have been with me *in The Nam....*✐

*Mom & Dad,*                                                           *Dec. 24th,*

*Well it's finally Christmas Eve! Thought I'd spent it in the rear but didn't quite make it. At least we're out in the Rocket Pocket & just below this hill you can see the lights along Highway 1. Sure wish I had camera cause it's really pretty here. No jungle or undergrowth here. Looks sort of like the badlands in South Dakota. And most of the rain passes over, further inland, because we're so close to the sea.*

*Actually stayed 6 days in rear! Real nice. & going back in 26th, then 31st! For New Years. Bob Hope didn't make it to Chu Lai. I'll write soon. Cease fire starts in 15 minutes, at 6:00 PM.*

*God bless you. Hope you had a real Merry Christmas!*          *Bob...*

*...Plugging in the* lights, Dad stood back to admire the plump, brightly-colored bulbs radiating their frosty glow onto long strands of tinsel and an array of ornaments, a few new, but mostly old, now showing the wear from Christmas' past. Crowning the tree was an ancient five-pointed poly-glass star Dad had bought a dozen years ago, its beam still as vibrant as it had been during its first Christmas season. Moving to the front porch, he turned on the outside lights and the flicker of hundreds of tiny bulbs sent a cascade of color onto a thick blanket of snow. To complete his role in dousing his small

162

portion of the gray night, Dad switched on the green twinkle lights that adorned a large spruce pine wreath hanging on our golden *oak porch door....*

*...The sun crept* to a position just above the western slopes, then, pausing for a final look, slowly rolled over the distant lavender hills. I lit one of the small candles I had bought at the PX, its glow enabling me to read for a few precious minutes more before the night *closed over us....*

*...Mom and Kent* patiently waited inside the car while Dad brushed off the slushy snow. Sliding behind the wheel of his pea-green 68 Impala, he carefully backed into the Brown's gravel driveway across the street, Mom praying he wouldn't get stuck like he did last week, having to seesaw his car till he got enough "umphfff" to send the car careening onto the ice-covered avenue. At the end of the block he turned onto Seventh Street and covered the half-mile between Cottage Grove and downtown where he made the short hop through several busy lights before gunning it to the top of the bluff. First Baptist Church was only eight minutes from home and they were soon greeting everyone as they gathered to celebrate Christ's birth with the traditional candlelight service. Picking up their candles and bulletins from the brightly lit foyer, they took their usual seats, halfway back and on *the right side....*

*...By seven-thirty* the encroaching night demanded I quench my light to prevent detection from enemy eyes. Settling into my bed, I listened to the soft hum of mosquitoes overhead that were perhaps scheming a way to penetrate my barrier of bug juice. Outside, the evening stars resumed their priestly glow in the eternals, their presence reminding me of the night nearly two-thousand years ago and I began to softly hum "Silent *Night, Holy Night."...*

*...Spiny green wreaths,* decorated with red velvet bows, hung in the center of each of the colorful stained glass windows bordering the pews. Strands of blue lights and red and gold ribbons joined the wreaths as they skirted the windows, making their way to the stage area where a huge spruce tree sat, bending with colorful trinkets the kids had spent several Sundays crafting. Beneath it waited presents the children would receive after the lighting of the Christmas candle. "Will everyone please stand and join me

in singing *Joy to the World*," Cletus Foiles, our song director, began. "Page 372, *all four stanzas!*"...

   ...*Wad took his* place outside the hootch to begin first watch, he and I sharing up since Fritts wasn't there. He stared past the scrubby bushes toward Chu Lai, perhaps gazing at the soft glow of far away lights dotting the coastal horizon and maybe thinking of the parties and friendly get-togethers going on right now in those distant patches *of human camaraderie*....

   ...*The songs sung* and the sermonet delivered, Pastor Carter nodded to Art Woodrum and Denny Shave to come forward to begin the highlight of the evening: the lighting of the candles. The lights dimmed as the ushers walked down the aisle, lighting the first candle on each side of the center aisle. The parishioners in turn lit the candle next to them and so on until the sanctuary glowed with the radiance of God's hope. Beginning as a whisper, *Silent Night, Holy Night* increased in volume until the rafters echoed its sentiments of peace, hope and love. Mom, Dad and Kent held their candles high, swaying to the gentle wave of light moving to and fro, perhaps saying their own private prayer for their loved one in that *strange far-away land*....

   ...*The twelve-hour* cease-fire wrapped around me like a blanket of hope. This would be a peaceful night, and Wad, guarding stoically just in case, lulled my eyes to close as the hum of the mosquitoes still sang silently *in the night*....

   ✎...*7:50 p.m., Friday, November 12, 1971, Day 386 / 39 to extended DEROS, Chu Lai Naval Center...Our mood was* mellow in the candlelit Quonset hut, empty now but for John and me. Our metal-framed beds guarded the corner near the door where our few meager belongings sat. Studiously taped to the cambered walls above us were several *Playboy* posters from magazines we'd found left behind in the hastily abandoned abode. We'd taken over the corrugated bungalow during American's Last Stand; only three days till embarking on the journey north, transporting the remainder of the Americal Division on a fleet of Army transport ships to Da Nang. Once there we would inventory, process and ship the remaining equipment to other bases throughout the world. Americal, then, would be no more, its remains as scattered as my beloved Second Platoon.

On the first of September we had undergone the motions of stand-down ceremonies and I had had the honor of being chosen as Color Guard, again, though this time without George's kooky crossed eyes. I had no idea where he was now, maybe in Da Nang. I had run across Nelson and Yoss, though, several months back. They, too, had landed rear jobs on the main chunk of Chu Lai. But they were all gone now, only a skeleton crew of volunteers remaining. I'd extended my tour of duty for up to 60 days to assist in the American pullout, which would assure me of a six-month early out; I thought it'd be worth it to avoid the stateside hassle I'd heard about.

We called ourselves Task Force Americal, the last paper pushers as the 1/52nd Infantry guarded our perimeter until the last nut and the last bolt were expediently processed. From dawn till dusk I assailed the keys of my electric *Underwood* in our lonely outpost, just south of the Replacement Center in the now abandoned Naval Center. We sat up shop in their CQ– several dozen men furiously working to meet the November fifteenth deadline. Even Captain Watson, another TFA volunteer, had already moved up to Da Nang. Before leaving, he had told me that I was the best damn clerk he'd ever had. That'd meant a lot to me; he was a good man. My new boss was LT Biggett, only nineteen but already a second lieutenant. Man, I was a year older than he was, though it felt more like ten.

"Bob."

"Yeah, John?"

"Hear about the dogs?"

"What about the dogs?"

John inhaled deeply before passing the bowl. "The fuc-k'n' dogs, man. The fuc-k'n' MP's blew the fuc-k'n' dogs away. They took out their fuc-k'n' *45*'s and blew every one of them fuc-k'n' dogs away."

"Why?" I blew out slowly.

"Didn't want no gooks getting 'em, man." –he brushed a wrist through his blond hair– "They eat dog, you know. Don't even use 'em as pets. Like they was a chicken or cow or some shit."

"I know."

"That's right. You were an infantryman."

"How you gonna act."

"How you gonna *fuc*-k'n' act, man. Wish I hadda chance to get out there."

I stared at John's pudgy arms. "No, you don't."

"Maybe not. Hey, how's your honey doing tonight?"

I turned and gazed through the smoke at my blond sweetheart hanging on the wall. "She's okay. Man, I think I am in love."

John picked up his guitar and strummed a few rusty bars, out of tune, as usual, but it was music. "Let's get the fuc-k'n' *fuck outta here!*"...✎

Christmas Day, Friday, December 25, 1970, Day 65 / 300 to DEROS
—too hot for Jesus—

Several drops of sweat accumulated on the end of Wad's nose as he leaned over to take the ruck's weight off his shoulders. "Guess LT wants...to make an impression." –the drops fall to the dust– "Don't know why else he'd be in such a fucking hurry."

I was leaning over, too, sucking in air. "Got something to prove I guess, being only his second day and all."

"Hey, guys," Yoss called from behind. "Merry Christmas!"

The temperature was topping one hundred degrees as we humped past the three o'clock hour, and the raging sun was showing no mercy, evaporating what little cloud cover there had been in the morning hours. The alkaline soil allowed only a trace of vegetation as we continued our trek, now nearing the limits of our southern border.

Looming in our path was a huge hill.

"We *are* going around this, right, Nelson?" All I got was a shake of the head.

"Break!" LT hollered near the hill's base. "Chopper coming in, bringing Christmas dinner!" Looking for looks of approval, he only found tired stares.

We closed ranks and threw off our rucks to await the Christmas bird. Five minutes later a chopper crew was handing out three canisters of hot turkey with all the trimmings, not so cold pop, red wine and egg nog. We scooped our paper plates full with Christmas. The chopper pilot had two more stops to make before nightfall, so after a ten minute gorge we threw the empty canisters into the bird and he was off in a cloud of dust. *Merry Christmas to all, and to all, a good night!*...

✎...*6:29 p.m., Wednesday, May 30, 1984, outside of Oquawka, Illinois...The horizon stretched* in front of me forever. Fourteen miles ahead and still out of sight was my destination, Burlington, Iowa, where a hot shower and dinner waited. Seven miles behind me I'd left the small river town of Oquawka, nestled just above Lock and Dam 18 on the Mississippi River, where I'd been based out of all week. The afternoon was hot for the middle of spring, but that was okay. I'd been looking forward to this run all week to clear out the cobwebs and reflect on the last couple of weeks. The ever-present fear I'd had of my heart doing weird things had been quelled, at least for now, by a book I had read by George Sheehan, claiming most long distant runners experienced such anomalies in the natural course of their running careers. Maybe it was the result of a runner's heart, or maybe it was all in my head. All I knew was– I had to run to feel good.

But besides that, my son was over a year old now and surveying the river week after week was beginning to take its toll on the home front. *Got to figure out a way to get off the road,* I thought, pounding through a dust cloud kicked up by a passing truck. *Ya know, this road life is a lot like the missions in The Nam. Stand-down on the weekends, then hit the bush again. Wonder if it means anything? ...*✐

*...I knew something* was wrong as we turned into our third switchback up the monster's craggy side. Christmas dinner was stalled in the pit of my stomach and it had no intention of going any further. One more switchback sent my stomach bubbling with partially processed turkey and dressing as the late afternoon sun opened its door and invited us in. *Bet those lucky guys are in Da Nang right now ogling some scantily clad chick at that "Bob Hope Show",* I thought as we rolled into another switchback. *Holding up a brew and toasting Christmas in style. And here I am. How you...gonna....* I barely had time to turn my head as I spouted like a gushing fire hydrant, decorating an unfortunate bush with Christmas red, green and brown bile. The second heave had just as much punch but not as much content, evolving into a series of dry heaves that kept up for a couple of gut-wrenching minutes. I wasn't the only one. Langley and Spurlin were also engaged in an impromptu food-flying fare. After a few minutes we continued on, not reaching the top until no less than three others lost their lunch– including LT.

When we finally claimed the top of this mountain of misery, it was five thirty. I fell to the ground with my ruck still on my back, wondering why we had to climb this thing in the first place. It was desolate– not a drop of shade or speck of water. What possible tactical advantage could there be in staying up here? Giving it five more seconds, I dropped it as a fresh pounding in my head turned my stomach again. Fortunately, we had had the foresight to hump the support poles for our hootches, so as the approaching darkness signaled an end to this cruelest day of our short lives, we escaped within to *await its demise....*

*...Dad pulled off* Seventh Street to return his family from a long day of gorging on turkey, shuffling cards, sharing the latest gossip and playing board games at my Uncle Chicks. Kent hauled in their cache of Christmas exchange gifts while Dad went straight to that coconut cream pie that had been beckoning to him all day. Meanwhile, Mom made some hot coffee to ward off the night's chill as Kent tuned in to Perry Como's *Christmas Special* on channel six. After the two-hour special and then the evening news, Dad unplugging the Christmas lights and checked once more on our dog, Tator, to make sure she wasn't wrapped around the swing set pole again and was unable to get into her *house of straw....*

✎*...12:03 p.m., Thanksgiving Day, Thursday, November 25, 1971, Day 399 / 6 to DEROS, Da Nang...I found an* isolated spot and sat down in front of my tray, brimming with all one could expect from a home-cooked Thanksgiving feast. *What a way to celebrate my twenty-first birthday, Uncle Sam springing for a huge dinner and inviting every soldier in The Nam to my party!* I gobbled down a big bite of mashed potatoes, steaming with hot turkey gravy. *Only six more days, a whole twenty days less than they said!* I rechecked my cargo pocket to make sure my marching papers were still there. *I'm actually going home! Home...man, it feels good to say that. And not only going home, but with a six-month early out!* Swallowing a big gulp of eggnog, I looked around the huge mess hall located in the center of the Da Nang R&R Center. Most of the soldiers were waiting for orders, eager for either a few exotic days out of country– or the big one– the Freedom Bird! Just ten days ago we'd left Chu Lai in the hands of the 1/52nd Infantry to prepare the RVA for the final phase of the take-over of the huge base. Since then, LT Biggett and I'd been frantically cranking out equipment transfers at assembly-line speed, hurrying to meet our deadline before I rotated out of The Nam.

But now, I was alone– just like before I had joined my Second Platoon. I gazed from my seat at the throng of happy GI's as they wolfed down their bounty. The echo of their chatter filled the hall with the sound of good times, for the migration of troops leaving the country was now affecting even this military post. It wouldn't be long; it wouldn't be long before all of us would abandon Vietnam. What would happen then– I didn't want think about, although I knew; *we all knew.*...✐

Saturday, December 26, 1970, Day 66 / 299 to DEROS
—TR—

Like a thoroughbred out of the gates the sun blasted off the horizon to push the air temperature past sweltering before we could reach Highway 1. It was no contest, twenty-eight Grunts huffing to its black-tarred shoulder bathed in a thick layer of sweat.

"Trucks...should be here soon," LT huffed, unshouldering his ruck.

"So, LT," –Hillbilly dumped his ruck on the edge of the road– "how ya fee'n' this fine morn'?"

"Like shit. Shouldn't have drank that second egg nog."

"Maybe that'll learn ya," Hillbilly advised. "Hey, if ya don't mind me a ask'n', where ya plant *yer* corn at?"

LT looked at Hillbilly for a moment before deciphering his meaning. "You mean where am I from? The great state of Pennsylvania."

Hillbilly eyeballed him for a second. "Enybody ever tell ya that yer the spitt'n' image of Teddy Roosevelt? Ya know he's one of ma most admirable presidents. He kicks ass."

"As a matter of fact, quite a few have shared your opinion."

"Then ya wouldn't mind then if we call ya by that brave man's name, you know, it being a compliment 'n' all?"

"If you don't mind me calling you Hillbilly, I don't mind your naming me after a president."

"Then that settles it." –Hillbilly walked to the middle of the road and held his lanky arms over his head– "Second Platooners! Listen up! I want ta introduce ya to the man who's gonna be a leading us into the bush...Teddy Roosevelt. But I think we'll just call 'em TR, ta save time."

"Here here!" LT said, raising his hands to accept Hillbilly's knighting. "Thank you for that commanding introduction and I will do my utmost to live up to the president's good name."

"And hey, Buffalo," Hillbilly concluded as two deuce and a-halves rumbled in from the north, "Best keep yer eye peeled, cause ya know about ol' Teddy's hanker'n' fer bagg'n' big game trophies."

169

Only Hillbilly, spewing his homespun rhetoric, could pull together our platoon's diversity into a common melting pot. Maybe that was one reason our casualty rate was so low compared with Third, who'd been averaging two to three hits a mission. *In my opinion,* I thought as I boarded the truck, *Hillbilly is our most valuable guy....*

✎*...9:11 a.m., Wednesday, December 1, 1971, DEROS DAY!... Returning from the* restroom, I make sure my ribbons are in plain view as I pass three green soldiers sitting like a row of ducks in the huge 747 airliner. I settle into a plush window seat and watch the grainy blue-gray spread of Idaho's Bitterroot Mountains pass below. *Thank God, I made it! After thirteen months and ten days, home, here I come!*

I eye the green soldiers. *How you like this Bronze Star, guys? Man, just how you gonna act? And this Air Medal? It's way too big for even three FNG's. Or maybe this Combat Infantry Badge, think you can handle it? Not even!* I remember my humiliation on my flight home after AIT. There had been a soldier returning home from Vietnam, eyeing me as if I were the lowest thing on earth, he with his string of fancy ribbons while all I could display was a limp private's insignia over a marksman badge. I look down, admiring the two rows of glory adorning my dress uniform. *Got more 'n he had anyway.*

*...3:14 p.m., Chicago...*"Right!" *I have* to yell into the phone to hear over the airport din. "Chicago! Should be there in..." –I spot a large clock hanging from the ceiling of the huge concourse– "...in about two hours!" My voice is shaking, my throat dry toast. "Okay, Steph. See you then!"

*...4:58 p.m., Moline Airport...*"Steph!" *I wave* over the crowd of departing passengers, trying to smile through my dry mouth. She makes the short push through the crowd, giving me a tight hug and whispering, "Welcome home," in my ear, squeezing a moment longer before remembering Jennifer is waiting behind her.

"Jen!" I give her a hug, Steph's perfume still lingering in my mind.

"Welcome home, Bob!" She tries to sound natural, but I know it's rehearsed.

"I can't believe I'm actually home."

"Well you are and we're not going to let you go."

*...5:33 p.m., Blackhawk College, Moline, Illinois...Suddenly I can't* wait to take off my uniform. *What is their problem?* My face flushes and my

skin pricks as I pass some staring, some scowling faces. I glance at my medals, so proud of them on the flight from Seattle. Now I want to hide them in my pocket. *I should be a hero here, right? What is it with these guys? And I left my friends halfway around the world.*

"It's right up here," Steph says, approaching a cluster of small offices. "Be just a minute."

"Okay. I'll stand guard out here." Jen smiles at my joke, but I'm not so sure that I'm joking. *Wish I had my 16. That'd wipe the smirks off their faces.* "So, how's school going?"

"Boring," Jen says. "These kids still act like they're in high school, you know?"

"Yeah, I guess. They're giving me some pretty nasty looks."

"I noticed. Don't pay them any attention. They don't have a *clue* what's really going on, you know?"

My lungs feel like they're collapsing as I pull in a breath of air. *This ain't what I thought it would be like. Feel like I just landed on Mars. Am I really home, or did I leave it back in The Nam? ...*✍

Tuesday, December 29, 1970, Day 69 / 296 to DEROS
—round and round and round we go—

"Just like Ky Tra, huh, Adams?" Ski was sitting by his ruck during a break on a narrow trail, squirting bug juice at several leeches attempting to climb onto his boot.

"What do ya mean?" I was threading one of my dog tags onto the laces of one of my new boots, not even yet baptized by a Vietnam paddy.

"What I *mean,* Mr. Adams, is having to baby-sit the goddamn CP every freaking day."

"Ain't that bad...least we're close to the RP."

"That's your problem, you can't keep your mind focused on the bad side of things."

Yoss pulled his legs tightly to his chest, as was his way. "If he did that, Ski, all he'd ever think about was you."

The hook-up signal passed down the line and we were off again, skirting south toward the 198th's AO in the foothills between the RP and the mountains. We'd been working the southern section of 196th's AO since the twenty-sixth, seesawing between the CP and our NDP's. Our only diversion had been on the night of the twenty-seventh when a wandering mongoose had picked the wrong bush to sharpen his claws on and set off our MA. Today our squad was defending the rear of our strung out platoon as it humped a maze of trails that riddled the hills, the breaks becoming more and more frequent as the afternoon wore on.

"I wish I knew what the fuck was going on up there," Wad complained during another break. "See that hill over there?" –he pointed at a saddled hill, its left hump almost devoid of trees– "I swear I saw that fucker before we stopped for chow this morning." A surprise visit from a Fat City bird had delivered a hot lunch.

"So, wadaya saying?"

"Think about it. New LT. New AO. Nothing but a shitload of small hills. What does that add up to?"

"Lost?"

"Fucking *A*. We've been walking in circles all afternoon."

The signal to hook up brought us to our feet. *Walking in circles, just like that stupid Escape and Evasion course*, I thought as we began to wind our way up a narrow trail of a long, shallow-sloped hill.

Sunday, January 3, 1971, Day 74 / 291 to DEROS<br>—volunteer pilot—

I rubbed my eyes, weary from writing in the dim light and gazed outside the hootch. The rain beat steadily against the plastic roof...*what, five days now? Six? I don't know.* It made it difficult not to drift into a mesmerized state of nothingness. *No wonder the Chinese use dripping water as one of their torture methods,* I thought as I forced my hand back onto the damp paper....

"...*constantly raining out here and the cloud ceiling won't raise enough to allow the choppers through to pick us up. We've been on this hill for I think five or six days now. Comfortable though. Built a good dry hooch for 3 men. - The most common type. It's getting terribly boring though... Iv'e written to everybody I can think of and now starting on second rounds. My last letter to you was written from this same hill. I've finished the book 'Christy' several days ago. Fantastic book! You should read it! When I send it, and all the other books Ive read home, probably this next time in. To show how much time we've got on our hands, I read 'Around the World in 80 days,' (your Christmas present) in one day (230 pg.). – a long trip for just one day.*

*Hope your getting all my mail. I write about 2 letters to you a week. Please tell me what letter you received last when you write to me. I'm sure your camera is waiting for me in the rear. If only we'd make it back.*

*Our stand-down should last a whole seven days this time. With all free time!*

*Run out of words. So please be careful. Tonight at 9:00 you should be getting up for church. New Year's was spent out here on this hill. Uneventful, but that's okay. Write soon.*

*Love, your son, Bob"*

Carefully folding the letter, I slid it into an airmail envelope and ran my tongue along the seal. Then I artfully drew the address in large ornate caps, adding the word "– FREE– " where the stamp would normally go. I placed it next to my growing stack of letters in my ammo can, closed the lid and looked at Nelson's hootch. Its inhabitants moved restlessly as they endured the overpowering boredom. *This is life in the bush,* I thought as I watched Ski practice blowing smoke rings. *A week of absolute nothing, followed by a few minutes of absolute terror.* Right now I wasn't sure which sounded better, the nothing...*or the terror....*

✎*...8:19 p.m., Thursday, May 23, 1985, Quincy, Illinois, journal entry...All day my* nose was plugged up bad. Could hardly breathe at all. So after work I figured I would go down to the pool and jump rope. At twelve minutes I flat run out of breath. It was almost like...I forgot *how to breathe....*

*...5:27 p.m., earlier that day...That's it, screw this jump rope. Try to run... play it by ear.*

I start at a slow pace, not much more than a walk while all the time thinking, *this gonna be like last time? I hate Quincy.* Up a long hill I crawl, past the graveyard to the park entrance. Slow. I have to stop. No breath, none at all. *Why am I so afraid? What's happening to me?* I walk a quarter mile, each step eroding until I stop, struggling to breathe and thinking, thinking about myself, my breathing, my heart. *Is this it? The end? Like this? Gotta try again!* I force my legs to a jog, but have to stop after a minute. *Try again! This hill, I can do it! Take it easy, slow, slow, slow.... God, barely made it, heart 150. Downhill now…walk, walk. I can't remember how to breathe! Why? But if I can't breathe, I can't run. It's not my heart! I don't care who you are, Bill Rogers or anyone, the fact is if you can't breathe you just can't run! Your heart hasta have air, it has to!*

Fear wraps around my heart, my lungs, my mind. *My diaphragm is so tight. Won't take air, won't let it in. Why? This is my worse run ever. Maybe my last…but who cares. Face it, damn it! What happens happens. Who cares anymore! I'm so sick of thinking about it! I JUST…DON'T…CARE!*

I jog again, more like a fast walk, past several geese feeding by a small pond, over a narrow bridge that ends at a steep, muddy incline. Up I go, stepping over oak roots. At the top I see the water fountain. *I can make it.* Close now. *I'm gonna make it.* Closer. *Water, good-good-good.* I stand erect and wipe my mouth. *Okay, Bob, this is it. Today I prove to myself…I have to prove to myself…that I can DO IT!*

I continue down the next hill, slowly jogging around the soccer field.

*Wait! Something's different!* Out of the park now. *Easier to breathe!* Up the incline I had barely made last run. *I want to run…to run!*

Ten minutes. *I can't believe it! Nine minute miles! It feels good. IT FEELS…SO…DAMN…GOOD!*

Fifteen minutes. *Eight-fifties. Wow! It's so crazy!*

Twenty minutes. *Eight-thirties. Incredible! Why? Because it's so simple. Fear, it was fear controlling me! It was fear restricting my diaphragm! My nose is as plugged as before, but now my diaphragm is so loose. It's so easy and so fun to breathe and it's getting better and better and better with each breath and with each step I take. God, this is freedom!…*✐

…*"Chopper inbound!" Tuck* shouted from the CP.

Wad stuck his head out of his hootch and gazed into a heavy bank of fog. "Who'd volunteer to fly through this shit?"

The eggbeater clicked in my ear and in spite of the rain I crawled outside to witness the eerie event. Most of the platoon had done likewise, watching TR on the horn, guiding in the craft by sound and compass heading alone. Soon the giant iron bird became visible, inching downward until the gunner could see enough so as not to drop the cases on top of a hootch. He pushed the cargo out and ten cases crashed to the earth, three of them splitting apart as they hit, a perfect shot, though, not five meters from TR's hootch.

"Four C's each," Nelson said, carrying two cases over.

I pulled out my P-38 and cranked open a can of peaches and pound cake and dug in. Outside, the rain beat against the plastic roof...*what, five days now? Six? I don't know.* Finishing my treat, I threw my empty can into the brush and drifted into a deep, contented sleep.

# STAND-DOWN FOUR

Monday, January 4, 1971, Day 75 / 290 to DEROS
—bad day for a new guy—

The word of an extraction ignited the NDP. An unexpected break in the weather had prompted the decision to get us out before another round of monsoon rains began. Within forty-five minutes we were securing a small abandoned potato field, straining our ears for choppers.

"Git that smoke popped, Yoss," Hillbilly bellowed. "The rear awaits ma arrival!"

A bright cloud of red billowed as four choppers thumped in under the cloud ceiling and the sight clicked into our weary minds that salvation from this mud-laden land was at hand. Next stop– hot food and a dry bed.

\*     \*     \*

"We're heading for our old re-train area!" Spanky yelled from under his poncho, eyeing the PX through a downpour drenching our convoy.

"Hey hey!" Chadborne shouted. "Some other poor fucks musta got stuck in that desert shithole!"

Turning right at the T, the trucks picked up speed as they headed down the hill toward our old unit area, but instead of gearing up, they braked to pull into a side road before stopping beside a CQ office similar to our old one.

"Let's go, boys," Retchin said. "I dunno where the fuck we are, but it's better 'n the dump we were in last time."

Good ol' Topp was standing on the CQ porch, a freshly lit cigarette doing the rumba as he spouted instructions on where to check our ordinance, always his top priority. I noticed a sign hanging behind him– 5/46th BATTALION GROUP, ALPHA COMPANY. *They must still be out in the field, or stuck at*

175

*that new re-train area.* Either way, I was grateful for returning to the oceanfront vista. The familiar smells of saltwater and fish carcasses rotting on the monsoon shoreline brought back an exhilaration I hadn't felt since my *first stand-down.* ...

✎ *...1:15 p.m., Friday, August 2, 1985, outside of Smokemont Campground, Great Smoky Mts. National Park, Tennessee...The redolent allure* of cherry birch and mayapple flourishing along the trail added to my sense of euphoria. Peering through the trees, the air was heavy with dew as dark clouds conjugated overhead. *Gonna rain,* I thought as I spotted a hiker coming down the trail. My legs moved effortlessly as I passed the lone hiker, making my way through the damp air on the pristine Smoky Mountain trail. *Can't believe how easy this is! There's another elevation sign up ahead.* "Elevation–5,280 Feet above Sea Level". *Wow, I started at 2,200 at camp! Must be the cool air helping me. None of that lousy heat like back home.*

Up ahead was a sharp bend in the trail. *Looks like good a place as any to turn back.* I checked my watch. *42:15... probably been going eight-minute miles so far. Five miles out, five miles back. Think this second half is gonna be sweet!* I made the bend and slowed for a few seconds to gaze as far around the bend as I could before pivoting on my right foot and starting back. *Whoa! Look out below!* I thought as gravity pushed me down the trail until my feet were fighting to keep up as they pounded the moist sawdust like a paddlewheel slapping the water. *How can I be doing this after the last couple months?* I remembered Quincy. *I must be dinky dau! Got to be doing sixes, at least!* Up ahead, the lone hiker turned as he heard my approach. He was wearing fringed high-top suede boots and carried one of those knotty-pine walking sticks I had seen down at the Cherokee Indian souvenir shop. Coming up quickly, I tossed him a friendly "Howdy" as I passed. He held up a hand and imparted a sagacious smile. My arms swayed to the beat of my stomping feet. My hips rotated smoothly as my chest barely needed to expand, my breathing seemingly non-existent. Thus unfettered I floated in *this mortal capsule.* ...✎

*...Checking in my* weapon, 60 ammo, smokes and frags, I returned to the CQ where Gilespie was passing out mail. He sorted through the pile until he found my name on a group of letters rubber-banded to a small package.

"That's it," I said aloud, as though x-raying the package with superman eyes and recognizing the silhouette of a camera. I found my barrack and tore open the package. The Kodak X-15 Instamatic was like what most of the guys carried except for one very important distinction– this one was mine! My folks had shipped two rolls of film with it, so after some brief reading I popped one in and asked the closest GI to take some flicks of me sitting on my bed.

Langley aimed the lens at my contrived grin as I sat cross-legged on my bed.

*BAMMMMMMMMMM!*

Screams from GI's replace the blast as we race into the rain and two barracks down. A GI hangs out of the splintered barrack's door. The young man's dying nerves twitch as his ashen face stares wide-eyed into the rain. I avert my gaze at the wooden steps, stained red with blood coupling with the rain.

"What the fuck happened?!" Third Platoon's LT shouts as he rounds the corner. "Get a medic!" though, at a glance, he knows it's too late. The fallen soldier is a new guy, judging from his new fatigues. "What was he doing with a grenade? Monkey Man?"

"I don't know, LT," responds a bearded Grunt who is kneeling beside the dead GI. "He must've forgot to take it off his ruck. Probably snagged the pin on the door when he opened the door."

Several medics arrive, including one from the Aid-Station carrying a stretcher. One of the medics closes the dead GI's eyes before placing his limp body onto the stretcher. With nothing else to do and since the rain is increasing, we return to our hootch. Any plans Topp has for the afternoon are canceled, so I settle down on my mattress and will myself to forget what has occurred, telling myself it don't mean nothing. Turning on my side, I open *The Chairman,* hoping to bury myself *in its pages....*

✎*...2:34 p.m., Saturday, January 4, 1986, Moline YMCA...Slamming the ball* into the corner for the third straight time put me over the top. It was a shutout.

"Good game." –I looked at the clock– "Guess our time is up."

Ray picked up the blue racquetball. "You were too good for me today, Bobber, but you wait till next time."

"We'll see."

Riding home, I knew I didn't want there to be a next time. During the second game, my heart had started racing as I had rushed in for a corner shot. Not wanting to let on, I had faked an untied shoe to give me time to recoup. Fortunately it kicked down long enough to finish the set. *I can run forever, no problem, ten, fifteen, twenty miles. But get me in a game, be it racquetball, basketball, softball, anything where I have to interact and sooner or later the anxiety takes over.* And it was getting worse. Doctor said it was PVC's. Doc Sheehan said it was a runner's heart. So why can't my *mind believe it?...✎*

Tuesday, January 5, 1971, Day 76 / 289 to DEROS
—Good day, sunshine! —

6:04 a.m.: I sit up, wide-awake. Everyone else is asleep. My muscles ache to stretch and get on with it. I pick up my boots and tiptoe bare-chested past my comrades and out the door. Pulling on my boots, I glance at the rain-washed steps where yesterday the dead man's body had lain. Before my eyes, the steps transform to gold as the first rays of the sun explode over the sea's horizon. I turn toward the glow, and it bends into my retina a million beads of light. I look around; everything is permeated with the hue of a spring dandelion. The rising sun lures me toward its radiance as a surge of euphoria fills me, the golden orb accentuating an inspiration as it *warms my face....*

✎*...6:13 p.m., Wednesday, December 10, 1986, Iowa Falls, Iowa, journal entry...Last Jan. 29 @ Quincy I promised myself I would be off* the road by Sept. 15th of this year. Well, it's been 3 mo. longer than I figured, but still that's not so bad. Next weeks my last week. My last day is the 19th. Maybe now I can start to repair the damage that living on the road for the past 6 years has created. With God's help it is possible. Believe it or not, it seems Art Davis has been an answer to my prayer to get me home. Amazing how God works, huh?

A tap on the door. "Be right there!" I closed my journal and grabbed *my field jacket....✎*

*...Chu Lai..."That's it!"* I shout aloud, suddenly aware this spontaneous eruption might awake the sleepers a few feet behind me. "That's it," I whisper, walking closer to the waking shore. *It's so simple!* I look at my watch and mentally record the time. *6:10 a.m. There's so much out there and*

*I've been going nowhere, stuck inside a mind with too many limits, too many walls.* I squint into the circle of life. *College! That's my way out of here! How could I have been so stupid to drop out? Maybe I was too young. Maybe too stupid. Maybe too spoiled. When I get home I'll start over. I'll make something of myself!*

The scent of bacon frying in the mess hall subdues my vision and I turn toward *the tempting aroma....*

✎ *...7:07 p.m., Iowa Falls, Iowa...Jim Cripe pours* a healthy shot of tequila. "Here's to getting off the road."

My glass kisses his with a clink. "To gett'n' off the road." I let it slide down, enjoying its fiery zing.

"Don't know how I'm gonna work out here without ya, Bob. Meek's gonna get your spot, you know."

"*You* put in for it, Jim. You know as much about survey as he does."

"You know I don't like being in charge."

"You'll do all right." –I gaze through the window. A crow is pecking on some scraps of bread lying in the snow– "Who knows, this might not work out for me, anyway. At six bucks an hour, I'll probably be broke by spring."

He looks at me with eyes somber and pushes another shot at me. "Nobody should hafta live on the damn road."

I pick up my glass. "I'll drink *to that, Jim."...*✐

\*     \*     \*

*...I knew I* was caught as soon as Topp eyeballed me. I sped up and lowered my head. "Hair's getting too long, soldier," he said, stopping me in my tracks. "After the floorshow, get it cut."

I found a seat inside as the band tuned their instruments. *Even at home it was a constant fight with Dad. It's my hair! What business is it of theirs how long it is. If I ever have kids....*

One of the Korean band members beginning his intro cut into my thoughts, telling us what a good job we were doing against the "hostile forces in the free-fire zone", and how proud everybody was of us. I leaned back and sipped on a Coke as the band jumped into their first song. I recalled the morning's inspiration. *Maybe if I put together a paper to analyze what I want to do with my life, that'd be a start. While I'm getting a haircut, think I'll pick up a notepad and get going on this.*

\*      \*      \*

Yoss and Nelson accompanied me to the PX; they went shopping and I got a haircut. I entered a long narrow building teetering on the edge of a rock shelf defying the sea's supremacy. Inside, a row of Vietnamese barbers dressed in starched white uniforms were busy cutting, combing and shaving GI's with assembly-line precision. Afterwards, they tenderized their patron's shoulders with miniature karate chops before dismissing them to begin the ritual again. I spotted an opening and jumped into the chair. The barber whipped a fresh apron around my neck, pinning it on while asking me how I wanted it cut.

The image of my father holding his sheers over me came to my mind. "Just a little *off the sides, okay?*"...

✎ *...8:41 p.m., Monday, March 23, 1987, journal entry...I was watching* a movie this evening about Vietnam. At one point they were humping in this field when one guy gets it on a land mine. It took me back, like I was there, & I freaked for *a few seconds....*

✏ *...7:14 p.m., Tuesday, March 24, 1987, journal entry...While riding my* bike to Art's this morning, it dawned on me that I hadn't gotten over Vietnam yet. That feeling that any second I could get blown away has been carried over into my breathing patterns, the way my nose stops up & I find it hard to breathe at times is based on a deep seeded fear of dying @ any second. But instead of dying thru enemy fire, I'm afraid my heart will stop thru lack of air. So when I run I begin to "panic", thinking I won't get enough air to breathe, which causes my diaphragm to tighten, making it difficult to breathe. It's a vicious cycle, but through it I've recreated the exact feeling from my Vietnam experience of walking through the bush, knowing any second a bomb could explode on top of me. So when I run, I become afraid that any moment I might keel over dead. I'm not sure why my subconscious does this, but at least I see the source of this problem now. Perhaps I can begin to work thru this by facing these facts & convince my mind that I no longer need to deal with this fear, since Vietnam is over & I must begin a new life in the *here & now....* ✐

# WIRE IN THE SHADOWS

Thursday, January 7, 1971, Day 78 / 287 to DEROS
—high as the sky—

I pulled the brim of my new bush hat to just above my eyes, pretending I was Clint Eastwood.

"Have anotha toke, man," Hillbilly cackled. I took the clip and filled my lungs with the magic blue smoke. Still holding my breath I handed it to Ski, who, I discovered, was ambidextrous when it came to things that made you feel all right.

*What a great day, man, only one short class on something about…. I can't remember. Tastics? Tacsics? I dunno. Then learning Nichols and his cohort Nick the dick 'ere outta here. I mean their time is up. Going home, didi mau, adios and good riddance. Spurlin is taking over as squad leader. A good man, that Spurlin. Yes he is. Then there was this floorshow at two. This time some little guys, from Australia, I think. Anyway, they had this lady lead singer and she was really, really good. I mean really good. Then after that I got me some cardboard from a C-ration box and cut a circle outta it–*

"Have anotha toke, man," Hillbilly cackled.

"Yeah, man." –a deep inhalation– "Here, Ski, have a toke, too, man." – *and then I put the cardboard into the top of my new bush hat to make it into like a flat top, you know? Then I took this clothes hanger wire thingy I found at the CQ and threaded it into the brim to make it stick out straight and stuff, you know, so it'd look like Clint Eastwood's hat, or maybe even the Sundance Kid. And I got me another idea–*

"Have anotha toke, man," Hillbilly cackled.

*–I feel like a space gypsy, man. No worries, you know. And I got me this other idea to bring out an extra pair of fatigues and take my sewing kit and stitch eyelets down the sides of the legs and then take bootstraps and thread them through like a shoe. Wow! That rhymes. And that would tighten them up like a pair of jeans like back in the World, you know? Like, I need some kinda identity out there. Uniqueness, you know? That would be soooo cooool. I don't eeeeven remember feeeel'n' soooo gooood. I mean everything's soooo mellow and soooo slow and soooo narrow and….*

"Have anotha toke, *man*," *Hillbilly cackled….*

181

✎...*9:51 a.m., Wednesday, June 24, 1987. Andalusia bottomland, Rock Island County, Illinois...I looked from* Jim Cripe to Gary. "Any ideas?"

"Scamp?"

"Take too long."

"Waders?"

"Too deep."

Gary waded into the Andalusia soup. The mud sucked him down to his waist in the knee-deep water, but he kept on, undaunted.

"You're fucking crazy!" Cripe shouted at him. "Least ya coulda took the tape with ya!"

"Throw it to me on the other side!"

"Look out for snakes!" I joked. A cloud of bees buzzed overhead, following the swamp's perimeter. "What?"

"Looks like they're moving camp, just like you did," Cripe said.

It was good to be back with the *Corps of Engineers again.*...✎

# MISSION FIVE

Friday, January 8, 1971, Day 79 / 286 to DEROS
—valley of the dragon—

Come on, Hippie, lean back! The scenery from three thousand feet was fantastic as I clicked off half-a-dozen shots of the other birds against the infused mosaic of green hues far below. Enjoying my new toy, I had recorded leaving the compound, the truck ride to Fat City and the array of aircraft zipping in and out of the airstrip. TR said we were going to work an area I was unfamiliar with– Dragon Valley. In previous years it had been one of the area's worst hangouts for the NVA. Word was they might be using the valley again to build forces for another Tet assault. *That's the VC's way of celebrating their New Year,* I thought as I clicked a shot at the chopper flying adjacent to ours, *blow away GI's.*

The ride to the valley was much longer than to Ky Tra as we followed the coast north before jumping inland. This time, though, my ears were safe from the blaring turbines and thumping blades since I had acquired a pair of earplugs. I had found a small canvas accessory bag to store them in, having attached it on the forward sling swivel on my 16. Before descending I snapped two more shots; the last one captured Hippie's profile as he held his hat while gazing into the celadon paddies below.

The jump from the bird was a rough one, sinking into almost a foot of mud under a tangle of weeds and two feet of water that turned black as we trudged to the morass' edge. Trying to catch my breath, I could only gulp the valley's stagnate, pollen-laden atmosphere in small doses. I couldn't resist getting in one last flick, though, capturing Retchin standing next to me and pointing his 60 into a ten-foot high mess of sawgrass and cattails.

The incessant drone pulsating around us signaled unseen danger and I breathed easier when we started to move away from the bottomland and gained higher ground. The January sun beat on us as we headed southeast towards the dragon's mountainous spine, traveling on narrow trails worn deep by sandal-clad feet. The threat of booby-traps was high, slowing our pace at times to a crawl as Hillbilly inched his way up a small couloir running perpendicular to the valley's main trough. Every time we stopped, silvery land leeches as lean as starving alley cats would sprint for my feet, hoping for a few drops of blood. The ring of bug juice I had squirted on my boots after leaving the swamp was still holding as Hillbilly cut off the main trail and to the top of a small knoll fifty meters in. On its summit, stunted trees and an explosion of plant life afforded ample protection from the sun and prying VC eyes.

We had a new guy with us, though he wasn't new to Vietnam at all. He was a young Vietnamese soldier assigned to our platoon, affectionately called a Kit Carson Scout because of his alleged knowledge of the local terrain. That remained to be seen. He went by the name Larry, an American name, though I wasn't sure why. He couldn't have been much more than sixteen, of small stature with a friendly, child-like demeanor. His uniform was ARVN, a crisp tiger-striped pattern printed on tailored fatigues that formed to his compact frame. First Platoon had also been assigned a Kit Carson Scout, who, strangely enough, also went by an American name– Bobby. It was nice to see them working with us; maybe they could help us figure out what this was all about.

Sunday, January 10, 1971, Day 81 / 284 to DEROS

—LZ Hardtack—

It had taken over three hours of sweat and muscle to reach the top of one of the giants guarding the southern edge of Dragon Valley. It was a tight camp, the brush so thick it took some time to clear our positions.

TR looked up as he pounded a stake into the hard-packed earth. "Nelson, need your squad to clear an LZ for a re-supply tomorrow morning."

Nelson shrugged. "What do you say, guys? Ready for a little more exercise?"

Nelson picked a spot along the narrow ridge sixty meters west of the NDP. "Got enough for four trees." –Nelson took out a spool of det-cord– "Pick 'em out, Ski."

Nelson wrapped the cord several times near the base of Ski's first pick, a tulip tree with a trunk the size of a man's thigh. He cut the cord, connected the end to a wire and unrolled enough to give him safe distance before hooking the end to a clacker.

"Fire in the hole!" he yelled, and the blast splintered the tree at the cord. The other three were dropped in like fashion, after which we shed our shirts to begin the job of clearing anything over waist high. The elusive clouds wouldn't give us a break from the afternoon sun, and by three-thirty we returned to camp with wood chips and dirt coating sweat-drenched bodies.

"What a motherfuck," Ski passed to Harv, watching us come in as he burned a cig.

Nelson threw down his machete. "LZ Hardtack. That's what that bastard is. Like trying to cut rock."

Hillbilly stood up. "So when we a gonna use this *LZ Hardtack*, TR?"

"Got a bird scheduled tomorrow morning–"

I tune out of the conversation to take care of more immediate needs. After toweling off the past few hours, I lay my head on the edge of my mattress. Before nodding off, a shiver slides up my spine that blinks my eyes open. I look up. The leaves above sway from a sudden shift in the wind. It doesn't bode well with me. I close my eyes again and it is a long while before I fall into *a troubled slumber....*

184

*...11:10 a.m., Monday, July 4, 1988, East Moline, Illinois...My tripping heart* slows me to a walk as I clasp my hands behind my head. *Not enough air! Got to breathe! Remember-how-to-breathe! Get more air in my lungs!* I stand still and wait. Soon my heart steps down to normal as a rush of calm washes away the biting tension gripping my mind. *Just oxygen debt, that's all....*

# DETONATION
## PART III

Monday, January 11, 1971, Day 82 / 283 to DEROS
—California spirit—

*July, 1963...* 🖎*All Danny and* I can do is watch. It doesn't take long either. Stupid Stanley Gorsney has to use a ladder to get to the first branch. Then he scoots out on his butt to cut the ropes and push the logs to four bullies gawking below– Clark, Rasso, the Roberts boys. Hooting and strutting like they're all hot stuff, hollering at Danny and me where we stand in the empty lot. *I should go over there. Should attack those creeps with my Tarzan yell and plow into the middle of 'em 'steada standing here. I'm not scared...just can't believe somebody'd do such a creepy thing. I never bothered 'em. Why'd they do this?...*✎

      *...TR announced he* needed one more volunteer for the re-supply bird.

Nelson cocked an eye at me with a mouthful of fruit cocktail. "Wanna help with the RS?"

"I dunno. Lemme get my boots on."

A muffled shout from Hillbilly, "Where's that other guy?! Bird's in the air!"

I struggled with my bootlaces as Hippie, in the next hootch over, grabbed his 16 and bandoleer, mumbling to no one in particular that he'd go. I breathed a sigh of relief, but a sting of guilt slid up my spine; I noticed his untied bootlaces whipping the air as he hurried past me. *Guy doesn't know I shoulda went.* I relaxed my grip on my bootlaces. *Now I can fix myself a nice*

187

*leisurely breakfast and then write a letter or two. Should get bookoo letters com–*

*KLAAAAMMMMMMMMMMMM!...*

✎...*2:16 p.m., Tuesday, August 2, 1988 Andalusia bottomlands...* "*Waddya think?*"

I gazed for a long moment through a faint mist guarding the swamp's crusty surface. My diaphragm wouldn't let me take in a full breath; maybe it was the vaguely familiar odor wafting from the brown water– I wasn't sure. "Let's radio back. Let 'em drive around and pick us up on that road over there."

Karl followed my finger to a graveled farm road hugging the base of the Mississippi Valley bluff. "Fuck, I don't wanna wait."

Kyle nodded in agreement. "Let's get it over with."

I didn't say anything as they picked up their survey gear and waded into the quagmire. Taking a last look at the gravel road, I sank my Army surplus jungle boots into the spongy grass that matted the swamp's floor. *Why did we need this anyway? Coulda guesstimated it. Bullshit engineers. Draw a line anywhere across their little maps....* I squinted into the hot sun. *What'd they say at lunch, ninety-six?*

Karl picked up the pace, anxious to cover the hundred yards of decaying soup and get out. Kyle was ten feet ahead of me. I held my yellow fieldbook above the tepid surface, rising above my navel. *Man, this water stinks. At least the blister don't hurt. Stupid idiot, running home from church in my Sunday shoes...what, almost seven miles? Why do I always get so fucking mad? Had to limp the last mile.*

Kyle was fifteen feet ahead. *Ray saying I looked like an ice cream man.* The thought of me peddling ice cream in the church foyer marched through my mind. *Me wearing my white pants and white shirt and white....*

Kyle was thirty feet ahead. *Better catch up, gotta get outta this shit. Reminds me of those stinking paddies...be a sitt'n' duck if some VC....*

My pace degrades as Karl maneuvers toward a dark slit in a wall of sawgrass we'd macheted through after lunch. I squeeze my hand against the fieldbook. *Feel weird. Breathe.* Karl disappears through the slit as I make the shallow reeds. Kyle is close to the exit, not looking back as I struggle with each step. *Legs...heavy.* I look up– no more Kyle. *Move...move your legs.*

*One more step. One more. One.... Dizzy. So stifling, nose burns. Gotta get air in me. Breathe!...✐*

*...Pressing my body* to the moist earth– I know. As Wad throws himself out of the hootch and triggers his 60– I know. While TR spills his cup of instant Sanka on his lap while trying to grab his 16– I know, and I close my eyes.

"Fucking Christ," breathes Blondie, "dink hit our MA."

*GOD! My fault...lazy...stupid...bastard! MY FAULT!*

"Was that our MA?!" I hear Hillbilly shout. *What's wrong with me? I know what happened. TELL THEM!* Everyone stares down the trail. I hang my head.

"IT'S A GI!" Hillbilly shouts. "Bring a poncho!"

I don't move as bewildered eyes dart around camp, trying to decipher who is missing. Spanky tears a poncho from the back of his hootch and runs out of the perimeter. Doc snatches his first aid bag and follows close behind. Ski drops his cigarette, letting it die at his feet.

"Who is it?!" TR shouts.

"Looks like Hippie...he's torn up good!"

"How the fuck did he end up there?" Buffalo growls at TR.

"Must've been trying to find the LZ."

*I knew where the LZ was. I CUT IT!* I stare into the ground. *I wouldn't a taken the wrong trail. I wouldn't a–*

"Get that bird in here!" TR orders and then to no one, "Why wasn't that MA *unhooked this morning?"...*

✐*...2:29 p.m. Andalusia...I key the* mike. "Something's wrong. Feel weird."

*"What is it?"*

"Dizzy. Can't get my breath...I...I can't move." Thirty seconds pass. I strain to suck in air. *Don't pass out.* I feel the blood rushing from my head. A forest of needles stab my wrists. I lean forward and place numb hands on my knees. Another minute. I hear motion.

"Hey, man," –Kyle wades toward me from the grass slit– "you okay?"

"Feel funny. Legs like stumps. Shaky. Can't move them."

Kyle takes my fieldbook and starts to open his canteen. "You want a drink?"

189

"Not thirsty."

"*Is Adams okay?*" –Kyle takes the radio from around my neck– "I dunno what's wrong."

"*Cripe thinks it's heat prostration. Maybe throw water over him.*" –a pause, then Karl– "*No, Kyle, don't go throwing water on him. I'm coming down.*"

*What's going on? Scared? Yes. I'm scared. But I'm ready for this. I've always been ready, ever since....* I smile through my fear at Kyle. "It's okay, man. Don't worr–" My jaws clench. A swell of convulsions consume my body. Kyle hugs my chest to keep me from falling. My body turns to stone. My arms fling into the air as if trying to pull out of the black water. *He's telling me it's okay. He's saying my heart's flying. He's telling Karl to hurry.* I look beyond Kyle's clatter. *I never noticed those hills across the river. I never took the time to look above the weeds. What are those specks under those trees? Cows? Trying to get out of the heat? I don't blame them; we should be there, too. I'm not afraid. I'm ready to die. What a stupid way to go, though. But it's okay. At last I can rest. I'm so tired.*

Karl crashes through the opening. "Hurry up, man!" Kyle shouts. "Gotta get him outta here!"

"Hey, Bob," Karl chops, "it's gonna to be okay. Gonna getcha out of here." They pull my stiff arms around their shoulders and start to drag me. My hands fling out *like a scarecrow....*

&#9758; *...January, 1955...*"*I no wanna* die!" I get in corner and feel all like fire inside.

"What, honey?" Mama stop making food and get by me. "You're not going to die."

"Yes I is Mama! Kent say I is!" Uncle Bill come in and get by me, too.

"Am. It's, 'I am,' Bobby and no, no you're not going to die, not for a long, long, loooong time. You don't have to be afraid, sweetie."

"What heaven like, Mama?"

"Oh, it's a wonderful place. People never grow old and never get sick. They're happy all the time."

"What it look like, Mama?"

"Well, it's a beautiful place. The sun is always shining, all of the streets are made of gold and everybody lives in big palaces...like castles."

"Will me be with you, Mama?"

"It's 'I,' Bobby and of course you will. All of us will be together. You don't have *to be afraid.*"...🖉

...*After that I* supposed they scooped Hippie onto the poncho and hauled him to the LZ. I could hear the chopper coming, its pilot unaware he would be leaving with a guy that shouldn't have had to go. A guy that should've come back carrying C's, ready for a smoke over a can of boned chicken and a perfumed letter from home. I imagine the chopper crew threw out its cargo and helped drag the shredded GI inside. Perhaps the gunner looked at the Grunts and wondered what the hell had happened on this quiet mountaintop. They came back then. Hippie's blood was splattered on them from the whirling chopper blades. I didn't want to hear Hillbilly compare Hippie's mid-section to ground hamburger. Didn't want to hear him say how he was blown out of his unlaced boots. I watched them stack the C's at the CP, along with my letters from home I had planned to read after breakfast. I suppose Hippie's perfumed letter was there, too. The re-supply crew returned to their hootch to clean up. Although I was already clean, I had never felt dirtier.

Tuesday, January 12, 1971, Day 83 / 282 to DEROS
—last rites—

*Sher –*                                            *Tuesday, January 12th, 1971*
*It is okay to call you Sher isn't it? I'm really glad you wrote cause nobody else seems to be at the moment & it can get kinda lonesome. I liked you're letter and the way you write. And if you had trouble writting the way I had trouble writting to you, I guess it did seem awkward, kinda dizzy?*

*That snowstorm you had the 2nd & 3rd must have really been cool. Wish I was there to go tobogganing with the BYF. Believe it or not it's been kinda chilly here the past couple weeks, specially at night. Monsoon should be over by the end of the month though & wow, it will get hot!*

*Well, as of this moment I'm in a little hooch in Dragon Valley. Dusk is coming on. I must admit, the platoon & I are quite scared. We're on top of a high ridge overlooking the valley. Not much danger up here but down in the valley there's a lot of booby-traps & other companies are getting messed up. So bad in fact we have to fly down tomorrow on choppers. And give em' a hand! Oh well....*

I rubbed my eyes, straining to see in the near dark as thick rain clouds cut short the evening light. We were supposed to have gone into the valley this morning, but an unexpected front moved in that made the CA too risky. We would try again tomorrow. We had a bad feeling about this one, so much so that a few of the guys had requested a priest be flown out to give us last rites. Higher-Higher, though, didn't think it was worth the risk.

The diminishing rain left a dampness that chilled our isolated mountaintop as I finished the letter and huddled under my poncho liner, tucking the end under my stocking feet as darkness enveloped us.

*What am I gonna do?* This morning Battalion HQ sent word that while they were taking Hippie off the chopper he...fell into two pieces. I stared at the ceiling in the hootch, seeing Hippie's broken body bursting apart over and over– seeing myself lying there and doing nothing. It was a long while before my mind would *let me sleep....*

✎*...2:51 p.m. Andalusia...*"*I'm feeling better* now."

They had helped me to the side of the skiff where the river's current eddied around my body. It felt good. I baked on a reassuring smile to old man Cripe, chewing on a camel straight as his bloodshot eyes gazed at mine.

"I dunno what happened."

"Heat prostration," Cripe told Karl as if I was still frozen in the swamp.

"Maybe swamp gas," Kyle threw back. "I mean, it *stunk* in there."

"You want a drink?" Karen offered.

"Okay." My wrists were still numb, but better. "Hey, thanks for pulling me out."

Karl jumped in the skiff. "Fuck, Bob, what would Long say if I didn't come back with my *damn crew chief?*"...✐

Wednesday, January 13, 1971, Day 84 / 281 to DEROS
—into the valley—

The sweat dried on my face as we gained altitude; the morning air was already hot and sticky, and as the bird lifted off the peak, my spirits did too– for I was grateful to be leaving that awful place. I stole a glance at where our old NDP lay under the mess of trees and vowed to leave it and its bad memories buried there beneath the foliage. Within a minute we were high above the tentacled valley and I started to take my camera out when I remembered the last shot I'd taken on the flight out, with Hippie silhouetted in the foreground. "Maybe later," I said aloud. Instead, I got a bead on the layout of the valley, which consisted of low narrow ridges running in odd angles with the main ridgeline, unlike the two predominately parallel ridges that framed Ky Tra's vast valley. I could see its strategic advantage for Charlie– bookoo hiding places.

The choppers set down at the edge of a dry field of sawgrass. Falling in behind Wad, we worked along the edge of several stubby hills that appeared to have been burned off in the not too distant past. The day was dry, as was the wide hard-packed trail and it wasn't long before we neared our day's goal.

TR stalled us at the base of a small rise where he engaged in a stream of radio communication. Twenty minutes later Ski pointed toward an approaching platoon. I recognized them as First.

Jimmy Ross, from Nichols' old squad, decided to stay with Wad and me. He'd been the odd man out ever since Nichols and his sidekick had left and had stayed in whomever's hootch could accommodate him. We were already down to twenty-three men– perhaps the reason we had hooked up with First.

With no patrol scheduled for the afternoon, I had a chance to start one of the projects I had brainstormed in the rear. I donned an extra pair of fatigues I had brought along, pulled the material tight on the sides of my legs and placed a mark on each side of the crease. Putting my other fatigues back on, I took out my sewing kit to began the lengthy job of sewing ten pairs of eyelets on the outside of each leg.

Thursday, January 14, 1971, Day 85 / 280 to DEROS
—ancient battlegrounds—

"Good shit, huh?"

I forked in a spoonful of mashed potatoes, savoring its heavenly taste. "Numba one, Ski." I flipped the letter from Sandy Johnson over to continue reading. I had taken a chance and dropped her a letter a month back, not thinking she'd write back. I mean, she didn't even *know* me. But I knew her– from a distance. Homecoming queen, straight sunshiny blond hair falling to the small of her back– face of a goddess. I had always been too shy to say anything to her. Instead I'd gawk as she sat cheering from the bleachers at the basketball games. Never got up the nerve– just like me.

This morning's hot chow, along with the letter from Miss Johnson, got me to feeling like my old self again. I was more than ready for a patrol. Our squad was teaming up with Hillbilly's and since Retchin was taking his 60 instead of Wad, I was relieved of carrying his ammo. I coaxed Ski into letting me take drag, which was the position I'd come to favor.

At the bottom of our hill we took a small trail, skirting eroding artillery craters from past battles the dense foliage couldn't obliterate. Occasionally we'd happen upon rusted chunks of exploded bombs laying half-buried in the earth. Hillbilly made sure to point out each one that encroached the trail, cautioning us not to let curiosity get the best of us and pick anything up.

At a heavily forested section of the trail an undetonated 1000-pound bomb lay partially buried with its tail jutting into our path. It was a few minutes before Hillbilly could coax TR into going around it. I judged it was over six feet in length with a two-foot diameter. *What a battle this must have been...Dragon Valley...maybe it got its name from all the fire it once breathed.*

It was a long patrol, not returning to camp until four. But it was good for my soul. Some dark clouds had leapfrogged into the next valley, which, from the looks of it, was getting our share of the rain. So, with a dry evening ahead, I pulled out my fatigues to do more stitching and responded to the curious stares with a, "You'll see."

Friday, January 15, 1971, Day 86 / 279 to DEROS
—dig it—

*WHOOOOOSSSHHHHHHHHHHHHH–*

"Mocko, get dow–!"

*–WAAAAAAAAAMMMMMMMMMM!*

Mocko gets the message as the shell splinters just outside the NDP. He squats awkwardly; even now his delirious smile pasted on his face.

*That's two.* The scream of air rushing from me slams my eyes shut.

*–WAAAAAAAAAMMMMMMMMMM!*

The earth dominoes beneath me and I raise my head in a rain of dirt and smoke. *I'm okay!* I see Mocko, still squatting by his hootch.

"Aim's gitt'n' better!" Hillbilly shouts. "Charlie gits nine points on that un'!"

*That's three.*

Another rush pulls me to the fetal position. *NO!* Two rockets thunder in, splintering wood behind me as a gale of leaves blow over me.

All is silent.

"...can't call in damn artillery if I don't know where it's coming from!" TR argued with First Platoon's LT as the blast died away. Now that our NDP had a big bull's-eye pinned on it, they decided to request a move. Word returned to stay put– Third was conducting a patrol nearby. They hoped that by us staying, the patrol could detect the source of fire if the VC opened up again. "So we're the guinea pigs?" TR asked Buffalo.

"You're beginning to figure out how things work around here, TR."

TR shook his head. "Listen up, men. Look's like we're staying the night, so we'd better dig in. I want a three-man foxhole in front of every hootch by 1500."

He got no complaints.

Wad drew a line in the hard soil with his E-tool to mark the hole's dimensions and rotating turns, we dug, chopped and hacked four feet into the earth, ending half-an-hour before TR's deadline.

"Imagine doing this every fucking day," Ross puffed after finishing his shift.

"Just hope this don't become some regular shit detail," Wad answered. "You know how it is with lifers after something gets started...they don't fucking know when to quit."

Ross smiled, wiping some sweat off his chin. "Don't hafta worry. You forget... TR's gotta dig one, too."

Saturday, January 16, 1971, Day 87 / 278 to DEROS<br>—in the nick of time—

No more rockets came. By eight o'clock we were hooked up, in case Charlie decided to hump more in for a replay. They did– not ten minutes after leaving we heard the *WHOOSH* of mortars soaring over us and exploding in the vicinity of the NDP. Another ten minutes and three more ripped over our heads. This time, though, we detected the faint "ploomp" of a rocket launcher somewhere on the ridgeline to our north. TR called in a fire-mission and minutes later a dozen *105*'s smashed into the ridge. I doubted they had found their target, though, since our directions were sketchy. Nonetheless, they must have gotten the message– they didn't fire any more on our two-klick hump west, following a thin stream and by noon, we began to wind up a large shallow-sloped hill, keeping to the northern side since its western slope was burned clean from napalming. Its top still held to a thick shock of trees and it looked to TR like a good spot to run patrols for a day or two.

This time I traded with Yoss and bunked with Nelson and Ski. To be honest, I was getting tired of humping 600 rounds of ammo for Wad. The position was less than glorious and I was beginning to feel more like a pack mule than a combat infantryman. So, maybe if I hooked up with my old roomies, Ross or someone else would take the hint– I hoped.

### Sunday, January 17, 1971, Day 88 / 277 to DEROS
### —23 minus 2—

Another dry morning greeted us. Ski and I were preparing our breakfast of beefsteak and turkey loaf, watching as First Platoon packed to head out.

"Wonder where they're heading?" I asked, distracted by Nelson's fumbling attempt to crawl out of the hootch.

Ski glanced at Nelson, did a double take and stared at his face. "What the fuck happened to your eye?"

Nelson rubbed a knuckle on it. "Can hardly see out of it. Let me see your mirror, Adams."

Nelson frowned at the reflection of his red, swollen eye. "Looks like shit." He got up and headed for Doc's hootch.

"Looks like that man is going in," Ski said. "Fucking guard is getting longer every night."

We didn't feel sorry for Nelson. We envied him. Any chance to get to the rear was a welcome one, barring, of course, Hippie's case. Doc diagnosed Nelson as having an eye infection, not from an insect bite but from one of the hundreds of strange bacteria roaming the equatorial ring. At ten-thirty Nelson climbed aboard a re-supply chopper along with Retchin, who was due for an R&R in Bangkok. First Platoon split soon afterward, leaving us with twenty-one men.

# DETONATION

—rooky bait—

"Wake up. Damn it, Adams, wake up. You're talking in your sleep."

"Wha...?" Wad's silhouette backed out of the hootch. Crickets chirping in the dead of night brought me back. Turning on my side, I noticed the bare floor where Nelson usually slept. I missed him– my mentor.

At 8:10, the dry leaf-like buzz from an army of grasshoppers pulled me out of a dreamless sleep.

"How far we going today?" I asked, crawling outside. Yoss had already downed half a cup of coffee while stirring a can of beefsteak.

Yoss paused before taking another sip. "Hooking up with First again. TR thinks we're too short-handed to be safe."

"Nothing wrong with that." Like a pro I tore off a chunk of C-4, the exact size to heat a medium-sized can of C's.

"Who's gonna play squad leader today?" Ski asked, sticking his head out of the hootch. "You, Yoss?"

"You're more than qualified, Ski."

Ski headed for his morning leak. "Just thought you'd like to move up in the world, that's all."

"*Shut* the *fuck* up," Ross scolded from inside his tent, "a guy can't get any sleep."

"Too late for that," –Wad was returning from the CP– "time ta get moving."

Minutes later, word came to stay put; First Platoon had received a wake up call: mortar fire. Right now a patrol from Third platoon was heading for its source. First was to send a patrol to flank and support Third should the need arise.

Nearing the noon hour, the CP gave word to go.

Leaning over to adjust my ruck, I waited in line for the point man to hack through the thick brush bordering the western side of the virgin treeline. After that, it was nothing but short grass in the rocky soil that stretched to the bottom where an abandoned potato field waited. Baby-stepping into my shadow, my mind was occupied with how to resign as AG. *Maybe Fritts will take it back.* I doubted he would fall for it, though– best to get a rookie who didn't know any better.

197

Making my way through the thinning bushes, a small cloud of dust pops close to my foot.

Ross is walking slack and hears a clink under his web belt. "Hey, looky, guys. My canteen's leaking." He smiles, watching a thin stream of water ebb through the canvas. Two more puffs at Ross' feet triggers in my mind what is happening.

Blondie, who is figuring it out, too, attempts to shout, "AMBUSH!" But all that comes out is an empty wheeze. "We got incoming!" He yelps, regaining his tenor. He cups his hands. "TR, get up here!"

"Let me by!" Wad snaps, squirming around a bush. I watch him lift the sling off his shoulder and step in front of me while attempting to lower his tripod. He stumbles, nearly dropping his 60. Our attention is drawn to his leg; a jagged hole appears in the middle of his right thigh. Its frayed edge turns red as the blot increases in diameter.

"GOD! I'M HIT!" He shrieks like a kicked dog as he falls to his knees.

"MEDIC!" –I fight for another scream– "WAD'S HIT!"

"Christ, get the other gunner up here!" Blondie screams. And then softer, "Where's fuck'n' LT?"

Doc rushes to Wad's side. I squeeze in front of them and drop my ruck. *Where's it coming from! I can't hear nothing!*

"Get a dust-off in here!" Doc shouts. TR moves past me with Tuck on his heels. He finds a few small bushes to hide behind before grappling to unhook the phone.

Doc pulls a syrette of morphine out of his med-bag, pops the cap, sticks it into Wad's hip and squeezes the drug in. "Looks like you're gonna get your ass out of the shit, Wad. How you gonna act?"

"It fucking hurts, Doc."

"Bird's on its way. You're gonna be okay." –he ties a combat bandage around the wound– "Now let the juice work. You'll be higher than the colonel in a few minutes."

Dust explodes around us as Wright and Chadborne move up next to me.

"Where they at?" –Wright swings forward his 60– "SHIT!" –I jerk my eyes at his bloody crotch– "Whatha...? Fuck, Doc. I'm hit."

Staring at Wright's red crotch a gush of warm blood splatters my face and arm. At the same instant, Chadborne doubles over and clutches his right leg.

Wright staggers, trying to hold his 60 and upright himself. He rattles a laugh. "Don't hurt a bit." –he sits down; his 60 rolls to the ground; he looks at me with a crazy grin– "I am going back to the World, Mr. Adams."

I wipe Wright's blood from my arm and squat behind my ruck, my heart looking for the quickest way out of my ribcage as I listen to Wad begging for the pain to go away. *This is it. We're all gonna die! We're all gonna die!* I lower my head behind my ruck– it never dawns on me to pick up Wad's 60.

TR fumbles his grid map, banging out numbers for a dust-off while trying to re-chamber his 16.

"Fuck!" TR spits as the slide on his 16 jams.

"TR!" I yell, opening a side pocket on my ruck. "Catch!" I toss a small can of WD-40.

Catching it, he sprays the slide and pulls back the cocking handle. It falls into place, running smoothly as it ejects the unspent cartridge.

"*Thank you,* Adams!" –he re-chambers a round– "You deserve a medal for that!" He turns toward the valley and lets off a burst of three.

*I can't hide behind this ruck all day!* My thought burns off enough fear to low-crawl it to the bushes by TR. I point my 16 and let off a clip into the treeline on the opposite side of the wide valley. *TAKE THAT, YOU FUCKING DINKS!* "Where they at, TR?"

"I don't know," –he grabs his grid map again to call in an artillery strike– "maybe on the edge of that treeline."

Doc turns, catching in his glance Wright's bloody crotch and arm.

Spurlin low-crawls to Wright and drags the 60 to his position next to Spanky.

"Where's the extra ammo?" Spanky asks.

"Fuck, I forgot." Sperling spots Hillbilly coming down the trail in a crouching run with two others from his squad. "Hillbilly! Grab Chadborne's ammo and barrel bag!" Hillbilly pulls the ordinance off Chadborne and does a feet-first slide into Spurlin's position.

"Enyth'n' else I kin hep ya with?" –he swings his 16 to his eye– "Whacha firing at?"

Doc turns Wright over and pushes a compress into the wound. "Keep that right there and don't let go. And don't sit up, I'm counting on you, man." He moves to Chadborne, who is holding a bloody towel over the upper part of his thigh.

"I'll be okay, Doc. Take care of Wad."

Wad rolls onto his back, bringing up his good leg. "It hurts, Doc. It hurts!"

"Okay, I'll give you another shot. But no more. Don't want you turning into a junkie."

"Chopper!" Blondie yells from behind the hot muzzle of his 16. Shimmering in the morning's heat, a lone dust-off beats in from the northeast, hugging the ground as it turns up the shallow valley in front of us.

"Gimme your poncho!" Hillbilly commands Ross.

The chopper blows a hurricane of dust at us as Spanky, Hillbilly, Ross and Blondie lift Wad onto the poncho. Doc assists Wright and Chadborne; the others rush Wad to the cabin. Two medics pull him in and Hillbilly snaps a thumbs up. Twenty seconds and it's on a reciprocal course.

"I'm hit!" Spurlin cries out over the departing chopper. He grabs his right arm and drops the 60.

Blondie notices the angle of trajectory from Spurlin's wound isn't quite right. "FAAAA–!" –his scream breaks– he detects a faint rattling across the stream from where we had humped up yesterday– "They got us in a cross fire!" –white fear sears my lungs as his words slam into me– "They're firing at us from across the creek!" Blondie shrieks, pointing north.

We try to protect ourselves, but it's impossible to find concealment from both west and north. They'll cut us down one by one unless we nail them with artillery. TR is calling off coordinates. "No smoke!" he shouts into the phone, "Just DROP IT!"

"Here they come!" Hillbilly cries as the resonance of eight-inchers streak toward us.

Behind me several more GI's approach from the treeline as the first round blasts the base of our hill. I stare wide-eyed as they work their way toward us.

*VROOOOOOOMMMMMMMMMM!*

We press into the ground as the last round slams into the earth fifty meters below us. "CHECK FIRE! CHECK FIRE!" TR screams into the phone. Checking his fire grid, he discovers the mistake was his– transposing the last two numbers on his grease-smeared map. Hot lead from an AK-47 rips through the flesh in Spanky's left forearm as TR calls in a correction and holds his breath. A second barrage streaks into the valley. It slams into the creek, the potato field, the treeline on the far side.

"*FIRE! FIRE! FIRE!*"...

✎*...12:24 p.m., Tuesday, August 16, 1988, Little Maud Campground, CO...The pine-scented* air buoyed my spirits as I carried my five-year-old, Craig, up the mountain trail in his yellow backpacking seat. Our tent was still visible through the mountain foliage. Stefanie, my youngest daughter, was playing tag near the creek with her cousin, Gloria. Jennifer, my oldest, wore a bored look, visible even from here as she sulked in a lawn chair.

"How you doing, buddy?"

"I'm hungry."

"Cool. I brought some treats."

"What, Daddy?"

"You'll see. It's a surprise."

A steep ten minute hump took us to a clearing at a bend in the trail on a rocky ledge. I was breathing hard, this being only my fourth day in the thin mountain air. Our first night was spent at an off-season ski motel at Steamboat Springs. After checking in, I had started on my usual run. Two blocks later my lungs were burning. But I had kept on. By the time I'd covered a mile, I had to stop as a stitch hit me deep within the center of my chest. It scared me. But after the attack in the swamp, what didn't?

I force several deep breaths. "Let's get you down. Daddy's feeling funny."

I sit down and squeeze my tingling nose. *What if something happens to me, with Craig? He'd be lost and....* The thought sends me rising on shaky feet. *Can't breathe, chest tight, like the swamp...dizzy, wrists numb, heart's....*

"We gotta go back."

"What's wrong, Daddy?"

I don't answer. *I can't carry him. I'll die!* "You walk ahead of Daddy, okay? Can you follow the path?" *Can't breathe. Gotta get my son back before I die!*

We start back. The empty backpack weighs me down. *Can barely keep up with him.* "Keep on the path, Craigy." *God, what he must be thinking. Don't pass out. Please, God, I can't pass out! He'll be lost. My legs...like stumps.*

*Keep moving...please! Can't think...I'm losing it. I'm losing it! This is the end! I know it I know it I know it!*

*There's the switchback! That's where I can see the tent. If I can just make it to there....*✐

\*     \*     \*

*...It was over.* I gained my feet and looked at my watch. Tapping its face, I was sure it had stopped at 12:10– but it was okay. *The whole thing started twenty minutes ago?* Making the treeline that led back to our NDP, I turned and looked at the barren stretch below. *If they had waited just a few more minutes...woulda wiped us out.* I turned and let the trees *swallow me up....*

✐*... Little Maud Campground... I see the tent!* I smile. *God, I feel better. I can breathe again. Must be the altitude, not used to it yet.* "Come on, buddy," –I swing the backpack to the ground– "lemme carry ya the rest *of the way."*...✐

..."*What do ya* think, Doc, Purple Heart?" Doc turned my arm, checking for more shrapnel after wiping off Wright's blood.

"All you got is one little piece in your bicep, Adams. Should work its way out in a week or so. Don't worry about it." –he smeared on antiseptic and applied a bandage– "Keep it clean so it don't get infected."

"Yeah, Doc, no problem. Spanky and Spurlin gonna be okay?"

"They'll be back in a couple of weeks, humping it with the rest of us." He headed over to the wounded duo, who were talking to TR. Blondie and Ross were downing several small trees to increase the diameter in a sparse section of the forest canopy, for another medivac was on its way– this one equipped with a device that could be lowered through the trees to avoid having to pick them up in open terrain.

Tuck informed TR that the bird was only a few minutes out. "Somebody pop smoke," TR ordered. Larry had already rigged up a smoke grenade wedged into the top of an empty C-ration can. He pulled the pin and a thick cloud of purple smoke began to filter through the trees above. Proud of by his clever stunt, he walked the smoking grenade around the camp.

"Larry!" Doc scolded, pointing him toward the area designated for the pick-up. "Stay right there!"

"I do what TR say! I pop smoke!" He answered in protest, though he did stay where Doc had told him.

Soon we heard turbines humming above us as Tuck confirmed with the pilot the smoke's color. I grabbed my camera from my ruck and peered through the leaves above. In a few seconds the medivac came into view and I spotted a metal arm that extended about four feet from the top of the cabin's starboard side. Hanging from the arm was a yellow, bullet-shaped object that TR had referred to as a jungle penetrator, about four feet long and attached to the end of a cable that was threaded to an electric wench inside the cabin. Beside the door gunners, two medics in white flight helmets waited to lower the device.

As the pilot hovered above the small hole in the canopy ceiling, one of the crewmen switched on the wench and lowered the penetrator through the trees, stopping at ground level on Tuck's command. Doc pulled down two arms that were folded vertically into the unit, forming two seats for the ride back up. Spank and Spurlin climbed on and interlocked their legs and their good arms. At Doc's command, Tuck radioed the chopper they were ready and the wounded pair were lifted through the trees. The seat clicked onto a track under the arm as it hit home, enabling the crewmen to slide our companions into the cabin.

As the sound of the chopper faded, TR looked at the remaining fifteen men. "Okay, listen up." –he studied his watch– "It's too late to make First Platoon's camp, so we're going to secure this hill tonight. Each squad take its old position and get some rest, because guard will be double of what you're used to. I don't want anybody dozing off."

Ski, Yoss and I set up our shelter. The loss of Wad was amplified since Ross had to move to Hillbilly's squad. Yoss immediately began clicking off a letter to who knows who while Ski, foregoing his usual attempts at ribbing Yoss, opted instead to knock off half-a-dozen cigarettes before retiring. I reassessed the day, replaying in my mind the scene of Wad falling as he stepped in front of me. The only conclusion I could draw was that the bullet had been meant for me. At that angle it probably would've hit my mid section. And now Wad was lying in the hospital with my bullet in him– and Hippie was lying in a body bag because I had been too lazy.

Tuesday, January 19, 1971, Day 90 / 275 to DEROS
—radio patrol—

Tuck clamped his hand over the phone. "Shutup! You wanna fuck this up?" Then into the phone, "Ahhhh, November Alpha, Echo Foxtrot, arrived checkpoint Tango 4, break."

*"Roger, Echo Foxtrot, Quebec 6, ETA ten zero mikes."*

"Roger Roger, gotcha Lima Charlie, out." –Tuck snapped his phone down, looking disgusted– "*Next* time we call in a checkpoint keep the *shit* down."

"Sorry 'bout that, Tuck," Blondie responded as he dealt another hand. "But you know running these patrols is hard work. Harv, you motherfuck, waddya bid?"

I checked my watch again: *3:46. Thirty more minutes and we should be clear.* After arriving at First Platoon's NDP, Higher-Higher had directed our platoons to conduct a search and destroy mission to scout out the NVA from yesterday's ambush. TR, conferring with First's LT, decided it would be too risky splitting the few remaining men. So, knowing the colonel would be listening in on the proceedings, they mapped out a bogus patrol.

TR jotted down the numbers for the next checkpoint. "Okay, Tuck, here's the ETA for Tango 5." –he stared at Tuck– "Why don't you act more out of breath next time."

"Shit, TR, I ain't no actor. Why don't *you* call it in?"

TR took the phone from Tuck and almost hyperventilated after taking a few deep breaths. Then he called in the confirmation for checkpoint Tango 5. A surge of laughter broke out from several GI's congregating outside one of the hootches, causing TR to throw his hand over the phone. "Ah, say again, November Alpha," he said as he motioned for silence. "Ah, last transmission not received. Ah, Charlie Papa Sierra 5, ETA, ah, one five mikes. Over." Not sure if he had made sense he slammed down the phone. He fell back on his ruck and lit up a Lucky Strike. "*Why* did I ever promise my father I'd follow in his footsteps?"

# STAND-DOWN FIVE

Wednesday, January 20, 1971, Day 91 / 274 to DEROS
—mud & water—

Fucking mud," Ski whines as he sinks up to his knees. "Why can't we pick a dry LZ for fucking once?"

TR shouts for us to hurry. We struggle through the morass, for the birds are already dipping to the surface. Unable to gain a solid footing, more than half of us fall in our scramble for the birds.

I climb inside and lean back as the birds lift us above the valley. The mud on my fatigues seems a fitting way to leave this valley. Anything that enters leaves tainted: Nelson, Spurlin, Spanky, Wright, Chadborne, Wad, Hippie– me. I check the bandage on my right bicep and wonder how close I had come to death– and how much longer I can evade it.

We ended up at the new re-train area in the middle of nowhere, but it didn't seem as bad this time. I shed my fatigues and jumped into my first shower in half a month. I was surprised by how a simple shower could lift my spirits.

After chow, I grabbed my stack of mail and retired to my cot to shuffle through my letters. I picked a letter from home. *Nothing much going on,* I thought while pecking through Mom's chicken scratching. *Man, wouldn't that be great. Just put in my eight hours, then have the rest of the day to do whatever. Maybe wet a line down at the dock, play b-ball and pool at the Toad's, or catch the Panthers playing down in Peoria or Bloomington. I could go for a lifetime of nothing much going on.* Ski barged into the room with word that they were gathering in Hillbilly's room. "Be right there, man." I stuffed my letters into my ammo can. *The lure of the magic smoke is strong,* I mused as I entered Hillbilly's abode.

Thursday, January 21, 1971, Day 92 / 273 to DEROS
—Purple Heartbreak—

Tying off the thread on the last eyelet, I took out four new bootlaces and crisscrossed them up the pant legs to the belt line. I pulled them on and drew the laces tight before tying them off at my hip. *Look 'n' good!* Satisfied with my tailoring, I took them off and stored them away for the next mission.

It was a busy day: a morning trip to the PX, boring classes in the afternoon and a letter writing spree before being served chow in a makeshift "picnic area" outside of Barrack Four. The clouds whipping above sent sand blowing through the compound that stung our flesh.

I spotted Fritts in line as he shielded the wind with his back.

"Hey, Fritts, good to have you back, man. Hear anything about Wad?"

"Yeah. Dude is taking it hard. It was a round from a 16 that hit him. Broke his thighbone in half...had to put a pin in it." –Fritts held out his tray– "Flies," he commented, noticing several black dots in his potatoes, "protein of the Grunts."

With full trays we retired to one of the picnic tables where Ski and Yoss sat stuffing their faces. For being such an antagonist in the bush, Ski still didn't mind hanging around Yoss, or Yoss him– their bond was deeper than either wanted to admit.

"Hey, Fritts, nice to have you back in our merry band of Grunts." –Ski raised his soda– "Here's to our fallen comrade risen from the rear." We tapped our cans in toast.

I forked in a large bite of potatoes, careful not to squish any of the flies– better to let them slide down.

"Fritts was telling me 'bout Wad. Sounds like he's screwed up pretty bad."

Fritts told his story again, adding that when the colonel had tried to pin the Purple Heart on him he threw it back and told him the whole fucking thing was bullshit.

"Fuck," Ski said, sliding his tray closer, "that's one messed up dude. He going home?"

"Oh yeah."

"How's Wright?"

"He'll be okay."

"His nuts weren't blown off?"

"He lucked out. Got 'im just below."

"Jeez," Yoss said while chewing on a morsel of roast beef, "so what about the others?"

"They'll be back...all flesh wounds. Oh yeah, Nelson's coming back and guess what? We're gett'n' some new guys."

Ski pushed back his tray and lit a Winston. "No shit? Maybe we can give Wad's gun to one of them, unless you want it, Mr. AG."

"*I* don't want it," I replied. "Hard enough to survive out there carrying a 16. Anyway," –I patted Fritts on the back– "*he* was AG before me."

"I don't *even* want nothing to do with that 60. And in case you weren't looking, both gunners *and* an AG are stretched out right now. But, since you *were* kinda forced into it," –Fritts thumbed at a deuce and a-half puffing into the compound– "maybe we can kill us two birds with one stone here."

The truck stopped and a dozen FNG's jumped to the ground, along with Nelson.

"Welcome to yer new home, boys!" –Hillbilly held up his grape soda– "Come grab some hot chow, man!" The FNG's stood like lost sheep, watching us stuff our mouths like wild animals until First Platoon's LT herded them toward the supply shed.

"Well," I said, picking a fly out of my chocolate pudding, "it'll be nice to have a full platoon again."

We got five of the twelve. Two filled in Spurlin's squad, soul brothers who soon found a home with Doc and Tuck as they traded their soul greeting. Slim, one of the FNG brothers, looked to be a prime candidate for the 60– tall and sturdy. He'd have no trouble hauling the big gun.

The other three were Jim Harding, Pat Sesnewski and Mike Vignola. Jim and Pat were assigned to Blondie's squad, replacing Wright and Hippie. We got Mike, filling in for Wad.

*　　*　　*

"You can grab a cot in here. Name's Adams...Bob Adams."

He lay his new ruck on Wad's cot and offered his hand. "Mike Vignola," he said in a guttural, almost whisper-like voice. "So I'm in your squad?"

"Yeah, but squad leader's Nelson Birch. He was the Grunt in the truck on your ride over. He's a good guy...you'll like him." –I sat on my cot– "Where you from?"

"Floral Park," he said, running fingers through steely black hair as thick as his physique. "It's a burg near Queens, in New York City."

"We got a guy in our squad from New York. From the Bronx."

"Yeah? That's pretty much in my back yard but hey, the Bronx is a whole other world."

\*   \*   \*

"Gentlemen." –Hillbilly paused to light his ivory pipe– "This first bowl I dedicate to the memory of Hippie, who died defend'n' our motherfuck'n' ideals of mom and apple pie." Hooking up to a rhythm in his head, he continued. "And who I know, would not deny, he'd ratha git high than take that gawdamn ride in the sky." –he passed the bowl to Pane– "So, we got us two new members, I see. Welcome to the Second Platoon Heads, man."

"This is Mike," –I nodded at him while taking the bowl from Pane– "and that's Pat." Pat gave Hillbilly a gangly smile that showed a mouthful of crooked teeth.

Ross leaned against the wall, crossing his arms behind him. "Where's your buddies at, man, didn't want to join the party?"

"Don't know about the brothers," Pat began, picking at a festering pimple on his chin, "but Tex don't smoke no dope."

"Tex?" Ross asked.

"Jim Harding, from our AIT unit at Polk."

"Got ourselves a Texan with us, huh?" Mocko broke in. "You know what they say 'bout Texans." –he paused as if originating the ancient slam– "Only two things come from Texas…steers and faggots."

"And which of 'em you be?" Hillbilly inquired. " A steer or a gawdamn queer?"

"I ain't no Texan."

"Well, maybe ya should consida chang'n' your gawdamn place of birth when ya git back to the World." Mocko's weird grin left him, but gained ground again as he took the bowl.

"Mocko," Ross inquired, "don't you ever wipe that shit-eating grin off your face?"

"Now, now, fellow Heads," Hillbilly stated while raising his hands like Moses parting the Red Sea. "Let's keep us a civilized tone. We're all on a mission from God hea, 'n' we hafta put our gawdamn differences behind us.

After all, eny one of us might hafta rescue our buddy's ass out there in the bush…'n' you know it."

We fell into silence after that, satisfied with the knowledge that the bowl would continue to glow late into the night and all that mattered to each of us would be preserved till morning light.

Friday, January 22, 1971, Day 93 / 272 to DEROS
—Monkey Man's bad old lady—

A face peeked in as the door cracked open. His leathery tanned, bearded face looked like he'd just come off the set of *Lawrence of Arabia*. "Hey, man, I hear this is where the party's at. Mind if I join?"

"Come on in, Monkey Man," Hillbilly said. "The more the merrier." I recognized him as the bearded guy who was kneeling over the fragged FNG several weeks ago.

"My platoon eats shit. Ain't a fucking head among 'em."

"Well, ya come to the right place. We are the 198th's *pride and joy.*"

Pat dug into a patch of dandruff under his black spaghettied hair. "How'd you get that name?"

"The dude goes apeshit over a hot plate of monkey meat," Hillbilly instructed.

"It's good shit, man." Monkey Man revealed a thick crop of coal-black hair as he removed a purple beret that accentuated his already dark persona. He picked up a tattered shoebox and removed the lid. "I knew you guys would appreciate this treat I got from my old lady." Nested in tin foil were several dozen chocolate chip cookies. "She baked these up special with some Cambodian Red I sent her a while back." –he took one and passed the box– "Shit will kick your ass, man."

The munchies were getting the best of me. I finished my second cookie, washing it down with my Coke before going for another. Meanwhile, Hillbilly kept the bowl glowing, this evening's stash procured from one of the village kids always looking for a sell by the perimeter wire. Hillbilly claimed it was laced with smack, whatever that was.

Monkey Man dominated most of the banter, rattling off a string of stories and by the second hour the conversation was echoing in my head. Not wanting to let on, I faked a smile as Monkey Man went on about a joke that had something to do with elves. Their laughter bounced off the walls, growing until it approached the screech of an incoming mortar round.

Monkey Man's face– it seems to glow. I chomp another bite, trying to make out his words, but they are no longer intelligible– just grunts, the grunts of a wild boar rooting through the guts of his kill.

The light from the room's lone bulb begins to fade. It flees Hillbilly, abandons Mocko, Pat and Mike, retreats from the cots, the ceiling, walls, floor, everything– everything but for the face of the Monkey Man. My stare cements to a trickle of blood that begins to slide from the dark man's eyes. It slides down his cheek and runs into his beard. Like a blast from hell's furnace the room turns to pitch– except for the glowing head of Monkey Man. The face of the devil. Bloody ivory planted in a charred skull over bobbing, laughing, red-stained face. Beard slick with Hippie's blood. Eyes yellowed with greed and staring into me with black slits that pierce my soul and lusts to add me to his plate.

*The DOOOOOOOOOOOOOR! Get out! Run! Words hitting me! I dunno what they are! Open the door! Open it! Open it! Close it!*

*Whoa...the floor...ain't even close to the ground, man. Wow! What was that monkey guy doing in there, man? Okay, okay, I got to act normal. I got to go outside and I got to act normal. Okay, there's the floor; where's the door? Walk slow, slow and act normal.*

*Oh no, here comes that new guy. Mex? Hex? No, Tex. Yeah. Tex, the steer, Tex, the queer from Tennessee. Here he comes. He's looking at me, man. He's gonna do it. He's gonna say something. There he goes, he talking at me and looking weird at me, man. Think of something. "Hi...man." I did it! He don't EVEN have no clue what it's all about. Now, get past the steer and go to the outside part of this place.*

*it          is          BEAUUUUTIFUL*

*Look at that sky. Feel that black wind. Dancing with my hair. Rushing on my face. Diving into my lungs. I'll go to the next place way over there. Ground so far away. Not feeling my legs at all. Floating. Floating in a tank. A glass tank. So smooth and so slow I can float anywhere I want. Nobody can see me or talk to me. Let's go into the night. Take me wind. Take me to your leader. Wow that big wall in the light. I see my shadow stuck on the wall. So black black. Hey shadow, Mr. Shadow-man, dance for me, if you will. Dance for me, my Shadow-man. Oh. Oh. Go. Yeah. Go. There he goes. I'm not moving, but my Shadow-man, he's dancing like a ghost. Don't eat me. Don't turn me to toast. I have to get away from my Shadow-ghost!*

*run*      *run*      *run*

I run from the wall and the dancing shadow retreats behind me. Stopping at a bunker by the deserted picnic area, I lie against the cool sandbags, and sleep.

\*     \*     \*

Monkey Man was gone and the room was empty. Everyone had gone. I walked the length of the barrack and exited the far end. I stopped. Hillbilly was sitting on top of the bunker, his legs squeezed to his chest, head pressed in his arms as he rocked back and forth. I slowly backed into the barrack and closed the door.

# MISSION SIX

Saturday, January 23, 1971, Day 94 / 271 to DEROS
—hook up Mocko—

I paused to admire my new image: laced up fatigues, Clint Eastwood hat, an assortment of beads, bracelets and headbands, sleeveless T-shirt, combat knife strapped to my hip– and no 60 ammo. A combat warrior: I was ready.

TR had passed over Slim as the new 60 gunner, wanting an experienced man instead. So without much coercing, Bromlow had volunteered to replace Wad and switched from Hillbilly's to Blondie's squad. Mocko volunteered to be his AG. *I wonder if Mocko's pasted-on smile will still be there after humping all day with twenty extra pounds on his back.*

"Hook up, motherfuckers, you're going to the bush!" Mocko proclaimed to no one as he leaned against the barrack's door. Scads of 60 ammo were draped around his neck– I swear he took it just to look cool.

Monkey Man was wandering among our ranks with a kitchen-sized can of peaches, trying to get rid of them by spoon-feeding anyone who'd take a bite.

211

The memory of his old lady's cookies prompted me to avoid his eye as I pretended to busy myself with my ruck.

We were full strength. Nelson was leading our squad again and the imposing Retchin was back on the 60. Langley would be his new assistant, stepping in for Chadborne. Another unexpected change occurred before trucking to Fat City. Buffalo was replaced by a new E-7– Sergeant Trainor. He was a thick, salty looking old dog with graying sideburns that tagged him in his forties. A voice like he'd swallowed a mouthful of rocks and a mean, timeworn scowl told us he'd put up with no guff. I had liked Buffalo and he had the full respect of the whole platoon. I would miss his rock solid confidence and *easy going manner....*

✎ *...Monday, September 26, 1988– Air Eater's Digest...*

Quincy, IL                                                        7 p.m.   68°
Ran 6.8 miles                                                  (1:01 07)

Dark thru Quincy Park, fear factor slowed me. I'm probably still leery from Colorado trip, plus tired from *Saturday's run home....*✎

*...It was a* short hop to our AO, this time to a section of the Northern Rocket Pocket in the foothills that preceded the foreboding mountains of the interior. Our mission was to check out several villes overdue for a pacification checkup and– I was ready for a mission with as few surprises as possible.

It was a dry landing on a thick brush-covered knoll and a short hump to our NDP on top of Rocket Ridge, the first ridgeline framing the expansive rice fields filling the Rocket Pocket like a chef's salad. In short order I was set up and preparing a hot lunch of boned chicken.

"Hey, Bob, what do you use to cook your C-rations?" Mike Vignola asked, pulling out a can of beefsteak.

I remembered when I had asked Yoss that very same question, just a few short months ago. Looking back at that first mission, it seemed no different than any other– like I had been here forever. "Look in my ruck, Mike, there's a bar of C-4 in there. Just tear off a hunk of it and roll it *into a ball....*"...

✎ *...Wednesday, September 28, 1988– Air Eater's Digest...*

Quincy, IL                                                        6:45 p.m.   75°
Ran 7.8 miles                                                  (1:01 19)

Equaled Monday's time even though 1 mi. further. Felt as if 2 different *people had ran. ...✐*

Tuesday, January 26, 1971, Day 97 / 268 to DEROS
—Sundance—

The last few days had found us working south along Rocket Ridge. We were scouting for VC trails that might lead toward the villages, readying to take on our primary role for the mission. The new guys stood out like unripe bananas next to the hardened Grunts– except Sergeant Trainor. He was working on his third tour and had seen more action than all of us combined.

No longer Wad's assistant, I was bumped up to walking slack and it was not a position I aspired to. They say the slackman is the most likely to hit a booby-trap– the pointman usually lucking out and leaving his cover man to eat his mistake. So it had been several long days of humping and by last evening, as we descended to establish our NDP in a grove of bamboo, I had earned myself a splitting headache. But if that had been the cost of the last few days, the reward was finding a new friend. Mike Vignola and I hit it off from the start, rapping through the evening hours, sharing our hopes and our dreams.

*       *       *

"Beautiful." Mike's square jaw stretched into a smile as we passed beneath an arched stone gate, each side topped with a RVN flag curling in the breeze.

A dozen chickens scratching for a morning meal scattered when TR halted us in front of several well-manicured flower gardens. "The sergeant and I will confer with the Honcho. We shouldn't be long."

Soon a flock of children surrounded us, always the first to overcome shyness, hoping for a handout of chocolate or other GI delicacy. We meandered with them through the courtyard, watching as the villagers busied themselves with trimming and cleaning in preparation for the Chinese New Year. By the central fountain, several mamasans were constructing a colorful green and yellow paper-mache` dragon for the upcoming Tet parade through Tam Ky.

"You cowboy?" asked one of the boys as I handed him my last chocolate bar.

I couldn't help grinning, imagining myself the Sundance Kid sauntering down Main Street. "I *bookoo* numba one cowboy. My name Bob. What your name?"

He grinned. "I Duc. I be you numba one fend."

"Okay, Duck, you be numba one friend...but I'm out of chocolate bars."

"That okay, Bub...*you still fend.*"...

✎...*Wednesday, October 5, 1988– Air Eater's Digest...*

Hannibal, Mo.                                   4:35 p.m.    60°

Ran 8 miles                                        (1:07 14)

If every run could be as this one. After an hour it was effortless, to sprint or whatever I *wanted...a joy!...*✎

Thursday, January 28, 1971, Day 99 / 266 to DEROS

—red at night—

*This has got to be paradise...* A rash of goose bumps retreated from my back as the sun cleared the last cloud. After a vigorous swim, my body sponged the heat from a sun-warmed boulder while watching Doc get the best of Duc and his friend, engaged in a water fight. I smiled at a nearby pagoda, where a satiny sunglow from its bleached tessellated stone wall threaded onto the velvety carpet-like grass at its base, clipped short by the Vietnamese cows roaming the countryside. ...*yes, paradise.*

After spending a good portion of yesterday munching through the village, we had again moved before nightfall. Closer to the village, we continued our monitoring by setting out a listening post– so far, so good.

"Duc," Doc said, standing bare-assed and reaching for his camera, "you take picture, okay?"

"Sho', Doc, I take pitcha. But you no have cos on."

"That's okay, Duc, you take picture." –Duc snapped off several flicks of Doc standing nude in the knee-deep water– "Just like the Garden of Eden, huh?"

I sat up. "You said it, Doc." A glimmer of light winked at me from below the surface of the stream. "Wow! Look at the fish."

"Now wouldn't that taste good for breakfast? Baked trout with a side of grits and red eye gravy."

My mouth watered at the thought. "Don't forget the orange juice."

"Fresh-squeezed grapefruit juice," Doc corrected, "served with crushed ice and a maraschino cherry."

"Man, Doc, you do live high."

"I can live anyway I want in my head, right, Duc?"

Duc was squatting on the bank, his head resting on crossed arms. "If you *say so, Doc.*"...

✎...*Friday, January 6, 1989– Air Eater's Digest*...

@ Home                                            5 p.m.   36° windy

Ran 7 miles                                       (0:59 28)

Bad run. Fear factor getting the best *of me. Sucked!*...✐

...*Duc led the* way back to our new NDP, retracing his tracks with ease through the maze of dikes that bordered the flourishing green fields. Before returning to camp, I stopped to take several flicks at a picturesque scene of a Vietnamese cow with her red calf standing in the middle of the path at the base of our hill.

"Hey, Doc!" Tuck yelled as he spotted us coming in. "Dust-off's been canceled. That other Doc can't make it out today."

Doc tossed his medic bag by our hootch. "Breaks my heart. Guess then it's sweet-ass R&R for the rest of the day."

In the last few days the continuity of our squad order had begun to erode. Doc and Mike were bunking with me and Ski had hooked up with Retchin and Langley. Yoss and Nelson were in the other hootch beside us, with Ross joining them. TR didn't seem to mind, though. In fact, there wasn't a whole lot that TR seemed to mind– a stark contrast to Lt. Owens' spit and polished ways.

Toward evening we moved again, partly for safety and partly for convenience. With the kids visiting our camp, our location was well known by the end of the day, so after their curfew we'd find a new location in case any VC had caught wind of our whereabouts. But also it made for a shorter hump to the village. We found a beautiful hill just outside of the ville, parallel to an adjoining rice paddy. From here we could see all around since only shrubs and grass surrounded our camp.

By seven-thirty, I was finishing up another letter to my phantom sweetheart, Sandy Johnson. *Wonder if I'll have the nerve to meet her if, I mean, when, I get outta here.* I sealed the envelope shut. *I hope so.*

Upon arriving at our new NDP, TR had asked if Doc, Ross and I would rotate with one other threesome for a listening post. It didn't sound bad since we wouldn't be by the main trail and wouldn't have to hassle with command-det claymores. Earlier, Sgt. Trainor had spotted an outcropping of boulders that overlooked the main trail just a short distance from camp, an ideal position to spot any mischief coming in or out of the ville. So as a cool evening breeze replaced the sun-baked air, we quietly walked the short distance to the appointed area. It was strange having Doc with us, he without a weapon, but being as high up as we were and concealed behind several large boulders, it seemed relatively safe. If we did spot anything suspicious, TR wanted one of us to hightail it back and report it anyway.

Having first watch, I crawled up one of the large boulders forming a natural ring around us and eased my head over the top.

The faraway lights of Chu Lai catch my attention first. *One of these days it's gonna be me sitting there instead of here.* I crawl forward enough to scan below where the trail skirts the base of the hill. "Damn," I whisper. A short distance from the trail was the distinct red glow of a cigarette. Staring at it for another few seconds to verify it was not an illusion, I ease down the rock.

"Doc, Ross, wake up." –they sit up in expectation– "Somebody's out there...smoking a cigarette."

"Keep an eye on 'im," Ross whispers. "I'll go tell TR." Ross disappears into the night.

"Come on, Doc. I'll show ya."

"I'm right behind you."

Doc peeks over the top. "Shit, I see *three*."

I thumb my safety as the breeze clicks up a few notches, causing me to shiver. I hear something behind me.

"Coming up." I look down as the whisper drifts up, seeing nothing at first until Blondie's yellow hair floats toward me.

Soon, Ross, Harv, Rickard, Pane and Tuck are stoically lined up with Doc and me on top of the granite.

"Waddya think?" Harv whispers.

"Jesus," Blondie says, "could be a whole battalion out there for all I know. Tuck, give me the horn."

Tuck crawls to within Blondie's reach. "Whacha gonna do, man?"

"Call in some fucking lums to get a light on this. Right now, we don't know shit. Could be three or three fucking hundred." Blondie takes the horn and ducks below the rock's apex to shield his voice.

"Charlie Papa, Charlie Papa, Echo Foxtrot. How copy. Break."

Ten seconds. *"Echo Foxtrot, Charlie Papa, got you Lima Charlie. Go."*

"Roger, Charlie Papa. Request lums at our November Papa. Break."

*"Roger, Echo Foxtrot."* –a five-second pause– *"Echo foxtrot. ETA zero three mikes. Go."*

"Roger, Charlie Papa, I copy. Out." –Blondie hands the phone back– "Okay, boys, when she's lit up, let 'er have it. I'll send smoke on those mafucks to confuse 'em." Rolling on his back, Blondie takes a smoke grenade from his web vest and gingerly opens his over-under to shove it home.

Dead silence. We lie like stone gargoyles. *They have no idea this is the last few seconds of their lives.* I flip to full auto and push my lips against the steel barrel and breathe a short prayer. I catch a glimpse of the glow, sometimes three, sometimes more. *They must be chain smoking, or–* The faraway thud from an artillery cannon hammers my heart. I brace my weapon against my shoulder.

*KRACK!*

The shell detonates a thousand feet above us; its incandescence transforms below a ghostly image of fast darting shadows– rats escaping a sinking ship.

A typhoon of sound encompasses me while blindly spraying my first magazine, breaking the cardinal rule by allowing adrenaline to do the firing. I throw in another clip and search for a target, but Blondie's smoke has obliterated the ground and makes it impossible to tell how many are down there. Red and orange flames flash through the smoke as Blondie now pummels the ground with HE grenades and overhead more lums ignite the sky with white light.

In minutes it is over. Only the dying crackling of the lums returning to earth can be heard. Then silence. No return fire.

Blondie let out a whoop. "We wasted those motherfucks, boys! Didn't *even* know what hit 'em!"

"That'll make 'em change their smoking habits," Pane exclaims.

We were all in high spirits. Back in camp, everyone was waiting for a report. Blondie conveyed to TR the mission was a complete success.

"Any confirmed kills?" Trainor inquired.

"We'll check it out in the morning," TR broke in. "No sense taking any unnecessary chances."

Sgt. Trainor looked skeptical. "Be too late by then, they'll be dragged off, only find a blood trail."

"We'll wait," TR said, *concluding the subject....*

✎ *...Wednesday, January 25, 1989– Air Eater's Digest...*

Arsenal to home                                    5:40 p.m.   29°
Ran 6.2 miles                                       (0:54 02)
Knees sore, rain, *dark, gloom, despair....* ✐

Friday, January 29, 1971, Day 100 / 265 to DEROS
—stuffed GI—

The mamasan pushed the plate in front of me. "You have *mo'* cookie?"

Patting my stomach, I pushed the plate away. "Much full now. Bookoo good, thank you."

"I can't do this again, man," I whispered to Nelson.

"No shit, isn't this our fifth meal?"

"Think we broke yesterday's record." I sipped on my mixed drink of *bac si de* and grape soda in a Loony Toons glass with Sylvester the Cat staring hungrily through the bars of Tweety Bird's cage. *This is one crazy war,* I thought, regarding a psychedelic blacklight poster hanging next to an intricate wood relief carving of a young Vietnamese girl sitting beside a pagoda decorated with delicate cherry blossoms. *One crazy war.*

The morning had been a complete embarrassment. After unhooking our MA, we ventured into our "kill zone" to search for bodies from last night's ambush. There were none. We searched for blood trails– none. Instead, we found two tree stumps, charred black by a recent lightning strike.

"So this here's yer VC, huh, boys?" Hillbilly bleated.

"Don't fucking add up," Blondie sputtered. Our eyes followed a trace of smoke rising from the stump's open wound. Several embers were glowing in its bowels, fanned by the morning breeze. The rest of the platoon got quite a laugh out of it. Now, as I sat in bloated misery, I couldn't resist grinning, engaged in a firefight with a tree stump, not the brightest thing *we'd ever done....*

# DETONATION

Hannibal, Mo.                                    5:40 p.m.   25° windy

Ran 5 miles                                              (0:45 00)

Slow & stupid. Scared. Last part though got back *some common sense.*...✐

### Saturday, January 30, 1971, Day 101 / 264 to DEROS
### —invasion of the food snatchers—

My eyes opened to the hubbub of children chattering in sing-song voices. Crawling outside, nearly a dozen of them were wandering through our positions. It had turned cool during the night and a gusty easterly wind was adding to the morning's chaotic beginnings.

"I no got C-ration," Nelson was saying as he staved off three of them seeking a handout. "You go see big guy." He pointed toward Retchin, sitting in front of his hootch, stirring instant coffee into his canteen cup. Nelson raised his voice an octave and looked wide-eyed at his tormentors. "He got bookoo food, bookoo candy! You go see now!"

As the kids ran off, TR was putting a stop to their mischievousness, making it clear that if they wished to stay they would have to stop begging and keep quiet; their banter could drive a GI insane within minutes. Setting them down, TR passed out crackers and chocolate disks Tuck had collected and told them a chopper was coming in and to sit back and watch the show.

The chopper arrived in short order. The kids sat rigid with fascination, unblinking eyes riveted to the chopper as it spun around to land into the wind. The medic from yesterday exited first, followed by cases of C's, mail and other supplies. What we most sought after, though, was a box full of banana clips, the 30-round magazines for our *16*'s we'd been promised. But there was a treat for us, too. A couple boxes of LRPS (lurps) were thrown off. It was a new type of freeze-dried rations packaged in waterproof canvas envelopes, a fraction of the weight of our C's. I managed to grab two before they disappeared.

"One apiece!" TR shouted as Blondie picked up the box of banana clips. "Save enough for the other squads." Yesterday, TR split our forces, sending Hillbilly's and Spurlin's squads across the paddy from us.

Once the supplies were unloaded, all of the soul brothers but Doc climbed aboard. The Miss Black America show was coming to Da Nang this evening and they had been granted permission to attend. Doc would be joining the brothers later when his work at the village was done. TR also decided to take advantage of the lull in action to attend some classes on combat tactics, though we knew that wasn't the real reason *for the sham.* ...

✎ *...Wednesday, May 17, 1989– Air Eater's Digest...*

| | |
|---|---|
| Morris, IL | 7:15 p.m.  81°gusty |
| Ran 7 miles | (0:56 15) |

Bummer! Too hot! Knees very sore. Had to walk *last half mile.* ... ✐

*...At ten o'clock,* eight of us headed for the ville. The flock of kids followed until they caught sight of their ville. Shouting *"Bac-si come! Bac-si come!"* they ran laughing through the gates.

Just a few patients remained for the Doc and the medic to examine, so I hung out on the honcho's patio and rapped with the kids while watching them perform their medical magic. Remembering that I'd brought along a couple of letters, I pulled one out from the "Greek", but it was impossible to concentrate due to the bombardment of attention thrown upon me by the enamored kids.

Noon came and so did the chopper. It dropped off several cases of C's to divvy up among the villagers, then swung toward Chu Lai with both Docs; ours was to continue to Da Nang to check out the black beauties. The NDP was quiet when we got back– only a handful remained since half of us were still parked on the other side of the rice paddy that shimmered below us in the afternoon heat. I decided that an afternoon nap would do me good. Mike had the same idea, so rigging our poncho liners to shade the sun off the front of our hootch, we settled in for an afternoon siesta.

Sunday, January 31, 1971, Day 102 / 263 to DEROS
—peace flag—

The wind shifted overnight, pushing muggy mountain air into our camp. Yesterday evening we had moved further from the village. Our forces were still divided, the other two squads mimicking our movements step for step before settling on a small knob at the base of Rocket Ridge. It was a hard hump for the rest of us up the craggy slope and we were exhausted when we had gained the top of a narrow crest.

I changed into a pair of cutoff fatigues and took off my shirt to catch some sun on a large boulder close to my hootch. Simon and Garfunkel were crooning *At the Zoo* on Blondie's transistor as I stretched out to unwind. Checking the wound on my bicep for the hundredth time I pinched it hard. It popped open and spurted. I squeezed harder and the tip of a lead fragment peeked out enough for me to grab it between my fingernails. I eyed the gray chip of lead. *To think this came from some VC bullet.*

Just beginning to relax, an incoming chopper dropped off four smiling brothers and a grim-faced warrant officer– it was payday in the bush.

"Get in line, boys," Mocko bayed, his frozen grin beckoning us as he walked toward a card table the officer was setting up to deal out his payment vouchers. "The eagle's about to take a shit."

"Mocko, I thought you did this shit for free," Ski said as he came up behind him.

"For what they pay me, I might as well be." Mocko crossed his arms, anticipating a long wait. He wasn't too far off in deciphering his hourly rate. Awhile back I had computed that even with the extra fifty bucks a month in combat pay, I was earning only twenty-seven cents an hour, considering that we're on the clock twenty-four hours a day, seven days a week. But I guessed we weren't here to get rich.

After sending $180 of it home, I pocketed $20 and volunteered to join a patrol to take the Pay Officer the half-klick to our sister platoon. He didn't seem too thrilled about it, but gave in begrudgingly after Sgt. Trainor assured him that this was a relatively safe area. Myself, I was looking forward to washing up in a stream that was *near their encampment....*

✎ *...Tuesday, June 27, 1989– Air Eater's Digest...*

Hannibal, Mo.                    5:25 p.m.   80°, 80% humidity
Ran 5 miles                      (0:40 00)
Left knee worse again. Spent 4 1/2 hrs. today cutting with machete at Bay Island. Extremely *hot and humid....* ✐

*...With gravity on* our side, it was a short trip to their NDP. Duc and Anh-Ten were talking with Hillbilly as we dropped off the officer to do his thing. Mike, Yoss, Ski and I continued to the stream, sandwiched between the paddy and Rocket Ridge. We quickly washed and shaved and made it back to Hillbilly's camp just as the Pay Officer was finishing up.

He was anxious to get back, so we headed out, the boys also joining. Ten minutes out an incoming slick spotted us, landing on a small flat in front of us. Ramos jumped out, back from an appointment with the dentist, or so he had claimed. The bird immediately jumped into the air before an irate Pay Officer had a chance to hop on.

"Hey, guys!" Ramos shouted over the chopper's noisy departure. "Where's my squad, man? Heard the platoon's split up?"

"Fuck," Ski grumbled, "it's down this motherfucking hill."

"Hey, I didn't know where to go. The pilot spotted you guys, so here I am."

"How's your tooth, Ramos?" Yoss inquired.

"It's doing okay...for now." –he paused– "It might need more work later, though."

"Yeah, right," Ski muttered under his breath. Then louder. "Let's get this man to where he belongs!" On the way back, Ramos informed us of a rumor predicting that sometime during the Tet holidays Chu Lai was to be overrun. Although Ramos was convinced by the tripe, I wasn't so sure, but still I was glad we'd most likely be in the bush then.

By eleven-thirty we made our hilltop NDP. The Pay Officer was now visibly upset that his entire morning had been frittered away running back and forth. Duc and Anh-Ten, though, wasted not a second as they scooted hootch to hootch like a couple of mongooses ferreting for a handout.

*　　*　　*

Blondie rose to his feet. "Who wants to take a patrol to Hillbilly's squad? Ain't shit going on here." I was tired of reading, so I decided to join his band. Three others came, plus Duc and Anh-Ten, who, for some reason, Blondie insisted should tag along.

In twenty minutes we were sitting around Hillbilly's hootch.

Hillbilly crossed his legs and lit the cherry blend in his pipe. "I tell ya, man, ever since ol' LT Owens left us, this platoon's been a gitt'n' more womplejawed every day. I's beginn'n' ta think TR's useless as tits on a boar hog."

"So what the fuck do we do about it?" Ski asked.

"*Nut'n'!* We don't lift a golldarn finga. 'Cuz soona or layda, 'n' probably soona, his shit's gonna hit the fan and when it do TR will hafta get that shit back together or ske-daddle with his commissioned tail tucked between his legs." –he blew out a perfect smoke ring, admiring it for a moment with narrow slits– "But…never ya mind that now, we got us a afternoon ta kill and I's for one's a aims ta kill it."

"How 'bout these kids snatch'n' us some boom-boom from their ville?" Blondie popped, revealing the real purpose for his visit.

Hillbilly, whose morals tended to drift like the smoke in his pipe, agreed. They promised the two boys all the soap and food they could carry if they delivered no later than five o'clock and sent them packing.

As the boys went their way, Hillbilly reached into his ruck and dragged out a large flag he had procured from one of the local soda girls. Embroidered within the red-fringed border was a white peace symbol thumbing its nose at the establishment on a field of deep blue silk. "How 'bout some flicks?"

A short walk was rewarded as Hillbilly pointed to a small thorny hill. Ancient black granite crisscrossed its steep slope and a huge sun-washed stone crowned it– a perfect spot for posing. I macheted a pole ten feet in length to which we attached the flag.

Pane collected our cameras and waited at the bottom while the five of us soon reached the top. Planting the pole on its summit, a brisk wind unfurled the flag in rebellious splendor while Hillbilly and I held it steady. Larry sat cross-legged at the flagpole's base. Standing behind us and holding his arms high was Harv, while Ski stood beside him flashing the peace symbol.

"This should be on the cover of *Look magazine!*" *Pane hollered.…*

✏️ *…7:11 p.m., Tuesday, August 1, 1989, Morris, Illinois…Come on, man. It's less than a mile now.* But I knew it was stupid to continue. Had been for over a year. I slowed to a walk; my left leg limped from the pain in my knee. *Shit, all these running years….* Route 47 shot like an arrow from the Illinois Waterway to I-80, now smothered with fumes, dust and the heat of gas and diesel engines. I scouted for potholes on the narrow shoulder, staring from time to time at the vehicles dancing over the interstate; my motel lay on the other side.

The pain shot up my leg. *…had to happen sooner or later.* I was hoping for later. I'd seen it coming. An inch at a time I'd seen it coming, but I hadn't taken any precautions. *Shoulda took a layoff last month. What is it with me anyway? Why don't I learn…cause I'm addicted to it, that's why. If I couldn't run….* I squelched the thought– that was *not* an option. Not run? Hell, it was all *I had left.…*✏️

Tet holiday, Monday, February 1, 1971, Day 103 / 262 to DEROS
—too little, too late—

12:52 a.m.: "Guys." –I pry an eye open– "Wake up." –it's Nelson– "Echo Recon's been hit."

Behind Nelson, TR is talking in hushed tones on the radio as the soft thumping of a distant firefight brings me to my senses. The night air is motionless– not a blade of grass stirs beneath the quarter moon. TR snaps down the phone and stands in his stocking feet. The gathering crowd watches as a silent red beam of tracers spits from a distant gunship.

"Ol' Puff's giv'n' 'em shit tonight," Blondie softly exclaims.

Sgt. Trainor figures if we take off now we'll be sitting ducks: humping in the dark, we might end up in the same boat– better to wait for near light. Recon Platoon is stuck on Hill 76 Firebase close to Fat City, more than seven and a-half klicks east and since HQ refused to send choppers to fly us over, TR's decision to wait is an easy one.

4:36 a.m.: LT moves us out. The black trail beneath us tests our agility and it takes thirty minutes to make Hillbilly's camp. They wait with packed rucks, silently falling in as we leave the massive ridge and begin to work across a maze of earthen dikes that stretch to the horizon.

5:28 a.m.: a faint rustling from the sky signals the beginning of a restless day. The world begins to gray. The stars dim. The first light of dawn pushes back the darkness with broad strokes of midnight blue. From a distance ville, the shrill cry of a rooster drowns the bullfrog's grunting at the paddy's edge.

On the far side of the paddy, we climb onto the last remnants of Rocket Ridge where several large blackened boulders intrude on the delicate stalks of green rice. TR finds it a suitable place to check in. An eastern glow raises his head and he pauses with the rest of us to watch the sunrise's red and orange glory spread across the quiet fields before us.

"Fuck'n' outstand'n'," Hillbilly comments with somber respect as the sunrise steals our hearts.

9:15 a.m.: the sun turns on us; a strong westerly wind becomes like the blasts from a firebrick kiln. TR knows it's no use; Recon Platoon is still over three klicks away. TR halts the platoon to request they either fly us the rest of way or take us back.

Before he can call, we spot two Vietnamese men walking through a nearby rice paddy, yet unaware of our presence.

"Lai dai!" Trainor commands. The two men look startled. "LAI DAI!" Trainor reiterates.

Not a freefire zone, we can't shoot first and ask questions later– though we train our *16*'s on them. They appear not much more than eighteen and dressed in muddy, black silk pajamas. Walking through the paddies rather than on the dike can only mean they're in a big hurry.

"Khong biet," is all we can get out of them, so TR requests a chopper to pick them up to be interrogated. "And while you're at it, how about picking us up as well?"

10:22 a.m.: a single chopper snatched up the dinks, leaving us staring at the departing bird; there were no more choppers available.

2:49 p.m.: we plodded into our old camp and began to re-build out hootches.

"Fucking kids got radar," Blondie frowned, watching a dozen kids entering the perimeter.

"I got boom-boom! I got boom-boom!" Duc exclaimed, running up to Blondie. "Numba one boom-boom! You pay Duc now!"

Blondie smiled as he spotted the answer to yesterday's request and began to collect the boy's payment.

One of Duc's friends approached Hillbilly. "You buy numba one koon-sa, GI?" Hillbilly's eyebrow lifted as the boy opened a small canvas bag, exposing a dozen sandwich-sized plastic bags full of wacky weed. "You buy. Ten dolla' bag."

Hillbilly pulled one out. "Numba one Cambodian Red," the boy sang, praising his stash. "It give even Budda bookoo numba one high."

"It not Cambodian Red," Hillbilly said, tossing the bag in the sack. "It local weed. I pay three dolla'."

"No loco weed. Numba one! Try...you see!"

"Bullshit. Three dolla'."

"Eight dolla'. It bookoo hard for me to find. I walk bookoo to get."

"Four dolla'."

"Six, GI. I loose bookoo for six."

"Five, 'n' not a nickel more."

"Okay, GI," the boy grimaced, "you bookoo smart. Five dolla'."

Hillbilly handed over a twenty dollar MPC for four bags. The boy snatched the twenty– it would go a long way at An Tan.

Hillbilly stuffed his stash in his ruck as Blondie finished inspecting the tousled prostitute. "They'll be plenty more to go around when I get back," Blondie exclaimed, disappearing with the whore.

Tuesday, February 2, 1971, Day 104 / 261 to DEROS
— "...*that Tet thing.*" —

A muzzle flash. Harv pauses with a spoonful of fruit cocktail halfway to his mouth. A puff of smoke on top of Rocket Ridge. The repercussion reaches our ears as several more flashes blink in the evening sky.

"They're shelling Chu Lai!" Tuck yelps.

"Fucking Tet," Sgt. Trainor spouts.

TR scans his grid map to call in a fire mission. He soon discovers other Grunt units are calling in sightings all along Rocket Ridge.

The day so far had been one typical of the Rocket Pocket. This morning we had moved off the main ridge and back toward the ville, settling on the island hill again. The kids had overrun our camp as soon as we had arrived and continued to harass us until TR kicked them out just after lunch. Mike and I had taken advantage of the confusion to didi it down to the swimming hole to clean up, that is, until a rain cloud sent us hustling back to camp.

"Everybody down!" Spurlin shouts, spotting the white streak of a short round spiraling toward us.

We glue to the rocket, sounding like a gyrating whistle tumbling end over end. *Fall! Fall!* my minds commands. It does, exploding into a blinding flash that reflects off my eyes a hundred meters in front of me.

Sit-reps fly as fast as the rockets; the firebases have their hands full meeting the demands being heaped on them. Soon our own artillery thunders over, though missing the top of the hill and hitting its eastern face. Like most grim events in this war-torn country, it is over after a few long minutes. The evening turns to dusk and dusk to night and for this day, at least, Charlie is done celebrating his Chinese New Year.

Wednesday, February 3, 1971, Day 105 / 260 to DEROS
—shade of things to come—

"I take one, no more." I took the gold-banded bottle of fermented bananas and stuffed it into the side pocket of my ruck.

"We're moving out!" TR yelled over the commotion. "Time to didi it back to the ville, ladies."

The soda girls ignored him.

"DIDI MAU!" Sgt. Trainor shouted while running towards them with outstretched hands and the indignant ladies began to flock down the hill.

The China Sea pushed in a cool northeast breeze that accompanied us on our hump across several rice fields. At two o'clock, we threw down our rucks on top of one of the hills where the rockets had been fired. Our position established, I sat down to open my bottle of wine, gazing to where the VC had shot the rockets. During the shelling, it was all I could do to not run out of the NDP. I didn't want to admit it, but as I poured the brew in equal amounts to the outstretched canteen cups, I knew my reactions to these episodes were getting worse. Before, I'd ride it out– no more, no less. But now, I was apprehensive, to the point where I'd cringe at the *hint* of an explosive, whether real or not. Yes, there was an unfamiliar monster growing within me– still small, still harmless, but I feared it wouldn't be satisfied until it *had its fill.*...

✎ *...Tuesday, October 21, 1989– Air Eater's Digest...*

| | |
|---|---|
| Peoria, IL | 5:50 p.m.  64° |
| 4.4 miles | (0:40 00) |

Terrible terrible. Knees bad, breathing bad, fear factor kicking my butt. What's going on? I'm scared and I don't have the *slightest idea why!*...✐

Thursday, February 4, 1971, Day 106 / 259 to DEROS
—dew dump—

Hillbilly pulled the pin and tossed it into the deep pool. A muffled explosion erupted, followed by a surge of turbid froth effervescing to the surface. Within seconds, half-a-dozen good-sized fish appeared.

"Now that's a how we fish back home." Hillbilly slapped a branch over the fish to begin reeling them in. "Don't go a wast'n' time with poles 'n' lures 'n' all that shit city-slickers use. When we're a hungry, we're a hungry *now*...and we git our food the quickest way we kin."

Yoss and I pulled out our cameras as Fritts strung the plump fish onto a bootlace. "Hold 'em up, Fritts."

We were still more than a klick from camp before stopping to try our luck in the natural spring, just off a small stream we'd been following as it cut through the middle of one of the narrow valleys falling from Rocket Ridge's eastern slope. Conducting an afternoon-long patrol, there wasn't a trace of VC to be found. Most likely they'd skied over the ridge before the last rocket had found its mark.

We made our perimeter by three o'clock. Fritts showed off the catch to the rest of the platoon before handing them over to Larry, who was eyeing them greedily. While Larry cleaned the fish, Mike and I killed the afternoon over a rousing game of spades with Tex and Pat Sesnewski. I thought we would've gone in on stand-down by now, but the VC rocket attack must've delayed it. So far all was quiet, convincing me that the rumor to overrun Chu Lai was bogus.

The flames licking at a skewering fillet sent a sumptuous aroma throughout the platoon. With a re-supply not due until tomorrow and since I'd finished off the last of my C's this morning, Larry let me have several chunks since I had been kind enough to have invited him into our hootch. The smell of roasting fish lured Retchin over, but before he could ask, Larry let fly with a string of Vietnamese expletives that made him back off. Instead, he feigned his hunger by asking to borrow some C-4.

I backed away from Larry's adolescent temper and joined Mike, who was eating a can of chicken and noodles and sitting cross-legged on one of the many boulders interspersed throughout the hilltop.

"Hey, Mike, Larry's got some temper, huh?"

"Yeah, how do you say…bookoo dinky dau?"

"Something like that. That your last C?"

"Affirmative. What do we do if the re-supply bird doesn't come tomorrow?"

Mount Hell popped in my head. "We starve." We were silent for a few minutes, content in our own thoughts. Finishing his dinner, Mike opened the other end of the can with his P-38 before crushing and tossing it down the hill.

"Hey, Bob, I was talking to Tex while you were on patrol. He was telling me he saw you in the hall the night Monkey-Man showed up. Said you were totally wasted. I just remember you getting up and walking out. What happened?"

"Man, like everything in the room just went black. I freaked, man, had to get outta there. Thought I'd never even come down. Weirdest thing I ever had." –I paused– "You ever have a bad trip?"

"No and sure as hell hope I never do. Hey, remember Hillbilly said the weed was laced with smack? You know that shit is heroin?"

Larry let out another barrage of expletives, this time aimed at Harv, who'd come over to see if he could get something out of him. Mike stretched and uncrossed his legs. "If you don't mind me asking, how long you been smoking?"

"Don't mean nothing. Couple months."

"What made you start?"

"It's weird you should ask. Back in the World I was always curious about it, but I never touched the stuff. Maybe I didn't want to disappoint my parents. Or else maybe I was just scared. I dunno. But then when I got over here and out in the bush and all, I dunno, it just seemed like the natural thing to do, know what I mean?"

"Yeah, yeah, I do. I've been smoking about a year now, with a couple buddies in the neighborhood. I really don't see why everybody makes such a big deal out of it." –he paused– "Unless it's got shit in it you don't know about." –Mike leaned his head back on the rock– "Getting stoned should be mellow, not like what happened to you."

"Well," I said as I gazed into the encroaching twilight, "it may be mellow back in the World, but there ain't nothing mellow about it in The Nam."

# STAND-DOWN SIX

Saturday, February 6, 1971, Day 108 / 257 to DEROS
—stretching home—

I couldn't help grinning at Ski's perplexity; his legs were stretched to the limit. "Come on, Ski," I chided, "you can *do* it!"

"Fuck you, Adams." He aimed the knife and let it fly. It plunged into the ground six inches outside of my left boot. Ski looked at me with a smirk, but it faded as I easily stretched my leg to the knife's edge.

"Now!" Duc laughed. "Now you sho' him, Cowboy!"

It was a great day and it was going to be a greater night– we were heading for the rear! Yesterday, Higher-Higher told us to start moving towards Chu Lai.

Last night had been a happy homecoming as the villagers visited our camp and today the reunion continued: rapping, purchasing last minute gift items, playing cards. Blondie even got up a game of touch football, using a squash as an improvised pigskin.

At one o'clock we were hooked up for the hump to Highway 1. Glancing over my shoulder at the waving villagers, I wondered if I would ever see them again, for they had become a part of my life in these few short days. I remembered my first impressions of these strange little people as I had ridden through the cluttered streets of Cam Rahn on that first night. Waxy-looking skin, bony bodies with shocks of jet-black hair, reminding me more of animated puppets from some circus sideshow than real, living, flesh and blood human beings. No, there really wasn't much difference between us. All we wanted was to have a roof over our heads, a full belly, good friends and peace. I prayed that one day, our peace would come.

\*     \*     \*

*These showers after getting out of the bush will be one of the best memories I'll carry from this tropical land,* I thought as I leaned my head back into a gush of hot water. Although I'd kept fairly clean on this mission, those dunks in the stream couldn't come close to a hot soap and suds scrubbing, followed by a minty shave and thorough brushing of the canines. Afterward, Hillbilly and I traded off doing razor cuts to the back of our necks, my motive being to avoid another confrontation by Topp.

I'd almost forgotten about that red-nosed excuse for a non-commissioned officer. But here he was, blubbering out god-like decrees as we checked our supplies into the new armory. He must've convinced himself that by now we were accustomed to this desolate re-train compound and retaliation was no longer within the capability of our bush-dulled minds.

After tidying up my space, a cot and several feet at the end for my ruck, I decided to organize the disarray of papers, pictures and knickknacks in my ammo can. After all, this box represented my only link to a civilized life still on hold in another hemisphere.

"Adams! How ya doing, man?"

I looked up as Bromlow walked into the room. "Hey, how were the eagle flights?" He and three others had volunteered for them in order to get an extra night in the rear.

He threw his ruck on one of the cots and plopped down beside it. His fatigues were still wet up to his crotch with paddy water. "I am fucking beat, man. Didn't see shit, but we did *six* touchdowns in five hours. By the fourth one that fucking 60 was wearing me down."

"Was it worth it for the extra night?"

"Fucking *A*, man. Skied over to the EM Club soon as we got in." –he couldn't help but smile– "Man, did we get shit-faced." –Bromlow stood up and started unbuttoning his shirt– "Hey, man, I'm heading for the showers. Take it easy."

"Oh," Bromlow said, pausing at the door, "hear Chadborne's got a rear job?"

"You're kidding."

"Yeah, working in the motor pool. How you gonna act? Hasta almost get blown away to get a rear job...fucking weird."

Sunday, February 7, 1971, Day 109 / 256 to DEROS
—repentant—

As I awoke, I knew the day was going to be a bad one. Last evening word came that we'd be heading for Dragon Valley again next mission and all I could think of was the man that I had only known as "Hippie".

With an afternoon of classes staring at us, Ski, Hillbilly, Harv and I passed the morning hours with a hung-over game of spades that did little to lift my spirits. One good thing did happen, though. They picked me to be barracks guard during the mock high school classes, made worse by Topp's presence as he hovered over them like a hard-core football coach presiding over study hall. Completing one revolution around the row of barracks lined up like the cars of an abandoned train, I stole away like a hobo into my barrack to sleep the afternoon away.

The pent-up hoot and hollering of returning GI's awoke me. Quickly rising at the sound, I almost fell back onto my cot from the rush of blood leaving my head. I glanced at my watch. *Two and a-half hours?* I quickly slipped out of the back door so as to appear to be on my eighty-seventh guard-duty lap.

My depression deepened as evening approached. Dutifully joining Hillbilly's group, he shared more of the stash, acquired from the kid atop Rocket Ridge. I tried to put my heart into the ritual, but after three hits I knew it was stupid to continue. Excusing myself, I returned to collapse on my cot with a vow to stop smoking and start anew.

Monday, February 8, 1971, Day 110 / 255 to DEROS
—backslider—

The slimy blue thing captured us tonight! Wow! Good flick, man! This morning we kicked off the day at nine o'clock with a couple of classes by our *LT*'s, followed by an exclusive dinner at the mess hall– if we had one. Then with pop and beer in our guts, we skied up to Phoenix! That's when the slimly green thing got us. Fine grass tonight, man. Hooking up tomorrow. One o'clock. Trip...bang...pow!!!

Tuesday, February 9, 1971, Day 111 / 254 to DEROS
—redeemed—

I pulled up my collar, staring into the slate-gray tarmac glistening from a steady drizzle accompanying a monsoon front moving in from the south. We were into the third hour of waiting for the cloud cover to raise enough to be flown out. I had a bad feeling about this one. Maybe it was the endless line of gray clouds pushed toward the mountains by a stiff breeze that could zap your energy in a few minutes. Or– maybe it was me. I'd made it okay now for over a hundred days, but compared to a year, it seemed my tour was just starting. Last night I had awakened in a wild-eyed pool of sweat, sure that Hippie's rotting corpse was hovering over me, his eyes staring into mine as he pointed an accusing finger at me. I was too horrified to pull my eyes from his emaciated face and into his *disemboweled mid-section....*

✎*...3:31 p.m., Sunday, February 18, 1990, journal entry...I realize now* that these anxiety attacks *are* related to Vietnam Post-Traumatic Stress Disorder as I had suspected several years ago. Funny, I had always scoffed at other veterans who claimed to have this disorder. I thought they were faking it for a free ride with Uncle Sam. But this unknown, mysterious feeling of fear I am going through *is* like the same fear I had to deal with in a very concentrated form in Nam, where for over a year I knew at any moment I could die. It first started to surface in 1979 or 80, while working for Tri-State Aerial Engineering. There, I experienced vague feelings of deep fear from an unknown origin. Since I had no rational explanation for these feelings, I assumed the problem must be physical. It was then I started to relate these feelings to a heart problem. That only worsened my fear and the circle began. The more concerned I became about my heart, the more fearful I became, which shot adrenaline into me, causing me to become even more fearful. Yesterday, I could hardly shovel snow– felt weak and shaky, until I refused to give in to it. Almost immediately the irrational fear left me and I continued to shovel for 1½ hours. But how much longer can I *hold this off?* ... ✐

...*"TR, we a* go'n' or not?" a frustrated Hillbilly complained as he sat down hard on his ruck.

At four-thirty, the decision to cancel the CA was made. A hundred and twenty relieved Grunts climbed onto the convoy of trucks to begin the ride through Fat City and back to the re-train area.

Chowing down the evening meal, I gave thanks in knowing that I'd be falling asleep tonight without the worry of Charlie or the rain, not to mention a two-hour guard. Mail call came at six and I retreated to my nest with news from Davy Jones and Art Davis II. An added bonus was a package from my parents, filled with homemade goodies that I'd share at the evening gathering of the Second Platoon Heads.

Before heading for the evening smoke, Mike stopped by with his guitar.

"You ever think of loosing your part?"

"What?"

"Stop parting it to the side like that." –Mike ruffled his hand through his black hair– "Give it a rough look. Let it do what it wants. Natural like, you know?"

"Guess I never thought about it."

"Try it down the middle or something different. Do it, man. You'll like it."

It was a mellow party. A half-dozen candles cast a soft glow on eight young faces absorbing the fullness of life as we passed the pipe. Above us, a steady beat of rain drummed the tin roof, accompanying Mike's melodic acoustics.

I hope it's raining again tomorrow.

# MISSION SEVEN

Wednesday, February 10, 1971, Day 112 / 253 to DEROS
—shades of summer—

The hard pounding of rain brought me to consciousness. I stretched under my poncho liner, savoring the musty sweet odor from the wet world outside, content in knowing that this would mean a welcome delay in hooking up. My thoughts trailed back to that day several weeks back when I had the inspiration to make something of my life if I ever got out of here in one piece. I had to stay focused, or the fire I had kindled to better myself would soon be extinguished. The harsh realities of the bush, though, made it difficult to look ahead; my future could end with my next step. I had to think of something to keep my aspirations moving forward. In short, I needed an attainable goal!

The gray morning blended to a brightening afternoon and by four the sky had cleared enough to attempt another stab into the Vietnam interior. The totality of D-Company, including Spanky and Spurlin, who'd recovered sufficiently from their wounds in the Dragon Valley ambush, climbed into the wet beds of the deuce and a-halves to begin the convoy to Fat City. Soon the sun broke through and poured onto the rich, green landscape. The paddies sparkled from the light magnified through the rainwater still clinging to the succulent stalks.

By the time we drove onto the Fat City airstrip the air had turned oppressive, covering us with a steamy blanket that transformed our fatigues into soggy furnaces. Worse– Higher-Higher had decided that it would be in the best interest of the mission to hump from Fat City toward the outer perimeter of Dragon Valley to detect possible re-supply routes being used by the VC and, worst still– we had to detour to Hill 270 to hook into a long valley that would eventually lead to the Dragon's back door.

We headed out in company formation, each platoon spaced neatly apart and continued for several klicks until a convergence of several streams running from the interior marked the point where we were to begin our separate journeys toward our assigned *AO*'s. Before leaving the stream, though, TR decided it was time for a break.

"Hey, TR," Mocko said, letting his ruck slide to the ground, "why didn't we get to take a bird from Fat City?"

"Somebody hates us," TR mumbled as he stripped off his sweat-drenched fatigue shirt and swatted at several mosquitoes diving at his bare arms. Monsoon was losing its grip; the first signs of a scorching summer were pawing at our door.

Mocko sat down and leaned against his ruck. "Like to see some fucking colonel hump it out here." –he kicked at several leaches racing for his boot– "How you gonna fucking act." I peeled to my sleeveless T-shirt and applied a liberal dousing of bug juice before laying my head on my ruck for a few napping moments.

The evening hours did little to cool the steamy heat that slowly dissipated from beneath the thick mat of brush and briars as we finally achieved the base of Hill 270. We grunted up the bare side of the north saddle, kept clear by a firebase on the south saddle. Reaching the summit at quarter of nine, we were near total exhaustion.

"Coulda flown us here in ten fuck'n' minutes..." Retchin exhaled as he lay his 60 down and peeled off his ruck. Looking up, he spotted a lone light twinkling from across the saddle from one of the firebase's bunkers. "...and somebody tell that shithead to squelch that goddamn light!"

Thursday, February 11, 1971, Day 113 / 252 to DEROS
—Bobby—

Etched through the mist were the rugged, bruised slopes that belonged to Dragon Valley. But for today, we were to begin the long hump into the desolate two-canopy jungle that stood between us and our objective. We learned from radio chatter that one of the guys from the mortar platoon had been dusted off late last evening from heat exhaustion– not surprising after the intense hump from Fat City.

Last night's full moon was replaced by an orb full of fury as we broke camp at nine to begin our northwestern journey. Blondie took point while I dangled at drag like a worm on the end of a hook. The hump was fraught with hills that continued to our first checkpoint, four klicks distance. From there we followed one of the many streams spawned from the heart of Dragon Valley. My sense of caution, usually my utmost priority while walking drag, was running thin by two, as the combination of the heat, the humping and a heavy feeling in the pit of my gut were taking its toll. By three, we caught up with First Platoon and after a quick break to chat, another junction in the narrow, fast-running stream split us once again. One more hour and TR called it a day as we set up a short distant from the stream.

"I think I've got a little of what that guy who got dusted off musta had," I told Doc, who was again staying with Mike and me. Our bond, unlike most of the other guys, was the desire to keep as clean as we could in this almost impossible environment. "Got a gut ache, 'n' feel nauseous."

Doc felt my forehead. "You do look a little peaked. But I wouldn't worry about it. Just cool down and we'll see how you feel later." –he pulled a can of peaches out of my ruck– "Eat these. It'll help get some complex sugar back into your system."

It did help– a lot. By seven, I'd forgotten all about my stomach and was clipping off a letter to the "Grif", Bob Ahlgren.

\*　　\*　　\*

"I'm awake." I scoot to the end of the mattress and toss the liner aside. The air is cold. Condensation drips from the tent, spattering onto the end of Doc's blanket. I stand to my full height and check my watch: 1:40. The full moon throws eerie tree shadows onto the ground. So quiet, except for the occasional grunt from a frog and the ever-present crickets. I pull my collar up as a wave of goose bumps shiver through me. The air is motionless. What few stars I can see through the leaves seem ready to burst as they hover too close above. *This has got to be...*I snap my head around. I prick my ear and stand motionless. My heart gears up as I *finger my safety....*

✎...*Monday, February 26, 1990...109 glowed bright* orange on the EKG apparatus. "Pulse is kind of high," the nurse says.

*She ain't seen nothing yet.* Waves of fear wash over me like a tsunami. "Guess I'm kinda nervous."

"Try to relax."

*Relax? Yeah, right.*

"Okay, that's it. That wasn't so hard now was it?"

The rest of the physical is a breeze. Rectum probe? Be my guest. Urine? Why not. Lung capacity? I'll blow all day if you want. Blood test? Hell, take it all. Just don't *even* wrap that blood pressure thingy around my arm. Whatever you do, don't *even* listen to my heartbeat, ma'am.

The nurse places gauze over the needle in my arm while sliding it out. "That's it. All done."

Bill and Jed are waiting for me in the truck, ready for the long *drive to Joliet....*

"*...Bobby–*" *The ghostly* whisper blasts an icy chill through my heart.

"...Bobby–"

*Mike?* I kneel beside him and shake his leg. "Mike, wake up."

"...BobbyBobbyBobby–"

I crawl in further and shake his shoulder. "Mike, hey. Wake up."

"Bo...wha, what?"

Doc's voice comes out of the dark. "What's wrong?"

"It's okay, Mike had a nightmare."

Friday, February 12, 1971, Day 114 / 251 to DEROS
—bad moon rising—

I poured a packet of Sanka into the bubbling water.

"What was wrong with Vignola last night?" Doc asked.

"I'm not sure, but he–"

"–had another one of his damn nightmares." –Mike crawled out of the hootch– "Guess I should have said something but, I was hoping I was over them. Guess you guys should know, in case it happens again." He pulled on a boot. "Last night I was saying, 'Bobby,' right? Well, Bobby is my kid brother. Several years ago I started to have these nightmares. In them he was always in some kind of danger and I was trying to save him. Sometimes they weren't too bad. Other times well, I'd end up screaming my head off. The last few years they've been almost non-existent– thought I'd outgrew them. In fact, last night was the first time it'd happened since before I was drafted."

237

"Maybe you should let TR know," Doc suggested. "Least, then, everyone would know it was you instead of a gook."

"Fair enough. Just hope he don't think I'm trying for a Section Eight."

\*　　\*　　\*

The dew burned off as the Vietnam sun sizzled over the clear blue horizon. We continued to follow the blue-line. So far, there were no signs of VC activity, which was fine with me. By four, we caught up with Third and the CP. Third was on break while the Mortar guys were cutting through heavy brush and not making much headway. After a thirty-minute wait, TR realized we weren't going to get anywhere by dark, so he told Hillbilly to do an about face and retrace our steps for a hundred meters where we'd again set up close to the stream. It was nice knowing the mortar guys, who were treated like royalty, had to do their share of cutting this time. Tomorrow morning, we'd just didi down their trail like Red Riding Hood going to Grandma's.

Saturday, February 13, 1971, Day 115 / 250 to DEROS
—bookoo letter, bookoo time—

Today was a carbon copy of yesterday: follow the blue-line northwest. Rickard and Pane went in on the back-haul bird, their R&R time having finally arrived– for now I could only dream about R&R.

The bird had delivered letters from my folks, the Greek, the Grif, Sue Davis and Valerie Perkins, sister to Ron, a Basic Training friend. The highlight, though, was a cherished letter from Sandy Johnson. I placed the letters in my ammo can where they'd be safe until setting up. It was a long morning hump, but by mid-afternoon TR surprised us by deciding to set up early. I quickly settled in, anxious to catch up on my writing, reading and also, I thought I'd take Mike's advice from last stand-down and try parting my hair in the middle. TR put a chink in my day, though, picking our squad to conduct a listening post; tonight would be a long one as we monitored the incoming trail.

Sunday, February 14, 1971, Day 116 / 249 to DEROS
—the hard earth—

The moon held full stage as my guard ended. It was bright enough to write a letter home.

238

Mom & Dad,                                    *Feb 14, 1971, 1 AM*

*Hello, Just got off guard & since it's such a clear & bright night decided to write a letter. Really sorry I'm not writing too much lately. But it hasn't been easy so please don't worry. We've been humping every day now since this mission started the 10th. We started out from Fat City (a fire support base outside Chu Lai) & now we're 10 clicks inland. I don't mind the humping so much, it's just that it doesn't give me much time to read our write. Monson's definitely over now as it hasn't rained for quite awhile now. It gets quite hot & sunny during the day & cool at night. I'm really getting a good tan though. This mission is 9 days long. We're looking forward to a 4 day stand-down & 3 day re-train totalling 7 days in the rear.*

*I've heard from some of my friends that the G.I. Bill is much more than I thought. They say it's up to $210.00 a month. I'll look into it while in the rear.*

*You remember that jammed thumb I got playing basketball the day I left? Well the swelling still hasn't gone down much. Probably due to continuous aggitation from humping guess I should see someone about it. It's my ring finger right hand. I got your letter today dating I think Feb. 6th. I was in the Rocket Pocket while Chu Lai was rocketed a couple weeks ago. In fact 2nd Plt. was nearest to whoever fired them. I could see the muzzle flashes about a click away. Some short rounds landed to close for comfort too. But they weren't trying for us...no sweat.*

*Guess it's really getting bad in the rear. But I'm never back long enough to see what's going on.*

*Hope you got my letter about the bible payments.*

*I received your package last retrain. Thanks very much!*

*Could you please send a lightweight ($1.00) brown T-shirt– maybe from Pennies to where out here.*

*Guess I should get some sleep now– it's 1:20 AM.*

*Take care & write.*                          *Love, your Son. Bob*

\*       \*       \*

"Fucker's a deep one," Hillbilly commented dryly before committing his body to slide into the stagnant water. Separated from the other platoons, we were on our own, having blazed trail now for a day and a-half. TR was determined to make our AO today, in spite of rugged terrain and scorching heat.

The marsh stretched a hundred meters before hitting another tangle we'd no doubt spend an hour cutting through. The rotting vegetation permeated my nose– my mind adding this to its collection of bad memories I would carry from this land. We had to hold our weapons overhead in the chest-deep water as the lumpy, tangled bottom tried to trip us. Water leeches, big enough to make their land cousins go screaming for cover, attempted to wrap their black rubbery-like bodies on ours, another reason to keep our arms out of the stench. We drug out of the bog on the far side, covered with black slime.

After a short break, Hillbilly's squad threw themselves to cutting, switching every few minutes until Blondie's squad took over smacking, hacking, kicking and cursing for another hour and a-half until we hooked into another stream.

A klick later, we found Third Platoon resting by the side of the blue-line, our paths crisscrossing as we moved down the widening streambed: I realized we were now knocking on the Dragon's back door.

TR picked the first hill closest to the stream and since it was a clear night, we decided just to throw ponchos over our heads.

"Great," I grunted while attempting to inflate my bed, "there's a hole in my mattress."

"So much for the comforts of home, huh, Adams?" –Ski pulled out his mattress– "What does it take to get an *oh shit* out of you, anyway, don't you ever cuss?"

"It just ain't my way."

Monday, February 15, 1971, Day 117 / 248 to DEROS
—boxed in—

My luminescent dial read 12:10. *Of all the nights....* I adjusted my poncho to make sure the water would drain to the ground. After a few moments, a light sprinkle tapping the plastic lulled me into a sweet world of sleep.

\*　　　\*　　　\*

A nudge on my boot. It was Yoss. "Adams...your guard."

"I'm up." It seemed I had just drifted off, but my watch made me a liar– it read 2:40.

"Keep an eye on Vignola. He was talking in his sleep again."

*So which lump is Mike?* In the dark they appeared more like fresh graves than sleeping Grunts. *Guard duty sucks. Hump all day, up all night.* I sat cross-legged with my poncho draped over my head, peering into the night like a lonesome owl searching for a mid-night meal. After a long half-hour, I heard the heavens opening up on the next ridgeline. *Here it....* I picked up the sides of my poncho as a curtain of rain swept over our camp. It was useless. I succumbed to the inevitable– a soaked butt and poncho liner. One thing was sure– guard duty sucked.

*      *      *

Last night's drenching had made everyone's life that much more miserable. We were taking our first break of the day, now two klicks from last night's NDP. Our stream was still widening in our quest for Dragon Valley and if it hadn't been such a dreary day, this indeed would have been a beautiful valley to behold. Once populated, the burned-out remnants of white stucco dwellings were now buried in an avalanche of brush and vines.

I picked up a flat piece of quartz lying beside the streambank. "Hey, Mike, this'll make a perfect sharpening stone."

"You know they have things made for just that sort of thing back in the World?"

"Yeah, but we're not back in the World." –I paused, considering if I should bring up an uncomfortable subject– "Hey, did you know you were talking in your sleep again last night?"

"*I* didn't hear nothing," he said in his usual jest. Then more seriously. "Did I wake the whole camp?"

"Only Yoss...but he was already on guard duty."

*      *      *

Our stream entered a series of steep ravines that cut its width in half. The trees hovered far above white water roaring and twisting through the half-light of the forest.

Hillbilly halted our Platoon and waved TR forward.

Ski squinted down the row of Grunts. A thin ray of sunlight spotlighted Hillbilly kneeling on the muddy bank. "Hillbilly found something."

I eyeballed the steep slope. "Good place for an ambush."

"They'll hafta see us first," Ski responded. "No way they can hear us."

I pulled out my camera and shot a flick of several Grunts ahead of me, the white water careening beside them framing the picture. Soon TR motioned the platoon to continue, waiting till his spot came up so he could fall in. As I passed where TR and Hillbilly were conferring, a chill bubbled up my spine; sandal imprints were freshly imbedded in the soft mud.

We continued along the stream's edge for another half-hour until TR indicated to Hillbilly to find a way to cross. He found a suitable ford a hundred meters further, a logjam that took us to the opposite bank where TR started to look for an appropriate NDP hill. Ten minutes brought us to one. Approaching its base, Hillbilly discovered several sprung bear traps that might had been used for booby-traps– or worse, to bait a GI into picking up a souvenir that had an explosive surprise waiting for him.

"I don't like it," Hillbilly said as he conferred with TR. "No tell'n' what's on top of this fucker." –he lit a cigarette– "Think we should look for another hill."

"You're the boss."

We found another hill and with investigation it proved free of VC tampering. The top was thick with undergrowth, as bad as any I'd yet experienced. What was worse was the gooey mud that clung to our boots, making it difficult to walk, let alone establish a hootch in the tangle of undergrowth. We finished our shelters, but couldn't prepare our meals until gathering several armloads of elephant grass to keep the mud off our butts.

Hillbilly and I were assigned MA duty. But TR, deciding it would be apropos to send out a short patrol to check the immediate area, made us wait until they returned. It was in the pitch black we groped to where the trail dropped down the hill. Stopping, we had to wait several minutes until our retinas could adjust to the sparse moonlight.

"This fuck'n' sucks," Hillbilly whispers. It takes a full twenty minutes to tie on the wire, thread it across the trail and clamp the spoon between the waiting clothespin.

"Just don't fuck up," Hillbilly warns as I ready to push in the blasting cap. "Don't wanna end up with my head stick'n' out of ma ass."

Tuesday, February 16, 1971, Day 118 / 247 to DEROS
—shadows from the past—

Harv, Pat, Yoss, Hillbilly and I were returning to where we had found the bear traps. Our mission was to blow them. Hillbilly, though, had different ideas.

"No sense a tempt'n' fate," he had said on the way over. "If I was a fuck'n' dink, soon as we'd didi'ed last night, I woulda booby-trapped the shit out of 'em, think'n' they'd a be com'n' again tomorrow, a which we are. Nope. We ain't *even* gitt'n' close to the mothafucks."

"Eight months?" Pat reiterated.

"That's right, twenty gawdamn more days and I'm a motherfuck'n' short-timer. I'll be so short ya hafta pull me outta my boots every gawdamn morn'n'." –he pulled a frag off his web belt– "Now... let's git this done."

He tossed his baseball grenade down the stream's bank and the rest of ours followed. A sequential *BAM! BAM! BAM! BAM! BAM!* resonated.

"Now far as ol' TR knows, those traps are out of commiss'n'. Let's git back."

I was glad Hillbilly had decided not to take the chance, his backwoods logic again keeping us out of a potentially dangerous situation. The platoon was resting by the stream upon our return and I quickly joined several others bathing in a deep pool bordering a rock ledge to wash off last night's mud and this morning's sweat. At eleven-thirty we continued to follow our stream, ever widening as the day wore on.

At the sixteenth hour of the mission's sixth day, we arrived. Before us now lay landscape that belonged to Dragon Valley: a new generation of dense flora struggling to rise above hard packed earth that still held the remnants of dead trees, once ravaged by what must have been a horrendous assault of napalm. We solemnly passed the pale monoliths of wooden decay, the last witnesses to that reign of death and sobering testaments of a valley we were lucky to get *out of alive. ...*

*✎...Friday, September 2, 1990, home of Art and Sue Davis...* "Then," *Joany continued,* "since the compressor broke, I had to blow them up myself. Could you see a clown passing out from blowing up twenty-five balloons? By the time I was done, I'd hyperventilated so bad my nose and hands were numb."

My mind clicked at her last statement. Till then it'd been just another birthday party, celebrating with cake and ice cream, the kids storming Art's basement, turning his poolroom into a battle zone. But her last statement zoned everything out. *Fate, that's why I'm here. To hear Joany say that– her nose and fingers turned numb? God, that's how I had felt in the swamp– and in the Rockies.... Hyperventilated? I was breathing like crazy, trying and trying to get.... Could I have been OVER-breathing, getting too MUCH air, rather than too little? Then, all that forced breathing while running before my knees gave out. Quincy? Hannibal? Man, what a concept. This never would have occurred to me.*

*...Journal entry, 9-3-90 Sa.*

Read for 1st time definition of hyperventilation, & am convinced this is the root of my "panic attacks". Symptoms include "faintness" or impaired consciousness w/o actual loss of consciousness, tightness of chest, sensation of smothering, apprehension, palpitation or pounding heart. Fullness in throat & pain over stomach region. In prolonged attacks, victim may exhibit "tetany" (spasms in extremities, numbness) w/ muscular spasms of hands & feet.

'Tetany: a syndrome manifested by a sharp flexion of the wrist & ankle joints (carotidal spasm), muscle twitching, cramps & convulsions caused by inadequate amounts of ionized calcium in the blood. This can be caused by hyperventilation. Tetany is often accompanied by alkalosis, sometimes produced by hyperventilation.

Alkalosis: a pathologic condition resulting from accumulation of base or loss of acid w/o comparable loss of base in the body, & characterized by a decrease in hydrogen ion concentration (increase in PH). It is the opposite of acidosis, although the blood is normally slightly alkaline. A drastic shift of the acid base balance toward alkalinity can produce serious symptoms, including shallow or irregular respiration, prickling or burning sensation in the fingers, nose, toes or lips, muscles cramps, numbness of extremities, & in severe cases, convulsions!!!'

This describes exactly what had happened in the swamp in August of 1988. For some reason, I had been breathing too fast, which began my hyperventilating. It didn't take long before I began to feel dizzy, which made me apprehensive. So, thinking I was out of breath, I breathed deeper, which is a common occurrence during hyperventilation. The increased breathing started my heart to pound, which made me more fearful, which made me breathe even deeper until my extremities began to numb (tetany). The worsening physical manifestations increased my fear, causing me to breathe faster until my blood was so saturated with oxygen I went into convulsions (alkalosis). If not for the same symptoms several weeks later in Colorado, I might be convinced this was contributed to swamp gas (methane), or heat exhaustion. But there was no poisonous gas on that mountain trail and it was not hot or humid to produce heat exhaustion. Although, I must admit these factors might have contributed to the collapse in the swamp, I am sure the primary reason for the attack was over-breathing. And since that physical last Monday, I can understand why it is easy for me to hyperventilate. I discovered my lung capacity is above normal for my age group (113%), probably due to my running. Therefore, my oxygen intake can easily be too *great* rather than too little. This explains away each panic attack over the last 10 yrs. To think ignorance can alter one's life so. I hope God can somehow salvage what is left *of my life....*✐

*...Just after six,* we found a suitable hill. It had once been occupied by a large GI element, for on its top were the remains of foxholes, now half-buried from the erosion of past monsoons. We judged it had been a company size unit, indicated by the large perimeter formed by the deteriorating pits. They were the only GI evidence, though– the VC had stripped the hill bare. We sat up in the middle, forming a much tighter NDP than our predecessors.

"If this hill could speak," I commented to Mike while driving in the hootch corners, "bet it'd have quite a story to tell."

"Hear the shit really fell several years back," Mike responded. "Hardcore NVA filled this valley at one time."

"Just hope they don't come back."

"They will, Bob. Don't forget the one thing they have that we don't."

"What's that?"

"Time."

Wednesday, February 17, 1971, Day 119 / 246 to DEROS
—cross at Red Cross—

"Betcha a can of peaches you can't."

"You heard 'im, Mike. A can of peaches. Man, they are gonna taste *so* good."

"Head first. It's gotta be head first."

I backed away from the shallow ledge, sitting two feet above a sharp bend in the stream. Exhaling sharply, I paused, then ran three steps, hopped, snapped my legs to my chest and spun one and a-half times.

245

"I don't believe it," Pat gasped as I speared the water with outstretched arms. My head popped out of the water. "You win, Adams. My hat is off to you."

We'd been on water patrol for an hour, enjoying our first non-humping day of the mission. The morning had been like R&R– sleeping late, leisurely breakfast followed by a game of spades. After lunch, I re-enforced the eyelets on my fatigues after changing into a pair of shorts. It was great to have a break.

We returned in time to greet a re-supply bird. I received several letters and withdrew to my hootch to enjoy the peaches while reading news from the home front. An official looking letter with a Red Cross logo imprinted in the corner got my attention first.

"Mike, look at this."

He glanced over its contents. "Shit, Adams, you better write home fast."

"I'm gonna do more 'n that. Be right back."

TR was sipping a cup of coffee and reading one of his letters when I approached.

"What's up, Adams?"

"Got this from the Red Cross. My parents think I've been badly wounded and want to know what's going on. Sounds like they're pretty upset. Any way of letting them know I'm okay, like bookoo fast?"

TR scanned the letter. "Write them right now and we'll get it to them quick as we can. Afraid that's all we can do. How do you think they came to the idea that you were wounded?"

I thought for a second. "Bet one of my buddies said something to 'em 'bout that ambush we were in. Maybe I sort a mentioned I got a little shrapnel from it." –I paused– "Hey, you know how guys can exaggerate."

"You didn't tell your folks?"

"Nah, guess I kinda sugar-coat stuff that goes on."

"Can't fault you for that, but if you're going to tell your buddies, let 'em know not to spread rumors, especially to your folks, okay?"

"You got it, TR. And I'll get started on that letter right now."

*Mom & Dad,*  *Feb 17 –71*

*Wow! Really surprised when Red Cross contacted me & said you thought I was badly wounded or something. Hope you find out I'm okay before this letter gets to you. It sure will take a long time. I don' know how you could* *have came to that conclusion. I can imagine how worried you'd be. About 3 weeks ago in Dragon Valley we <u>did</u> run into an ambush. But I just got a little scratch in my right bicep, no sweat. It did take a little blood though so perhaps I was put in for a purple heart & you heard it through the paper (?). Wad, that machine gunner, was hurt in the leg. He got to go back to the World & is coming along fine now.*

*So I'm still out here in the same area as told in my last 'midnight' letter. We go in in a couple of days, really looking forward to it. This has been declared a "dry" area, or no dinks.*

*This afternoon we took a swimming patrol down to the stream at the bottom of the hill. We're way downstream now & it widens quite a bit. I found a perfect swimming hole there. There was a rock ledge 2 feet high & then a 12 ft. depth of clear, sparkling water. It's just like a paridise if there wasn't the element of danger. All the water is clear & perfectly safe to drink. Even through 12 ft. of water it's easy to see bottom.*

*We've finally been given a couple days break while waiting to go in. I'm just playing spades & reading. Weather's really nice too.*

*Well, guess I'll stop. Take care & <u>please</u> don't worry. God Bless.*

*Your Son, Bob*

Thursday, February 18, 1971, Day 120 / 245 to DEROS
—swimming hole bully—

"Bo...Bo...Bobby...BobbyBobbyBOBEEEEEEE!" Mike shoots straight up, exploding the hootch and ripping the corner stakes away. "BOBEEEEEEEE!" Mike holds his arms to the sky as adrenaline snaps me to my feet. I tackle him to the ground and clamp my hand over his mouth.

"Mike! Mike! Wake up!" –I straddle his chest– "Wake up, Mike! It's okay! It's okay!"

Mike's eyes open as he swims to consciousness. "What?"

"You had a nightmare. A big one."

"I...sorry...I–"

Doc cut him off. "It's okay. Get some sleep."

It isn't okay and as the camp settles back, I hope that a VC ear didn't get a bead on our location. *He'll get a section-eight for this.* I try to stop my hands from shaking. *My best friend yet.* I look at my watch in the moonlight. *2:20. Why does everything happen on my shift?* ...

*...6:43 p.m., Tuesday, September 27, 1990, Lagrange Lock, Illinois...Close enough, Jed, close enough. Give it gas now, come on, scoot it up. That's it, that's it. Now ease it in there.* I toss my line at the eye; it makes a sweet "taloop" as it finds the yellow cavel. *Gotcha!* I hold the bow fast while Jed shifts to reverse and swings the stern into the wall so Bill can secure it. Behind him, the stern is fifteen feet from the wicket gates that hold back the flow at the Lagrange Lock and Dam.

I jump into the engine compartment and switch off the water and gas. The radio squelches before I can kill the batteries.

Jed leans out the door. "Bob, you have a message from your wife to give her a call. You go on ahead; we'll finish up."

His words tap a yellow spike into my spine: getting a call from home while in the field– never good news. "Guess what, honey, we won the state lottery!" "Darling, we inherited a million dollars." *Riiiiiight.* My legs are wobbly as I approach a thirty-foot steel ladder that leads to the top of a huge tainter gate seventy-five feet across. *I can do this!* My heart jumps. *What's wrong?! Craig? Stef? Jen? Dad?* The ladder towers before me. My saliva turns to paste. *Why do I always do this to myself? Remember what I read about this shit. It's the breathing!* I step onto the ladder. *God, I'm more afraid of climbing these steps than making that call. Why do I do this even when I know what's going on inside of me?*

I make the top, cross the plankway and climb down the steep metal-grated steps on the other side. *Okay, get control of yourself.* My heart starts to palpitate. *Shit! Not that! Relax! Don't breathe too deep! Control! Come on! It's gonna be okay!* I walk across the lock gate, down the walkway and into the lock house. Palpitations slap my chest. Legs– rubber– melting wax. The office is on the third floor. *I can make it!* "You got to." One flight. Two. I can't breathe. Dizzy. No spit.

"Hear...I gotta message?"

"You Adams? Yeah, your wife wants you to call."

Two tries. *Stop misdialing!* Fingers– cold– shaking. Two rings. Three. Four. Five. "Sheryl? What's wrong?"

"You're mother called." –My heart jumps between my lungs– "It's your grandmother. She passed away this morning."

I'm relieved. I'm ashamed. She'd been *sick for months.....*

\*       \*       \*

...*"I'm in charge* of this patrol and I say *no* swimming."

Ski bristled. "Fuck you, Ramos. I don't need no chicken-shit telling me what I can or can't do."

"I'll tell LT."

"Go the fuck ahead and tell LT, maybe he'll give you a section-eight, too."

Beneath the hot noon sun the crystal-blue pool was like heaven waiting. Harv, Pane and I followed Ski's lead and stripped off our fatigues. Ramos sat with his back to us, holding his head like a bully who hadn't gotten his way. With the first splash, the hellhole morphed into paradise.

First thing this morning, we patched the result of Mike's nightmare with duct tape. Nobody had said anything, but I knew they were thinking it– Mike was too big of a risk. Last night we were lucky– damn lucky. Next time, the fate of the entire platoon could be compromised by his unpredictable behavior. And I knew TR couldn't chance that.

It began to look like we'd be sitting it out for the rest of the mission, for TR was not at all anxious to venture too far from his perch. Hillbilly thought he'd lost his nerve. TR didn't appear to be the bush type, anyway; a desk job would've suited him better. But I guessed he wanted that CIB on his chest to enhance his military career, not to mention make his papa proud.

Saturday, February 20, 1971, Day 122 / 243 to DEROS
—oops!—

Good news came early. Hook up!

"Guess what, Mike?" I said as we packed, trying to get his mind off of the other night. "I hear Hillbilly's got some good dew for tonight."

"That Cambodian Red *can* kick your ass." –Mike fell silent and then– "Think I could *use* a kicked ass about now."

"Don't forget to get your guitar out of storage. When you play that thing, man, it really mell–"

*BAM*!

"SHEEEEEEEEEET!"

I snap my head toward the scream and lower my 16. TR sinks to his knees as he clamps bloody hands over a hole in his hip. His 45 pistol lies at his feet.

Doc forces his hands away. "Shit, TR, you did it proud. Clean through. Tuck, get a medivac."

TR is on the brink of crying. "Shot myself with my own gun!? What's my father gonna think?"

"Teddy!" Hillbilly hollers from across the perimeter. "Ya oughtn't a play with guns, man. But would ya mind keep'n' it down? We're try'n' ta pack our shit here."

"For Christ's sake, TR, Hillbilly's right," Blondie says, throwing in his two cents. "Your hollering's gonna bring a whole NVA regiment on top of us."

Finishing the field dressing, Doc gives TR an injection of morphine as the thud of an approaching medivac spares TR any more badgering.

"Why can't I get any respect?" TR muddles while being placed onto a poncho. Fritts tosses a blue smoke onto the west side of the perimeter and they carry him to his impromptu Freedom Bird. We watch as it picks up, leans port and throttles its turbines to clear the trees guarding our slice of heaven.

# STAND-DOWN SEVEN

Saturday, February 20, 1971, Day 122 / 243 to DEROS
—happy smoke—

The surf was strong, making it difficult to keep my balance as I bounced toward deeper water. Up to my chest, I paused to let the sea rock the tension from my body. *If only the war was over...* —I inhaled the beauty of the faraway mountains peeking over the wooden barracks like a watercolorist rendering– *...this would indeed be paradise.*

Ski walked to the shoreline and cupped his hands. "Hey! They got a riptide warning out!" –but even paradise can carry a threat of danger– "Topp says everyone *outta the water!*"...

✎...*1:03 p.m., Friday, January 4, 1991, home*...*"...then we'll impound* the vehicle and sell it at a repro auction. And unless we recoup the full amount, you'll be liable for the balance...immediately."

"*You* can't *do* that–"

"We have every legal *right* to do that, Mr. Adams."

"You can't! The motor's shot, the transmission's shot, the power steering's–"

"Mr. Adams, if you renege on the loan we are well within our legal me–"

"Look, *Roadway* promised to 'Tote the Note,' and two weeks later they transfer the loan over to you clowns knowing full well it was going to fall apart. You're probably in on the scam with them!"

His monotone bass voice didn't waver. "It was a no-warrantee purchase, Mr. Adams. Law's on our side. Either you continue your payments, or we *will* repossess–"

"You're a bunch of crooks!" I slammed down the phone. *Floyd's Finance? What a fucking joke.* But I was more scared than angry. Helpless. After all, the car had cost nearly four thousand. And now I needed over three thousand to fix it– and I was broke.

"What am I gonna do?"

Sheryl looked up from the paper. "Will your dad give you a loan?"

"Ask my dad? I'm going *for a walk.*"...✎

*        *        *

...*"Damn your joker!"* Pat slapped his ace of spades on the rough wooden floor, doubling as a card table.

"Sorry, boys," –Hillbilly raked in the trick– "looky likes yer ass is set, Mr. Sesnewski."

Ski lit his third joint. He'd been making them from his cigarettes by first removing the tobacco and replacing it with finely ground marijuana leaves from Hillbilly's almost empty plastic bag. I wasn't smoking; I had evening CQ duty.

"Cut?" Ski asked.

I tapped the deck. "I trust you, ol' buddy. Now deal me a Boston." As Ski flipped out the cards, a familiar tingling radiated in my skull.

I blinked hard. "I bid four."

Hillbilly took a puff on his pipe. "Put me down fer five."

Pat: "Three here."

Ski: "I'll go four."

The room moved on me.

"You gonna play or sit there all fucking night?" Ski was leaning his head into my face.

"Guys, would you believe I'm getting a buzz just sitting here?"

Hillbilly held out his hand. "Mr. Adams, you *have* arrived. *Ain't it cool?"*...

✎ *...1:21 p.m., Friday, January 4, 1991, East Moline...Fuck! I don't need this!* I stop by a driveway, just past the dip of a shallow saddle. My heart races. My spit paste. I try to look inconspicuous, though I know the sight of a grown man standing in front of someone's house looks anything *but* inconspicuous. My mind is scattering like the snow, falling heavy and wet as it covers me with its claustrophobic curtain.

*It will pass. It will pass. It can't kill me.* Thirty seconds. *Can't stay here. Gotta keep going. Gotta make it to the top.* The thought pumps my heart faster and I check its beat against the bruised side of my neck, bruised from the constant– checking– checking– checking.

*I can't make it. I can't...go home. I don't fucking care no more. Just go home.* I retrace my steps. My heart strums like Dixie as I make the rise. I dare not act like anything unusual is going on, in case some curious eye is probing me as they sip their coffee or brandy or whatever their pleasure on this cozy winter day– while icy terror tightens its grip on my fragile heart like *a boa constrictor....*✐

Sunday, February 21, 1971, Day 123 / 242 to DEROS
—rats—

I excused myself from another get-together with the Heads and ran through the rain to enter one of the many barracks that sat empty during stand-down. Shaking the rain off, I sat down and crossed my legs in the middle of the aisle.

"The world is one." –I slowly raised my head– "This barrack...is *so* cool." –I held still, listening as the rain tapped the tin roof– "Look, there's a roof up there, man. You can't *even* get me, rain."

My eye caught movement by the door. A rat was peering at me through the propped-open screen door. Its matted slate-gray hair covered a corpulent body no less than a foot in length. The rat paused to shake the water off before lumbering down the aisle.

"Hi, rat. *What's up, man?"*...

✎...*1:52 p.m., home...I open the* backdoor, lean on the dining room table and sit down. My head rushes and my heart skips to normal, but the usual peace doesn't wash over me– it always had before. *Damn Floyds. Damn Roadway.* Ten minutes. Sheryl comes into the kitchen, asking again about the loan. *Damn Roadway. Damn Floyds.*

I stand and walk outside. *I can do this. I have to do this!* Grabbing the shovel by the back door, I begin to peel a fresh layer of snow off the chipped concrete sidewalk. At the bottom of the steps, the snow is half a foot deep by the garage. *Big driveway, wish it.... No!* I drop the shovel and creep *to the backdoor....*✎

...*The rat stops* in front of me and rises on hind legs. Our eyes lock– his inquisitive stare gives me the distinct impression he wants to ask a question. I wait expectantly, but instead he drops to all fours to continue his sniffing stroll down the aisle. At the far end, he stands on his haunches for a last inspection before pushing open the screen door.

"Bye, rat." –he gives me a departing look, then waddles down the wooden steps and disappears into the downpour– "The world is one," I say as I return my stare *to the roof....*

✎...*1:59 p.m., home..."I can't do* this anymore."

"What?"

"My heart."

"You're just having anxiety. You need to get some help."

"It's more than that."

"No. It isn't."

"I ca–"

"Get some help."

"Where?"

"Call the Pastor."

"Why him?"

"He can help you."

"Nooo–"

"Do it."

I walk downstairs to our bedroom and lay on the bed. *See the wall. See the wall. Relax. Come on. There. There it goes...relax...relax.* My heart gears down and I know it is now or never.

Three rings. "Pastor White? This is Bob Adams."

"Well hi, Bob, nice of you to call." –he sounds busy– "What can I do for you?"

My face flushes. "Well, I got a problem and, I think I need help. You see, I'm having...I'm having, anxiety...major anxiety. I guess. I think it has something to do with Vietnam...maybe. I'm not sure. Would you mind coming over to talk?"

Silence. "Ah...let me, check my calendar." –silence– "Okay. Let's see...I think...yeah, okay, I can be there in an hour."

*    *    *

The scrap of concrete as Sheryl shovels the driveway– the sound of a car pulling in– a car door thudding shut– a greeting– the door opening– the click of shoes coming down the stairs– a knock– the bedroom door opening.

"Hi, Bob." –he shakes my hand– "Boy, it's cold out there." He takes off his coat.

"Thanks for coming, Pastor." He lays his coat on the couch and sits down beside it. "So, Bob, how can I help you?"

"I'm," *–just say it!–* "I'm afraid, Pastor. I...I don't know what's happening to me. It's like...I'm going crazy. I'm afraid of everything... maybe...it's guilt."

"Guilt from what, Bob?"

"Vietnam. This guy there. He died. It's my fault."

"Why do you say that?"

"His name was...Hippie." –a tear blinks into my eye– "I can't remember his real name...if I wasn't so...if I wasn't so lazy...he'd be alive right now...claymore got him...ours...shoulda been me. It should have been me."

Pastor White paused to take out a small notebook. "I'm not a therapist, Bob. And to be honest, I believe that's what you need." –he began scribbling on the pad– "I'm going to refer you to a Christian psychiatrist who can help you. He's a good friend of mine and I trust him." –he handed me his number– "You've taken the first step, Bob and I'm glad you had the courage to take it. But for now, let me leave you with a verse that's always given me hope when I'm down." –he opened his Bible as the tear left my eye– "Here it is. Jeremiah

29, verse 11. 'For I know the plans I have for you, declares the Lord, plans to prosper you and not to harm you, plans to give you hope *and a future.* '"...✐

Monday, February 22, 1971, Day 124 / 241 to DEROS
—lifer games—

"Guess what, Mike?" –I stuffed a fork-full of powdered eggs into my mouth– "Got four months in country today."

"Four months? Shit. Hey, congratulations, man. Why don't you buy me breakfast then, okay?"

"My treat, 'n' that goes for you, too, Yoss."

"How much time you got, Yoss?" Mike inquired.

"Going on six months," he answered with a mouth-full of sausage.

"Halfway there. Cool."

"Yep," he said before gulping down half of a carton of orange juice. "Since you're buying, Adams," he said, standing, "think I'll get some more sausage and eggs."

"That guy eats like a horse," Mike commented as Yoss headed for the chow line. "How does he stay so skinny?"

"Probably by worrying about his buddy, Ski."

"What is it with those two, anyway? They're always in each others shit."

"All I can think is you got a hard-headed Catholic Wisconsiner and a hard-headed Jewish New Yorker– need I say more?"

*     *     *

Ducking under Retchin's arm, I found myself in good scoring position. "Ski!" He attempted to pass, but Harv's spidery reach pushed the ball off court.

Ski bent over to catch his breath. "Harv, you sorry-ass son-of-a-bitch."

"If ya can't handle the mudafuck'n' heat, Ski-bo, then get yer–"

"Okay, ladies!" Retchin boomed before taking a long draught of beer. "If you don't fuck'n' mind, we're trying to play a serious game here." He set his beer on a weathered picnic table and took a drag on his cigarette. "Your ball, Ski."

Ski passed it in. Before Retchin could react, I zipped around him, going in for an easy lay-up before he could get his cigarette to his mouth.

"Goddamnit!" he complained. "Don't move so fast."

255

"We *were* gonna play the winners!" Langley shouted as he and Fritts approached. "But the way it looks, there ain't gonna be any with all the goddamn bellyach'n' going on. Heard you fuckers clear from *the mess hall.*"...

✎...*6:34 a.m., Monday, January 7, 1991, home*... "*Breakdown?*"

"Yeah, I guess...from Vietnam...or something. I think I need to take the week off. Got an appointment this morning with a psychiatrist, so I'll bring a Doctor's excuse."

"Okay, Bob. Get yourself some help and don't worry about it. I'll take care of everything on this end."

"Thanks, Weiss."

I hung up the phone and looked at the empty kitchen– emptier than I ever remembered. My nerves were wired, pricking my wrists. Pricking my nose. *Just hang on three more hours.* I went into the living room and sat on the sofa, leaned back and closed my eyes. *God, I once held the world in my pocket...sitting warm in my hootch while midnight guard ate away the minutes. Dreaming of life after The Nam. Wife, children, home with a white picket fence, a cottage by the ocean, or nestled deep in the mountains.* Idealism. Perfection. Hope. Life as it should be. Having kids young enough to enjoy them. Dad was forty when I first saw the light of day, in his fifties by the time I had wanted to trade some fast balls with him. But his arm was slow and I felt a tug of compassion as I let up on that burning slider I had perfected. Now I feel so much older than he'd ever been. My own son...what's happening to him now that he's traveling the same path I had taken so long ago? I can't even play catch with him anymore. Too afraid that.... *I'm so sorry, Craig. Can you ever forgive me?*...✎

...*The day was* clear and sizzling, with just a hint of a breeze flowing from the sea that shimmered just a hundred meters from the round ball court. After breakfast, Ski and I had taken a morning dip, yesterday's tumultuous rollers now tranquil. By the time I had arrived at the basketball game at ten, my back was already feeling the effects of the sun's hot rays.

Fritt's and Langley took on the winners and thus we seesawed back and forth until we dragged ourselves over for a late lunch just before one. I couldn't eat much, partially from fatigue, but mostly from an overdose of UV rays and after a feeble attempt at downing some meat loaf, I shuffled to my barrack to crash for the rest of the afternoon.

*　　*　　*

Nelson pushed on my shoulder. "You going to the floorshow?" –he pushed again– "Shit, Adams, your skin's burning up."

I start to turn on my back, but the rough woolen blanket sent me back to my stomach. "Too much sun, man." Ski, two beds down and struggling to pull on his boots, looked in as much misery as I.

Nelson headed for the door. "Let's get going."

Nearing the USO, the discordant blare of guitars and drums warming up competed with the noisy banter of Grunts gathering outside the building. We worked through the crowd to where a cluster of Grunts were attacking several tubs of iced beer and soda, complements of Topp. We grabbed a drink and stopped to talk to Retchin, Blondie and Harv before entering the building.

"*What* are you wearing, soldier?" A CO barked, pointing to my fatigues as we approached the door.

I stopped, coyly looking down at my laced-up pants. "Fatigues I've altered for a better fit, Sir."

The CO glared at me. "Well, *I* don't like them. After this show, you *will* change into regulation dress, soldier. We are *not* running a style show here."

I gave him an awkward salute along with a feeble, "Yes, Sir," my face feeling as hot as my burnt shoulders.

"Woo-hoo! Did he get in your shit or what!" Ski teased as we searched for a seat. "That's what you get for being such a damn rebel, Adams."

"Shut up, Ski. Why can't these lifers leave us Grunts alone?"

A roar from the inebriated Grunts drowned out any further attempt at intelligible conversation as four scantily clad Korean women danced onto the stage in sync with the bands opening number. Blondie was already in high spirits, swinging his hips while several behind him tried to get him to sit down. *This is a juicer's paradise. Us Heads prefer a calmer, mellower form of entertainment. Like watching a fly crawl across the floor…or a rat.*

The Korean band did justice to the dozen or so American hits they shoveled out. What followed was a disappointment. A group of GI's took the stage to impart their interpretation of such hits as *American Woman* and *Born to be Wild*. The lyrics were indistinguishable under a dominating rhythm guitar that blew a typhoon of notes through our ears. But, like saving the cheap wine for last, the juicers didn't mind as they sloshed their beer, shouting and gyrating at the expense of us who had to endure both the crudeness of the band *and* them.

Thursday, February 25, 1971, Day 127 / 238 to DEROS
—a little emptier—

Hillbilly placed the remnants of dew into his well-used ivory pipe like a parched man draining the last precious drops of water from his canteen. Two days ago we were dumped into the *Gobi Desert* re-train area. With monsoon winding down, there was nowhere to hide but the un-air-conditioned, adobe-like barracks as the hours crawled by.

Mike had been re-assigned to bunker guard at the Fat City Firebase. After what had happened last mission, we weren't surprised. I looked at our small group of patriots as Hillbilly passed the last bowl around. The room was a little emptier. I already missed Mike's dry sense of humor and creative strumming while endeavoring to stretch the evening hours. He may have been with us but for a short while, but in those few weeks, his presence had somehow made it easier. He had, in fact, *renewed my hope....*

✎...*10:21 a.m., Monday, January 7, 1991, Bettendorf, Iowa...Dr. Hansen peered* at me through the top of his bifocals as the florescent lights in his office reflected off his bald head.

"You have Post-Traumatic Stress Disorder, Bob." –I wiped at my eyes– "It stems from repressed guilt about Hippie. Bob, his death was not your fault."

"But I shoulda gone."

"You could not have known, Bob. Nobody could have. He made a mistake, that's all. You've been holding this in for twenty years and it's going to take time to get back your joy of living. Think of it as learning to walk all over again."

"How? I'm scared of everything. And I don't understand how this has anything to do with Vietnam."

"It's all tied together. Over the years your guilt has manifested itself in the form of an anxiety disorder and this, too, will take time to work through. In the end, Bob, your success at beating this is entirely up to you."

"Okay. But what about my heart. It starts to flutter or something."

258

"That's perfectly normal for panic attacks."

"You don't understand. I swear sometimes it's doing two hundred beats a minute."

"It's *normal* for panic attacks, Bob. It can *not* hurt you. This is the first thing you have to accept."

"You don't know what it's like when it's happening. I can't think. I can't move. It's...it's like I felt when a rocket was coming at us."

"Listen to what you just said: 'It's like I felt when a rocket was coming at us.' You're mind, it's recreating your near-death experiences, and now this sensation has become a real entity to you." –he paused– "But it is *not* real, Bob. It can *not* hurt you. The next time it happens, go to a quiet place until it stops, but better yet, stay and go through it." –he picked up a notepad– "Look." –he spelled out the word, *F E A R*, vertically on the page– "Do you know what fear really is? Read each word as I complete them."

"*F*-alse, *E*-vidence, *A*-ppearing, *R*-eal."

"And what does that mean?"

"It's all in my head?"

"Pretty much. The actual physical symptoms *do* take place, though there are some who would dispute that. Its source stems from your brain, released by a variety of chemicals into your bloodstream that creates the symptoms you're experiencing."

"How do I stop it?"

"By understanding yourself and what's happening within you." –he flipped to another page on his notepad– "Write the letters *A B C D* vertically on the page." –I did– "Now beside the *A* write 'Activating event'. In your case, this is facing a situation with which you're uncomfortable, like walking up a hill, or shoveling the driveway. Now write 'Belief' beside the *B*. Here you have a choice as to what you believe about the activating event. Are your past beliefs rational or irrational?"

"Irrational?"

"And this brings us to *C*. Write 'Consequences'. Because of your irrational belief in the activating event, you cannot perform the task you wish, which stops life's joys, does it not?"

"Yeah. I guess so."

"Beside the *D*, write 'Disputations'. This is where your human intelligence can counter the natural occurrences taking place in you. Since you now know that palpitations, heart flutters, or a racing heart, are normal for panic attacks, you do *not* have *to fear them.*"...✐

# MISSION EIGHT

Friday, February 26, 1971, Day 128 / 237 to DEROS
—Ski free—

A man approached our platoon. At first I thought it was LT Owens, for he was a similarly built black man in his mid-twenties.

"Second Platoon? I'm replacing Lieutenant Hunter while he's recovering from his wound in Da Nang."

"Ya mean he's a coming back?" Hillbilly asked, disparaging.

"I can't answer that for sure, but I assume he'll resume command. Anyway, I'm Lieutenant Carter, so if you have any questions, I'll be happy to address them now."

\*　　\*　　\*

"Here we go again," uttered a perturbed Yoss as a swarm of female entrepreneurs descended on our truck convoy at the Fat City Airbase. I, on the other hand, didn't mind it at all– a chance to stock up on souvenirs and talk with the fairer sex– what could be better?

"You Cowboy, no?" –one of the soda girls pointed to my laced up fatigues– "I rememba you visa my village."

It was good to be remembered and after the transaction I mingled with the other GI's, enjoying the carnival-like atmosphere while bartering with the local ladies.

Two o'clock brought fourteen choppers, returning a shipment of haggard Grunts so they could begin stand-down. It was a fast switch, the choppers hovering long enough to throw out Company A in exchange for Company D. I braced myself as the now familiar exuberance of lifting into the sky engulfed me. At three thousand feet we slid onto a southwest wind and turned toward a region unfamiliar to me, an area of the 196th AO that hadn't been checked out for the last six months.

Entering a range of mountains towering over the southern section of the I Corp, the choppers split like geese seeking refuge before nightfall. There were four in our flock, soon alighting onto a dry field near a fast running stream. Making my way to the edge of the field, I noticed a heated altercation by the last chopper in line. The chopper ended the argument by ascending into the air, leaving seven unhappy Grunts staring at its departure.

Moving closer, I recognized them as members of the CP Platoon. "This is good," I said to Yoss, "I don't see Tex, Ramos, Pat, Sergeant Trainor...."

Yoss stood with a big grin on his face.

"What?"

Yoss took off his ruck to wait while LT Carter got on the horn. "Ain't no Ski, neither."

Saturday, February 27, 1971, Day 129 / 236 to DEROS
—I got me the rucksack blues—

An early morning switch returned our platoons to normal.

"Fucking CP," Ski whined. "I had to pull *double* guard last night. My shift, *plus* radio watch for an hour. My sorry ass was dragging this morning." –he tried giving Yoss a hug– "Oh, I missed you so much."

"Jeez, Ski, get outta my face, I ain't one of your Wisconsin lover cows."

First break found me pulling off my shirt. The shoulder straps had turned my sunburned shoulders into a blistered mass of raw flesh.

"You, too, huh?" Ski winced.

"For a nickel I'd leave half my supplies behind."

Blondie continued to pick his way on the thin trail, following the stream we had landed by last night. No longer able to stand the straps cutting into my shoulders, I was forced to pull up on the bottom of my ruck to relieve the pressure. It was awkward –I had to carry my 16 by the handle– and dangerous, since my weapon was not as accessible.

The valley narrowed until the terrain on both sides of the stream rose a hundred feet over our heads. Déjà vu– we found ourselves again boxed in with no way out but forward. The dark trail remained well worn, another ominous factor.

"You can almost smell 'em," Ski whispered during one of the endless stops. "Like burning shit." He was right. Though faint, the same smell from

261

the burning hootches during the eagle flights. "If they ain't here now," Ski continued, "they were."

A break signaled down the line and I released my burden. Another message came asking for volunteers to go on a short patrol to check the trail– Blondie had seen something he didn't like.

"Come on guys," I encouraged, "beats staying here like a sitting duck."

"You go." –Ski pulled off his shirt– "I'll stay and practice my quacking."

Yoss and I stepped over a tired Grunt here, a rucksack there and joined LT, Doc, Hillbilly and Sgt. Trainor at the front of the line.

"We're going to check out that structure," LT said, motioning ahead. "We'll take it nice and easy, then find a place to set up for the night."

Nearing a large iron pipe that bridged the stream, Hillbilly spotted several shallow tunnels beside the trail. "Gunny holes," he said, pointing with the muzzle of his 16. "Gooks use 'em to hide in."

The pipe was nearly two meters in diameter, its rusty exterior anchored on both sides of the narrow stream by massive concrete headwalls. Once used as an aqueduct, it still looked operable, had there been any buildings standing for it to supply. We tight-roped across one at a time, in case some gooks were waiting for an easy kill. On the other side we continued our search, but found no sign of VC activity.

<br>

Sunday, February 28, 1971, Day 130 / 235 to DEROS
—don't bug me—

Ahead of us, the remains of an ancient bridge shimmered through the heat. Other French structures dotted the landscape, now overgrown and in total ruin. We had humped all day, retracing our trail from yesterday. Now we found ourselves right back where we had started.

Nelson let his ruck slide off his shoulders. "Shit. Why did I complain about monsoon?"

The heat hammered us as Blondie and Tex set out an MA at the base of the bridge, waiting for us to cross over before connecting the battery. We raised our NDP on a small grassy knoll beyond the other end.

Too hot to cook and too hot to eat, all that was left was to retreat into the plastic shelters. I stripped to my waist and bathed my exposed flesh with bug juice before stretching onto my poncho liner.

As the sun retreated below the horizon, bugs began to retreat into our hootch. Hard-shelled beetles, greasy cockroaches, slick millipedes, rubbery leeches, a flurry of gnats and a stream of mosquitoes flew, slithered or crawled inside and made themselves at home. Unable to fall into a deep sleep, I swatted, slapped, picked and brushed through the night on my *sweat-soaked blanket....*

✎...*6:10 p.m., Wednesday, January 16, 1991, Wildwood Baptist Church...There was a* rock in the pit of my stomach. *6:10...it's started.* The night was blustery. The snow zinged against the church's huge oaken door as I pulled it shut against a biting wind. *Why does it bother me anyway? Desert Storm ain't my war.* But it did. It'd been dogging me all week. *They're gonna do it like I did it and they don't have the slightest fucking idea that when it's all over it ain't all fucking over...it's never all fucking over.*

I walked down the hall with Sheryl, heading for the Wednesday night Bible Study Group. After last week's breakdown, it was time for a change. A time to reset my priorities. On Sunday, I'd gone forward at the invitation. I was determined to leave everything at the altar, to let God take this cracked vessel that could barely move without twitching, palpitating, or going numb. I was going for broke.

The study came and went. Everyone talked like everything was cool. "God will take care of all your needs." –I hoped so– "Give him a chance, you'll see." –he'd better– "In him, all things are possible." Maybe so, but it had better be quick. What are those guys thinking right now? Stuck in the desert, spitting out sand, eating their MRE's. *"How you gonna act, GI? You bookoo dinky dau. You come to desert to fight? You get you domommie head blown off, dinky dau GI."* What do they know? Not a damn thing.

I had volunteered my art skills to create a poster to show where all of the church's soldier boys and girls were stationed in the Gulf region, with a picture tagging them to their location. *Since when is a war like some damn advertising campaign? Desert Storm? Step right up for Desert Annihilation! Gas masks marked down 20%, this week only!*

About to leave, one of the parishioners approached me before I could avoid his eye. "Bob, would you give us a hand? Evelyn's car needs a push to get her off an icy spot in the lower parking lot. I think the three of us could handle it."

His words spear my heart like an icicle. *I can't do this! I can't! Please, God, why the fuck are you doing this to me!* "Okay, I guess so." *My legs. I can't feel my fucking legs!* Down the steps, hold the rail. Don't fall. *God! I got no spit!...* ✎

Monday, March 1, 1971, Day 131 / 234 to DEROS
—sweet relief—

A grim roar from the March lion resounded as the diamond sphere launched over the horizon to pour its fury upon our waking NDP.

"How's that feel?" Doc asked as he applied the salve.

"Tight. Feels tight. So, you think it was a spider?"

"That'd be my guess. The swelling should go down in a day or so."

I took my mirror and gazed through swollen eyes at my red-puffed face. "Man, I look terrible."

"There's a water patrol going out soon. Why don't you tag along? The cold water will do your face good."

"You read my mind."

Seven of us skied up as soon as the tasteless breakfast was over. Through sweat-streaked eyes we spotted an ideal spot to take a dip.

"Heaven's gate is just below the top of that water," Pane said. "You coming?"

I'd be a fool not to.

Tuesday, March 2, 1971, Day 132 / 233 to DEROS
—lucky strike—

I glanced at my watch. "We better be getting back. It's past three-thirty."

"One more dive." Ski climbed to the top of the outcropping and turned his back to the pool before jumping feet first and spearing the water with just a wisp of a splash.

"Not bad. We keep this up and we'll be Olympic divers by the time we get out of The Nam."

It was a repeat of yesterday– not a hint of a cloud. By the time we returned to the NDP, we felt as if we had spent the past three hours digging a foxhole in a river of molten lava rather than frolicking in a cold mountain stream. It had been another buggy, sleepless night, but as morning dawned, my face was beginning to shrink back to normal, although it itched like crazy.

With rucks full– after an early morning re-supply– we hooked-up at four sharp and crossed the French bridge to continue along a well-traveled dink trail. In less than five-hundred meters and forty-five minutes, LT informed us that we had reached today's goal, a spiny bush-covered hill rising only fifty feet above the trail.

"Not much of a hump, LT," Hillbilly commented as Lt. Carter approached the front of the line.

"As long as it's far enough to keep the dinks off our ass, that's all I care about."

Hillbilly studied the craggy terrain in front of him. "Ya picked yerself one helluva a hill, LT. Gonna take a while to cut up this un'."

LT looked around at several carbon copy hills close by. "You see anything better than this one, be my guest, Mr. Glidewell."

"You 'n' me's gonna git along jis' fine. I kin tell that, LT."

"That's good. Now you want to start cutting up this fucker?"

Hillbilly began to hack through the thorny plants with Pat and Spanky while the rest of us waited at the hill's base, careful not to cluster in groups along the narrow trail.

"Shit! Cock...suck'n' motha...!"

LT cupped his hands to his mouth. "Hillbilly! What is it?!"

No answer. Instead, the sound of brush being pushed aside told us they were heading back. Seconds later Hillbilly appeared, supported by Pat and Spanky. He was holding his left leg off the ground as a stream of blood trickled from a four-inch tear in his fatigues over his shinbone.

"Don't even say it," Hillbilly warned Blondie.

"Christ, Hillbilly, I wasn't gonna say nothing. So ya cut your leg. You want a fucking medal?"

"Fuck, no," Hillbilly grimaced, "jis' a week of sham time."

Doc pulled up Hillbilly's pants leg, revealing a three-inch slice diagonally across the shin. "Right down to the bone, Hillbilly," Doc sniffed. "You did it proud, man."

"That's the way I do things, Doc. It's all or noth'n' with me."

"Okay, Tuck. Get a duster in here. This man's going in."

"What about the hill, LT?" Spanky asked. "You want us to keep cutting?"

"Fuck no. Far's I'm concerned, this hill's jinxed. We'll set up down here tonight."

Given low priority, it took close to forty minutes before Hillbilly's bird came. "Y'all keep cool now," were his last words before two volunteers whisked him through a whirlwind of orange smoke.

"He'll be sitt'n' pretty tonight," Spanky commented as we watched the bird dip over the next ridge.

Wednesday, March 3, 1971, Day 133 / 232 to DEROS

—don't tread on Tex—

Last night fulfilled our dreams. As the evening light faded, so did the heat; a cool northerly breeze washed over our NDP. The bugs, too, left us alone, opting instead to nest comfortably in their own abodes. And I, exhausted after several sleepless nights, slept like a baby. With the morning light, my appetite returned full force, feasting on two cans of boned chicken, followed by an encore of sliced peaches, coffee and pound cake.

We moved out earlier than usual, eight o'clock and although the sun did its best to wilt our renewed energy, it couldn't compete with the blast furnace reputation it had earned the last couple of days. We had only moved a short distance when Blondie found a bunker complex hiding under some freshly cut brush, only ten meters from our trail that paralleled a wide stream as it wound its way into our AO. The half-buried, ten foot square structure was constructed of mostly clay and was covered with several layers of small diameter trees, each layer reinforced with a mixture of more dried clay and grass.

"Don't look like much," LT announced, "but if the VC had a couple RPG's in here, they could waste a platoon in a mad minute."

"LT!" Blondie pointed to several other lumps of brush distributed randomly on a twenty-meter radius. "Looks like they're planning a party."

With further investigation, we located four bunkers in all. LT speculated that this possibly could be the sight from which the nearby firebase was getting peppered in recent weeks.

"Good thing we got bookoo C-4 in that re-supply," LT said. "We're gonna need it. Blondie, pick three men to help blow the bunkers. I'm going to radio in our *find to CP.*"...

*✎…12:46 p.m., Tuesday, March 26, 1991, Rock Island, Illinois…I reach into* the storage box atop the *Motor Vessel Sweatt* and hand two transponder units to Bill, who begins to screw them onto the tops of the tripods. Scotty is on the helm as we head across a choppy river created by a stiff west wind to survey the upper side of Lock and Dam 15. The boat bobs like a cork as he gingerly pulls up next to the concrete seawall protecting Davenport's shoreline.

"Just punch 'er in," Bill advises and the rubber fender scuffs two feet up the wall. Scott throttles in tight to the seawall while my heart palpitates with the waves. *Why won't it STOP! I felt great during lunch, felt great all morning, but soon as I get out here…IT JUST WON'T QUIT!* As soon as the boat steadies, I jump on top of the narrow wall with transponder in tow, thankful for the steady ground and walk it to the horizontal control point fifty feet upstream. *Come on, man, relax, remember what Hansen said.* I spread the tripod legs over the survey point, struggling to position them so the gale wouldn't push the unit over.

"Need a safety line!" I yell through the gusts to Bill, who is watching from the bow. He ducks into the cabin and soon returns with a short length of three-eighths inch line.

Approaching, Bill scans the wall on the landside to the bottom, fifteen-feet below. "There's nothing to tie it to! Try putting the legs out wider."

"It'll hafta do," I tell Bill as I check it for stability. "Let's just hope it don't go in." We jump back on board and Scotty heads for the next transponder point, just above the dam. My heart thumps like Peter Rabbit's foot. *God, I'm sick of this! End! Please! Please, God, help me do this!*

*…Journal entry, 3-26-91*

PVC's continued right up to 4:30, but the second I got into Bill's car to go home– BAM! They stopped just as quickly as they began when I stepped on the boat! Crazy! It's now 8 pm & feel fine, no PVC's at all. What a day. I believe all this is going on because of that stupid physical I have to take Fri. morning. This is dumb. I mean, realizing what's going on & yet it's happening anyway. And then, for it to stop so suddenly, right at quitting time, when my responsibility has ended. How much longer will this go on? Hansen says it might take the same amount of time as it did for all of this to develop. It's been coming on for ten years. I don't know if I can hold on for another ten years. Even today, I thought I'd be *better off dead.…✎*

*...I slowly rolled* my head and rubbed my blistered shoulders before continuing to swing the blade at the twisted mass of thorny bushes in front of me while behind me Nelson, Spurlin and Tex waited their turn to attack the barbed labyrinth. We were less than a klick from last night's NDP; LT was satisfied to slowly leapfrog into our AO. And with each hill looking like it was pressed out of a cookie cutter, it left us with no option but to pick one and grope to its spiny pinnacle.

Two hours after Nelson's first swing, he took his last to open the door to the top. Amazingly, there was little growth on the hill's apex. Instead, a field of elephant grass painted the top with a dusty green hue, along with a few prickly bushes that intruded like the greasy pimples on Pat's chin.

"Looks like we weren't the first ones here," Nelson said as he sat down to rest. "Hope we're the last, though."

After a short rest, we returned to retrieve our rucks and lead the platoon back up, the loop taking less than ten minutes. "Is this shit or what," Tex declared in his Wayne Newton slang, "two fucking hours of cutting, followed by a five-minute hump."

Blondie dropped his ruck to claim a position on the far side. "Tex, this small-ass hill would look like a mountain in Texas." –he winked at Retchin, who was unloading his 60– "Why, if I was standing on top of a hill this big in the middle of Texas, I bet I could spot your momma changing your diaper right inside your nursery."

"Blondie," Tex said, pulling out an arrow from his quiver of Texan comebacks, "if you were standing on a hill like this in the middle of Texas, everybody in the whole fucking state would get to see just what a lazy, backwoods, good-for-nothing pussy you really are."

Thursday, March 4, 1971, Day 134 / 231 to DEROS
—this ain't Kansas—

"There it is again," I whisper as the echo fades in the night breeze.

Ski leans forward to pick up his 16; he slowly lets out his breath. "Shit. Nelson...you hear that?"

Nelson didn't. He was sound asleep. Ski and I sit like jade Buddha's until another ominous growl confirms our fear.

"Think he's coming up the hill?" Ski whispers.

I grip my 16 tighter. "If he is, he's gonna get one big surprise."

"*If* he takes the trail," Ski rattles back.

The hair on the nape of my neck bristles as a slithering sound shoots my head toward the corner of the hootch. Exhaling, I relax; a gecko is checking us out. *Great timing, lizard.* I turn my stare back into the night. Ten minutes pass without a sound. Ski's steady breathing denotes that he's asleep– he had pulled guard just prior to me. *Who woulda thought I'd be spending tonight worrying about a tiger attacking us. Just think, a wild Bengal Tiger, roaming just outside our camp. Wonder if it's ever killed any villagers around here?* I look into the night sky as a cool breeze caresses me. *Musta didi'd. Maybe the scent of man scared 'im off...who knows? Lions, tigers, bears? Man, this ain't even Kansas.*

Friday, March 5, 1971, Day 135 / 230 to DEROS
—tiger butter—

A seven-thirty wake-up had us packing for a re-supply chopper that was already heading to drop a load of C's at the base of our hill. While stuffing my gear in my ruck I asked if anyone had heard anything unusual last night. Nobody had. They thought we'd imagined it, though Ski didn't buy it, saying we weren't *even* short enough yet to be *that* dinky dau.

*       *       *

"For Christ's sake, why the fuck can't they schedule the dump *after* the hump?" Blondie retorted, cramming six new meals in his ruck as the chopper disappeared over the next rise.

"Be too much like thinking," Langley answered. "Don't *even* want 'em to ruin their reputation."

We began our usual five hundred-meter leapfrog along the valley floor, continuing along the same trail until we found ourselves at the base of one of the taller hills. The scrubs were just as thick as on the previous hill as a new machete crew wielded its way up. At its summit we were treated to a spectacular view of our AO, including a view of the firebase that guarded this sector. Other GI's had used the top of this hill at least once, so we were on the lookout for booby-traps as we established our positions.

Our hootch was almost up when a flurry of chatter broke over the radio. Tuck and LT exchanged confused glances. "What the fuck's going on?" Tuck queried.

A few more exchanges over the radio. "Fuck if I know." –LT picked up the horn– "Charlie Papa, Charlie Papa, Echo Foxtrot. Break." –no answer– "Charlie Papa, Echo Foxtrot. Break."

*"Echo Foxtrot, Charlie Papa, I gotcha good, how me. Break."*

"Same same, Charlie Papa. What's the chatter. Break."

*"Roger, Echo Foxtrot, Hotel November's got one confirm. Scared the shit out of them. Break."*

"I copy, Charlie Papa. Why the scare? Break."

*"Echo Foxtrot, Hotel November bagged one Bengal striper. Break."*

"Roger. Out."

LT slowly lowered the phone, noticing our curious looks. "Adams, you were right. First Platoon just killed themselves *a fucking tiger.*"...

✎*...11:14 a.m., Tuesday, June 4, 1991, home...What the hell am I doing?* My gaze to the first fork of the elm tree starts my heart to palpitate. *Do I really want to do this?* I stand still, practicing the breathing technique that Dr. Hansen had showed me. *Breathe in... nice and easy...eight, nine, ten. Out... nice and easy...eight, nine, ten.*

I drive the first nail into the *2 x 4*, the first rung of a makeshift ladder that will lead to the elm fork twenty-five feet above. Ten feet above the fork is the rotted rope swing that I plan to replace with a new nylon rope. I *could* use a ladder but– I have something to prove.

The trunk is tough and I bend several nails before securing the chest-high board. I reach over my head and nail in the second rung. My chest palpitates. *Come on...relax. Okay, here I go.* Grabbing onto the second rung I pull myself to the first and begin banging in the third.

Thus up I go, rung-by-rung, all the while my heart jerking and bouncing inside my chest in protest that I dare defy my fear.

I look to the ground, twenty feet below. *Woulda been a walk in the park before the swamp attack. But now, it's life and death. Keep going.* The most challenging is ahead– over the bump by the fork. I continue to drive in the rungs, the hardest part of which is starting the first nail. I have to free my grip on the tree and hold the *2 x 4* with one hand while hammering with the other. To do that, I must wrap one leg around the tree to free my hands.

Sixty minutes finds me placing the last rung a foot below the fork. The task has taken my mind off my heart, which had surrendered to my determination several rungs below me. Now it is tapping as steady as my hammer. I start a new nail and drive it home. The last rung is secured and I place my life in its hands and pull myself onto the fork above it.

I scan the hilly neighborhood and relax. *I can't remember the last time I had a victory like this....✍*

Saturday, March 6, 1971, Day 136 / 229 to DEROS
—rage—

"Now what?" An agitated LT listened to another burst on the radio as he gulped down some early morning grub. "Fuck. Not again."

"Whatsamatta, LT?" Blondie was sipping his coffee and eyeing LT's disconcerted expression.

"One of First's hit a toe popper. Leg's torn up good." –LT paused to listen– "The point man tripped it, but the slackman got the full force of it." – he listened to a few more lines– "Some guy called, 'Bobby'."

"That's their fucking *Kit* Carson Scout," Spurlin broke in.

Everybody fell silent as we watched Larry stand up, who was cooking some noodles that were just coming to a rolling simmer on his C-4 stove. "Christ, Larry. I'm sorry, man," Blondie offered in condolence. Larry and Bobby had been best friends since childhood. Bobby had been looking forward to a trip back to the World with a GI friend of his who was going home on leave. Larry just stood there as the rage simmered on his high cheekbones. Larry's mother and father had also been victims of VC terrorist. "Doncha fucking worry, Larry," Blondie continued. "You'll get your chance at the motherfucking VC."

I looked down at Larry's canteen cup as the noodles boiled over *onto the earth....*

✍...*Monday, July 6, 1992, Peoria Boatyard...It's 1:43 in* the afternoon. I'm at the Peoria Yard office watching the clock hoping to get out early and maybe catch an early swim at the Fairfield Inn.

The phone rings. Betty takes it.

"Jed, it's your office."

"Hello?" –a pause– "Hey, Weiss, what's up, man?" –another pause– "What?!" Jed jerks his head as if someone had just kicked him. "You're shit'n' me!" –his voice goes up an octave– "Ed?!" –he holds his body rigid, only his bobbing head acknowledging Weiss' news– "Shit. No way!"

"Guys!" Jed says. "Ed Holling just *died!*"

My spit dries up as the blood deserts my head. *No–*

Bill is standing by the door; he doesn't move.

"He had a heart attack! On the elevator. Scott was with him when it happened and *he* passed out."

I stand up and walk into the communications room just off the main office. *Gotta sit down.* I plead with my lungs for one full breath. But it isn't there. *Not Ed!* After several minutes, Jed walks in.

"You okay, man?"

"I dunno. Don't feel so hot."

"Well, I can't blame you. It's a shock."

I stare at my chalky hands. *He just got married this weekend. Showed me his ring not six hours ago. Maybe he sensed something. He'd been complaining for months about some kind a reflux in his throat, or something weird like that. Scotty said there were times when Ed couldn't even walk around the lock chamber. Had to get the cart to pick him up. Man, I just had dinner with him last week in Clinton. Talking 'bout The Nam and he joking about how nothing'd gone on while I was there just cause he went through the '68 Tet offensive.* I fill my lungs as far as they allow. *Wrists feel weird. Man, can't nothing happen without me thinking about myself? I'm not the one who just hit the dirt....*✏

Sunday, March 7, 1971, Day 137 / 228 to DEROS
—mad minute misfire—

My sunburn was much improved as we neared the Rocket Pocket. Good thing, too, for the sun was back in full force after taking a few days R&R. We were two hours into the hump when I began to notice a definite change in the terrain. Smaller hills, covered with thick elephant grass and an occasional scrub tree, spread before us as the valley flattened.

By eleven-thirty we reached our pre-designated coordinates for the day. "Gonna split elements tonight," LT informed us during a break at the base of a small saddle. "Blondie, Spurlin, take your squads up the south saddle and the rest of us will take the north. That'll cover our ass since we'll have an eyeball on all sides." It made sense to me this time. Both hills mirroring each other, we'd be blind on one side if we had occupied either the north or the south side. This guy knew his stuff.

"See those buildings?" –LT pointed with his 16 at the ravaged remains of some old French buildings several hundred meters to the east– "We're going to do a little recon by fire when we reach the top. Open up for about sixty seconds on 'em in case we got us some dinks hiding in there. And it'll be a good chance to check out your weapons since we haven't had a chance to use 'em yet this mission. Okay, Blondie, Spurlin? See you at the top."

For the first time this mission, it was an easy hump up, requiring little clearing as Nelson led the way. Both elements reached the top at about the same time. LT allowed us a minute to get our weapons in order and to spread out on a rough firing line, then, raising his arm to synchronize both sides, he raked down his arm to signal open fire.

A deafening *RRRRRRRIP!* rattled in my ears as I emptied my first magazine in only a few seconds on full auto. I popped it out and shoved in another and immediately squeezed the trigger. Three rounds flew out the barrel and then stopped. One of the cartridges was jammed at an odd angle in the ejector flap. I pulled back the cocking handle and pried the round out and chambered another. Again, the same thing happened. *What's going on?* I thought as LT waved his arms to signal the cease-fire.

"Double-feeding," Nelson said, answering my thought as he spotted my predicament. "Hey, LT. Adams' 16's double feeding!"

LT came over and took my 16, pulling back the handle to free the stuck cartridge. "Gas port might be plugged. Shit, Adams, we'll have to order you a new one tee-tee." –he handed it back and winked– "Just hope we don't get any action till then, huh?"

Monday, March 8, 1971, Day 138 / 227 to DEROS<br>—pith?—

Before reaching the bottom of the hill, the distinct *BRRRRRAAAAAPPP!* of a 16 on full auto resounded.

"All clear!" came Blondie's familiar rasp. "Spotted a dink!" he shouted as he came around a turn in the path. "Fucker was trying to cut across the trail at the bottom of our hill."

"You get 'im?" LT asked.

"Christ, no. Sure as fuck missed."

"Keep sharp, men!" LT announced to the rest of us. "Gooks might be setting us up for an ambush."

A light mist began to fall from a blanket of thick gray clouds as we continued southeast. Yesterday we had left the stream that had served us so faithfully through much of the mission, which continued to wind toward the sea with the maze of other streams draining the wide delta valley. Replacing the stream were a number of gunny holes bordering the trail. Blondie moved the platoon slowly so as to check out each one, in case the gook he missed was using it till we passed. A klick later we arrived at the base of our new NDP. I had counted no less than thirty-six holes along the way, all invisible except when I was directly adjacent to them. *A VC gauntlet,* I conjectured as we took a break at the bottom of our hill.

LT must've overheard Blondie's complaint the other day, for he had scheduled a re-supply at the end of the day's hump instead of the start. Nearly forty-five minutes later the muffled thumping of a Huey drowned out the gentle sound of a shower spritzing the surrounding growth. It was a quick swap in a fog of blue smoke as the chopper dumped our load of supplies in exchange for a small stack of homeward-bound letters.

"Adams," Ross yelled, "here's your new 16!"

I looked at my old one and then at the departing bird, making hay for the rear. "What about—"

"Oops," Ski said from behind me, "you're gonna be well armed *now.*"

The bird's delivery of a D-ring, a stack of letters and especially a new air mattress offset my ire at having to hump two *16*'s for the rest of the mission. "Least I'll be able to sleep better at night." I told Ski as I packed my mattress and tied my old 16 to the top of my ruck. "Be right back, Ski. Gotta take a pith...I mean...a piss," I said as I quietly correcting my stumbling attempt at using the taboo language.

Ski snickered. "Adams, you know how dumb that sounds to hear you say that? Don't *even* fit you, man." My red face didn't answer. He was right.

By the time we reached the hill's top, the light misting shifted to a steady shower. Doc, Ski and I retreated into our hastily built hootch to wait out the end of the rain or the afternoon, *whichever came first....*

✎*...Tuesday, July 7, 1992, Peoria, journal entry...Raining hard. Did nothing @ Boatyard all morning. PVC's start at 8:30. Feeling uptight no matter what. They kept up till 1:45. 24 hours after hearing about Ed. But that's not why they stopped.*

Rain finally ended, so went to boat to install hatch openers (shock absorbers). I was scared to death for some reason– just to do a little work– PVC's going like crazy. Dave asked me to take the sander and cut some weld off. I wasn't sure if I could do it. I did though. Then I helped Dave put a pin on one of the shocks and as I was helping, (@ 1:45) a wonderful peace came over me. My PVC's vanished. I felt fantastic. The answer was simply to face and overcome a challenge I thought I couldn't handle.

Never had the PVC's ended so dramatically– again God has showed me that my problem is in my head. Went on 2-hour walk this evening. *Feel @ peace....✐*

Tuesday, March 9, 1971, Day 139 / 226 to DEROS
— 'Smok'n' Joe, smok'n' hill—

I gazed into my mirror and rubbed my hand over two week's of stubble on my chin. *Never had a beard this long...cool.* The beard wasn't the only thing growing on me: three days without a dip in a stream, combined with two days of rain had transformed me into a picture of grime.

LT gave us a treat before leaving our hill. He offered Blondie's radio so we could listen in on the pre-recorded Clay-Frazier fight on the Armed Forces Radio Network. Dubbed the *Fight of the Century*, it was the first time in the history of the heavyweight division that two undefeated boxers would face each other in a title bout. The bell rang in Madison Square Garden and for the next hour we felt the stinging jabs of Clay and Frazier's powerful body shots as they took the fight the full fifteen rounds. In the end "Smoking Joe" came out on top, retaining the title belt from a frustrated Cassius Clay.

*       *       *

I stood to stretch my back. "This look familiar?"

"Ain't this where we were at Christmas?" Yoss said.

Ski was concentrating on blowing a cloud of smoke onto a leech, stretching gumby-like for his boot. "I knew we'd been here before. Must be outta the 196th's AO. Don't know why they put us there anyway."

"Least there weren't any dinks to deal with," Yoss said.

"No, just your breath, Bronx-head."

"Ski..." –Yoss kneaded his eye– "...nothing."

275

After the break, we continued for another klick, passing more familiar country; we were traversing the very trail we had used on Christmas Day. Ahead of us loomed the monster hill TR had made us hump up after gorging on that luke-warm Christmas dinner. Carter proved to have more common sense than Hunter, instead choosing one of the smaller grassy hills. By two o'clock, we were set up and preparing a late lunch.

LT informed us the mission was about over: a ball game was on the roster for tomorrow afternoon. With rejuvenated spirits Nelson and I set out to establish the MA's: one on the main trail, the other on the path leading to the NDP. To speed things up, Nelson took one and I took the other. About finished, I looked up to rest my eyes, fixing my gaze on the evening horizon. I squinted at one of the hills across the valley, some five to six hundred meters away.

"Nelson. Stand up slow and turn around." —he did— "Look to your right, that hill way over there, see what I see?"

Nelson studied the hill's side. "Your damn eyes. How mucha got left?"

"Just about to hook up the blasting cap."

"Wait a second." —he quickly finished and slid around me— "Okay, let's didi," he said as I pushed the cap home. We made camp in a few minutes and headed for LT's hootch.

"Adams spotted gooks."

"Where?"

There was too much brush at LT's position, so I directed him toward the south side of the perimeter where there was a clear view. "That hill over there. There's three or four of 'em."

"I got 'em." —LT adjusted his binoculars— "I see, no, wait, five, six, fuck, maybe more and they ain't got a clue we know about 'em. Way to go, Adams. Tuck, get me the horn and my map." —scanning the grid map, he located the hill— "Oscar Sierra, Echo Foxtrot. Break."

"*Gotcha, Echo Foxtrot. How me? Break.*"

"Same same. We got unfriendlies at hotel 167, Bravo Sierra...468...852. Request fire. Break."

"*Echo Foxtrot, I copy. Unfriendlies at hotel 167, Bravo Sierra 468852. Do you have visual? Break.*"

"Affirmative, Oscar Sierra. Break."

*"Roger, Echo Foxtrot. Correct smoke. Break."* It wasn't a minute before a distant "THUMP" was followed by a ripping sound that ended in white smoke, short and south of the target.

"Oscar Sierra," LT said as the dull pop of the explosion reached our ears, "adjust up three zero zero. Right one zero zero." Ten more seconds and another smoke slams into the base of the hill. LT studied the smoke with his binos. "Adjust up one zero zero and fire for effect, fire for effect." A series of thumps brought in a barrage of *105*'s, pelting the scattering VC and turning the hill into a typhoon of dense black smoke.

Wednesday, March 10, 1971, Day 140 / 225 to DEROS
—blue rainy blues—

*"Now* what time is it?" Yoss asked: his watch had died two days ago.

"Three minutes later than the last time you asked," I answered, "but if you gotta know, it's five-sixteen." We'd been waiting for our CE since two o'clock and the prognosis didn't look good. At five-thirty our suspicions were confirmed as Tuck received a call that our mission was being extended one more day. Making our way back to our old NDP, the thickening clouds began to bleed a steady stream of warm water that added to our depression. In ten minutes we had our hootch reset. With no food and not able to read in the waning light, I resigned myself to an early retirement, hoping to glean a little hope from my dreams.

# STAND-DOWN EIGHT

Thursday, March 11, 1971, Day 141 / 224 to DEROS
—hardcore—

Blondie stands up. "Get your ass out there, Adams! Bring 'dem beautiful birds to papa!"

I yank the pin and let a smoke grenade fly into the middle of a narrow rice paddy as four slicks roll over the nearest hill. Spotting the orange cloud, the choppers drop while I hold my 16 overhead with one hand and grip my camera with the other. I get off a shot before having to tuck my head, close my eyes and lean into the hurricane. We jump aboard and the birds rebound into the air. Like segments of a caterpillar the choppers approach the hill we had called home before banking back toward our LZ. The swaying paddy grass sweeps beneath my faded combat boots and we race into the sky and toward the first evening star.

*     *     *

"Get in formation, men!" an unfamiliar face commanded as we entered the desert re-train area.

"Who the *fuck* is that hot dog," Retchin bellowed from the truck bed.

"*That* fuck'n' hot dog, you mangy Grunt, is our new CO."

Retching jumped clumsily to the ground. "Hillbilly! You sonofabitch! How the fuck are you?"

"I'm jis' dandy. But *you* folk are in fer one big shake-up. Lot's happened since last stand-down." –he turned and squinted at the new CO, standing rigidly in front of the armory– "Fucker's a *Green Beret.* Hardcore clean to his eye-fuck'n'-teeth."

There was no more time for small talk and the late hour wasn't about to spare us from the man's wrath as the CO studied Topp's attempt to form us into ranks: shouting, pointing, pushing and pulling. Finally roughing out eight ragged rows, we stood, watching with apprehension as the CO's glare flashed against the setting sun.

"Men," –the CO paused for effect– "my name is Colonel Gander. You have been detailed to the 196th Brigade. Until your return," –another long pause– "you belong to me. Rumors have been flying as to the future of the brigade but, before we enter into that arena...."

The colonel removed his cover and blistered a stare across our ranks from one end to the other. "*What* kind of outfit is this! You bluelegs look more like a band of pirates than representatives of the United States Army!" –I shifted left, trying to conceal my laced fatigues behind Harv's slouching body– "Haircuts *will* be enforced ASAP! Facial hair *will* be within military specs. No more sideburns, no more goatees. Your TA-50 *will* be according to regulation. This means steel helmets. This means all point-men will be assigned one each flack-jacket. This means foxholes at your NDP *will* replace the," –an ominous glance at Topp– "air mattresses someone has erroneously issued you. Until a unit *looks* proper, it cannot conduct itself in proper fashion. Is this understood men?"

No response.

"*Is* this understood men?!"

A feeble, "Yes, sir."

"I CAN'T HEAR YOU!"

"YES SIR!" echoed among our ranks.

"That's better. Sergeant!" –Topp almost stumbled in his rush to the CO's side– "Dismiss the men!"

Topp brought a sloppy salute to his forehead before facing the company of tired grunts. "ATTENNNN-HUT!" –we stiffly pulled our feet together– "D I I I I I-SMISSED!"

Hillbilly accompanied us to the armory to get on with the standing down of our weapons. "So, CO Gander thinks he's a gonna shovel us some sorry shit, huh? We'll jis' see 'bout that." –he looked back at Ski, Pat and me– "We'll see who lays the golden egg, boys. Rememba, Ol' Gander Goose hadn't faced *the Hillbilly yet.*"...

✎*...1:18 p.m., Thursday, August 20, 1992, Joliet, Illinois...*"*Back me in,* Dave." Jed settled behind the controls of the sixteen-foot skiff like Bogart taking out the African Queen. *Why does HE always have to drive?* Avenarius backed the trailer down the narrow concrete ramp, stopping as Jed clenched his fist to signal me to release the bow from the wench. *Especially now.* He powered up the 25-horse Yamaha and backed off the trailer before giving Avenarius the thumbs up to pull the trailer out. *Two more days. Just two more days of this shit and it's over.* Avenarius and I got in as Jed bowed into the bank. I sat on the center bench seat; Avenarius leaned back on the bow seat and lit *up a cigarette....*✎

*...I checked in* my two *16's*, grenades, smokes and ammo and headed for mail call to collect a modest stack of letters and a package from home. Inside the package were a box of cookies along with several requested items of long standing, among them a spelling book to increase my word skills and a brown T-shirt to add a little variety out in the field. *Wonder if I'll be able to wear it now that we got the new CO?* I thought as I neatly folded the shirt into my rucksack.

Linda Sheesley's letter was next, mostly about her new beau that led me to conclude it would be a waste of time to write back. Sandy Johnson's letter I saved for last. It was small talk, but I savored her words like *manna from heaven.* ...

✎...*1:29 p.m., Joliet, Illinois...Ever since the* Nam I've carried an uncanny sense of knowing when danger was just around the corner. Call it a sixth sense, I don't know, but as we headed in silence down the narrow Hickory creek, I knew we were in for a bad afternoon. This morning the lock guys had the Brandon Road Lock and Dam's far gates wide open to keep the suction away from the towboats as they head into the lock chamber on the upstream side. Unfortunately, those gates were at the point where our creek emptied into the Illinois Waterway below the dam. As we came out of Hickory Creek, we discovered that the nylon tape that we'd set out the evening before to help us eyeball our distance from the dam had been sucked into the hydraulic created by the gate's thirty-five foot high by fifty-foot long wall of water thundering into its self-made scour hole. If you've never seen a hydraulic close up, it's something to behold as the crash of water creates a backward spin, or "hydraulic". Get caught in it and it'll slam you to the bottom and roll you back up behind the water curtain, just to get sucked back down again, over and over and over like a croc's death roll....

Anyway, Jed sees the tape sucked into the hydraulic and immediately heads for the concrete wing wall that butts against the open gate– without first calling the lock to close it off. I could see what could happen– any idiot could. But Jed gets lucky, driving the flimsy bow into the bank just ten feet from the waterfall. I jump out like a scared rabbit, ready to kiss mother earth as I scramble up the wing wall and pull the tape out. The tape is all tangled so I go to untangle it. Jed finally calls the lock to send a guy over to close the gate, so I take my time, praying he'll get here before I have to get back in that skiff before Jed backs out. A 25-horse motor in reverse isn't much stronger than using a couple oars. *Jed, what if the engine conks out?...*✎

...*Hillbilly was full* of news from the rear. "Guess what boys?" –he passed a new yellow bowl he had purchased at the PX– "One of 'dem rumors the ol' Goose is gonna di-vulge tomorrow is that we're a gonna be on Da Nang bunker guard start'n' April First. Check it out."

"Far out!" –I bit into a chocolate chip cookie– "hear anything about next mission?"

Hillbilly blew out a perfect ring of smoke. "Northern Rocket Pocket."

I took the pipe from Pat, inhaling deeply. We just might coast right on out of Chu Lai yet.

Friday, March 12, 1971, Day 142 / 223 to DEROS
—no way out—

As the afternoon wore on, my untrimmed hair stuck out more and more as one by one the GI's succumbed to the inevitable: a regulation haircut and shave. The CO had set up an impromptu barbershop in one of the re-train classrooms, meanwhile doing spot inspections and making good on his promise. Walking across the sandy compound I tried to keep some Grunts between the CO and myself, but I knew it was useless. Before the hour turned over I gave it up and entered the shearing barn. Taking a seat in the barber chair I looked from the shiny stainless-steel scissors to the Vietnamese barber. "Just a little off *the sides, okay?"*...

✎*...1:46 p.m., Joliet, Illinois...So, here we go again. Am I stupid or something? If I survive this guy, I SWEAR, no more Jed's in my life. NEVER!* Rounding the last bend, we again face the thunder of the dam. *Fuck! The gate's open again! Is there no God?!* Jed throws the boat into neutral and picks up the radio as we drift toward the end of Hickory creek. "Brandon Road Lock, survey skiff."

*"Brandon Road back." Thank you, Jesus. And please...hurry.*

"Yeah, could you send someone over to close off these gates at the east end?"

*"Yeah, someone'll be right over."* The boat drifts smoothly down the center of the creek toward the roar of water. Jed sits behind his steering wheel like some seafaring god as we meet the end of the creek and enter the narrow basin below the dam. Avenarius sits erect on the bow, his cigarette still in his mouth– but he isn't sucking, instead his eyes glare at me in bewilderment as if to say, *"You guys play with your fucking lives like this all the time? I'm just a damn temp, man! I don't need this macho bullshit!"* The motor idles roughly. I scan for the oars, noting their exact location and exactly how I will have to pick them up should the motor just happen to die from a drop of water in the

281

fuel line or a hiccup of air passing through. Jed sits like King Neptune; *nothing* can *happen to Jed....*✐

*...A knock on* the door interrupted our festivities. "Come on a in!" Hillbilly cackled.

"Hey, man, I presume this is the home of the Second Platoon Heads?"

"*Mike!*" I proclaimed wide-eyed.

"Heard you guys were in town," he said as he took his guitar from its case, "so I skied up from Fat City. Thought I'd spend the night."

I refilled a new bowl I had purchased on a morning run to the PX– after getting scalped. We spent the next few hours *renewing our hope....*

✐...*1:54 p.m., Joliet, Illinois...Our skiff drifts* slowly toward the outer rim of the hydraulic.

One hundred feet: the chasm slowly draws us in; its mist fails to cool my worried brow. Not able to sit still any longer, I motion Jed with a shy whisk of the hand to back up.

Seventy-five feet: he ignores me as the boat rocks gently. The roar of the approaching death-hole tenses my muscle and nerve. *What the fuck is he thinking about? He's a fucking idiot!*

Sixty feet: "Hey, Jed," I blurt, "back up." He looks at me like I had just hit him with a rock. Avenarius could've sprouted wings.

Fifty: "What?" Jed snips, "*I'm* not going to let anything happen to us."

Forty: *the fucking guy has fucking lost it!* "Hey, Jed. Back up!"

Thirty: Jed glares at me as he pulls the throttle back. The engine falls into reverse. *Thank God! It didn't stall!*

Twenty-five: Jed jams the throttle down and the whirling prop pushes the engine's lower unit out of the water. *Fuck, it ain't even locked down!*

Fifteen: I leap to the stern and push the propeller into the water. He feeds the motor more gas; the boat begins to back up. Five feet. Ten. Fifteen. Twenty-five. Fifty. As the current releases its grip, I lock the motor down. Jed pulls up on the throttle a hundred feet from the dam, then flips it back into neutral. *Now why'd he stop?* We again begin to drift toward the vortex.

Seventy-five: Avenarius is gripping the boat's sides with white knuckles.

Fifty: my jaws clench. "Back UP, man!"

Twenty-five: Jed eyes me like I'm crazy and slams it into reverse. Ten feet. "This far enough?" –fifteen– "How 'bout this?" –twenty-five– "Here?" – seventy-five– "Want me to back all the way to the *damn boat ramp?*"...✐

Saturday, March 13, 1971, Day 143 / 222 to DEROS
—dress right...dress?—

Topp drew his skinny legs together. "Company. ATENNNNN-HUT! DRESS RIIIIGHT! DRESS!"

"Fuck'n' ridiculous," I overheard Retchin comment from behind me, bringing a snicker from those within earshot. The cool morning breeze had picked up considerably and as I stood waiting, the cold air whipping through my shirt took me back to that October formation in Cam Rahn, the day my orders had come down.

The CO advanced gallantly and snapped to attention as he saluted Topp. "GOOD MORNING, MEN! You look more like soldiers today! First, as of fifteen April, the 196th will be moving to Da Nang. I won't divulge any details, as we are still in the planning stage. This information is being disseminated to squelch the recent rumor that we are standing down in the near future. View this as a transfer and nothing else. Second, let me take this opportunity to introduce you to Major Hazard, commander of the 196th Infantry Brigade. As you well know, your last mission was conducted in his AO. He would like to personally thank you for your service."

He did a stiff left-face and instructed Topp to prepare the men for inspection. Topp shouted for us to stand "at ease", though he appeared as anything else but "at ease" as he subordinately trailed the brass.

The ordeal wore on for almost a full hour as Gander and Hazard scrutinized each Grunt for proper dress and hair length– the real reason for the walk-through. I was glad I hadn't decided to hold out yesterday– didn't *even* need *that* hassle. After the inspection we were spared the lifer games for the remainder of the day. I retreated to my barrack and changed into my brown T-shirt after clipping off the sleeves– it was surely going to be a good night.

It wasn't, though. With each joint I became more depressed and by the fourth one I knew it was no good. *Place is getting too tight, man, now with that hard-core lifer running the show, upstaging Topp like that. Man, I liked it better the old way. At least Topp stayed outta our business. And I ain't gonna wear no steel pot out in the bush. No way, man! And why didn't Mike show up tonight? He ain't got nothing else to do. I hate this re-train area. Why can't we get back to the ocean instead of this...prison?*

# MISSION NINE

Sunday, March 14, 1971, Day 144 / 221 to DEROS
—role of the lifer—

Blondie stopped short outside the barrack's door; a pile of camo-lined steel helmets sat in a waiting deuce-and-a-half truck. "Jesus H. Christ, what the *fuck* is this bullshit?"

"One-half of Gander Goose's promise," Hillbilly answered, walking around Blondie to pick one up. "Fucker's weigh a.... What in Sam Hill? Looky here, boys!" –Hillbilly picked up a faded, bulky flack jacket from the bed of the truck– "Guess who's hump'n' ta dinner."

Harv was kneeling, strapping a new combat knife to his ankle. "Y'all ain't gonna wear that now, are ya, Hillbilly?"

"We'll jis' fuck'n' see, Harv."

I picked up one of the steel helmets and tried it on. "Just like on bivouac, huh, Nelson?"

Nelson put one on. "Looky me, I'm GI Joe!"

At ten, we loaded into the trucks with the steel pots adorning our heads like WWI doughboys to make the journey to the Fat City airstrip. The soda girls swarmed us with their wares as we arrived, not at all intimidated by our strange looks. I did my part, purchasing a purple and yellow headband from Suzy and a copper bracelet from Molly, the same lady who had manicured my nails on my second mission. Soon, Gander broke up the carnival and moved us out of Fat City in columns of four, but failed to stave off the band of soda girls as he marched like some crazed drill instructor toward the first range of mountains.

"Bet he's up there calling out cadence," Ski joked. "Your left, one, two, three."

Retchin, catching on to Ski's line, started us off on one of our own–

# DETONATION

*"I want to be an Air-borne Ran-ger,*
*I want to live a life of dan-ger,*
*I want to go to Vi-et-nam,*
*I want to kill some Char-lie Kong..."*

\*      \*      \*

Word for break passed down the line. LT was standing in a small clearing, motioning us in. We'd left the main element thirty-minutes ago; most of the soda girls had decided to follow us as we veered north toward our designated AO.

"I *know* what the CO's wishes are," LT began, "but out here, *I'm* the one who calls the shots, not him. The way I see it, your lives are in *my* hands and I have to do my best to see that all of us get back in one piece." –LT removed his helmet– "If you guys don't want to wear these fucking steel pots, tie them to your rucks." –he tossed it down by his ruck and it thudded with a deadening finality– "Never did like the fuckers." –he looked at Hillbilly– "And the pointman doesn't have to wear that fucking flack jacket, either. This is my second tour and I *know* how hot it can get humping in the dry season. Wearing that will only get you a heat stroke."

"Oh, now ya don't hafta worry 'bout that." –Hillbilly turned a sly smile– "I dumped that lead coat at the end of the airstrip."

Monday, March 15, 1971, Day 145 / 220 to DEROS
—down unda—

Halfway during my guard the rain started, baby tears at first, but soon swelling into tantrum-sized drops. First light stirred our wet and sleepy world and by full light the rain matured to a full-fledged cloudburst. I had a new air mattress and I was thankful Gander's threat to eliminate them was unfounded. It afforded me a dry island as I pulled up my blanket and ammo can to rescue them from brown jungle water streaming through our premises.

LT spread the word we weren't moving, so I took the opportunity to get out a couple of letters, followed by some note-taking on a book I had received from home that contained brief descriptions of colleges throughout the U.S. By mid-afternoon, I whittled down my choices to five colleges: one in each of Illinois, Wisconsin, Minnesota, Colorado and Florida. By my crude

285

calculations, I'd be able to swing it between the GI Bill, my meager savings and working part time. I couldn't wait to start.

Dinnertime rolled in and Pat lit his stove just inside the curtain of water. He was staying with Ski and me since Doc had moved over to chum with his brothers in Spurlin's squad.

"Guys," Ski said, opening a can of turkey loaf, "how does the word, *Australia*, sound to you?"

"You mean as in R&R?" I asked.

"Yeah. Let's put in for it, man." –he placed his can on the stove– "You know we deserve it."

"What the fuck's in Australia," Pat interjected, "besides kangaroos and Aborigine?"

"Round-eye pussy, man!" Ski said, reprimanding him with a look of disbelief. "Monkey Man was telling me about Sydney."

"What's Sydney?"

"You never took geography? It's their fucking capital. There's a place there called King's Corner, or something like that. He says getting laid there's easy as walking out the hotel door. Anyway, there's shit-loads to do down there."

I stowed my book in my ammo can. "Isn't that where they're building that *Opera House* I read about in *National Geographic*?"

"There you fucking go, Pat!" Ski said, enthusiastic. "There's the goddamn *Opera House*. What more you want?"

"Round-eye pussy? *Opera House*? Man, let's do it!"

That settled, Pat suggested a round of his favorite card game over dinner: Pinochle. Ski and I had never played the game, so it was a learning experience that soon evaporated the evening and as the fading light called time out till another day, the new game mixed well with our newest seed of hope– *Australia*!

Tuesday, March 16, 1971, Day 146 / 219 to DEROS
—firebase follies—

It was drizzling as we left the hill. Heading north, we skirted the edge of the Rocket Pocket for several klicks– at least we were *close* to the land of milk and honey. The mist pricked us like icy needles throughout the morning, turning the grassy slopes into sliding boards.

Two hours brought us to a dense thicket between two grassy hills. I detected the boom of a 105 leaving Firebase 270. Seconds later I heard another, then another.

The first round rips the atmosphere. *Must be close. Hope we're–*

"DOWN!" LT begs and the shell slams the side of our hill.

The scream of more.

The second missile explodes on top. Two more on the far side.

The blasts are replaced by screams from LT on the horn ordering them to check their fire, that there are friendlies in their AO.

"Bet they don't know the fuck where we are," Ski wheezes, "cause LT's lost."

I look at my left hand; a handful of mud is locked in white knuckles.

"You see how evenly spaced those shells landed?" Ski says as I release the mudball. "Bet they were doing one of their routine fire missions."

We pushed on, humping straight through the noon hour before LT finally called a break. Ravenous, I tore into a can of fruit cocktail. We were soaked and exhausted, but that wasn't the worst; news filtered down that LT *had* been following the wrong ridgeline.

It wasn't until early evening that we reached our hill; we had to backtrack almost the entire distance we had gained this morning. I was volunteered to join a cutting crew to hack a path to the NDP. Pat, Langley and Ski were behind me as I macheted a clump of brush halfway up the slope.

My foot kicks against a hard object that echoes with a distinct metallic clang. I freeze.

I pull the grass away. "Oh, man. I got me a live 105 round."

"Shit," Langley exhales.

I take a deep breath. "Back up."

As if the day was cursed to the end, Ski ran into a larger 155 artillery shell. Skirting the deadly cylinder my only thought was to be far away from the firebase, for I was beginning to fear it more than the VC.

Wednesday, March 17, 1971, Day 147 / 218 to DEROS
—sweet angel of sleep—

My eyes pop open. Something is wrong. Call it intuition. Call it one of those things Grunts develop after being in the bush for awhile. But my heart is scraping my rib bones as I stare at the black plastic over my head. My guard had ended over two shifts ago; it's well after midnight. After a few seconds, the veil of sleep falls from my ears– *phoo!mmmmmmmm*– I hear the muffled pounding of *105*'s walking up our valley like some primordial carnivore on the prowl for red meat on a black night.

*PHoo!mmmmmmmmmm.*

I strain my eyes in the thin light. Pat is sound asleep on the far side of the hootch; Ski, sandwiched between us, stretches his neck out of his poncho liner like a giant old tortoise wondering what the hell is going on.

*PHOO!mmmmmmmmmm.*

*No way...not after yester–*

*KARAAM!mmmmmmmmm* thuds the base of our hill. My torso turns to ice. "SK–!" But a tinny stream of bile rising in my throat chokes off my wor– *shrrrrrrrrrrreeeeeeeeeeeeeeeeeeee–*

*WAMMMMMMMMMMMMMMMMMMMMMMM!*

My every muscle warps to concrete as the round quakes me six inches off the floor. Steel fragments, hot and ugly, zips a few precious inches over our hootch, severing limbs and brush and ripping into the trees. I grip the hard plastic floor.

It is over. I find myself in the low crawl position, my arms holding my torso above the floor as the taste of the missile's steel settles on my palate. My sleeping gear has disappeared. So has Pat. A silent cloud of sulfur invades my nostrils as blackness washes over us and *we are okay....*

✎*...1:32 a.m., Thursday, September 9, 1993, Red Lion Inn, Havana, Illinois...My eyes snap* open. My heart gallops through my chest like a sprinting horse. The room is black but for a thin streak of yellow creeping through a slit in the curtain from the deserted parking lot. The red digital display reads 1:32 a.m. *Not again. Please, God, not again. Everyone is asleep and I'm in the middle of nowhere.* I press my finger against a carotid artery. It taps my skin thirty times before I can pull it away in a cold sweat. *1:33. This can't be! Third night in a row. Always one-thirty. Why always one-thirty?* My thoughts spin away. *This gonna happen every night for the rest of my life? I'll go crazy!*

*It's okay. It's gonna be okay!* My legs tense like stretching rubber bands. *Relax. I can't! So scared! I dunno why, but I'm so scared!* My legs begin to tremble. *Not the shivers. I can handle the heart, but not the shivers! Relax. Don't lose it. Don't...*. It rises to my jawbone. *Relax, please*. It stops. It starts again. My jaw clenches like a vise. Stops. Starts. Teeth rattling. Stops. *Starts. Stops. Starts....*

      *...But we aren't* okay and never will be again. Ski isn't moving. Instead, an eerie rattling falls on unwilling ears. *Is this the death rattle I'd heard about? That sound when the human organs are exposed, gasping as their precious fluids bubble from the body? Is this that sound?* "Ski?" *–he's dead! –* "Ski?" *–I know it! –* "Sk–"

"Shit! I was thinking the same thing about you. What the fuck *is* that noise."

I listen again, concentrating on the ugly sound. "It's coming from underneath the floor. It's a...*BUG,* man!" –I explode with laughter– "A June bug caught under the floor. We're all right. We're all right!"

On adrenaline-pumped legs we escape from our hootch. *"There* you are." I grin, seeing Pat's silhouette at the back of our hootch. A form clawing the ground in front of LT's hootch catches my attention.

LT is on the verge of screaming. "Tell them to check their fire, Spanky. Do it now!"

Spanky scrambles for the radio, kicked aside during the chaos. His hands grab onto a hard object and paw at it until they find the phone.

"Check your fire check your fire! Firebase 270, I say again. Checkfire!"

"Are you keying it?! You're not keying it!" LT screams. "Key it key it!" As Spanky keys the mike and shouts again, a single and very distinct "phoom" silences *the entire NDP....*

      *...1:42 a.m. ...I crawl out* of bed and slip on pants and shirt. *Gotta get outta here. There's nowhere to go. But I gotta get outta here!* I hurry into the night. The moon is gone, the night black but for a mothy light illuminating half-a-dozen ghostly vehicles in the motel parking lot. I walk to our truck and lean against it. Burying my hands in my pockets, my jaw locks like a mad dog. I fight to control my shivering. My heart flies beneath my shirt. *What isss going on with meeeee? ...*

289

*...It hits Ross* first. "Gotta get outta here!" He crawls toward the edge of the NDP.

Blondie jumps on top of him. "Stay here, Jimmy! Jimmy! It won't do no good!"

"DOWN!" LT screams.

I drop, pushing face and terrified thoughts into the moist earth. The shell howls. Closer. Its moan brands into my soul a horror I've never known. Closer. The very trees seem to vibrate. Closer. Then sound. Complete. Total. Encompassing. Then light. Hell's storm. The flash blisters the air. Cauterizes the night– my eyes– my courage. Again I ride the bucking earth as hot steel rapes the far side of our hill. What shrapnel still free flies into space– a few rip into the opposite sides of our undeserving trees– but better *them, than us. ...*

✎ *..."Bobby?" Startled, I* turn toward my name. Dick Baker is leaning against his car, smoking a cigarette.

"Can't sleep either, huh? I got in an hour ago. Came down from Kingston after second shift. Gonna start laying out Quiver tomorrow."

"Yeah?" *What's he saying?* "Couldn't saleep, cooold."

"Yeah, these damn drafty motel rooms."

"Yeah." I fight to control the shivering. *No good.* "Well. Tink I'll turn in."

"Okey-dokey, see ya manana."

I crawl under the covers and pull the blanket up to my chin. *Freeeeezing.* I pull the Gideon Bible out of the top drawer of the nightstand and flip it open.

*'Praise be to the Lord, my Rock,*
*who trains my hands for war, my fingers for battle.*
*He is my loving God and my fortress,*
*my stronghold and my deliverer,*
*my shield, in whom I take refuge, who.... '*

*...'who subdues peoples...under me....'* Fifteen minutes of forced reading passes. My body floods with warmth. The shivering stops. My heart returns to normal. I sink into *a dead sleep.... ✐*

*...The light tried* to pry my eyes open, but having no luck, it settled to wait for Nelson.

"Re-supply coming. Gotta hook up."

Ski pulled his blanket from his face. "We still here?"

I knew what was on everyone's mind. Last night was somebody's fault and as we got our things packed, LT admitted to it. He had given the firebase the wrong coordinates, thinking we were half a klick east, which we would've been if we'd stayed on his messed up course the day before. But, since he was big enough to admit his mistake, we let it slide. After all, nobody got hurt and it'd provide good fodder for the next couple of write-ins home.

Not getting to sleep till near dawn, I was dragging by the time we hit the trail at seven-thirty. It was good to see the sun shining again, though, absent now for more than a week. But it betrayed us as it engulfed us in its quest to vaporize the recent rains that had replenished the abandoned rice paddies stretching before us. Hoping to out-distance the firebase's damage path, our legs turned to stone as LT pushed us through the day with few breaks and by late afternoon, I was tipping the last of my water onto my face. We achieved our goal and for today– that was enough.

*     *     *

"Your guard, Adams." Ski is asleep before I can drag myself from the hootch. Too tired to think, too tired to care, I prop myself against the front pole and fight the sleep that is determined to take me back. *I can't sleep. I hafta make it! There's no other choice!* An hour and a-half later finds me pinching myself to keep from falling over.

At last my time is up. The precious angel of sleep takes me back into her sweet arms and at this moment, I can think of nothing better on this planet– nothing.

Thursday, March 18, 1971, Day 148 / 217 to DEROS<br>—circle of terror—

I sit up, push aside the mosquito netting and step into the cool night air. The stars are brilliant against a black sky as a new moon begins its ascent over a distant mountain. I feel refreshed, fit, eager to go. The others are still asleep. *Why shouldn't they be? After yesterday, we're lucky to be alive, so let them sleep.*

A nearby brook invites me and soon I am peering into its black ribbon of glass. My feet sink into the shimmering moon and I wade across. *Should have brought my 16, but it looks safe enough, so why let it bother me?* Several thickets stand in my way, so kicking them down I discover a well-used trail

291

beyond. I follow it for over an hour until the path becomes narrow and weedy, ending at another stream.

I begin to wade across, but throw myself back onto the bank. Three VC are on the far side. A strange yellow glow emits from their faces as they seem to float above the trail while methodically searching the terrain right, then left. A thread of fear slides down my throat. *Gotta tell the others! They're gonna kill us all!*

I swing around. I'm standing outside of my hootch. A soft blue light inside illuminates a form– my own; I lie asleep, unaware of the danger. *Can't be. How–? If I'm–? My Jesus. My Jesus I gotta wake up! I gotta know I'm gonna die!* I tear at the netting, pounce on my body and shake it, but my eyes won't open. I strain to set my body up. Nothing, my body is paralyzed with exhaustion. I try again. I pull with all my might. "Wake up! Wake up! Bobby! BobbyBobby! WAKE! UUUUUUUP!!!!"

My eyes open and stare into mine. At the same moment, my fear vanishes....

I sit up, push aside the mosquito netting and step into the cool night air. The stars are brilliant against a black sky as a new moon begins its ascent over a distant mountain....

*       *       *

We continued northeast, hitting more and more decaying paddies near the fringes of the Rocket Pocket. The pace was to a crawl. Stopping for the hundredth time to maintain our ten-meter spread, I leaned over to take the weight off my back. My new boots were giving my feet trouble, my toes feeling numb as my back as I flexed them inside boots buried in a foot of mud.

A little after noon, we gained higher ground that took us from the paddies and into several klicks of rolling grass-covered hills. Plodding into the hot afternoon, last night's dream kept haunting me. I'd never had such a series of nightmares and prayed never would again. Seeing my own body lying there....

It was going on three-thirty when we rose high enough to catch a glimpse of the lush green fields belonging to the Rocket Pocket. LT called it a day. We found a grassy hill that skirted a narrow stream feeding the lowlands and we dropped our rucks and soon built our plastic shelters. At last I had a chance to peel off my boots. I rubbed my hand across the wrinkled sole. *Starting to look bad again.* Something else caught my eye. At the top of my boot line, a small dime-sized sore tattooed my left instep. Its reddish color meant it might be infected. I wasn't sure.

*     *     *

"You won't *even* believe how good the shit tastes," Pat said between bites.

"I dunno. I've never even drank vodka."

"You can't taste it, man, especially in fruit punch."

I looked at my cup of creek water. "You know, the more you talk about it, the better it sounds."

"It's *gooooo-ood*," Ski said from his air mattress. "We get back, Adams, we'll drink the shit out of it."

I was feeling much better than this morning– catching some Z's to make up for that firebase fiasco a couple of days back. For whatever reason, I was now ready to head out with Pat to set out the nightly MA.

Friday, March 19, 1971, Day 149 / 216 to DEROS<br>—mail delay—

*March 19-71. Fri. 9 AM*

*Hi. Were moving about everyday so no time to finish this. It finally cleared up yesterday, it's real nice out now.*

*Planning on setting a date for my R&R– probably sometime in May. I'll have a year in the army & 7 months in country. I'll be going to Australia with 2 other guys from this platoon– Ron Lazenski (Wisconsin) & Pat Senesei (New Jersey). I'm going to save my next 2 pay checks so don't expect any money till the end of May. The R&R is 7 days but it will end up being 2 weeks including travelling time. I'm really looking forward to it. It's something to split the tour up. I'm going to purchase a Yashica camera ($60) for the R&R. it's a real good brand. I was thinking instead of buying civilian clothes it would be much cheaper for you to send them over. You could use the money from my savings– so if you won't mind I'll send you a list: shoes (the pair with the big brass buckle) 2 pair sock (thick brown & green), pants (white hopsack Levis & old denim jeans for wearing out in the Australian bush) 2 belts (wide black & brown) 3 shirts (brown shirt– 2 body shirts– expensive $20 brown one & yellow striped)(brown sleeveless sweater), wide brown watch band & Speedo swim trunks (jungle print– red & black(?), newer ones)*

*That's about it. I can buy T-shirt & underwear at the PX.*

*Can't think of too much more. 6 more days left on this mission. So take care & God Bless.*

*Love your Son,        Bob*

*PS. Average spending on an R&R is from $250 to $350.*

Saturday, March 20, 1971, Day 150 / 215 to DEROS

—family feud—

Yesterday evening had been my first chance in days to enjoy a stream bath and as I awoke, I felt like a morning dove, in spite of a canceled CA this morning to the southern end of the Rocket Pocket. A patrol yesterday morning had yielded several VC bunkers, so the CO had kept us around, wanting us to blow them before leaving.

We hooked up early and headed west away from the RP, stopping long enough to take care of the bunker business on the way to our NDP. By noon, LT was ready to set up beside a small stream bordering a low, flat knoll in the middle of a rice paddy. The site was just a few feet above the water, but still afforded an excellent defensible position as it sat like a grassy island in the middle of the other low profile hills. Taking advantage of the early break, I shed my boots and stuck my bare feet out of the end of the hootch to let them bask in the Vietnam sun. The rest of me was sound asleep.

*       *       *

"Get your shiny ass *down* here!" Tuck awoke me from a sound sleep and I crawled outside to see him shouting at an inbound chopper, hovering a hundred feet above him. "My rucks empty, 'n' so's my gut! I wants me some meat!" Yellow smoke from a discharged grenade momentarily covered Tuck's form as the chopper dipped its metal feet just a few inches into the paddy– this pilot was good. Tuck, Mocko, Ramos and Slim waded out to retrieve our goodies, making sure the cases of C's didn't spill into the quagmire as they tossed them onto the bank. They returned to haul the other supplies: letters, some medical supplies for Doc and an assortment of other requested items.

——"Be nice to get some fucking hot chow for a change," Mocko complained as he dropped three cases of C's in front of his hootch. "Get'n' so a man can't remember what real food tastes like."

294

"How kin you complain about this shit?" Tuck said, picking up his squad's ration of C's. "Uncle Sam went to all the trouble sending you a free can of shit, 'n' all *you* can do is complain?" –he winked at Blondie– "Why when I get my ass back to the World, I'm gonna stock my pantry with this good-tasting shit. Think you should do the same, my Mocko Man."

Mocko's grin widened, shaking his head as he knelt down to split open one of cases. "Tuck, you eat shit."

"Fuck, Mocko, gimme a can of your goddamn C's and I will!"

Sunday, March 21, 1971, Day 151 / 214 to DEROS
—catch up—

*Dear Parents,*           *March 21 – 71*    *10 AM – clear & hot*

*Hello again. Got our re-supply yesterday & a letter from you. #16– right now were right outside the Rocket Pocket looking the area over. There's not much of anything out here. There is a stream though so we can keep fairly clean. I must have covered most of the area surrounding Chu Lai by now. I seem to recognize everywhere we go.*

*Tomorrow I've got 5 months in Nam. Time does pass quickly here. Especially out in the field. The rumor now is that there's a 60% chance of not going to Da Nang. I kinda hope we stay here. Don't even want to go up north.*

*Answers to your letter #14– one can buy film for producing slides from my camera. But next time in I am buying a new camera– Yashica– $60.*

*We get back in rear twice a month. Missions last from 9 to 14 days– spend 3 days in rear.*

*I'll probably have to spend 11 months in Nam. 8-10 months in field.*

*Wad won't be back to our platoon. He got sent back home because his leg bone (femur) was broke in half. He'll have to have a steel rod put in his bone to hold together.*

*#16 letter: We won't get out of the field– the most we could do to getting out is to run patrol in Rocket Pocket surrounding Chu Lai...someone has to secure Chu Lai.*

*I heard the Clay– Frazier fight live via satilite at 11:25 out in the bush.*

*The Maypo you sent in the plastic bag wasn't too good (not enough sugar, mild, no butter) half the apples you sent were smashed– C rations never change.*

*We still hump about every day.*

*The water tastes a lot better than water at home.*
*I got my PFC raise– $255 a month. About $50 taken out of check.*
     *Love, your son, Bob*

### Monday, March 22, 1971, Day 152 / 213 to DEROS
### —Grunt's foot—

I squeezed the toes inside my boots to get some feeling into them. Already three klicks into our hump, we had started early, heading south after reaching the northern end of our AO. The colonel had extended our southern edge by eight klicks, pushing it to the same area where we had been at Christmas. Rumors from intelligence that another attack on Chu Lai within the next few days was imminent, so they wanted us to search out possible VC rocket and mortar caches. With twenty checkpoints ahead, we were humping the edge of the RP to avoid going through the mountains.

By four, we were a little over halfway there, stopping a little past hill 76, where Echo Recon had been overrun. Some boys who were tending their water buffalo spotted us and sent out an alert that we were in the area. Soon, the same soda girls that had followed us out returned in full force. They buzzed around us with shouts of greeting while pushing their pop and souvenirs. LT decided to position the NDP along a shallow slope that rose near a rice field. It was getting late and since one of the mamasans promised no rain for the night, we decided to crash under our ponchos.

### Tuesday, March 23, 1971, Day 153 / 212 to DEROS
### —Deno's last hurrah—

I tap Pat's shoulder. "Your guard." The rumbling of a storm sweeping over rocket ridge sends me scurrying back to my bed. I curl beneath my poncho as the sky drops a sheet of rain that clap the ground like a standing ovation at a Pavarotti opera.

Thick bolts of lighting fracture the night when I detect another sound– rockets. Then another– artillery– ours– ripping toward Rocket Ridge to answer the VC challenge.

The thunderclaps intensify as friend and foe exchange fiery handshakes of death. I squeeze my body under the plastic until my shoulders ache, praying it will all go away. *I must escape. But to where?* I lift my poncho; the storm flashes against bloodshot eyes witnessing a world losing its sanity. Around me, the black lumps of my comrades are revealed as charcoal blue bolts buckle into mustard-colored streaks of fire that shoot my heart into overdrive. I can't tell if I'm looking into the heart of a thunderstorm, or shattering remnants of my final *moments on earth. ...*

✎*...2:46 p.m., Saturday, August 6, 1994, home...Blood and sweat* mix with a thin coating of gun oil as I press the muzzle against my temple. Upstairs, life goes on. My wife and son watch the tube, relaxing after a long day of yard work. The sting of cold steel fades as it absorbs the heat of my skin. *Can't tell a soul what it's like inside of my brain. Rotten week. Going to work like nothing is wrong. If I only KNEW what was wrong! What good did that shrink do...nothing! No matter what I learn about this shit, it don't do no good!* I crack a smile as a movie image from *Joe versus the Volcano* flashes in my head. *"You have a brain cloud, Mr. Banks." At least he had something with a name he could hold on to, something to pass around like a favorite appetizer at a party.* I lower the gun. *I can't do this. I'm not that big of a coward...not yet.* Wiping a smear of blood on my temple, I release the magazine and begin to clean my virgin Glock like it's my newborn, oiling the barrel, spring and slide, pushing the bolt into place till I hear the erotic click as it seats. My head falls forward. A full minute passes.

I snap up and shove the magazine home.

"VIET!" –I chamber a round– "FUCKING!" –I point the barrel– "NAAAAM!"

The explosive charge ignites in the small room; a neat hole appears in the gray paneling, above *my office phone. ...*✐

*...In the crumpled* folds atop my poncho heave tiny seas created by a troubled wind. Beneath, I sway with the gale's rhythm. I am soaked, but *I am alive.* As light dawns, so does Hillbilly's voice, rousing my curiosity to rise, spilling the oceans onto the earth.

"Wake up there, ol' Birch. Ya know yer one lucky sonofabitch."

Nelson pulls his poncho back far enough to peek over and follow Hillbilly's finger to a spot in the rock-pocked mud. Less than ten meters away brown water from the rain-swelled paddy seeps into a fresh artillery crater.

A dozen soda girls slid in at eight-thirty; it looked like they came to make a day of it. They had brought tote sacks, filled with pop and souvenirs and maybe a few extra rice cakes to curb their paltry appetites. We clumped our soggy gear together and like pack mules strapped it to our backs to continue our journey south. Within the hour a stampede of drizzle began to assault us, driven by a steady eastern gale that neutralized any chance of drying our wet clothing. At noon, LT called a break. I dropped my ruck and sat down on its leeward side, hoping to close my eyes for a few minutes, but gave up when a legion of goose pimples began to march across my spine. I thought the soda girls were crazy to stay with us another second, but they didn't seem to mind, huddling together, squawking like a gaggle of geese.

At twelve-thirty a lone gray chopper droned toward us. Its racket slapped our ears as it passed, turning sharply before driving into Rocket Ridge. Facing the wall of wind, it inched back, lifting its yellow snout to feather down a few feet from LT's weary boots. The crew threw off a dozen boxes of C's, followed by a scant offering of the good stuff– letters and such. The pilot signaled for LT.

"Doc!" LT shouts through the gale. "This is it! Your Freedom Bird!"

Doc stands up. We had known he was short, but not this short. We rush forward to offer him a quick farewell– he gleams like a man reprieved. Picking up his ruck, he leans against the wind and jumps inside the chopper, raising his fist in salute as the gale pushes the iron bird to a hundred feet before leaning into its drive to Fat City.

*That's the way it is in The Nam,* I think as I catch a last glimpse of my brave friend, Doctor Deno Belton.

It was going on two o'clock and the girls decided to return to their village. I gave Molly most of my C's and told her I would miss her. I didn't know if sharing this sentiment was the right thing to do– but I would. My heart echoed with emptiness as I watched her leave with the others, carrying much of our re-supply to their village– our way of showing our appreciation for their company.

By three-thirty, we entered an area of the RP we had visited when we aided the sick in the village that housed Duc and Anh-Ten. Finding the same clearing outside of the village, we settled in and I, crashed straightaway and slept like the dead.

# DETONATION

Duc and Anh-Ten approached LT, who was lashing his bamboo hootch poles to the top of his ruck; there wouldn't be any where we were heading today. "You want to take point?" LT asked. "You know...lead platoon?"

"We do this for you?" they answered in unison, their eyes like saucers. "We be numba one pointman! You see!" –with heads high they strutted over to Hillbilly– "LT say *we* be point, Hillbilli. You folla *us!*"

Hillbilly caught LT's wink. "We walk *bookoo* today. You no be babysan. Bic?"

"*We* no babysan, Hillbilli, *you* see."

"Lead on then. I'll be a foller'n' right behind ya."

The boys picked up their bamboo walking sticks and began to high step it from camp, looking back every few seconds to admire their new status. LT wasn't too worried about the boys: we'd be humping the RP all day, hoping to chew up the last leg in search of our southern limit. So far we hadn't seen a thing. The VC seemed to have vanished.

The VC weren't on *my* mind this morning– my feet were. Streaks of pain flowed from my toes to the top of my ankles, telling me sooner or later they were going to give out. At each break I'd tear off my boots to knead the numbness out. And that neat dime-sized sore on my left instep was now as big as a quarter. I flaked some dead tissue away, revealing a puss-filled hole. Though the sore was painless, I guessed it was worse than it looked.

Lunch came and went, followed by a short siesta. Four-fifteen found us at the base of our hill.

"This is it, men," LT announced. "Hill 437. By tonight it'll be ours." We pulled our heads back and gazed at its summit.

Hillbilly shook his head and turned toward Duc and Anh-Ten. "You heard the man. You're a gonna earn yer damn pay *today*."

The talking ended then; we needed every ounce of air to feed our burning lungs in our ascent up a gravel-filled washout cutting a narrow trench into the red clay, rock hard after eons of monsoons. Twelve-inch steps degraded to six. After ten minutes we were panting for a break. I collapsed to the ground, not bothering to remove the ruck, waiting with clenched teeth for the burning to subside from my lungs, thighs and shoulders.

Thus upward we inched, from break to break to break. Two-thirds up the monstrosity, a mass of gray granite stopped us. From its base it rose straight up. Its pinnacle well over two hundred feet above us. Dove gray moss taunted from the shadows of the mammoth rock as we searched for a route to the top.

Fritts, dragging his feet thirty meters ahead of me, collapsed in a heap of spent muscles.

"Man down!" Nelson shouted. "Get Doc...get whoever's got Doc's bag down here!"

Sgt. Trainor showed up a minute later, expelling a "Shit!" while sliding the last five feet that ended on his butt. "Hey, Fritzy," he said, getting to his knees, "some dumb-ass put us on one fucking hill, huh?" Trainor began pouring some water on Fritts' towel, noting his drenched shirt and flushed face.

The sergeant began bathing Fritts' face and neck. "Get that ruck off him. We're gonna cool you down ol' Fritzy boy. You're like an overheated radiator, that's all."

Nelson pulled the ruck free. "He can't carry this shit, Sarge. We'll hafta split it up."

"Gimme your canteen. I'm gonna need more water."

Nelson helped remove Fritts' shirt so Trainor could sponge his upper torso. Next, he tore apart the ruck and began distributing Fritts' gear as the Grunts filed by.

*　　*　　*

"Looky here!" Pane stood on the brink of the gray slab wall that had taken us two hours to bypass. To the east lay the golden white coast, to the west the purple-hazed mountains of the interior– we were above it all! The brisk air smelled of fresh pine and nothing was to be heard but the wind in the grass. For the first time in the bush, I felt safe.

"Let's push some rocks off!" –Pane jumped at one of the smaller ones– "Come on!"

"Why the fuck not," Blondie answered. The boulder was ten feet from the edge and the two of them slid it along the smooth granite until it teetered on the edge.

"Ready?!" Pane shouted. With a heave, the boulder was airborne. It picked up speed to a thunderous explosion below.

"Damn!" Blondie shouted. "Loud as a rocket! Let's do another!" Their fervor was infectious; the whole platoon got in on the act. Duc and Anh-Ten were delighted at our GI craziness. Even LT and Sgt. Trainor joined in the ruckus. After depleting the supply of small boulders, Hillbilly eyed a six-foot slab of black granite sitting stalwartly on the brink.

"Retchin, git me some C-4."

Thursday, March 25, 1971, Day 155 / 210 to DEROS

—on top of old baldy—

I turned on my back. Rain splattering softly on the roof motivated me to take a look outside. A blanket of grainy white fog had settled over the bald mountaintop sometime during the morning hours, for during my one-thirty guard, the stars had still peeked through party cloudy skies. Sitting up for a closer look, I couldn't even see the CP, only ten meters away.

"Everybody desert us?"

Ski was sitting cross-legged on the edge of his mattress enjoying a morning cigarette. "Hey, what's happening? Looks like it, don't it?" –he shot me a quick glance– "You wouldn't have my brand in that can of yours? This is my last pack."

"No sweat, Ski. Think I got three."

"You're a lifesaver, man. Think we'll get that re-supply today?"

"Better. Got one can left...and peanut butter."

"Like Ky Tra, huh?"

"Don't *even* want *that* again." –outside, I heard the first stirrings through the silent mist: a smoker's hack, the clank of a canteen cup, an unintelligible curse– "Huh, they didn't desert us after all."

The rain turned to drizzle, preventing the sun from burning off enough fog to get our re-supply. Duc and Anh-Ten had decided to head back to their ville after chomping on Blondie's last can of beefsteak. They had slept in the corner of his hootch last night, according to Ski, who had picked up the latest gossip after a morning visit. Blondie had tried to get the kids to send their village prostitute to our next stand-down by promising them a tidy cut of the profit. Whether or not they'd come through was anybody's guess. But that didn't stop Blondie from making the rounds to take orders for his latest business venture.

With no supply in sight, LT decided to take out a patrol to at least get some water, while at the same time following the CO's orders to scout for enemy rocket caches. LT picked ours and Hillbilly's squad to accompany him. Our descent took us down the northwest side, much gentler as it was broken into several smaller hills cascading off the back door of Rocket Ridge. After several detours, we finally wormed our way to the bottom where a good-sized stream was waiting for us. Our uneventful patrol was back before five and with the prospect of a hungry evening, I looked for an outlet to vent my disappointment. I found it tied to the back of my rucksack.

"I'm digging me a foxhole, Ski. Wanna help?"

"You fucking crazy? LT didn't say we had to dig one."

"Gotta do something to keep my mind off my stomach." –I unfolded the E-tool and began digging several meters from our hootch entrance– "Who knows, maybe we'll get rocketed tonight and this'll save your life."

"Fuck, if we do, I will certainly thank you. But for now, I'll just watch."

# STAND-DOWN NINE

Saturday, March 27, 1971, Day 157 / 208 to DEROS
—tuckered out—

The sound of eggbeaters chopping through the thinning fog impelled Hillbilly to look up. "Here come the chow wagons!"

I dragged my tired ruck onto heavy shoulders and limped toward the LZ. The bald mountain was leaving us with few of the pleasant memories when first conquering its crown. Yesterday had mimicked the day before and today, likewise– fog, fog and more fog. There had been a brief window yesterday afternoon, enough to get off some shots of the panoramic landscape. But it had closed again before we could get a re-supply. Following Pat and Ski, I grabbed the edge of the chopper floor and crawled on board as my ribs pressed against my thin flesh. I leaned back and closed my eyes.

\*      \*      \*

Food was all I cared about. Hot food. Food with flavor, food with bite–none of that tepid, tasteless stuffed-in-a-green-can crap. The chow line was waiting for us as our convoy pulled into the re-train area– they knew. Gander Goose was nowhere in sight and I was thankful for that, too. Topp was there, though, standing at the front of the chow line like a man who had seen the light.

"How ya doing, soldier! Good to have ya back, soldier!" he sang like a drunken sailor at an Easter Sunrise Service. I didn't know *what* his problem was. But it was okay by me. The fragrance of roast beef smothered in brown gravy drowned out Topp's sweet-talk as I floated toward its magnetic lure. Potatoes came first. Piles of 'em. Then diced hot-buttered carrots. Two, no, three slabs of roast beef and an avalanche of steaming hot gravy. Pick up eggnog. Go sit down. Stuff it in. Go for more.

\*      \*      \*

Several beads of sweat lost their grip from my nose as my gut heaved again. Ski was standing several paces behind me, leaning on the door jam, fingering a half-smoked Winston.

"Why don't you fucking crash. You look like shit."

I booted some sand over the remains of my supper. "Could you tell the Heads I won't make it?"

"No sweat. Just get some sleep."

Sunday, March 28, 1971, Day 158 / 207 to DEROS
—Blondie's scam—

Ski waltzed into the barrack like a man who'd just won the Irish Sweepstakes. "Adams! We ain't in the goddamn 196th no more. No wonder ol' Topp was shoveling us sweet shit last night."

I swung my legs to the floor. "You mean we're back in the 198th?"

"Fucking *A*. Let's celebrate. Breakfast is on me."

"Let me shower first."

"How ya feel'n' this morning?"

"Bookoo better 'n last night. I'm starv'n'."

"My momma always told me that was the first sign of getting better."

303

After shedding two weeks worth of the bush under the steaming water I felt considerably better. A fresh shave and a pair of clean fatigues helped boost my moral enough to enjoy a hot breakfast with my inner circle– Yoss, Pat, Nelson and Ski.

The morning passed with no chance to escape the isolated re-train area and one o'clock found us sitting in a stale classroom searching for a safer way to approach and infiltrate VC tunnels and bunkers. The mind-numbing experience lasted till three-thirty; by then most of us were ready to toss the inept instructor into one of those damn tunnels of his, followed by a fresh bouquet of baseball grenades.

*    *    *

Father sun teetered for a long moment on the brim of the hushed horizon, perhaps wondering what mischief would transpire after he closed the day's door, but, having a schedule to keep, he continued his eternal slide into the curried abyss.

With the sun safely out of sight, the thin corners of Blondie's conspiratorial lips turned up in satisfaction.

"One night only, gentlemen, step right up for the sweetest *poontang* in all of *Chu fucking Lai!*" Soon Blondie was clinching a wad of twenties in his left hand while he meticulously combed his way from barrack to barrack– sometimes bartering, sometimes bribing, sometimes begging. His whore was doing the horizontal hula in a small room at the far end of the armory building, attracting to her dirty red door a straggled line of swaggering Grunts, whose sacred shadows cringed beneath dingy boots. It was, indeed, a good night for Blondie.

Across the compound, a clean-cut Robert Horton was in heated battle with *The Green Slime*, the latest flick playing in the classroom that a few hours earlier had been torturing its captive students. Meanwhile, six pallets of beer and soda were going fast, chilling inside four ice-filled fifty-five gallon drums placed outside of every other barrack.

I was ready for a good night. A wild night. A night to celebrate. And I had come dressed for the kill. Adorning my tanned forehead was a golden headband with the words V*I*E*T**W*A*R**N*A*M sewn with ultramarine blue thread across its front. Brown sleeveless T-shirt, stitched fatigue pants, copper bracelets on my wrist and an assortment of beads adorned my neck like trophies from a raid on an Ozark souvenir shop.

I didn't like what Blondie was doing and as I packed more smack-laced dew into my yellow bowl, I wondered how anybody in his right mind could participate in such debauchery. Soon he showed his smug mug in the door to snake his oil at us. Hillbilly swallowed it, excusing himself for, as only the Hillbilly could spin it, "Ergent business down unda," while flipping Blondie a twenty.

It was as wild as an evening could get, considering we had to work within the confines of what was no more than a glorified desert prison camp. Yes, Blondie was doing well, perhaps better than he had imagined. And as for the whore? Well... it was business as usual.

Monday, March 29, 1971, Day 159 / 206 to DEROS
—no pain—

Five sets of eyes shimmered in the setting sun as its last remnants streaked through the dusty air of the small room.

This morning, Pat had made a run for the PX, returning with a collection of vodka, rum and cherry fruit punch. "You're gonna love this shit!" he kept swearing on our return. By evening he had me so pumped I couldn't wait for him to set up a makeshift bar: a *2 x 10* placed across the tops of two chairs.

Pat refilled my plastic cup and pushed it into my hands. "You were right, Ski, can't *even* taste the vodka."

Pat kept mixing and we kept drinking as the night digressed into an incoherent ramble of shouts, grunts and guffaws. I was feeling good. So deliciously good! Face flushed red as Topp's, I staggered towards Pat's bar.

"Gib me one of dos...'n' don hoed da, bodka."

"Yeah," Nelson purred from the corner. "Don't hoed da...BODKA!" Pat's unsteady arm sent a double shot to the floor.

"Arrest that man!" Ski blurbed from his cot, pointing a swaying finger at Pat. "He's...he's aboos'n'...abruis'n'...." His voice trailed off, buried in an avalanche of laughter. Yoss was laughing so hard he couldn't make a sound, his mouth frozen open as some of the brew bubbled out of his big nose.

"Lemme do it!" –I pulled the bottle out of his hand– "Dis how *I* mix a dink!"

"Dink!" Ski shouted, coming up for air. The laughter swelled as I took a swig of punch followed by three big gulps of vodka before Pat could grab it.

"Ya knows...I Steelzz...houz youz zay it? Steelzz...I can't taste it." I backed up and collapsed on a cot. Attempting to stand, the room spun so that my head couldn't keep up with it. My head fell back as somebody swung my legs off the floor and onto the cot. After that the banter terminated as quick as my dad would click off TV on *a school night....*

✏️*...2:06 p.m., Wednesday, December 13, 1995, Belgium Village, Moline, Illinois...*"You're up, Bob." I felt good– all of my friends, playing our annual Christmas rolly-bolly game in the basement of the Friend's Circle Club. Sitting my Old Style on the bench, I positioned the vinyl disk in my right hand. We held onto a thin twelve to eleven lead. I eyed the stick. Both Kenny and Karl's disks were close enough for a point– Karl's a foot away. I assumed my bowling stance, stepped off in the packed dirt right, left, right, left while gracefully bending and releasing the disk. The disk moved as if embodied with of a life of its own, rolling to the far right edge of the court before smoothly arching on its beveled edge at the mid-way point. It rolled past Kenny's, nicking off Karl's to fall six inches from the stick.

"Yeah!" Sammy shouted. "Point!"

I slapped Sam's hand and picked up my beer. "How you gonna act?!"

My twenty-minute interval for a leak was overdue. "Bill, take my turn? Be right back." I moved past the shuffleboard, dodging a lightbulb hanging from the low ceiling before walking up the narrow steps. *Man, I am dizzy.* But it was a good buzz. I embraced the warm glow of camaraderie I'd missed for so long, since, when? Last Christmas? What made it better, though, was the fact that at last my path was leading me toward a rear job. My months of studying the computer books was paying off with an opportunity to take a crack at an office job, processing the surveys we'd crank out on the Illinois and Mississippi Rivers. *Kinda like the way I got out of the bush, huh? Practicing on that typewriter when I had that gook sore.* I passed a gaggle of women clucking over a game of Bunko in a large room skirting the bar; their voices mingled with my buzz. *And with any luck, I'll stay in the rear too!*

The throne-room was down a skinny hall and to the, right? No– left. Karl's voice filtered up the stairs, hooting at a shot Kenny must've nailed. *How many beers now? Karl bought, Kenny, me, Sam, then Karl. I dunno.* I leaned my head against the wall in front of the porcelain urinal and turned my gaze at a lightbulb hanging from the cracked ceiling by a frayed wire. The bulb spun slowly. *Man. I am...drunk.*

I twitch as a rusty *clunk*! from an ancient heating duct echoes in the small room. My heart starts to race. I lower my head and stare straight ahead, noticing the spidery network of pumpkin cracks in the old plaster. *It ain't fair, God. Not! Fucking! NOW!...✐*

Tuesday, March 30, 1971, Day 160 / 205 to DEROS

—pain—

✐*...3:38 a.m., Sunday, July 14, 1996, home...Thunder echoes on the far horizon. A storm is coming. In the black of night, its crawl over the plains still the air. The moon falls away and the locusts cease their grind as the leaves become as stone. I lie, eyes wide, body tense, for another storm ravages, not spawned by the night or by the day, but by the dark forces that rule my mind. In its mist reigns Death, wielding its scepter of deception as I struggle in its cold embrace. So close, its icy breath rakes my face. On the day of the Swamp it had pierced my mortal soul and has since been my preternatural companion. I smell its stench. A thousand times I have smelled it...tasted it...felt its sticky arms enshroud me, as a spider with its prey.*

*I see the lightning now. It flicks against my eye. The brown grass beneath me bends to my weight as I stare into my storm. If I stand, it shall again cast me down. In my youth, the Hope had made me strong. I would push into the gale that whipped through my body. In my youth, I had thought the storm would soon subside...but never...no never...it is here always. Now I am but straw, flimsy, brittle, waiting for my storm's blue flash to turn me to ash.*

*The tempest is upon me! Behold its rage! It hurls my body and cuts my flesh! My blood flows black onto the earth! I seek refuge, but there is none! Yet...no man can see it, nor can hear it. It moves with the stealth of the anaconda, yet wantonly feeds with the boldness of the lion upon my heart, my mind, my very soul! That is enough, enough to jolt my brain, enough to trip my bloody wire as it claps a silent hand....✐*

*...*"You alive?"

I pry one eye open enough to squint into the morning. A riveting pain hammers it shut again.

"We're hooking up. Gotta get ready."

My cottonmouth voices. "Yeah."

"Hey," the voice says, "get some food in your stomach. It'll help, man."

*Leave me–* a lightning bolt of pain fractures the thought. Another minute and the full weight of what I am up against crashes down. My head is a grenade, a mushy bloodshot grenade– and the fuse is burning.

I try to push hot bile welling in my throat back into what feels like hell's furnace. *It's coming out!* I roll off the cot, hitting the floor with a dull thud. Pushing to my knees I crocodile across the hall, out the back door and crash onto the sand. The volcano blows, bent on wrenching every vestige of matter from my paralyzed torso.

The contractions subside, leaving me a rack of spent nerves and muscle tissue. I wipe bile from my mouth with the back of my hand and sit on my haunches for a few minutes to find my breath, then zombie back to my cot.

LT appeared at the door. "Adams, you okay?"

I looked up from the fetal position. "Feel like crap, LT."

"That's what Nelson says. Why don't you hitch a ride on the supply truck and put yourself on sick call."

"Thanks, LT. Sorry about this."

"Just get better and see you in a couple days."

As he brisked outside, I sat up, dead sure someone was using the inside of my skull for a handball court.

"Adams," Ski said, stuffing his poncho into his ruck, "you *way* overdid it last night. Fuck. You ever hear of pacing yourself? Well, maybe this'll work out okay for you after all. Tomorrow you'll be hanging out on the beach while I'm humping my ass off." –he picked up his ruck– "See you in *a couple days.*"...

✎*...8:42 p.m., Sunday, October 27, 1996, home...I backed away* from the computer screen. Its pulsating waves clawed at my closing eyes. *That's it. That's the whole of it. At least for posterity, my children will someday know why their father is crazy.* I opened an eye and hit the print button. The printer's green eye blinked and hummed to life.

## MY LOSING BATTLE WITH PTSD

### Things that kick my heart to racing:

Anticipating anything, like when I have to go into an area where the only way out is up / walking too fast / burping (can you believe it?) / bending over / standing up / my pectoral muscles bouncing from an unexpected movement / breathing to shallow or too deep / at trigger points: places that have historically been difficult to proceed beyond, like the bottom of a hill, or a place where I'm far from a 'safety zone' (an area where I can stop to recover without looking conspicuous), or, just before achieving a goal (like arriving at my driveway after a walk).

**What stops it from racing:**

Standing still / lying down / going somewhere alone / controlling my breathing (taking a deep breath, then exhaling slowly while trying to concentrate on nothing) / entering a safe zone (home, bathroom, street corner, bus stop, etc.).

**What do I feel like during the episode:**

Intense, mind-numbing, breath-taking, lock-jawed, muscle-quivering fear / like I'm going to die (many times I will make my peace with God, believing these are my last moments on earth) / extreme anger (using profanity that would curl the toes of a dog) / thoughts of suicide (why not?) / symptoms of hyperventilation (can't get full breath, can't hold my breath for more than a few seconds, numbing and tingling of extremities: ankles, wrists, nose, lips) / no appetite / dry mouth / constant urge to urinate / feel as if I'm teetering on the edge of a cliff / out of control / mind in turmoil (can't concentrate on anything, at times to the point where I can't even count backwards from ten).

**How do I feel immediately after the episode:**

As the heart begins to recover, it kicks into some PVC's (skipped beats), then back to racing again, then into more PVC's and so on. It all depends on how frightening the episode was. If particularly bad, this process could go on for up to ten minutes, but usually lasts a minute or two. Great stuff, huh? Many times, as it is going away, I feel an euphoric calm sweeping through my mind, almost like a physical reaction from taking a drug.

**How do I feel later:**

In the early 90's, it was always fear. Now I react with extreme anger. Sometimes I break things, or slam my fist (concrete walls are a favorite). At times I feel suicidal. Other times I experience extreme depression and exhaustion (I go to bed as early as 6:30).

**What I avoid because of this disorder: (here we go!)**

Group sports like softball, racquetball, basketball, volleyball, playing pool / running more than fifty feet / bouncing / bending over / sweating / walking up hills / walking with anyone / helping someone carry an object / going into a remote area with another individual (they'd think I was crazy if a spell started) / mowing the yard / carrying the garbage out to the street / any morning activities that involve physical activity / drinking too much coffee or too little / getting up too early or going to bed too late / overeating (that full feeling) / not eating enough / anything extreme (in either direction) / any hard yard work (like building a retaining wall or re-shingling the roof, which accounts for my yard falling apart) / going to the doctor (a big one!) / going to church (sitting with a group of people) / talking in front of three of more people / going to any activity where I might be called upon to say something / participating in any activity where once I begin I am expected to continue until the job is completed.

**Conclusion:**

I believe if, for a moment, I could erase these unwanted thoughts from my mind– I would be cured. But instead, the more I try to avoid them, the more they hound me. It's as if part of me can no longer live without this fear, for after twenty years, it refuses to let go. Like those leeches in Vietnam, the malady clamps tight to my brain– sucking my courage, my manhood, my joy of living. Nobody knows it is there as it grows fat and strong, but me. Nobody can see it, but me. Nobody can touch it, but me. Nobody can taste it, smell it, feel it, hear it.... Nobody...BUT ME! Meanwhile, going by the wayside are my children, my wife, my friends, my self-respect *and my faith.* ...✐

*     *     *

*...I slid off* my seat and stood in front of the CQ office as the truck rolled away. In a strange way, I felt like I did on the day when I had first arrived at the 198th. Everything was still frozen in place. The CQ still wore its thick coat of blue paint, its plywood shutters were propped open like a rabbit trap to lure in the outside air. Inside, the gray floor fan spun its rusty tune. Behind the CQ, four rows of empty barracks waited with tin roofs crowning their hollow heads. A throbbing serenity rested over me. Pausing for a few more moments to take in the peaceful setting, I opened the door.

"Gilespie, how's it going?" –the screen door clapped shut like the one on my Grandma's front porch– "LT sent me on sick call."

Gilespie rolled his swivel chair from his cluttered desk, "You're–?"

"Adams, PFC Adams."

"Oh, yeah, I remember. You came in with that Mexican guy."

"Dennis Moreno."

"Yeah, Moreno..." –he averted his eyes– "...too bad about him." – Gilespie rolled his chair to the filing cabinet– "Here it is." –he filled out the pertinent information– "And, reason for illness?"

I scanned the rehearsed list of excuses in my head. "Been throwing up. Headache. I dunno, flu?"

He jotted it down and tossed his pen on the desk. "Good enough. PFC Adams, grab a bed and make yourself at home. Aid Station opens at 1300."

I found a bed in a barrack nearest the sandy coastline, dropped my ruck and let the surf lull me to sleep.

*　　　*　　　*

The doctor removed the thermometer from my mouth. "So, how you feeling?"

"Better, I guess."

He eyed me with raised eyebrows. "Rough night, huh?"

A shadow of a smile clouded my lips. "Well...maybe a little."

"Hey, don't think you're the first one in here with a hangover. Happens to the best of us."

"Hey, this was a super *bad* hangover."

"That's what they all say." He turned toward a white-enameled cabinet. I stole a look around the sterile room, crammed with medical supplies from probes and needles to scalpels and stethoscopes. A sudden urge to burst out laughing welled in my throat, As I had passed the CQ office on the way over I spotted Topp, wearing a flack jacket, hands locked onto his 16 as he roamed his paranoid world. I held my breath and pinched my hamstrings to extinguish the humorous scene. The doctor turned back and handed me a white envelope. "Here's some pain reliever tablets. Take two every four hours; you should be okay by morning."

"Hey, Doc," –I stuffed his offering into my shirt pocket– "since I'm here, would you take a look at my leg?" I dropped my left boot and pulled off my sock.

The doctor raised his eyebrows again. "Why didn't you report this earlier?" –he studied the red-streaked sore, now nearly big as half-a-dollar– "Looks like a tropical ulcer." He pulled on a pair of surgical gloves.

"A what?"

"Grunts call them gook sores. If that goes untreated long enough, you could lose your foot."

"You're kidding."

"Do you think I go to those re-trains to lecture about foot care just to hear myself talk?" –he grabbed a couple bottles from the cabinet– "The good news for *you,* mister, is that you just earned yourself an automatic seven-day profile."

I didn't answer, pursing my lips as he began cleaning the skin around the sore with an alcohol soaked cotton-swab.

He pushed the cotton stick against the abscess. "You feel that?"

"Nope, not a thing."

He pushed harder. "Now?"

"Nothing."

"Okay. At least we don't have to give you a local. I'm going to clean out the infection and dress it, then I'm going to start you on some antibiotics."

"Doc, my toes have been killing me, too. Going numb and stuff."

"When?"

"When I'm humping."

He pushed the ball of my foot. "That hurts, huh?" –he spread my toes apart and gave them a cursory inspection– "I'll wrap your ankle and give you a can of that foot powder I've been trying to pedal." –he picked up one of my boots and held it in front of my face– "And get a pair that fits."

*     *     *

A clip of VC rockets dragged me out of a sound sleep and hammered me to the floor. A siren began to peel and I expected Topp to career any second through the screen door and pull me kicking and screaming into the nearest bunker. But the door held as the siren continued its electric wail. I held my ground, too. I wasn't going to spend the night in some bunker this time, not when I'd fought so hard for this three- by six-foot *chip of paradise....*

✎*...9:24 a.m., Monday, February 10, 1997, Albany, Illinois... Karl lights another* cigarette. "You don't mind? I wouldn't have worried about it, but Kool says he needs it ASAP." *Why does he keep apologizing?* "It should only take a few minutes."

"I *said* it was okay, so don't worry about it."

"Just checking. Don't want to put you out."

"You're not, okay?" We fall silent as we head north out of Albany. Breakfast at Julie's had been a bust: no appetite, unable to finish while Karl wolfed his. I stare out the window as he cranks up *97X*, too loud for nerves pricking just below my flesh. At the morning meeting, soon as Karl had said "Potter's Marsh," and, "Could you help check my level loop on a couple of the ponds?" I had felt like I was about to face a firing squad. *Why? What's the big deal? You know what. Same old shit. Scared to get out of the office, hiding in my new cubicle like a caged animal...only this animal wants to be caged.* So I had said, "Sure, guess I can go." What else was I going to say? And now, here I am, feeling like a kid at recess about to face-off with the school bully– and recess is only a dozen miles away. *Get a grip!* But it's way too late for that– no spit, hands sweaty, head swimming– yes, it's too *late for that. ...✐*

Wednesday, March 31, 1971, Day 161 / 204 to DEROS
—reborn—

I awoke to the sound of sea gulls squawking over lunch. Turning over, the dull surf percolated in my ears, as if trying to brew some order back into my head. My hangover was just a blunted memory of a stupid night. *Fruit punch and vodka, wait till I get hold of Sesnewski and tell him what I think of his fruit punch and vodka.* This morning the Doc had removed the old bandage, squeezed out the gunk, packed it with some gooey white ointment and applied a sterile gauze. I was amazed at the scope of the ulcer. Almost an inch deep, there was no blood at all– just white puss oozing from the spongy sides. He gave me a green canvas slipper and told me not to wear my boot till further notice.

After a hamburger steak lunch, I changed into a pair of green nylon Speedos and found a spot on my beachfront paradise before sinking into reading *The French Lieutenant's Woman.* I read non-stop for nearly an hour before resting my eyes, gazing at a speck of a ship wavering on the horizon. Remembering Ski's R&R plan, I checked my watch. If I hurried, I'd have time to put in for it and buy that 35mm camera for the trip before my next appointment at the Aid Station. I gained my feet and limped to my bungalow, the bit of sanity I was hoping to find now flowing through my veins like saline solution through an IV, and I *was bookoo content. ...*

✐ *...Thompson, Illinois...Karl slows to* the posted speed limit, passing where the town cop usually sits in the small river community of Thompson, Illinois. We turn left onto Potter's Road, just a block from the country market where I had escorted Sheryl on our first date so many years ago. Reaching the town's edge, Karl crosses the causeway to a large island and our job site.

I fake a boring nod as he gives me a glance and says, "Be right back," before jumping out to unlock a cow gate. Continuing past the gate, Karl jumps onto a snow-packed trail that winds into the backcountry. Sliding around a bend on the road, he tosses me a mischievous smile. A few years ago I would have been the one slipping and sliding like a drunken bronco rider. But now? My jaws clench like a rusty vice. A mile in, he pulls up on a road beside two ponds, part of the expansive Potter's Marsh, a protected area the Corps monitors as part of its Environmental Management Project.

Karl points at an upstream pond. "That's one of the ponds we gotta check out." –he opens his field book– "Came in almost half a foot low when I closed the loop." –he points to another– "Let's take off on that one. That closed out just dandy."

"You know what you want, why don't I take the book?"

"No problem. I'll hafta take the spud bar to get a couple soundings."

I take out the level and mount it with shaky hands onto the tripod. *Relax, man. This ain't so bad.* Karl grabs the level rod and spud bar and heads for the pond while I ready the level on the side of the berm.

"Ready!" I shout and he extends the rod three sections and sets it on top of the ice. "Got it!" I record a 15.72 into the backsight column. Karl puts the rod over his shoulder and heads for the other pond. *Not too bad a day out. Man, wish I could work out here again.…*✎

Thursday, April 1, 1971, Day 162 / 203 to DEROS
—dusting off the keys—

Gilespie sank into his chair. "I can't help it, Adams, that's what Topp said."

"But the Doc said–"

"*I know* what he said, but what can *I* do about it that I haven't already done?"

"Well, I'm gonna go over there right now and get a note…or *something*. Man, I can barely walk here!"

"Do that. Then bring it back here and I'll see what I can do…okay?"

Nodding, I dramatically limped out the door and headed down the sandy street toward the Aid Station. Topp's self-centered order pounded in my head as had my hangover, blinding my eyes to the morning, now alive with the first streaks of the sun as it crept across the lane's golden surface. *How could he be so stupid, wanting to send ME to a firebase...paranoid bastard! Creep probably thinks I'm gonna frag 'im.*

*       *       *

My blue moon-shadow dogged at my heels as I grumbled toward the CQ office.

"Hey, Gilespie," I threw at him nervously as I pushed open the screen door, "here I am."

"Good news, Adams. You're staying."

"The note did it then?"

"Yep."

"Far out!" I exhaled, relieved at the bit of good luck. "So, what's up tonight?"

Gilespie studied his watch. "Your on till 0100. Just answer the phone and keep an eye out. That's about it."

"No sweat. Sure will beat pulling guard in the bush."

"I bet. Well, I'm gonna crash, been a long fucking day."

"Goodnight, Tom." Gilespie left me in the company of the aged floor fan, grating out a monotonous tune that I quickly terminated since a cool breeze was sifting through the screen windows.

I sat in Gilespie's chair. *I could get used to this.* Swiveling around to face a green steel cart sitting adjacent to the desk, I fondly eyed a lead-gray Smith Corona typewriter sitting like a steely-fingered octopus on the yellow-stained wooden tabletop. *Been a long time since I used one of these.* I spun back and opened several grumbling drawers under the gray-slabbed desktop. Finding what I was searching for, I turned back and cranked a sheet of stationery into the roller. A quick scan found the "ON" button and the cephalopod-like suckers began to plant their inky tentacles onto the virgin pulp.

*Mom, Dad –                                  Thursday – First of April*

*Hello again. Doing okay I hope. You may be surprised at this letter being typed. I'm on CQ now in our company orderly room and thought I'd take* advantage of the trypewritter. I'm surprised at how much I've remembered from high school - I'll have to know how to in college anyway.

Well finally I got some sham time (rear duty due to profile). Our company was on retrain 2 days ago. The day they hooked up I was feeling kinda sick, slight fevor, vomiting. So I got to stay behind. First time in 5 months. Am okay now so no sweat. While at Aid Station I had them look at these Gook sores on my foot (left– caused from lack of water to keep clean or dirt). Well, I got a seven day profile out of it. Not bad. Have to go back every day to change bandage. It's quite nice back here. Wouldn't even know a war was going on.

Went on the beach yesterday to soak up some sun, wore green speedo's you sent, thank you for sending. Also they show flicks every night free. Can't wait to get a rear job. I am staying in company area.

Have now got R&R put in with 2 of my friends– we will go to Australia. Get my list of clothes I'd like sent? Remember am saving next 2 pay checks. Requires at least $250 dollors to take. Plane fair payed both ways. I will land in Sidney. Bought Yashica 35 mm camera for occasion (half price - $62). A really good one. Kinda complicated but hope master it by R&R.

Found out for sure that GI Bill is presently $175 a month for no dependants. Each month in service counts as 1½ month for bill– total 36 months. That would give me $6300. With bonds for 2 yrs. $1200 I'd have $7500 to work with. Get college books I sent for yet? Figure can get near finishing art course while finishing duty in states. Hope so anyway.

I sent more (3) negatives home.

5/46 stands for 5$^{th}$ Battalion 46$^{th}$ Infantry.

198$^{th}$ Brigade in the Americal Division. Check it out!

One month ago 198$^{th}$ became the 196$^{th}$ Brigade. Now were back to the 198$^{th}$ again. So fortunately we wont be moving up to Da Nang.

Well again I run out of words so guess I'll have to stop. Please take care & God bless. Son– Bob

Saturday, April 3, 1971, Day 164 / 201 to DEROS
—Scott—

My suntanned toe kicked at a shell, half-buried in the seaweed-specked vanilla froth bordering the sand like a Santa's beard. I was feeling better than I had in weeks. My ankle and toes were better and thanks to the daily cleansings and antibiotics, the gook sore was showing signs of healing. Physically– I was on a high.

My bungalow peeped around a shore bunker five hundred meters ahead. I broke into a sprint, my parched lips licking the seawater splashed onto my flushed body as my feet pounded through the warm surf. Reaching the point opposite my hootch, I throttled back and quickly tiptoed across the hot sand to *the back door.* ...

✎ *...Thompson, Illinois...Taking the foresight* reading, I pick up the level while Karl spuds through the ice.

"Now what?"

"The other pond," he puffs, picking up the level rod. "Three-point six." – he drains the icy water from the level rod– "Ready?"

I record the depth and we head across the frozen pond to where a ragged snowmobile trail guts an icy path through the brush. What little spit I have abandons my mouth as the truck disappears from view. *It's okay now. Come on. Relax.* Karl throws me some small talk until we reach the next pond, where large ruts of frozen slush from snowmobile use hinders our progress. *Here it comes...dizzy, can't breathe...I can't get my breath!* The far end of the small pond seems a mile away as Karl pulls ahead. *It AIN'T gonna happen!*

He stops, waits for me to catch up and points. "Set up over there and I'll getcha a backsight on that other pond." –he points at another shot of hard water across a patch of dead grass– "Then I'll give you a shot over here."

"Okay," I say through a mouth of white paste. *Why am I so scared? Why am I so afraid to breathe? It's like I can't remember how. What a fucking phobia: the fear of being out of breath. Or better yet: the fear of breathing.* I look through the scope. My head shakes, making it difficult to focus. *Four. No Three. No. Four, four, four thirty, four thirty-two? No, thirty-one. Four thirty-one.* "Got it!"...✎

\*     \*     \*

*...I threw a* small paper bag from a trip to the souvenir stand on my bed and looked to where a GI was sleeping several cots over. *New guy,* I judged from his factory fresh fatigues. His pale, lanky frame pushed his shiny boots over the end of the bed. *At least he knows enough to sleep when he gets the chance.* Swinging my legs onto the army blanket, I pulled my hat over my face and closed my eyes.

317

Early evening shadows blanketed the barrack as my eyes drifted open. Cat-like, I stretched my arms and legs and glanced at the new guy's empty bed.

"Hey, you're awake," an unfamiliar voice said from the far end of the room. The new guy closed the screen door. "That CQ guy told me to bunk here since I'd be going to your platoon. Hope you don't mind."

"No sweat," I lied.

The new guy approached with extended hand. "Name's Scott Fitzgerald."

"Bob Adams." I returned his handshake, the strength of his grip masked behind fingers slender as his tall frame. Then as an afterthought, "Welcome aboard."

"So," Scott minced, sensing the awkward moment, "how long you been in the field?"

"Going on six months," I answered, studying his Sherlock Holmes-like face. I lowered my guard. "I'm from Illinois. How 'bout you?"

"A little burg called Hawthorn, northwest of New York."

"You mean New York City? There's a couple guys in our platoon from New York. One's from the Bronx. The other guy..." –I remembered Mike's transfer to Fat City– "...well, the other guy got transferred."

"Yeah? You got any idea when we're going out?"

"You'll probably take the first slick outta here. But it gets pretty crazy sometimes– usually don't know what's happening till it's over. Myself, I'm working on a seven day profile." –I pulled up my pant leg and proudly revealed my bandage– "Gook sore. It's like jungle rot." –I offered Scott my first genuine smile– "Well, my stomach's telling me it's time to eat. *Wanna come along?*"...

✎*...Thompson, Illinois...I climb into* the truck; my heart races like Ben Hur's chariot. *It's over, it's over! I'm going home. Home!*

"Since we're here, you want to go ahead and do that other pond? I got the sled in back." *He's taunting me.* "Just take a half-hour."

"Why doncha wait till you have more guys." *Is this stupid?* "Kool don't need it right now, anyway."

"Then maybe you should call Aidala and clear it with him."

I do. "He said don't worry about it, so let's get outta here." We do. He slides around the corners, threatening to get the truck stuck.

"Sure you don't want to do that pond?" he taunts again. "Just take a few..."

"Let's just get outta here." *I'm going crazy. I know it!* My heart isn't slowing down. Karl pulls past the gate. *Close it yourself, Karl, I can't even get outta the truck!* He does. We pull onto the causeway, out of Thompson, onto the highway. I lean back, try to relax, try to close my eyes. My lids jerking on me. *Calm down, it's over, it's over, it's over, it's over, it's over and I'm going home!...*✎

Sunday, April 4, 1971, Day 165 / 200 to DEROS
—a little slice of home—

"Dis da Sec'd Patoon Barrick?" Three FNG's tramped into my barrack and slung their gear onto several of the beds. I had been sound asleep, having talked long into the night with Scott, whose contagious friendliness had begun to fill Mike's void.

"It don't matter what barrack you use," I said, irritated by the FNG's tone.

"Well, da *man* toad us ta find da one with da Sec'd Patoon guy in it. Dat be you?"

I sat up, staring at the gangling black private. He was green as they came. "Yeah, man, that be me."

"Okay, den, we jes make oursales at home hea." He slowly lowered his tall frame onto his bed, as if not trusting it to hold his weight. Passing the test, he stretched onto it and slid his chocolate arms behind his head.

The second private carried his small wiry frame with a bouncing confidence and approached smiling. "Don't mind him, a bus just ran over his old lady. Hi. Mike Puccio," he said, spitting out the "P". He nodded at the third private. "That's Dennis O'Brien." Exchanging a quick shake and a smile, I liked these two guys.

"That big guy is Charles A. Brewster," Mike said, throwing a thumb at him. "He's from Leakesville, Mississippi. The three of us go clear to Basic. Right, Brew."

Brew didn't avert a lazy stare at the ceiling. "Fuck'n' *A*, ma man, Pucci."

"His manners suck. But we get in any shit out there and he'll be one hell of an asset."

"*No* motha-fuck VC gonna mess with tha Brew," he sauced out, keeping to his upward stare.

319

"Where'd you guys come in from?" Scott asked. "I didn't see you at the Replacement Center."

"We were there," O'Brien answered. "But only two days." His eyes shone in his brown face like little black nuggets. "Before that, we were at Long Binh."

I tugged on my boot. "You guys hungry?"

Brewster ran into a group of brothers, using it to split from us as they ate up several minutes of chow time doing their hand-jiving ritual.

"You know," I said, setting my tray of sliced hot dogs and sauerkraut on the table, "you sure your name is Dennis?"

O'Brien looked at me with a mouthful of kraut. "What you mean?"

"You look more like a George. You sure that ain't your name?"

He didn't miss a beat, shoveling another forkful of kraut to his mouth with a hairy paw. "Nope, not the last time I looked at my driver's license."

"Well, I'm sorry. But I'm just gonna hafta call you, 'George.' Dennis just ain't you, man."

"Hey, you keep an eye out for me out in the bush and you can call me anything you want."

"Deal, George," I said, pouring a mound of ketchup on my plate.

George was from the same part of New York State as was Scott, which initiated a burst of spirited recollections about some of their common haunts. Puccio hailed from San Diego and took us on an out-of-body excursion, spinning tales as only an exuberant Italian like a Mike Puccio could. We talked until the KP guys threw us out. We talked our way to the barrack and to the beach, where I shared with my new friends my slice of paradise.

*     *     *

Gilespie slammed open the screen door. "Fitzgerald, Brewster, you other two: you're hooking up. Grab your gear and throw it in the jeep in front of the CQ, pronto."

They exchanged nervous glances. I knew what they were feeling.

"Remember, hook up with Nelson Birch or Hillbilly. They're good guys and will treat you right. Platoon's probably working the Rocket Pocket and there ain't *even* nothing going on there."

# DETONATION

—paradise lost—

"TR? Man, what are you doing here?"

Lieutenant Hunter looked up while sorting through a stack of mail in the CQ office. "You know, that's a question I've been asking myself all day."

"How's your hip?"

"Good enough to send me back into the bush."

"Adams," Gilespie said, looking up from his paperwork. "what's *with* your platoon anyway? Last night a shitload of 'em came in for one reason or another."

"Well," I Yogi-Beared, "we always were smarter than the aaaa-ver-age Grunt."

On the way back, I visited the barrack closest to the CQ. Gilespie was right. Ross, Spanky and Bromlow were on sick call. Ross' right cheek was swollen from an abscessed molar and Spanky needed several stitches from a cut on his arm from a C-ration lid, of all things. Pane had gone and stuck Bromlow with a knife right through his boot while playing splits and it was bad enough that he might not have to go back out. Bromlow said when the CO got wind of it, all hell'd broken loose and he slapped an immediate ban on all "frivolous games". And last, Rickard was booking for a rear job.

There was a newcomer, too: John Webb, Doc Belton's replacement. Looked like he could've been Tex's brother. I thought we would've had a medic by now, which meant the platoon was still walking naked.

*     *     *

The doctor finished wrapping my nearly healed gook sore. "Okay, Adams, you can put your boots on."

"What do you mean, Doc?"

"It means the ride is over; I'm putting you back on active."

"Couldn't talk ya into a couple more days, huh?"

"I think you know you're ready," he chuckled.

As I walked back, I wasn't surprised by the verdict. He was right; I *was* ready, for I hadn't felt this fit in months. In my left hand I carried a small bag with enough bandages and antiseptic to treat my wound for the next ten days. In my right was the note that would send me back *into the bush*....

✎ *...1:13 p.m., Saturday, June 14, 1997, home...Shit! My motherfucking heart!* A bitter mix of fear and anger boils in my veins as I coast down the hill and into my driveway. *There ain't enough goddamn profanity in this world to show how I feel! Can't even take a bike ride without this fucking shit! How the fuck am I suppose to relax!* I throw my Schwinn *Varsity* onto the grass beside the garage. *Fifty goddamn minutes, ever since I passed K-fucking-Mart. Fuck! A little bounce in the road and...BAM!...there goes my heart. Give it to me, God! Give me your fucking worst! You say all things work for good? You say trust in me and I will give you peace? When? When? WHEN FUCKING WHEN?!*

I grab my ax from the garage. *You're not a God of love. You're not a God of anything. I don't know what you are...you might be nothing but a big joke.* I raise the blade over my head. *You want my fucking bike, God? Well...* –the ax torques down with all my might– *...TAKE IT!* The steel rips the royal blue main frame into two useless scraps of iron. *HERE!* The bike feels my pain as I fracture the handlebar and front wheel, cleaving the rubber with a soft eruption of stale air as the weapon cleaves into the rim. Two more swings take care of the back tire and the exposed pedal. One more takes out the seat, paring it like a melon to *its white pulp....*

# DETONATION

# THE FAR BLUE HORIZON
## PART IV

# MISSION TEN

Wednesday, April 7, 1971, Day 168 / 197 to DEROS
—reunion—

*July, 1963...⬖I squinted through* the rich tangle of oak leaves to the forest floor, more than thirty feet below. "How many more!" Danny disappeared while I leaned back and rested my elbows on the partially built sumac platform, secured to a sturdy fork fifteen feet from the trunk. *Can't wait to see their faces when they see this. Ladder won't getcha up here now, creepheads!*

Danny reappeared below. "Thirteen!"

I did a quick estimate on the remaining space the small fork provided, it being a third as big as the giant fork below. "Only five more! Tie one on!" *Heck, I can barely make it up.* I pulled the log up, swinging it to prevent it from snagging on a large limb below. *No way THEY can do it...clumsy idiots.* I pulled the log over the fork, untied the rope and lowered it down to fish for another. *Idiots weren't even smart enough to get rid of 'em* –I fit the smooth timber in place– *'n' now we're gonna have even a better treehouse than before.* The log secured, I began raising the next one. *This is still gonna be the best summer yet!...✎*

*...LT Hunter, Spanky,* John Webb and I climbed off the truck bed at Fat City. My ruck was chock full: eight boxes of C's, four each of frags and smokes, bar of C-4, six magazines of 5.56mm ammo, plus two thirty-

round banana clips taped back-to-back, secured in my 16. Under each arm I carried a case of soda I had picked up at the PX– my gift to the Grunts.

A lone slick by the edge of the airstrip revved its hot turbines and I pulled the two cases of soda beside me and let the chopper take me away. The slapping wind rushing through the cabin reminded me of what lay ahead. Sham time was over: muddy paddies, aching shoulders, scorching heat, bloody leeches, natty eyes, volcanic fear, sleep deprivation and heartburn-city C's would be on today's menu. But, in spite of the reality check, I still had this strange, pulsating attraction to life in the bush, a life that floated on an altogether different plane than the life I was leaving by that guarded beach. Out here, every pore on my racked body pricked with high voltage intensity. Maybe that was why Sergeant Trainor kept coming back for more: at no place else had I felt so alive.

Our chopper spiraled like a lone vulture over a tiny paddy somewhere near the bowels of Ky-Tra Valley, waiting for confirmation of the purple smoke smudging the olive canvas below. The pilot got the okay and we began corkscrewing toward earth, heading into a small pocket linked with countless other pockets riddling the southwest peripheral of Ky-Tra's main valley. Down on the floor the bird waited while Webb, Spanky and I, along with Hillbilly's squad, unloaded the shipment of C's and mail. It then spun out of the narrow watershed with TR, who was to hook up with the CP.

"Well, looky what the cat drug in," Hillbilly exclaimed as the bird cleared the paddy. "How ya doing, Adams? Ol' Ski's got bookoo vodka wait'n' fer ya at yer hootch."

"Funny, Hillbilly, real funny."

"My eye's a play'n' tricks on me, or was that TR on that bird?"

"In the flesh," Spanky answered, "heading for the CP."

"Poor fucks. Hey, Spank, ready ta tangle with another C-rat?"

"Long as it ain't fruit cocktail." –Spanky stepped out of the paddy– "This here's John Webb, our new Doc."

"Howdy doody, Doctor Webb. Welcome to our platoon." –Hillbilly readjusted his load– "See ya got yersef a 16. Last Doc didn't hanker much ta those."

Webb scrunched his round face, not quite knowing how to handle Hillbilly's twaddle. "Guy's gotta protect himself."

"That he does, Doc." –he slung his 16 over a shoulder– "Boys, let's go. Time ta git on back."

I greeted the rest of the squad as Hillbilly moved into the treeline. Retchin was there with Langley. George and Mike Puccio were there, too; George looked bush-jaded compared to Mike, who appeared to be thriving in the jungle environment.

The camp was nestled among a sparse stand of tulip trees atop a small rise butting against the same paddy that doglegged around the toe of our hill. My squad guarded its shady eastern slope, enjoying an excellent view of the marsh.

"Anybody for some soda?"

Ski's back was to me, stirring up some chicken and noodles. "Adams is back!" he chortled, cranking his head toward me. "How's your gook sore, man?"

"Scott told ya, huh? It's bookoo better." Fritts was engaged in a teaching session with Scott over the finer points of spades and turned long enough to wave. "Hey, Fritts, good to see ya." –I nodded to Scott– "See ya took my advice."

"They promised to take good care of me," Scott returned. "You see O'Brien and Puccio?"

"They were at the LZ. George was looking a little haggard."

"Who's George," Ski asked, "that new guy over there?"

"Nah, that's John Webb, our new medic. George is that O'Brien guy."

"But I thought–"

"Trust me," I grinned, "it's George."

"Whatever. Slide that pop over here." –Ski peeled off a coke– "And just in time for dinner."

"Hey, where's Pat?"

"Gone, shamming it with Mocko on 270. You believe that shit?"

"How'd *they* luck out?"

"LT picked 'em after Higher sent word they needed two guys for bunker guard. Don't *even* know why."

"And I was about to chew Pat out about his vodka. So what else's been happening?"

"Well, we *were* in the RP till they flew us into this shithole yesterday. Weren't off the bird twenty minutes when we ran into some gooks. Gave 'em some shit too." –Ski tested his noodles and finding them suitable, began spooning them in– "Ten to twelve of 'em, some kinda hospital patrol; ran right smack into the fuckers."

"Anybody get hit?"

"Wright got it in the arm by some shrapnel from Blondie's blooper."

"Wait a minute. *Gary Wright?* I thought he went back to the World after Dragon Valley."

"Not even. Hospital said his wounds weren't bad enough."

"Coulda fooled me. I mean, part of his arm sprayed all over me."

"I don't know, man. All I know is he hooked up with us the morning you stayed back. Carrying the 60 again, too, since Bromlow got stuck. You hear about that shit?"

"Yeah. Knew it would happen sooner or later. So how did Wright get hit by Blondie?"

"Wright was up front when Blondie's egg hit a tree. Can you believe it? Not ten feet from Wright."

"Wow, that guy's got bad luck."

"No shit. Anyway, we plugged three of their nurses before they could didi. Hey, did you check on our R&R date?"

"Taken care of. May twentieth we will sky up for down under."

Ski scooped out the last of his C's. "Round-eye pussy, here I come."


Thursday, April 8, 1971, Day 169 / 196 to DEROS
—day of rest—

As the sun burned off the morning haze, the stifling air dogged us like an obnoxious acquaintance you never could quite shake. I spent a drawn out lunch picking over my ham loaf and talking to Scott about the intricacies of a mechanical ambush before getting reacquainted with *The French Lieutenant's Woman*, my eyes greedily caressing every word as they swept me from the bush, the Nam and the war.

I read non-stop for an hour and a-half until the faint stench of rotting vegetation wafting off wet legs and mud-caked boots prompted me to rest my eyes: Spurlin and Blondie's squads were trudging into camp. They were returning from a four-hour patrol, having checked out the area where they had fired at the NVA nurses two days ago.

"So wudja find?" Nelson asked, standing to stretch.

"Notta thing, Birch," Blondie answered. "Fucking gooks just don't wanna play no mo'."

"Probably halfway to Hanoi by now," Nelson concluded.

"That or they're on fucking R&R in the nearest ville."

They filtered back to their positions, ready to enjoy a few minutes of rest. Brewster was beat. I could tell from the way he trudged back to his hootch, but his face refused to clue it to his bros, Slim and Tippy. They touted themselves as the Second Platoon Bloods, slapping hands and talking slams while inside I knew they were hurting as badly as we. And because of that, they had my respect.

Friday, April 9, 1971, Day 170 / 195 to DEROS<br>—duel—

The moment the word, "Break," shot down the line, I threw off my ruck. "Back's killing me already, Scott. How you holding up?"

"I can't believe the shit we gotta carry." –he lowered his ruck to the ground– "You got any more of that bug juice?"

I tossed him my bottle. "Don't go overboard, kin burn a hole right through ya."

"I don't care. I gotta get rid of these damn mosquitoes."

The path was a thread of hard-packed mud as we brought up the rear. Ski was on drag while Scott and I walked ahead of him. Less than an hour ago we'd found a clear enough spot to take a re-supply, which only added to our misery. We were almost out of our tiny valley when Blondie ran out of trail and into a wall of dense foliage that stopped him cold. Since then, it was cut and walk a few feet, cut and walk a few more.

The break over, I pulled on my ruck and leaned forward to adjust the straps. The sight of my boots reminded me of the crystal blue surf running between my toes just two days ago. I pulled the front of my shirt up to absorb several drops of sweat dangling on the tip of my nose. Looking up, I saw our thin line crook toward the slope on our right, heading for the far above ridgeline obscured in *the verdurous mist....*

✎...*10:28 a.m., Saturday, October 11, 1997, East Moline...This ain't gonna work.* I start up the hill anyway, pushing against a wave of apprehension swelling in front of me. Midway, the wave engulfs and nearly stops me, for I dare not breathe too deeply. As I near the top of the hill, though, the wave subsides. My head bobs to the surface. *This ain't so bad. Man, it's good to get outta the house. I don't know how much more of this I can stand...babysitting all night, working all day...sucks.* I near the driveway where my hearts usually starts racing. *Here it comes....*✎

*  *  *

*...I sank to* one knee to allow the heavy ruck to complete my calculated fall onto a plethora of grapevines that all but swallowed the small shelf, three-quarters up the steep slope. "Glad this LT's got some common sense. Our last LT didn't know when to quit."

"This is enough. Fuck." –Scott's lanky form buckled beside his ruck– "Think I ran out of sweat an hour ago. Why are we climbing this thing anyway?"

"Because," –Ski squatted on his haunches while trying to wiggle out of his ruck– "it's fucking there."

Nelson returned from the CP. "Come on, guys, let's get our hootches up. Got goddamn MA duty."

"You take Scott," Ski said, pulling out his machete, "*he* ain't been broken in yet."

"Okay, but *you're* on cutting patrol tomorrow."

"Why the fuck *me?* Fuck, I do all the work around here."

Yoss was searching for some level earth beneath the mat of vines. "Jeez, Ski, you won't even wipe your own ass."

Ski's lips flattened to a thin line. "I'll wipe it with your face."

"First you'd hafta figure out where it is."

"What, my ass or your face?"

"You figure it out."

"Look who's talking, a guy who can't even fart without his mama's permission."

"How would you know. You keep track of my farts?"

Scott looked at Fritts. "How long these guys go on like this?"

"Go on?" –Fritts tossed his support poles to *the ground*– "*Forever.*"...

✎*...10:42 a.m., October 11, East Moline...Shit! I expel* while passing the driveway that triggers my heart to begin racing. My mind registers the well-known routine– make it to the next safe spot, three and a-half blocks

330

away: the power pole by seventh street. There, at least, it won't look too weird if somebody is wondering why I'm not moving. I guard my pace and began to auto-rationalize. *Okay, this is a surge of adrenaline released into my bloodstream by some mindless fucking fear of being too fucking far from a safe fucking spot. Now does this fucking suck or what?*

I spot the power pole. *So...am I going to stop like a woose, or am I going to keep going? Okay, look, Bob, you didn't chose to be a warrior, hell, you didn't even want to be a warrior but...you became one...so whether you wanted to or not...you are one, so...FIGHT LIKE A GODDAMN WARRIOR!*

I keep going. *Keep a slow pace. Don't hyperventilate.* I hold my breath. Ten seconds. Slowly exhaling, my heart klicks to normal for a few seconds. Then starts racing again. *Try again.* I do and the same thing happens. Several more times, but I can't get it to last. "Fuck," I say audibly. *What's wrong with me? I ain't walking no fucking gook trails no more. I feel like I'm all scrunched up inside my chest, hiding behind my rucksack like I did in that ambush. Look around. It's safe here. The leaves are gorgeous, the sky is blue, the birds are singing.... Why can't you let me come home, God? Why do you keep me there? I did my part. I didn't run away.*

Next safe spot is Radden Park, over a half mile away, unless I decide to turn early and go through the back neighborhoods. In that case, I'd have to traverse a full mile before finding refuge at the Kennedy Square strip mall.

I decide for the long haul. *Maybe I can practice getting used to this. What do I fear? Dying? Yes. But so what? Doesn't everybody? Exercise then? Breathing? What? I know a racing heart is common to panic disorders. Hell, it can go like this for hours with no problem, so why can't I get it through my thick skull that I don't hafta fear this?* The only answer my brain can conjure is that this is now a habit and for some warped reason my mind now depends upon these attacks. It needs them. But why?

My confidence increases, as does my pace. *This is just a mind game. I got no choice but to deal with it. So, deal with it! It ain't gonna last forever.*

So I do. It's a slow mile; twenty minutes later I enter a Hardees restaurant by Kennedy Square. *Now get to the bathroom and get this shit stopped.* "Oh, great." The toilet is running over onto the floor. I relieve my bladder and exit to find a booth to see if I can knock it out there.

Several prying eyes across the isle motivate me to take some letters out of my back pocket I had intended to mail during the walk. I pretend to sort through them so as to calm any suspicions they might have of this foodless derelict sitting by them.

*There!* My heart proceeds into its typical adrenaline withdrawal with a series of wild palpitations, followed by a few seconds of normality, followed by another surge of racing and so on for five minutes until my heart clicks into a soothing lull of repetitious splendor. *It's almost worth having these fucking spells for the rush afterwards!* I sit for another five minutes before mustering the courage to get up and purchase a *small orange drink....*

Saturday, April 10, 1971, Day 171 / 194 to DEROS
—cutting up—

I lounged against my packed ruck, savoring the last few pages my book, made more enjoyable knowing that Ski was somewhere above me hacking a trail to the top. He, Tex, Puccio and Tippy, one from each squad, had been working on the mountainside since nine-thirty this morning. At least they had cooler weather to work with since the dawn had ushered in an influx of low gray clouds from the west.

The lunch-hour rolled in and our squad enjoyed renewed appetites with the break in the weather, not to mention the quiet of a Ski-free meal. Scott shared my stove, dropping in his ivory ball of C-4 as mine shrank into oblivion.

We were tossing our cans into the brush when a shout from above clued us the cutting crew was on its way in. The four appeared seconds later– shirtless, dirty and pants soaked with the morning dew that never seemed to evaporate. Ski sat down heavily by his ruck, rubbing his right hand.

"Webb," –he held up a blistered palm– "got anything for this?" Webb brought over his medic bag and took out some disinfectant and several Band-Aids. "Tomorrow it's your fucking turn," Ski said to Nelson through clenched teeth as Webb applied the suave.

Nelson didn't look up from a letter he was penning. "Don't mean nothing, Ski."

"Tell that to my fucking hand."

LT came over to inspect Ski's hand. "Shit, Ski, maybe you should be cutting trail more often to toughen that up."

"Funny, LT."

"Hey, Birch, need to get some guys together for a water patrol before we head up. Won't be none on top."

"No sweat, LT. Ski, you ready?"

"*Fuck you, Birch.*"...

✎...*12:16 p.m., October 11, East Moline...Soon I'm on* my way again, enjoying the beautiful fall afternoon, now warming into the lower seventies. *This is great! How could I have been so stupid to let that happen?* Enjoying my calm, I use the time to take up where I'd left off from yesterday's walk: going over in my head a name for my book as I juggled dozens of combinations.

*Silent Storm, Silent Thunder, Silent–*

"Fuck!" In my preoccupation I had missed a curb, my heart taking off as my chest muscles bounced from the unplanned maneuver. "I don't fucking goddamn need this shit!" –I turn around, seeing that I'm an equal distance between two safe spots– "Wouldn't you *fucking* know it!" –I slow to a crawl– "People must think I'm crazy, seeing some weirdo talking to himfuckingself. But who the fuck cares?"

I make it to Seventh Street and stop by a stop sign. *I ain't moving till this stops! Too fucking far to go and I'm too fucking tired to fight it. My brain is so tired....* I stand there, oblivious to the stares from the passing cars. *I'm a prisoner to my fear. To my mindless fucking goddamn fear!*

Two minutes.

Three.

Five: palpitations – exhale – slow – good – slow.

Eight: the racing stops.

I start again, daring not to breathe too deep or too shallow or jiggle or burp or lose my balance like I'm walking a high-wire a thousand feet over the street.

One block: a young lady pushes a baby carriage by me as fast as Carl Lewis can sprint by Howard Cossell.

Two blocks: I increase my pace – better.

Three blocks: *now maybe I can...fuck! Fuck! Fuck! Fuck! Fuck!* My heart speeds up like a bull seeing red. *That's it...no more...I'm done...I'm fucking done...walk...just...walk...maybe I'll make it...maybe I won't.* I look into the sky. *You want me to quit, God? Let me die if you want, but I am not going to quit!*

I make Crisis Hill, pausing at the bottom before slothing up the other side. Reaching the top, my mind is beyond exhaustion. My heart races wildly beneath a layer of paper thin chest muscles, now every nerve in my hollow hulk echoing the *PUMP! PUMP! PUMP!* of my renegade motor.

Another four-block crawl sends me up my driveway. I...AM...HOME! And my stupid, good-for-nothing brain knows it. In less than sixty seconds– though exhausted, though angry, though distraught– my heart kicks back into *a steady beat. ...*✐

Sunday, April 11, 1971, Day 172 / 193 to DEROS
—spoonful of fear—

The air burned my nostrils as I sucked it into my lungs. "Guess I'm gonna owe Ski an apology," I said, showing Nelson two red blisters on the palm of my right hand.

Nelson threw down his cigarette stub and poured some water over his face before handing me his over-under. "Least he got..." –he squeezed by me– "...his blisters on a *cool* day." –he swung his machete into the thicket– "This is...bullshit." Nelson's back was soon glistening with sweat as he fell into silent concentration.

Guarding our rear, my thoughts drifted back to last night's discussion with Scott about what we were going to do when we got back to the World. He wanted to go into law, of all things. His uncle had a practice in his hometown and had promised to make room for him should he pass the bar exam. *Pretty high ambitions for a guy beating the bush.* But then, so were mine– and why not? *We have as much a right to make it as the guys who got their college deferrals.* The image of Molly manicuring my nails popped into my head. *What would these villagers do if everybody got out of serving? They'd be dragged off to the Hanoi Hilton soon as those French guys left, or whoever was fighting before us. Somebody's got to do it.*

An angry mosquito chewing on the back of my neck dug me out of my daydream. I glanced at Nelson; his white back was now splotchy with red marks from a combination of mosquito bites, thorny brush and the heat.

"Need a break?"

Nelson turned and grinned. "Why, I'm having a good ol' time. I like cutting so much, I think I'll make a career out of it when I get back to the World. 'For Hire, Professional Bush Whacker'...think it'll fly?"

\*  \*  \*

I drop to the ground. "Just... WAIT!"

Yoss looks at me peculiarly. "Jeez, Adams, it's just a tree."

"I *know!* But I can't help it." –I take three shallow breaths– "Okay, do it."

"Fire in the hole!" Nelson shouts.

I press my hands over my ears like I'm trying to crack my skull and as the explosive splinters the trunk, I feel my body splintering with it.

"What's with the fucking jimjams, man," Ski asks from beside me.

"Gimme a second. I'll be alright." Another twenty minutes clears enough room for a chopper. We make a hasty retreat as night rushes in, anxious to get some chow. As for re-supply, it will have to wait till morning.


Wednesday, April 14, 1971, Day 175 / 190 to DEROS
—ow—


One member stronger as Ross had returned with a mended molar on the morning's re-supply, Nelson and I had been cutting a new trail since nine-thirty– only ten meters from the one we'd cut up last night. It was steep, slippery and so thick the tangle easily supported me as I leaned against it to catch my breath. The last three days made it seem as if we were cutting to China. Rotating cutting crews, LT insisted staying off the VC trails and blazing our own. It was probably a good idea, for there were bookoo signs of VC activity: cultivated potato fields, recently abandoned straw hootches, fire pits that hadn't yet seen a raindrop and even C-ration cans strewn along the streambanks. But cutting through the double-canopy had its downside: sore, grouchy Grunts and little headway. I estimated we'd covered only a klick since Saturday.

Nelson's feet slid out from under him for the second time, sending him crashing to his butt. "What kinda motherfucking hell is this? Take over, Adams. I've had it."

"How's your hand holding up?"

Nelson held up a callused palm. "Not nearly bad as my ass."

My blisters, too, had healed into a hardened layer of thick skin, at least one less thing to worry about as I struggled to keep my balance on the wet leaves and vines beneath the slick soles of my boots.

"WHA–!"

Nelson whipped his towel at my back. "Bees!"

The word shot my heart white. "Get 'em off!" –I felt a hot sting dig into my right cheek– "Back up back up!"

Collapsing fifteen meters from the hive of ground bees, I dug through my panic for a breath of air. "Any getcha?"

"One nailed my arm." –he looked at my back– "You got three. Fuck."

"And one on my face. I hate bees. Ran into a whole nest of yellow jackets when I was a kid...about killed me."

At two, we dragged ourselves into the NDP. LT let us get some grub while Webb treated our stings. Shortly before three, we hooked up and made the bottom– in less than five minutes. From there, LT conceded to follow a gook trail for almost a klick.

"Why do I get the feeling I've already been here?" I asked Ski while resting by the side of a stream that cut through a narrow gorge.

Ski studied the terrain. "I remember. This is where we got stuck sleeping in the rain after Fritts twisted his ankle. Remember that shitty mission?"

"That's right. Seems like a lifetime ago, huh?"

# STAND-DOWN TEN

Thursday, April 15, 1971, Day 176 / 189 to DEROS
—hello-goodbye—

I paused, crooking my ear for the sound of choppers. "Seven."

"Whoa, think you got some bad-ass cards?"

"You'll find out, Ski." The tricks started to fall, Scott and I gobbling up most of them, leaving Yoss and Ski with a set hand.

"Why didn't you trump that fucking heart?"

Yoss took a swig of water. "The same reason you laid off suit instead of trumping that king of clubs."

"I had my reasons." –Ski looked up for the hundredth time– "Where the *fuck* are those birds?"

Going on three, the birds were an hour late and we didn't want to stay another night. Between the bugs and the bee stings it had been a sleepless night, but as morning neared, most of the swelling in my face had gone down, though it was still red and tight from the poison. We'd arrived at the pick-up zone by twelve-thirty and LT had allowed us to fire half our ammo on some nearby abandoned hootches, partly to keep our trigger fingers happy and partly to send one last message to any VC who might still be in the area.

"Here they fuck'n' come," Hillbilly announced. "Let's git the *fuck* home."

Four choppers slid over the horizon and fell into a dive toward our blue smoke. Tex had the privilege of bringing them in; his oversized fatigue shirt flapped in the artificial gale created by the lead bird. As Nelson led our squad to the third bird back the black paddy water flooded my boots, imparting a barbed reminder to take back with me to Fat City. Scott looked apprehensive, being only the second time he'd saddled this wild stallion of wire and steel. I found a seat by the door gunner, secured my earplugs and leaned back to watch the untamed mountains of Ky Tra silently fade away.

*　　*　　*

"Hello, *boys!*" Mocko's pasty smile was waiting for us as we climbed from the trucks. Behind him, a gauntlet of food canisters waited. We'd been delayed at Fat City for two hours by the absence of Third Platoon, due to a mix-up by the chopper pilot as to their location in the hodgepodge of valleys on Ky Tra's northwest side.

Retchin swung his 60 over his shoulder. "So, Mocko Man, looks like your fuck'n' sham days are over."

"Mocko," I interrupted. "Where's Pat? I gotta beef with him and his vodka that 'bout killed me last stand-down."

"Hey, man," –Mocko's grin faded as much as possible for a Mocko– "dude's in the hospital."

"What?"

"Yeah, man. He was burning brush below our bunker when his flame-thrower blew up on him. He's in bad shape. Got burns on eighty percent of his body."

"Fuck," Retchin said, pulling his ruck off the truck bed, "gets out of the bush to get toasted on a firebase."

"He gonna be okay?" Nelson asked, handing down Yoss' ruck.

"Fuck, Nelson, *you* didn't see 'im. I don't think so."

337

The news of Pat rippled like a pebble dropped into a farm pond to the debarking Grunts, who granted Pat a few moments of silence as the wave bumped by. But too soon, the lure of hot chow overcame their respectful pause for a guy they barely knew.

Mocko joined us tonight. We smoked a round for Pat– it was the least we could do. Mocko told us how it all came down: how the flame-thrower backfired on him, how he fell backward in a ball of flame, how the blankets were thrown on him, how his hair got burned off, how his screams still follow him into the night– Mocko did have a heart after all.

By eight, we were sufficiently stoned and just in time for the evening flick: *Hello-Goodbye*. The movie kept our eyes rolling and by the time Harry drove the baron's vintage car into the swimming pool, I had nearly forgotten about Pat. In the end, though, the movie failed to boost my spirits. Afterward, I took a lone walk to the edge of the compound and gazed for a long time into the star-filled sky.

*Dear Mom & Dad,*                                          *April 18, 1971*

*So sorry for a delay in writing. At times I'm just not in the mood and won't write to anyone for a couple weeks at a time…so please bear with me.*

*I'm on a re-train right now. We go out tomorrow. My foot healed up fine & hasn't bothered me since. It was a good break for awhile.*

*I suppose you know that we're again the 198th again. Right now our division (23rd) is due to go on stand-down sometime in the fall. Right now the First Cavalary is in the process of standing down. The're south of here. The divisions are standing down from south to north. Although the divisions will start standing down this May. Our 198th Brigade will be the last to leave. Mainly because we're the closest to Chu Lai. So I may go home with the 198th. The're going to start giving us 60 to 90 day drops! With that I would have only 120 days left!*

*My R&R for May 20th has been revoked, due to too many people appling at that time. Only 10% of the Company is allowed to go at a time. "Ski" will probably still get his since he's more time in country. I'll probably put in for a leave for that date instead. Only difference is your not garenteed a place to go. You just have to take what's available. Plane fairs both ways still are payed for by the Army. I'll put in for my R&R at a later date. One is allowed a 7 da. R&R, & a 2 week leave. Either 1 or both weeks at a time, & a 3 da. in country leave.*

*Two days ago I received your no. 23 letter. The picture from my other new camera will be much better & bigger too. It cost $62. & it was half price as compared to state prices.*

*Lately I've really been getting into art study. I try to sketch some each day & am improving steadily. I hope to be quite accomplished by the time I go back to the states.*

*I shouldn't be in the field for more that 2 more months -less with a leave & R&R.*

*I can keep my civilian clothes in my foot locker in the baggage room in Co. area.*

*Did you know Linda Sheesley is going to marry a Fred Schulzt. from Orion? The wedding is planned for June 16 - 73 - don't mean nothing!*

*The weather here now really is nice. It's very dry now & hot but I like it that way. Went swimming down by USO today.*

*I think the next time in, May 5 - 12 is stand-down.*

*Decided one subject I'd like to take up in college is French Language & history. I've really become interested in it. Seems I can't read enough now. I've gone crazy for knowledge!*

*Well that's about all right now. I'll try & write more often. Please take care.*

*God Bless. Love, your son, Bob...*

✎*...3:19 p.m., Saturday, January 10, 1998, home...I'M TAKING IT BACK!* White knuckles crash into the Chuck Norris heavy bag I'd purchased after Christmas– I had to do something in my basement prison. I pace back and forth on the cold floor like a caged animal. *It stops here!* A right! Left! Right! Pacing. *You've taken everything I have!* I stop and lean against the whitewashed basement wall, my skull in my hands. *My fucking life's been stolen from me. Can't walk outside no more. Trapped in my basement like a scared fucking rat. Too scared to look outta my black fucking hole. The Nam wasn't that bad. Didn't see no heavy combat like some of those dudes by the DMZ, so why...?*

Over to the bag, slamming my fist. Pacing. *Doc says it's guilt, guilt from Hippie. But it's more than that. It's got a life all its own now. The fear itself. That's my monster. It's broken free...AND IT'S OUT TO GET ME!* Straight right, another harder, another, harder! *You think you're going to destroy me?!* A flurry of left jabs, a hard right hook. *You think it's over? NOTHING IS*

*OVER! GOD, I'M GOING TO TAKE IT DOWN! THAT BLACK BAG IS MY FEAR!* Red knuckles crash into the nylon surface. *I'M!...*SLAM!*...NOT!...* SLAM!*...QUITTING!...* ✐

# MISSION ELEVEN

Monday, April 19, 1971, Day 179 / 186 to DEROS
—junk yard guard—

The blades pumping over my naked head sent me hurdling over the first ridge guarding the Rocket Pocket. My boots, supple as moccasins and bleached white from the sun, swayed in the rushing wind as the chopper pulsed through the warm air. Fifteen slicks, our entire company, blazed toward an area well beyond our usual stomping grounds. Behind us, more slicks, carrying an Engineering Company.

An hour brought us gliding into a huge valley that narrowed in the middle like an hourglass. I guessed our destination was a large hill sitting by itself in the bottleneck. Our CO had disclosed on stand-down that we were to re-establish a long-abandoned firebase, hoping to slow the dink's relay of ammo and supplies to their coastal counterparts. From there, rumor had it, the 198th would remain until the demise of the American Division.

Falling into the shadow of the enormous hill, the choppers dropped us in a paddy at its base. First Platoon and the CP were already snaking up its side, burned clean from countless napalm attacks. Third and the engineers were waiting in line at the bottom when we closed in on them.

"Talk about a clusterfuck." –Ski looked at the peak– "How do we get ourselves into these things?"

"You're a natural at it, Ski," Yoss had to say. "How long we gonna be here, anyway?"

"Probably forever. Shit, look at the size of that mother."

"Too bad Scotty ain't here to enjoy the hump," I mentioned while unscrewing my canteen lid. He had stayed back to treat an ingrown toenail that'd become infected on his first mission– lucky stiff.

340

\*        \*        \*

I squinted at the Grunts disappearing over the crest like a column of ants. Resuming my ascent, I returned my stare to the red clay that crumbled under my boots as we inched behind the green engineers, trailing a hundred meters behind Third Platoon's last man.

Three hours took us to its summit. At first glance, it appeared as if some angry god had lopped off its top with a meat cleaver. There wasn't a shard of vegetation anywhere, just a heavy layer of red dust coating the surface like frosting on a cake. Blown up shards of vehicles, tanks, earth-moving equipment, buildings, cannon and bunkers were strewn over the landscape like a scene from *War of the Worlds*. They had clearly never intended the hill to be used again, but here we were, waiting to build a major firebase large enough to house a battalion.

As ordered, the platoons were waiting at the edge of the plateau.

"Listen up!" LT commanded. "The engineers have accompanied us to give guidance in rebuilding this firebase. As the first ones in, it's our job to secure it and follow their lead. Eventually, we'll construct bunkers around the perimeter. But for the next couple nights, do the best you can. Right now they're going to use metal detectors to search and clear any mines that might have been left behind. So hold tight." –LT scanned the company– "Any questions?"

Hillbilly squatted against his ruck. "Think I'll cut me some Z's."

\*        \*        \*

*WAM!*

"Medic!" cries one of the engineers. His buddy sprawls beside him on his back.

"Webb!" LT shouts. "Tuck, get a dust-off!"

Several engineers cradle the wounded soldier as Webb arrives, along with First Platoon's medic. As if waiting in the wings, a chopper appears in less than ten minutes, stirring a cyclone of red dust as it thumps onto the clay. The young man is sailing off the hill in less than a minute.

Hillbilly removed his hat and scratched his head. "How the fuck *he* git here so fast?"

LT was conferencing with the other platoon leaders in a small huddle near where the engineer got hit. The engineers stood silent with metal locators flung over their shoulders.

"You ask me," Retchin said, "I think we sure as shit should get off this hill."

"Okay, men," LT said, returning. "Here it is. They had hoped to clear out the mines with metal detectors, but they're finding so much shit buried they're useless." –he paused for a moment to let the substance of his words sink in– "So instead, they're going to get a Rome-plow and maybe even a D-9 to rake off the ground and blow 'em in place."

"What're we supposed to do till then?"

"Maintain, men. We'll set up over there." –he pointed to the southern rim of the hill– "That's our AO from now on. Just don't go wandering around too much."

Blondie stood up and brushed the red dust off his pants. "Oh, I don't think you'll hafta worry 'bout that, LT."

Tuesday, April 20, 1971, Day 181 / 184 to DEROS
—don't dance with Betty—

Nothing. I repositioned my bare back on my ruck and continued to stare at a red coating of dust on my arms. I wondered if my face looked the same.

Nothing. Nelson was on his fourth Salem. Webb was trying to write a letter as the stationery battled with his sweaty hand. George was sound asleep; his parted lips tinged with red dust. Puccio was wrapping his towel around his 16 to keep the dust out. Yoss was eating peanut butter crackers, doing a, "*thpppt*," every few minutes to get rid of a speck of sand. Ski and Ross were hustling Mocko in a game of cutthroat.

*Nothing. Not a shadow in sight.* The noon sun basted my shoulders, spurring me to throw my fatigue shirt over them. I braced at the sound of another Chinook coming in. Every thirty minutes they came, sandblasting the ground, infiltrating every crevasse and fold with another layer of red Vietnam clay a hundred meters in every direction...*no wonder they call 'em "shithooks".*

Supplies, how could there be so many supplies? Already several *105*'s were in place overlooking the hill's eastern slope, the one we had humped up yesterday. Boxes, bundles of sandbags, crates, pallets and canisters were

342

stacked like the Tower of Babel in the center of the sliced-off hundred-meter wide hilltop. Before the dust could settle, a skycrane helicopter, carrying a huge water canister nicknamed a "water buffalo", flew in to keep the dust flying.

I squinted into the dust storm. *I gotta try and eat.* "Yoss!" I yelled over the roar, "betcha I could set this can in the sun for ten–"

*BAMMMMMM!*

The skycrane is scooting off our hill as our eyes shoot toward where a GI is crashing onto his back. A box of 16 ammo he had been carrying is bursting open on the ground behind his head.

"Christ!" Blondie yells from two positions over. "This hill's gett'n' blown *all* to fuck!"

Ski jumps to his feet and begins to walk up the hill for a better look, but freezes after a few steps. "This is bullshit!" he shouts, retreating to his ruck.

A dozen guys surrounded the fallen man, doing what they could until help arrived. It soon came. A Chinook pitched in the thermals while maneuvering toward the CP. Talk floated over it had been a Bouncing Betty, a delay-activated mine that had gotten both this guy and the one yesterday. Stepping on it triggers a spring mechanism that causes it to "bounce" three or four feet into the air before detonating. It was ironic that it was meant for the VC and here we were clearing them by the not so brilliant tactic of walking around till you found it– or it found you.

I watched the Chinook as it started for Chu Lai with the wounded man and I thought of another bit of irony. This morning Higher-Higher had dubbed this bald hill, "Firebase Professional," a hill that, as in a game of Russian roulette, was taking out our brave men *one by one. ...*

✎*...8:32 a.m., Friday, March 6, 1998, Corps of Engineers, Rock Island, Illinois...I look up* from the plotter; Scott Kool is approaching. *Meeting must gonna start.*

Jimmy walks in and takes a seat in the black swivel chair. He leans back and crosses his legs. "Okay, Scott," he begins, "the reason I wanted to talk is to see how you're organizing your data sets onto the CD's for the vector files and the ortho photos. What we need is some kind of order that'll make it easy for us to access."

"Plot will be done in a minute," I say over the tapping ink pen.

Scott begins to explain the convention he plans to use while I lean against the plotter. Kevin Carlock walks in and takes a seat by the window.

8:36–The plotter stops. I turn it off.

"So, anyways," Jimmy continues, "we're getting data that takes too long to clean up...."

My heart begins to race. Ten seconds. It settles down.

8:41–Another ten second race. "If you guys got something to add here," Jimmy says, "*jump right in.*"...✎

\*  \*  \*

*...The air cooled* as the sun sank below the western mountains of the wide valley basin. Settling in for second guard, the shadows darting around me told me it was to be a repeat of last night. The mountaintop glowed with lums and star clusters the engineers were shooting like drunken Chinese at a New Year's party. What I couldn't figure out was why they shot them *above* the hill instead of out in front of them. Maybe they were trying to light up a card game, for they couldn't be seeing dinks *every two minutes....*

✎*...8:47 a.m., Corps of Engineers....Jimmy keeps talking* and Scott keeps answering and Kevin keeps interjecting as my heart races in my chest. *I got to learn how to handle this; try and concentrate on what these guys are saying.* I try. "...COT files would be useful later on," Kevin is saying. I pull out my pocket watch. *8:47...1 2 3 4 5 6...*I count my heartbeat for ten seconds. *19...about a hundred twenty per minute. What would they do if I chucked this coffee cup at the wall...hard as I fucking could? Or maybe ask Jimmy to feel my pulse.* I stare at Jimmy's black turtleneck while his words spill out. *God, the guy still acts like it all matters. Wonder how he'd be acting if his heart were racing away, no spit in his mouth, jaws tight as a vise grip....*✎

Wednesday, April 21, 1971, Day 182 / 183 to DEROS
—Chanel #5—

"You got *any* idea what we're doing?"

Yoss stood to stretch his back. "Don't look too bad to me," he said, admiring the two layers of sandbags forming a crude rectangle. Yoss leaned over to hold another bag while I shoveled in the clay. Nelson stood next to Yoss, ready to tie it off before stacking it onto the emerging bunker. Five

344

meters over, George, Puccio and Webb were attempting their own version.

"At least ours is square," I threw at George. "Yours looks like some kinda four-sided triangle."

George backed up a step. "You don't realize it, but you're looking at the future Taj Mahal of bunkers."

"Hey, guys," Nelson interrupted, "what about the roof?"

I backed away with Yoss and Nelson to study the structure. "Maybe if we sorta like start putting the bags closer and closer towards the top? You know, like a pyramid or something." Before Nelson could answer, LT and Sgt. Trainor approached with word that Echo Recon had run into some gooks several klicks to the southwest while conducting a morning patrol and we were to drop everything and pack our rucks for a possible CA.

Nelson squeezed out a last drag on his Salem. "Let's just hope they won't *send us back.*"...

✎ *...9:21 a.m., Corps of Engineers...Up and down,* up and down, up and down. *Don't mean nothing. It can't hurt me. Got to learn not to be afraid of this. Got to learn to function while it's happening. Haven't said two fucking words yet. But I'm going to stand right here till this fucking meeting is done. Not going to fucking run. Dr. Hansen said go somewhere quiet till it ends. But better yet...stay! Well, I'm going to fucking stay! Gotta take a piss, but I'm not gonna move, not gonna run. I said this was the year I'd kick this in the ass. If I can learn to function while it's happening, I'm halfway there.* "Yeah, the directory structure looks good," I answer Jimmy. *Hell, I couldn't give him a rational thought right now if my life depended on it....* ✐

\*　　\*　　\*

*...The evening was* as clear as I'd ever seen: a pure, silvery blue chilling in a gentle breeze. We hadn't been called on the alert; Recon, having wrapped up its business, was making our perimeter at this moment. Tomorrow, a D-9 would clear them a spot on the mountain's west side.

The sun was racing for the finish line as I lay in our bunker, now five layers high. Turning toward the wall for a little privacy, I took out a fresh sheet of stationery and began a letter to Jennifer, my new girlfriend. A month ago, Stephanie Ziegler, one of my regular correspondents, had introduced me to her. She was rooming with Jen in a small flat in downtown East Moline. We had hit it off great and were now exchanging letters once a week. Her penmanship was beautiful and her perfumed letters drove me up a wall. She said she had French ancestry, which added to her already mysterious persona. Heck, I didn't even have a picture of her yet.

*...I've been on this hill now for almost a week, Jen. It gets so hot during the day you could fry an egg....*

I moved my head closer to adjust my vision in the waning light.

*...So how's your job going? Stef says you're getting a raise starting next month? I got one a month ago. Making a whole $255 a month now...Army's going to make me rich, huh?...*

Rubbing my eyes, I looked up to see the darkness had gobbled the far treeline and the paddy, now speeding up our hill. The stupid engineers had already begun shooting their lums.

*...Did you get my picture I sent last letter? When do you think you'll send...* –I paused to light my candle– *...me a....*

A hissing sound prompts me to glance up.

sssssssssssssssssssssssss*LAAAAMMMMMMMMMM*!

A deafening flash from George's bunker sends me pancaking off my mattress. A gray dust cloud erupts from their perimeter and rolls over me, cutting off my breath. Nelson, grappling from a sound sleep, bangs my head with his arm while a blast of adrenaline rakes my brain. Raising my head I spot LT; he crouches catlike, his 45 in hand in front *of George's bunker....*

✎ *...9:31 a.m., Corps of Engineers...*"So I'm gonna go down and write all this out as I've interpreted it," Scott says. "Then I'll e-mail you a memo to see if you agree." He walks out. Jimmy walks out. Kevin walks out. I return to my cubicle. A long and concentrated exhale returns my *heart to normal....*✍

*...*"INCOMING!" *LT screams,* his eyes white as his teeth. His last syllable is drowned out as the hill ruptures like a grenade. I grab my 16, breathing shallow the acrid smoke and peer over the sandbags. Radiant dots of light punch holes in the black sky as I strain to spot the horde of VC that must be crawling up our hill. Behind me, the thundering peal of artillery sends its carriage of death to the nearby hills while the CP Platoon blankets the paddies below with their own *version of destruction....*

✎ *...9:42 a.m., Corps of Engineers...* "Got that plot done?"

My heart starts racing again. *Shhhhit.*

"Yeah, Kenny, in the plotter."

He picks it up. "Can't read it."

"They're right in front of you."

"Where's the upstream cells? Supposed to be four of 'em."

"Probably on the next sheet up. I'll get it."

9:46–"Here you go." *Go for it heart. I ain't afraid of you.*

"I only see three. Where's the other?"

"I don't know." *This is interesting, like an experiment.* I check the time. *Cool. Been an hour now.* I sit down, another long, slow exhale downshifts my heart.

9:47–"Bobby, you got a second?" It's Jimmy.

"Yeah?" My heart starts up again.

"Just got back from talking to Barb about small boat harbors. This might be something you want to hear, Kenny."

I look out the third floor window of the Clocktower. A towboat is waiting to enter Lock 15. Kenny looks, too. A man in faded coveralls starts to unwench a cable to separate the barges. Two guys jog on the sidewalk that runs by the lock. *Wish I could do that.* Kevin comes in. Jimmy talks. My heart spins, but I can follow what he's saying, can even answer his questions. The joggers disappear. "No, the TIN isn't imbedded in an AutoCad drawing," and, "Gotta export it as a Version 12 drawing," and, "I can't print the ortho with the soundings yet." *This ain't so bad. Can think now...I can think now!...*✎

...*"Cease fire! Cease fire!"* LT waves his arms. The cacophony fades beyond the next chain of mountains. All is quiet. The wind whips a lone dust devil where LT had been standing moments earlier.

"Medic!" George shouts. In the chaos I'd forgotten about the initial blast.

"Doc's hit!" Puccio choruses in. "Get a medic!"

"What the fuck happened?" I hear Nelson say from behind me. Third Platoon's Doc appears with Hillbilly and LT.

"Give me room!" their Doc shouts. "Knock out this wall!" Webb's pallid form is disclosed as the wall comes down. His legs are *splotched with blood....*

✎*...10:00 a.m., Corps of Engineers...Jimmy leaves. Kevin* leaves. Kenny works on plotting the missing cells' coordinates. I sit down.

10:03–Heart slows to normal. *Got some spit again...good.* Write some more notes.

10:07–"You want a copy so you can lay out your dredge cut?" Kenny says, "Okay." I pick up the sheet. My heart gears up. I ignore it. I make the copy. I bring it back. I give it to Kenny. I sit down.

10:12–I jot down: 10:12–my heart still races.

10:15–Heart slows to normal. I start to process another survey, *Treat's Island Lower....*✎

...*"How the...?"* I looked up to see Ski standing beside my bunker.

"One second I was writing a letter and the next, something hit his bunker." –I glanced down the hill– "If it weren't no VC...."

"...then it came from a GI," Ski said, finishing my thought. We turned our heads towards the engineers' camp. "Some goddamn engineer put a fucking H-E in his blooper instead of a lum– I'd bet on it. You know how they get off shooting those fuckers right over us."

Thursday, April 22, 1971, Day 183 / 182 to DEROS
—halfway home—

The morning sun warmed my bones. I shook a packet of *Sanka* into the rolling hot water in my cup while listening to the muted growl of a D-9 huffing and puffing on the far side of the hill.

"Guess what, guys?" I said, squinting through the coffee steam. "As of noon today, I am on my downhill slide."

Yoss raised his canteen cup. "Congratulations, Adams. You're now an official member of the 'Secret Society of Short Timers.'"

"The downhill side goes bookoo faster," Nelson added, lifting his head off his bed.

I stood to my full height. "I'll be right back, gonna take me a morning stroll."

"Hey," Nelson advised, "just cause you're getting short don't mean you're invincible. LT don't want us taking no chances."

"After last night? What else could happen? I'm just gonna check out the dozer and maybe get a look at those clowns on the other side."

Webb had been dusted off last night. Both of his legs were torn up good, though he wouldn't be losing them. Thank God for that. And thank God that George and Puccio, who weren't two feet from Webb, didn't even get a scratch. All we could figure was that the round must have hit the side of a sandbag and driven most of the shrapnel into the ground. Whatever had happened, we were damn lucky, except for John Webb. I didn't know what they were going to do about the ignorant engineers– probably give 'em a medal.

I fell in behind several unfamiliar faces while approaching the water buffalo. I recognized the castle on one of the men's shoulder. *So this is–*

### KLAMMMMMMMMMMM!

I slam into the ground as the lead guy triggers an explosive. One of the soldiers screams for a medic. A couple of his buddies hold the wounded man while Third's Doc bounds over and rattles out orders. *God, there ain't NO safe spot...* –I pick up my cup and push myself to my knees, spitting out some clay– *...except my bunker.* I look at Nelson and Yoss, crouching beside our sandcastle. Nelson wears a perplexing look on his face as he grips his over-under, perhaps wondering why we have to defend a hill that has become our worst enemy.

*Now what? Hightail it to my safety zone, or keep going?* I stood up and continued toward the CP, hidden behind the supply stack. A couple of important looking CO's were scanning a blueprint, turning to point this way or that every couple of seconds. I gave them a wide berth, not wanting to attract attention.

I stopped. Before me lay a uniform row of bunkers that looked like they had been stamped out of a press. The engineers' roofs were solid and flat, so much so that several of them were sunning themselves on top as they sipped on sodas. *Where'd they get the pop?* I wondered which one of these dunderheads had about killed our Doc. In front of each bunker sat a table like the one by the CP. *Chairs, too? They must think this is some kinda R&R, unless they get pampered like this all the time. Wait till I tell the guys.* I continued around the circumference to where First Platoon guarded the northwest front. Their bunkers, though not quite as polished, looked similar to that of the engineers.

Another minute brought me to my goal. A huge bulldozer spouted a thick column of tarnished blue diesel smoke as it sliced the top two feet off of a small saddle, thirty feet below the summit. Trailing in the red clay behind the gigantic two-track were the sixteen members of Echo Recon.

### KRAAAAAAAAMMMMMMMMMMMM!

On all fours, I whip my head up to see Echo Recon drop like a wet rag. My eyes freeze on a neat, round crater where a GI had been walking a moment before. Two others writhe like spastic worms. Several more do not move.

"Get some fucking birds!" First Platoon's medic screams.

Two Grunts fight to hold the struggling man still while the doc jams two syrettes of morphine into his remaining leg. Third and the CP's medics arrive with morphine and bandages, overwhelmed as they jump from man to man.

Ten minutes brings in a convoy of dust-offs, pulling me out of my surreal state. I get to my feet, noticing as I turn that I am not alone. Most of Third and Second Platoons are behind me, standing like specters as they witness the gruesome scene. Four dust-offs cruise in low, forcing us to lower our heads and close our eyes. The Grunts sling the dead into one of the chopper cabins like so many deer carcasses onto a pickup. Stretchers are supplied for the rest and the Grunts run back and forth to fill the remaining choppers. The birds rise in a cloud of red dust and leave behind a mind-numbed firebase. In a few moments, all is quiet. Only the crater and the blood soaked soil remain to tell us that Professional is falling *apart from within....*

✎ *...4:23 p.m., Sunday, March 8, 1998, home...Four days of this shit and –*I slam the bag with heavy right hooks– *NOW I feel fine. Why? IF I ONLY KNEW WHY! Maybe...hell, maybe it doesn't matter why. Ever since that meeting it's been like I've lost all my confidence...like starting at zero again. Friday at work was a white hell, heart spasming on me every few minutes till I went up to the exercise room. Then yesterday...same thing, all day– at least got the taxes done. But scared to work out, walking slow for an hour downstairs, heart banging in me while I tiptoed around it. Then first thing this morning here it comes again soon as I wake up. So instead of going to church I'm down here pacing the floor, slamming the wall...surprised I* *don't break my hand. Bet my knuckles are a half-inch thick now from twenty years of punching walls, bricks, anything in its path.*

I deliver three left jabs. *Shrinks say it's free-floating anxiety. Like I don't even know what's going on or how to stop it. Maybe it's like being on that insane hill back in Nam, "Professional". Maybe that's what started all this– never knowing if my next step would be my last. Shit, the only safe spot was my bunker. Safe spot. Huh, just like on my walks...wonder if there's a connection? I wonder if it matters if there's a connection? God, maybe it's something I don't even remember, like when I was a kid. Like all those weird nightmares I used to have. Then what chance is there?* I notice a Robin digging for a meal just outside the basement window. *Maybe it don't matter what the reason is.* The Robin stabs at the earth, sensing his reward is near. *Maybe I just got to deal with it right where it's at and not worry any more about how it got started.* The Robin flies away, a fat morsel trapped *in its beak. ....*✐

Friday, April 23, 1971, Day 184 / 181 to DEROS<br>
— "Would you believe it?"—

The sweat was falling from me like Smok'n' Joe staggering into the fifteenth round. Our bunker was now eight rows high, due to the events of the last twenty-four hours. Yoss and I pumped the bags full, tied them off and heaved them over to Nelson, who was putting the finishing touches on the walls. We were using the engineers for our example, Nelson and Yoss having taken my advice to check out their handy work earlier this morning.

At eleven, a slick dropped off a surprise.

"Scotty!" I shouted, spotting him coming over the rise. "Welcome to paradise! We've got your room reservation ready."

"You mean *that*?"

Scotty threw his gear outside the bunker while we cogitated on how to put on the roof. We decided to go with Nelson's plan of laying *2 x 4*'s across and then layering the bags on top. The trouble was, the engineers had nearly depleted the supply of *2 x 4*'s, so we could only scrounge up enough to place one every foot apart. It seemed to support the weight okay, though, and by early evening we were moving our gear into our new home.

I spat a grain of sand out of my mouth. "I'm gonna wash up. I'm starved." I ducked into the bunker, grabbed my soap, towel and helmet liner, which

351

doubled for a washbasin. Twisting out of the small opening, I placed the helmet on the roof to grab my 16.

"Ahhhh...." The sandbag beneath the helmet began sinking. Reaching for it, the bag slipped between the wooden rafters. The bags on either side followed, causing a chain reaction that continued the length of the two by four. Instantly, the next board bounced up as the bags deserted their posts. In a cloud of dust, the roof collapsed.

I tugged on my torn air mattress while behind me, Nelson and Yoss stared, dumbfounded. Next door, Ski was rolling on the ground in laughter, looking as he had on that fruit punch and vodka night.

I slowly turned around. "Ah...sorry about that, Chief," I said, doing my best "Maxwell Smart" impersonation.

Saturday, April 24, 1971, Day 185 / 180 to DEROS
—dust break—

I couldn't wait to get off the ground. The slicks snatched us from the helipad one squad at a time, climbing the hill's thermals before drifting with the morning breeze over its western edge. "Maybe *this* is our R&R," I had told Yoss as I shook the dust off my ruck early this morning. After the accident, everything we owned was caked with brick-red powder. Nelson had cleared out enough sandbags to make himself a small nest. Yoss, Scott and I slept behind the bunker.

The birds carried us a half-dozen klicks west of the firebase, landing near a well-manicured potato field in the next valley over from Professional.

"Let's do it," LT said, deciding on a well-used trail heading southeast. The field of potatoes lay to our right as we skirted its edge. I was amazed how the gooks did it– without detection. I thought of my Grandma's garden in Winfield, Missouri. She was so proud of that immaculate plot of fresh cucumbers, sweet corn, beets, carrots, spinach greens, leaf lettuce, radishes, onions, pole beans and potatoes. As I'd grown older, I, too, had contributed to its care, plowing the furrows with the old side-bladed John Deere plow she stored in the garage, near the old barber chair from Grandpa's shop. How I loved to climb into that chair and spin, jack it up as high as it would go and spin some more....

I looked to my right; a thick grove of scrub trees had replaced the field. *Been out of the bush too long.* I regained my concentration. *Keep to business, gonna get blown away, or someone else.*

We humped till three-thirty with few breaks, covering over three klicks when LT took us up a hill of brush and elephant grass within sight of Professional. I pulled out my machete to begin clearing our space. There was no clay, no dust– just rich, black soil beneath the green. In no time our hootches were up and chow was bubbling on our stoves.

*　　*　　*

"Outgo'n'!" The thunder from the 60 pounds my head into the ground. Thirty rounds later Harv releases his trigger finger. Twenty seconds pass. "It's all right. Thought I herd someth'n'... prably a mongoose."

Sunday, April 25, 1971, Day 186 / 179 to DEROS<br>—bunker games—

Two crickets hummed a duet as a drop of dew smacked my cheek. I pulled up my torn poncho liner as another drop splattered my forehead. I had slept well for the first time in days, in spite of no air mattress and Harv's panic. My eyes drifted shut as the camp began to stir. Next door, someone was getting his morning rush from his first cigarette. LT was calling in a sit-rep to the firebase. I turned over and pulled my blanket over my head. *Just ten more minutes.*

*　　*　　*

"So Scott... waddya think? Steep... enough... for ya?" It was all Scott could do to keep sucking in air. We made the crest and our boots clanked across the grating of the helipad as we headed for our position. It was already going on three, humping since a hastily downed breakfast this morning– shouldn't have slept in.

"Cocksuckers," Retchin breathed as our side of the hill came into view. The D-9 had shaved off two feet of earth where our bunkers had once been. Our sandbags were lying in a pushed up heap below its path of destruction.

"What the fuck's going on, LT?" Hillbilly asked.

"Guess after Recon got hit, they wanted to make sure it wouldn't happen again." –he frowned– "We're gonna have to rebuild them."

353

\*        \*        \*

The moonless night lends little help in discerning the rustling in the brush thirty meters in front of me. *Just do it!* I pull the pin and shout, "Outgoing!" letting the pin fly as I toss the baseball grenade below. Ducking, I wait for the blast. *BLAM*! The report echoes over the hill as I stare into the night to see if I had done any good. Several long minutes pass. Nothing. *Probably a stupid mongoose. Wish I had a blooper; a lum would tell me what I need to know.* The guys are still sound asleep inside the roofless bunker; two plastic ponchos hang over it to keep off the dew. *That was kinda fun.* I look on either side. *Nobody seems to care anyway.* I pull out another frag, pull the pin and chuck it as far as I can down the slope. "Outgoing!" I yell as the frag is in midair. *Almost forgot to yell that time.* The frag flashes, sending a delayed blast a half a second behind as I huddle against the sandbag wall to try and absorb some of the residual warmth stored deep *within the bags....*

✎*...12:02 p.m., Monday, March 9, 1998, Davenport Wal-Mart...I picked out* a bottle of vitamin B complex. This morning I'd heard on *WOC* talk radio how vitamin B helps rebuild your nerves– like adding insulation to bare wire. *And right now my nerves are nothing BUT bare wire.* Next to me a Wal-Mart employee was talking to an older lady and her son about the benefits of St. John's Wort, saying it was a natural remedy for depression. Leery of any manmade substances, this sounded like a good alternative. I pretended to study the contents of my bottle, waiting for the couple to move on so I could grab one. *Okay, vitamin B for my nerves and this stuff for my head. We'll see....*✎

Monday, April 26, 1971, Day 187 / 178 to DEROS
—guarding the grates—

I wrapped my 16 in a towel to keep the dust out. Except for having to wear the steel pot, this wasn't half-bad duty. LT'd assigned me to guard the helipad, a duty I didn't even know existed until he told me to report for it at 0800. Only one slick had come in so far, its cargo just a couple of bags of mail and a guy from the artillery unit, from the looks of his patch.

The morning passed as slow as midnight guard duty. I passed the time watching a group of arty guys just below me, sending ordinance to Charlie Company, ten klicks to our south. Before firing, they calculated the direction of fire on a circular aiming device. *No wonder we hafta dodge them so much out there. Contraption don't look too reliable to me.* They alternated between a 105 and an eight-incher, the huge cannon thundering as it blew its projectile from its blackened muzzle.

At noon, I was spelled by a PFC from Artillery. Hurrying back to my platoon to stir up some grub, I slowed as I spotted a line of Grunts transferring sandbags from where they had been pushed into a ragged pile near the crest above our area– not one bunker stood.

"What happened?"

Nelson was pulling on a Salem, catching bags from Scott and throwing them near a crudely drawn line in the clay to indicate the bunker's outline. "Some fucking excuse about reshaping the hill. Hell...all I know is...we're gonna get...damn good at this before it's over."

"I'd help ya, man, but I gotta be back in thirty minutes."

"It don't matter anyway, Adams. Hell, they probably got that fucking D-9 waiting to fire up again soon as we're done here."

The rest of the afternoon was a repeat of the morning. I couldn't figure why they needed someone to guard the pad anyway; it was already surrounded by Grunts. Maybe they figured a sapper was gonna tunnel in from China and plant a satchel charge. It was hard telling, dealing with the kind of intellect that would re-establish a hill that was killing more GI's than it was protecting.

*     *     *

*Apr. 26<sup>th</sup>, 71*

*Mom Dad -Well, here I am again. It's really getting hot here now. Probably over 100 by now. Since the 19th we've (Delta Company) has been in the process of constructing a firebase. It's out about...*

Another round jarred my pen as the eight-incher rumbled above my head.

*...25 clicks from Chu Lai. As soon as we're through (this summer) the whole 5/46th will move out here. There's not much sense in it though. Soon as the 1st Calvary finishes standing down, our division will start. Therefore we'll have to give it to them (South Vietnamise) this summer. so I think it's just a waste of time. The 28th we're moving off the base and spending the rest of the time...*

355

Another blast sent my pen sliding off the page. LT had tacked on bunker duty to guard the artillery station just below the helipad. There were four of us, one from each of the Delta Company platoons.

*...in the bush. As you know my R&R for May 20th was cancelled. So yesterday I put another one in for June 1st & probably will get it.*

*We've been building bunkers, filling sandbags & digging holes. It's not much fun.*

*Well, I'm going to try and get off a couple more letters, not too much to say. So take care & God Bless.*

*Your Son Bob*

## Tuesday, April 27, 1971, Day 188 / 177 to DEROS
### —dominoes—

"Nine cans. That'll be...one...two...two fifteen." I handed a five to the supply guy and he counted out my change. It was great having a snack shack, which the engineers assembled yesterday. I bundled the cans in my fatigue shirt and headed for our four-layer high sandbag fort. True to Nelson's word, they'd done it again this morning, barely giving us time to clear out before knocking over our bunkers. "More earthwork," was the only excuse one of the drivers would give. Hillbilly, though, wouldn't leave without spinning them a bit of backwoods wisdom that had just about caused a fight between them and us; we were just having a little trouble understanding why they weren't doing the same thing to their AO.

I'd spent another day doing helipad duty, this time having volunteered to protect it from possible invasion by the underground Chinese– anything to get away from our sandbag hell. LT was passing out mail as I rejoined my squad, getting back in time to hear my name. With a couple of letters, along with a package from home, I returned to my bunker and ripped open the small package. Inside were several books and a box of crumbled-up chocolate chip cookies. "Grab your spoons, boys," I said, setting the box on one of the sandbags. I picked up a red-jacketed book. *Just what the doctor ordered: The Power of Positive Thinking, by Norman Vincent Peale. This one I have got to read right away.* My nose diverted my gaze to another letter. Unsheathing my knife, I carefully sliced open the top and inhaled the sensuous perfume effervescing from the letter's folds. I paused for a moment before delving into

Jennifer's words, gazing at my pitiful surroundings. *Here I am, in the middle of nowhere. Grubby, unshaven, unwashed, living in a house made of dirt and eating leftovers from a forgotten war.* –I unfolded her letter– *THIS is what it's all about.*

# MISSION TWELVE

Wednesday, April 28, 1971, Day 189 / 176 to DEROS
—racing for the sun—

Peering into the shadows spreading from the swelling sun, fear and relief shuffled through my brain like a badly dealt hand. We were finally leaving the accursed firebase, but it was already going on seven and the birds were nowhere in sight.

"Here they fucking come!" Hillbilly shouted.

A faint tapping sent my eyes to the far peaks, appearing as dipped in chocolate. At first I discerned one tiny slick, shimmering half-light, half-dark against the endless hills and valleys beckoning to the twilight, until others and still others emerged from behind, wavering to and fro, slapping their blades in the evening air. Our platoon was slated to go out first. One by one the slicks lined in to dump off Charlie Company's mud-wearied Grunts. Hillbilly and his boys climbed onto the first chopper. Blondie's squad, along with LT and Sgt. Trainor, swung into the next cabin, then Spurlin's bunch and our crew took drag.

We quickly rose to three thousand feet where the cold air quickly recharged my spirit. Somehow, for these few minutes, flying with the clouds as my footstool, all my troubles became as small as the rice paddies passing far below. My flying escort became my time machine, whirling me to a late evening of fishing for channel cat on the end of the dock down in the Grove, or scaling the rock wall at Devil's Lake in Wisconsin. The memories were always pleasant and always took me home.

Turbulence popped my dream-bubble as the birds began a steep plunge for a tiny valley that looked too small for one chopper to land in, let alone four. Behind us, the rest of the company branched off to their pre-designated *LZ*'s, looking like stray crows running against the sunset. Hillbilly's bird lit on the edge of a tiny paddy, engulfed in the evening shadow while we hovered above in the last dull rays of the setting sun. A few seconds and his slick careened out of the way for Blondie's bird. Spurlin's bird dumped at the same time as Blondie's and our bird left the sun behind to heave in for a rough thump where we shuffled through the dark water for shore.

Hillbilly was already cutting up a small hill next to the paddy. We fell in behind him as each man searched for danger in the waning light: Charlie Company had been hit several times during its week in the bush.

It was a quick cut to the top, so with the few remaining minutes of light we had time to put our hootches together.

"Adams," –Puccio tossed me a small nylon bundle– "it's a hammock I bought at that souvenir stand. You can use it if you want." –a grin licked his thin lips– "I won't be needing it."

"Thanks, Mike, maybe I will." Looking from the poncho to the hard earth inside the hootch, I decided to give it a try. Two small trees were sitting eight feet apart near the hootch. *Right there.* Tying it on, I straddled the webbed leaf. *Here goes.* My butt cleared the ground by six inches. *Cool!*

"Whatcha gonna do if it rains?" Yoss inquired.

I looked into the deepening blue. "It *ain't gonna rain.*"...

✎ *...1:58 p.m., Saturday, April 11, 1998, home...Wouldn't it be nice if–*I looked to the top of the slope– *if I could just run right up that hill as if nothing was wrong....* "Craig! Let me have the mower!"

It was the first cut of the year, well, not really a full cut; that would come later. For now it just needed a trim off the high spots that'd taken off in the unusually warm spring. My heart gears up as I spin the mower around. Three more passes on the high patches of grass and the clipping is done.

"Okay, Craig, take the mower up!" –I ignore my heart– "Want to burn some leaves? I blew a pile of 'em out in front!"

"All right!" –he holds out his hand– "Matches?!"

"Be careful!" I hand him a dozen farmer matches and watch as he pushes the mower up the hill. *Breathe. Hold. Exhale. Relax.* My heart downshifts. I force a gaze at two squirrels playing tag in a nearby hackberry tree. *Better. God, I am so sick...* –I turn to look at the top of the shallow slope– *...wouldn't it be nice if...* –I lean forward and begin running up the hill– *...keep going...* –

past the deck– *...yeah!* Craig is just picking up the rake. "Hey, Buddy, *want some help?"...✐*

Thursday, April 29, 1971, Day 190 / 175 to DEROS
—Elsie the cow—

"So, how'd ya like it?"

"Like sleeping on a cloud, Scott."

"You lucked out, too," he said, dipping his hand in his canteen cup and flinging some water in my direction.

By seven-thirty, Blondie was leading us down our hill. We soon hooked into the most well used trail I'd seen yet. Wide enough to walk three abreast, the trail was so trampled I began to feel like we might run into a regiment of NVA regulars if we stayed on it too long. The path wound into a thick stand of trees that cut the light in half, considerably slowing our pace as Blondie deciphered his every step. A stream rushed beside us while overhead a thick lush of leaves and vines kept the forest floor clear.

The line came to a standstill. LT waved Nelson forward.

"We're gonna take a patrol up that hill on the other side of the creek," Nelson said as he returned. "It'll be our NDP if it checks out."

Dark water swirled around my legs as the water crept to my thighs. The far bank came up and soon my boots were draining as we hugged the steep hillside on a narrow path leading to the top. *This don't seem right; trail's been used tee-tee ago.* LT kept to it, though. Reaching the top, the sun filtered through the bamboo where the ground leveled out for a hundred meters before falling off again.

My eyes widened. Before me lay a sea of litter; it was once a huge NVA camp.

"Fuck," Ross said, gazing at an empty carton of Borden's Condensed Milk. "Where'd they get this shit?"

"The villes," LT said. –he pointed to a can of GI turkey loaf– "Shit, Ross, that could've come from your ruck for all you know." –he turned and held up his hand– "Let's get the hell out of here. Might be booby-trapped."

\*       \*       \*

*"Roger, Echo Foxtrot. Out."* I snapped the telephone down and leaned against Tuck's ruck. *That wasn't so bad. Remember "break" and "Echo*

*Foxtrot", then say, "niner", for nine and, "mike", for minute. No sweat.* This was the first time I had to pull radio watch at the CP hootch. I'd never paid much attention to the lingo Tuck or LT used on the horn; it was almost like learning another language. At least I had remembered most of the code words drilled into me in AIT. *Maybe I should go over them one more time: Alpha, Bravo, Charlie, Delta, Echo, Foxtrot, Golf, Hotel.... What's "I"? Oh well...Juliet, Kilo, Mike, November. India...that's it. Okay, "O"...now, what was "O"?*

Friday, April 30, 1971, Day 191 / 174 to DEROS
—swinging in the rain—

The clouds washed thick and ugly beyond the next ridgeline, still two klicks ahead. I watched Scott's long legs stretch in front of me. *Scott's getting stronger. Might make a Grunt out of 'im yet.* Tomorrow a re-supply would fill our depleted rucks with C's and would hopefully last until a CE somewhere on the ridge's far side.

By two o'clock, the ridgeline and the thundercloud were looming above us as Hillbilly followed a thin trail bordering a long narrow paddy. LT signaled Hillbilly to turn left and find a spot close to the paddy; it would make an ideal spot to pick up our supplies in the morning before continuing over the ridge. Without much debris impeding us, they were soon cutting our poles at the base of the mammoth ridgeline. I, on the other hand, was busy looking for a suitable spot to hang my bed.

"You ever gonna bunk with us again?" Nelson asked as he paused to watch me tie off one end of my hammock.

"You should try it. You'd never sleep in that hootch again, either."

"What if we get incoming? Your sorry ass'd be hanging out on that sling."

"Already thought of that. One little roll and I'm on the deck. I'm only six inches off the ground anyway."

"Okay, but I'll stick to my mattress."

He began shaking out his poncho while I contemplated a plan to construct an overhead shelter. I took my poncho, attached a shoelace on each of the center grommets and then tied them several feet over the hammock's lashings. There was an abundance of brush where I could fasten each of the four corners, forming an "A" that covered my sleeping quarters. Backing away, I judged that even a hard downpour couldn't infiltrate my bed. There was even room to lean my ruck out of the rain against one of the trees. I cleared the ground in front of my bed and positioned my stove. *Just like home....*

✎*...2:45 p.m., Saturday, May 9, 1998, home...Three layers down,* the original shingles looked almost new as I tore them from their grip on my garage. *Something's happening in my head. I'm not sure what, but –*I scooted down to the next row– *I ain't complaining.* Finally, enough shingles were removed from around the ragged two-foot gash, caused by the combination of a stiff wind and a dead elm on Easter Sunday, to begin the job of piecing in fresh one by six's. *Feel like I can do it now, like I'm not afraid to breathe.* I picked up my skill saw and squared the ragged edge. *All these projects I've put off,* –I looked over my run-down property– *neglected the house so long, rotting around me...just like my wasted years. Ten years...a decade of fear. Ever since the swamp. August 2, 1988. A day that, at least in my world, will forever live in infamy.*

Sweat was forming on my brow. *God, I love it. Work! Hard work!* I grabbed the tape measure and committed the hole's width to memory. "How ya doing, Lexi?" My granddaughter was sitting on a lawn chair that sat on top of the flat shed roof, connected to the back of the garage– she'd begged me to let her watch. Lexi pretended not to hear, her golden locks covering her eyes while she read *The Cat in the Hat.*

"Lex?"

"Grandpa!" –she lowered her book– "Can't you see that I am trying to read?"

"I thought you wanted to watch."

"I am...but I'm reading, too."

"Okay, okay." I picked up a board and marked the first cut. *Maybe it's the weightlifting, maybe the vitamins, or the coming of a new season.* I adjusted the blade on the saw. *Maybe rereading The Power of Positive Thinking has helped. It sure did back then, humping it in the dark to Professional.* I lowered the blade on the pencil line and began ripping off the first cut. *Or maybe it's the writing. Man, is this taking a chance or what? Starting a book and not even knowing if I can finish it?* Leaning forward, I fit the board over the bottom portion of the hole. *Good fit.* I grabbed the next board. *But that's why I started it, right? To come to terms with my past. And to explain to everyone why I've been living like a hermit. My God. Ten wasted years.* I paused to gaze into the crisp blue *over my head....*✎

    *...I opened my* eyes to the sound of large bulbs of rain smacking the roof. It was pitch black. I reached under me and felt my bottom. *Great.* I searched for a leak in the roof. Nothing. I followed the cords to where a trickle of rainwater was channeling from the bark to the hammock.

Saturday, May 1, 1971, Day 192 / 173 to DEROS
—feel'n' the power—

Sheathing my knife, I took one of the halves of the canvas LURP bag, wrapped it around the hammock cords and secured it with a length of shoelace. I watched as the raindrops slid from the cord to the canvas bag. After a few seconds the water began a steady drip to the ground. *Success!* I sat up to complete the other side.

It was going on eight-thirty and the rain was still falling, making the chance for today's re-supply slim. Patches of fog drifted throughout the silent camp, transforming the hootches into gravestone-like apparitions from a grade-B werewolf movie. The entrance to Nelson's hootch was dark. He, Yoss and Scott were still zonked out in the cool lull of the humid morning. A feeble trail of cigarette smoke was struggling to rise from Ski's lodge, sitting so close to Nelson's they could've used the same corner stakes.

The lower half of me was soaked, along with the hammock. But with the leak fixed, it would only be a matter of time before my body heat dried my clothing. I opened my ruck and pulled out the last of my C's: pork slices, crackers and a GI's favorite, peaches and pound cake. The crackers went first, then I munched on the chocolate disks hidden under the saltines while preparing my stove, anxious to stuff meat into my stomach.

*       *       *

I felt the seat of my fatigues. *Almost dry.* Reopening my latest read, *The Power of Positive Thinking,* I flipped to the next chapter, ready to devour another of Dr. Peale's precious anecdotes. "...*One of the most powerful facts about you is expressed in the following statement by William James, who was one of the wisest men America has produced. William James said, 'The greatest discovery of my generation is that human beings can alter their lives by altering their attitudes of mind.' As you think, so shall you be. So flush out*

362

*all old, tired, worn-out thoughts. Fill your mind with fresh, new creative thoughts of faith, love and goodness. By this process you can actually remake—"*

"Hey, Adams. What's up?" Scott said, crawling out of his hootch.

"Not much. How ya doing?"

"Gotta piss like a racehorse." –he stepped towards the bushes– "Must be the rain, huh?"

"It's gonna be a long day."

"What do you do on days like this?"

"Count raindrops. Hey, you got any food left?"

"I'm out. But we're getting re-supplied today anyway, right?"

"Look above you, man. Can't even see the tops of the trees."

"Maybe it'll clear by noon. I'm starving."

"You ain't *even* hungry yet, Scott." He parted with a, "See ya later," before darting back into his shelter.

I stared at his hootch. *Least he's got somebody to talk to.*

\*     \*     \*

*"...Whatever your situation may be, you can improve it..."* Late afternoon found me deep in thought, mesmerized by my new find. *"...First, quiet your mind so that inspirations may rise from its depths. Believe that God is now helping you. Visualize achievement. Organize your life on a spiritual basis so that God's principles work within you. Hold firmly in your mind a picture not of failure, but of success. Do these things and creative thoughts will flow freely from your mind. This is an amazing law, one that can change anybody's life including your own. An inflow of new thoughts can remake you regardless of every difficulty you may now face and I repeat...every difficulty...."*

\*     \*     \*

Yoss' touch on my shoulder sent my hand for my 16. "You're on, Adams."

A steady cascade of water clapped over my head, weighing my eyelids with its steady beat. I reached a cupped palm into the downpour and splashed some water onto my face. The night was void of light, my night vision unable to penetrate the darkness. I could only catch hints of what might be trees or a VC standing between me and the steep slope beyond.

My gut felt the telltale gnawing from the lack of food. *Don't even need another Mount Hell. Be nice if ol' Scotty could miss that one. And George, he don't belong here, either.* I craned my neck around, staring in the blackness at what would've been a dozen hootches. *None of us do. ...*

✎*...6:09 p.m., Thursday, May 14, 1998, home...One more... come on...DO IT!* I strained at the hundred and thirty-pound weight, pulling it behind my head to complete the set. *Gotta weight lift...it ain't no hobby or sport like for others...not any more.* I got off the bench and paced the basement floor to regain my breath. *Now it's the difference between surviving or drowning in my tidal wave of goddamn fear. In a few moments I lost a whole month of progress with this shit! Cutting brush like crazy and feeling fantastic. Next second, heart tripping and I wanting to crawl under that brush like a scared little mouse. It makes me so angry I could rip my fucking flesh off!*

I positioned myself on the bench for the seated military press, carefully spacing my hands on the Olympic bar. *Slinking into the house, afraid of my shadow. Push, damn it! It's like my brain sets me up for an attack just to see if I can survive this shit.*

*Come on, one more! push! I need this! This is my root! My beginning! It's from here that I'm gonna make it or lose it! It's from here that I'll know if I have a fighting chance at licking this thing! Don't <u>ever</u> give up. Reverse press next...go for it!...*✎

Sunday, May 2, 1971, Day 193 / 172 to DEROS
—the wings of eagles—

The rain was easing as the camp began to stir: someone making for the weeds to relieve himself, muffled voices, the clank of a canteen cup. Yoss exited to ask how I was doing and Ski came over to ferret my last pack of Winstons. I heard Scott asking about the re-supply, now a day overdue. Nelson, I'm sure, was thinking of Mount Hell when he answered that he had a can of beefsteak left that he was willing to share.

The morning dragged on. I swung my legs to the ground, dead sure what a caterpillar must feel in his cocoon– mine was stretched between two trees. *How many hours have I been lying here? All day yesterday. The evening*

THE FAR BLUE HORIZON

*before. No wonder by butt hurts. Maybe this hammock ain't so hot after all.* I reopened my book.

"*...A second method for drawing upon that Higher Power is to learn to take a positive, optimistic attitude toward every problem. In direct proportion to the intensity of the faith which you muster will you receive power to meet your situations. 'According to your faith be it unto you,' (Matthew 9:29) is a basic law of successful living.*" I flipped the page, not wanting a distraction to interfere with the flow of energy pulsating from the pages, in what would begin to change my life. "*There is a Higher Power and that Power can do everything for you. Draw upon it and experience its great helpfulness. Why be defeated when you are free to draw upon that Higher Power? State your problem. Ask for a specific answer. Believe that you are getting that answer. Believe that now, through God's help, you are gaining power over your difficulty.*"...

*       *       *

At three o'clock a brisk front pushed furrows of feathery white clouds into a steely-blue stratosphere. I contemplated the next few hours as water from the leaves hit my roof in waves from crisp gusts of wind batting the trees. Most likely we'd spend the night and take re-supply first thing tomorrow before attacking the ridge. Or better yet, with the fair weather coming in, the bird would *yet come today....*

✎ *...8:31 a.m., Thursday, July 23, 1998, home...*

>> -----Original Message-----

At 03:07 PM 7/20/98 -0500, you wrote:

Don!

So glad to find you on the net. Maybe you can help resolve a search I've been after for last quarter century. Early in 1971 our platoon lost a guy in a place called Dragon Valley, near Chu Lai's Americal Base. Only knew him by the nickname of Hippie. He walked into one of our own claymores on the morning of Jan 11th. I've always blamed myself for his death and I thought maybe I could contact his relatives to help get this off me. It's been a heavy load to carry. We were serving in the Army, 198th Brigade, 5th Battalion of the 46th Infantry, Company D, Second platoon. He was probably an E-3 at the time. I've done searches with some Vietnam "Wall" lists, but can't nail down his name, wish they would include your unit name to aid in the search, but....

365

You're offering a great service for a lot of guys who don't know where else to go. Thanks!

My name is Robert M. Adams

SSN: 309-44-5058

From: Donald [SMTP:cowboy48@ptd.net]

>> Sent: Wednesday, July 22, 1998 3:47 PM

>> To: Adams, Robert M MVR

>> Subject: Re: Americal Division Casualty Records

(www.americal.org/locator/laddonv.htm)

'Robert,

I could use your Rank, MOS and dates in Vietnam for my database. I checked my records and this is what I found. Your friend called Hippie was: EDWARD W. BETHARDS, PFC, his SS# was 546-74-4974. My records show the incident occurred at 8:25am and he was taken to CHU LAI. His COD: PMW BOTH THIGHS w/ALMOST COMPLETE AMPUTATION BOTH LEGS. The description of the incident is: FOLLOWING PARTY TO LZ, FRIENDLY MECH. AMBUSH. This is all I have on this gentleman. I can't guarantee the accuracy of these records, because remember, we were only 18 years old when we were over there, if you know what I mean.'

"Edward Bethards." –I enunciated his name– "Ed Bethards." I sat back, fighting a sudden urge to cry. "Forgive me, Ed."

'I hope this helps you out. Please read everything I sent to you and understand it before you react. If I can help in any other way, let me know. There is no cost to you, but you can make a donation if you wish. I use the donations to go to the Archives to collect more information. I travel to the Archives whenever I gather together enough donations to make the trip. It takes 3 days minimum to cut through the bureaucracy and find the information I am looking for. In that time, I need to sleep somewhere, eat meals and the cost of copying the documents themselves. There is a lot of work creating this database, but I am not in this for the money, just to cover expenses, as I am on disability just like a number of us Vietnam vets are. If you care to make a donation, know that it will be put to good use.

Donald Van Estenbridge
10 Gravity Planes Rd.
Waymart, PA 18472-9120'

"I will *Cowboy, I will.*"...✎

      ...*News spread to* start humping for Professional. It didn't make sense. It was ten klicks; the sun would be gone before we'd gone a quarter of the way. But the word was coming down straight from the colonel, so we couldn't fake our way out of this one. I shook off my poncho and packed.

Another message shot over the horn. Our long-awaited re-supply would arrive shortly.

"Tuck's taking that bird in for R&R, Adams," LT said as he approached. "I'd like you to take RTO till he gets back."

"But I haven't d–"

"You'll do fine. Just stick by me and I'll help you over the humps. Tuck, give Adams your radio."

"You got it, LT. So you gonna be the *man,* huh, Adams?" Tuck said, bringing over the steel box.

"I guess so. Hope I can remember those code words."

"Shit," he grinned, "just fake it like the rest of us. And tie that antenna down so no dink spots that flag pole."

He walked back to trade fists with his brothers, elated to escape for seven days of paradise while I picked up the case, increasing my ruck's weight by twenty-five pounds.

Hillbilly led us out and we emerged from the edge of the treeline as a bird clipped in, barely giving us time to throw out a red smoke. Its crew tossed out four cases of C's and a box of ammo in exchange for a grinning, fist-waving Charles A. Tucker before back-trailing down the valley.

Busting open the boxes, we each grabbed two meals and Hillbilly took off on the same trail we had come in on. I followed LT, feeling lost in this new world of radio chatter. The first hour fell to the second and then the third. Four checkpoints later, I had the lingo down. I closed the distance to LT in the waning light until I almost touched his ruck. The quarter moon was somewhere below the trees and as night took hold, it held me in its *grip of terror.*...

✎...*3:22 p.m., Friday, July 31, 1998, Yellowstone National Park...I stared at* the rows of steps leading to the summit of Mammoth Hot Springs as Sheryl, Craig and I passed Liberty Cap, a huge dome-like rock at the foot of the mountain. The manicured trail led us up a steep incline that bordered a frozen gold and vanilla rock waterfall rising to the second level, seventy-five feet *over our heads.* ... ✐

...*Deep within my* soul flashed a spark of calm; it slowly emanated through aching muscles, until permeating every fiber. *Draw on that Higher Power...guess that means you, God.* My fear vanished. A shield of peace washed over me as we descended a huge watershed that would eventually empty into the valley encompassing Professional, still hours distant. Breaks were few and short– better a moving target than a sitting duck. "Charlie Papa, Echo Foxtrot. At checkpoint Hotel 8," I said with confidence. "Checkpoint India niner ETA three-*zero mikes. Break.*" ...

✎...*3:31 p.m., Mammoth Hot Springs...Something was different* as I moved my legs up the incline. The fear was gone!

"Whew!" Sheryl gasped as the trail leveled off. She sat on a log bench. "I am out of shape."

I tried not to act out of breath. "At least it's flat for awhile."

Dark peppered clouds whisked overhead, the remnants of an afternoon squaw that had about blown us away while heading for a quick lunch in the bustling tourist town. So far our vacation had been marred by a succession of rainstorms, squelching our hike to the Grand Prismatic Pool, a picnic by Obsidian Creek and flinging a fly in the Firehole River.

Emboldened by the successful climb, I took on the legion of weathered steps skirting the colorful orange and white terraces of the frozen springs *with renewed mind.* ... ✐

...*The huge shadow* of Firebase Professional engulfed our platoon and we dropped our rucks at its base.

"So what's so fuck'n' important?" Hillbilly cried. "Don't look like it's being overrun ta me."

"Christ, maybe the fucking engineers run out of Grunts to blow up," Blondie popped.

"That ain't it," Retchin answered. "Higher-Higher needs his boots spit-shined."

"He can spit-shine this!" Spurlin bellowed, gripping his groin.

"I don't know what the fuck's going on yet," LT said. "They just told us to be to the top by morning."

"If that's the only way ta find out..." –Hillbilly stood up– "...then let's git to the top of this fucker."

We regained our feet for the last leg of the hump. The recent rains had turned the slope into a nightmare of slides and pitfalls. Stumbling in the black shadows, I was soon covered with red mud, spending more time on my knees than on my feet. The first break found me *wheezing for air....*

✎ *...4:11 p.m., Mammoth Hot Springs...*"*Think we should* go for it?" Sheryl asks while eyeing a steep incline of steps leading to the top of the mountain."

Apprehension stones my mind for a millisecond. "Why not?" –I look to the top of the mountain– "Long as the rain holds off. What do you think, Craig?"

"Nah, let's go back. We did this last–"

"All right then. *Let's do it!*"... ✐

*...Two hours takes* us to the halfway point. LT decides to give us time to break open one of our meals– lest we faint from exhaustion. He looks pretty ragged himself.

"How ya doing, LT?"

"Hanging in there, Adams." –he looks to the top of the mountain– "I'm hanging in there."

The radio squelches. "*Echo Foxtrot, this is Papa One. Break.*"

"Give me that fucking horn, Adams. I'm getting to the bottom of this bullshit."

"Papa One, this is Echo Foxtrot. Need to know nature of mission. Men are exhausted and I have nothing to tell them. Break."

A long pause. "*Roger, Echo Foxtrot, I copy.*" Another long pause. LT looks agitated as he peers at the summit. "*Echo Foxtrot, be advised, at your arrival, will begin stand-down procedures. Break.*"

"What are you saying? Break."

"*Word from S-3. The 5/46 is going home!*"

# FINAL STAND-DOWN

Monday, May 3, 1971, Day 194 / 171 to DEROS
—first out—

LT gives me a wink and Spurlin and I hop onto the first chopper of the day; we're heading for the rear! I'm not sure why Spurlin and I are going in before everyone else, but I don't care! *Could this be my last day in the bush?* I gaze at the western slopes, bathed in the morning's buttery glow. *Gotta be, just gotta be!*

I'm not the least bit tired, even after a sleepless night. Not reaching the top till almost four this morning, we found the base on fire with the good news. Wanting to release my excitement, the first thing that came to my giddy brain were my C-rations. Like baseball grenades I tossed them far down the slope, praying that these would be the last ones I'd ever hump.

The wind slaps my face as our chopper soars above my world of twisting streams and whitewater rivers coiling through a vine-matted maze of writhing ravines and canyons before catapulting off of Rocket Ridge and sailing over the clusters of villages and paddies that stretch to the edge of Highway 1. The chopper glides on, past Tam Ky, Fat City, past the desert re-train, the PX and past our Company area to light behind the Replacement Center, adjacent to the beachfront. *Talk about service!* Jumping onto a large concrete pad, the blades pull in a mixed aroma of sizzling bacon and burning fecal matter.

Topp is waiting. "Take your gear to Barrack Four and report back here at 1000 hours. You've been chosen as color guards for tomorrow's stand-down ceremony." Several brass-looking types on the far side of the chopper pad give Topp a wave and he hurries over without a second glance back.

"Why us?"

Spurlin shrugs. "Don't much know. Don't much care. But..." –he looks at his watch– "...if we hurry, we can grab us *some hot chow.*"...

✎ *...8:49 p.m., Sunday, August 2, 1998, Pahaska Teepee Lodge, East Gate, Yellowstone National Park... "Yep," I said,* staring at an elk head guarding the tavern door, "tomorrow we head home." I tipped my shot glass, letting the whisky slide down, looking like the reincarnation of Buffalo Bill Cody, sitting in his lodge, enjoying an end of day nightcap. "Too bad about the rain."

Sheryl stirred her seabreeze. "I got to see what I wanted. And tomorrow we'll visit Norris Geyser one more time. What time can we check in at Jackson?"

"Probably 'bout one o'clock."

"Let's get to the gate early."

"No problemo."

I raised a silent toast to a buffalo head hanging above our table staring glassy-eyed into the shadows, perhaps its spirit listening in as John Fogerty wailed the whimsical lyrics of *Green River* from the speakers behind the bar. *So this is it. August 2nd, 1998. Ten years from the day of the Swamp. The day when everything I'd ever believed in went straight to hell.*

*I can't believe I did so well at Mammoth Springs! Straight up that sucker, no sweat! Maybe it all evens out for everyone in the end...that is, if you live long enough. As for me, though, I know there's a lot more plowing to do, more mysteries to unwind...but it's easier now. I can use what I already know, use it to put down the lies from the past.* I turned my gaze to the buffalo. *I wonder if learning about Hippie's name helps somehow. I know it does. Ed Bethards. Why does it feel so damn good just to say his name? Somehow I gotta get hold of his family and make it right with them...somehow.*

"Another round?" a college-aged man inquired from behind the bar.

A nodding glance at Sheryl. "Sure." Outside, the night was closing fast on the mountain peak across the highway as a cowboy entered beneath my elk-head companion. He was escorting a woman that looked of American Indian ancestry. One of the patrons who'd been chatting with the barkeep hollered a greeting to the couple before joining them at a corner table. Above their laughter hung a weathered piece of stretched buckskin detailing the battle of the Little Bighorn, showing the immense Sioux and Cheyenne camp that had dwarfed Custer's six hundred strong Seventh Cavalry. *I'm getting closer.* My gaze turned to watch the mountaintop lose its golden halo and disappear. I picked up my shot glass. *Yep...closer.* With another shot in my gut, I escorted my wife to our cabin, the strong heart of the buffalo now firmly meshed *within my own....*

\*      \*      \*

...*"PA-RAAAAADE, REST!" The* sergeant barked commands that took me on an unwanted excursion back to Basic Training. I fought the urge to scratch at a twitch in the small of my back while gripping the flag of the 5/46 Infantry. Spurlin stood beside me, holding rigid the blue-starred flag of the Americal Division. We'd been at it all morning. The lunch hour was nearly over, the smell of frying hamburger taunting me from the nearby mess hall.

"RIIIIGHT, FACE! RE-DEEEE, HARCH!" We filed off the field for the twentieth time, marching behind the CO, Topp and other assorted brass and noncoms.

"DIIIIII-SMISSED!"

Topp's red nose glowed brighter than usual. "Okay, you men get chow. I'll pick you up tomorrow at 0700 to get your new fatigues."

"Man, my stomach's growling," I said, "can you believe we gotta wear starched fatigues for this sideshow?"

"Don't *even* forget the new boots...*polished* boots."

"Take me back to the bush, man. Well, maybe *not*," *I corrected*. ...

✎...*6:35 p.m., Monday, March 29, 1999, home...Spectre of the Gun*, a Star Trek rerun, was winding down. Finding my usual spot on the couch I curled my legs under me, ready to relax after a vigorous weightlifting session. It had been a long winter. The long, cold months had drifted over my confidence and I was grateful to see the changing of the seasons. Although I believed my mind was on the mend, there were still unresolved issues taking me to the dark world of the panic syndrome.

Sipping my beer, Captain Kirk is again faced with an unknown entity, this time the Melkotians, an alien race whose warnings to Kirk to stay away were ignored when he had beamed to their planet's surface. An unexpected surprise awaits Kirk and his sidekicks: the irate Melkotians decide to punish the crew by transporting them to Tombstone, Arizona, or a re-creation of it as plucked from the memory of James T. Kirk. The Melkotian objective is simple: test the humans to see if they measure up to the Melkotian moral code. If they do not, they shall be killed.

In this surreal netherworld, Kirk and his friends becomes the Clanton gang. It is October 26, 1881, the day of the legendary Gunfight at the O.K. Corral and at 5 p.m. they will face off with the legendary Earp brothers.

Chekov, in the role of Billy Claiborne, had already caused a departure from the historical event, having been gunned down by Morgan Earp. As the final hour approaches, Scotty fails to lose consciousness after testing the fumes of a tranquilizer bomb, created by Bones, who had hoped to use it to subdue the Earps. Before they are able to decipher the enigma, the saloon clock chimes five times and the aliens transport the unwilling foursome to face their fate within the gates of the O.K. Corral.

The team fears for their lives, but Mr. Spock explains his realization. He notes that the gas bomb should have worked according to physical laws. Thus when it failed, the physical laws were disregarded and when that happens, reality does not exist. In short, Spock surmises that this whole scenario is not real, but actually an elaborate illusion occurring in the minds of the crew or to be more precise, it is only as real as their minds accept it to be real.

While Spock's will is so strong that nothing can harm him, he has to convince the others of the same, but any lingering doubt will prove deadly since the mind will make it real.

"That's not possible," Bones says, "there'll always be some doubt!"

"The smallest doubt, would be enough to kill you."

Bone's eyes widen. "We're just human beings, Spock! We don't have that clockwork ticker in our head like you do. We can't just turn it on and off!"

"We must," Kirk says, eyeing Spock. "Spock. The *Vulcan mind meld.*"...✐

Tuesday, May 4, 1971, Day 195 / 170 to DEROS
—blanket party—

"Men of the 5/46..." –a long respectful pause– "...we are gathered here this day to pay tribute to all the brave men who have passed before us." –the colonel paused again– "Men, who under the direct line of enemy fire, laid down their lives for the cause of freedom, to further the cause of democracy to the far corners of the earth. We pass on this flag then, a symbol, not only–"

A drop of sweat slid down my temple as I held rigid the unit's colors. *How great is this, this morning getting my R&R orders for Australia! And only two weeks to go!* I fought the urge to scratch as another drop trickled down the inside of my left leg. *Man, I hate these. Here I am right back in a pair of FNG fatigues. Let's get this over with!*

"–privilege to have served under the Southern Cross, who–"

I made eye contact with George. A crack of a smile crept up my jaw as he gave me a cross-eyed stare. I pushed a fingernail into my thumb to quash a well of laughter fighting to rise up my throat. *Don't laugh! Please! Don't laugh!* But the more I fought it, the more I had to dig my nail in. *Think of something...anything!* But only George's kooky eyes came to me. I stared at the ground, breathing rapidly to get a grip on the urge. *No matter how long this stupid thing takes, do NOT look at that guy again, cause I KNOW he's just waiting for another chance!*

"–In the event that one day duty will again invoke this stalwart battalion to distant shores–" *I'll get him for this!*

*　　*　　*

I showered the day's sweat off in the washroom of the Replacement Center. After the ceremony, Topp had informed me that headquarters wanted to interview me for a rear job.

"Scott!" I yelled to the next shower stall over. "We having a party tonight?"

"Yes, sir. As we speak, Hillbilly's getting a stash of numba one Grade A Cambodian Red."

"All right! Hear anything what's gonna happen to ya?"

"Nope." –Scott's voice echoed in the small enclosure– "Wonder why *you* got called for that interview so quick?"

"I dunno, man, but I ain't *even* complaining." I finished rinsing the soap out of my hair and turned off the shower.

"Wonder if I'll be sent to Da Nang?"

"Hey, don't sweat it, man," I said over the splatter of residual droplets bouncing off the wet concrete. "I tell ya, they're wrapping this war up. *Everybody's* going home." –I toweled off and grabbed my clean pair of fatigues– "What the...!"

"What's wrong?"

"My wallet! It ain't in my pocket!"

*　　*　　*

The shower room rip-off seemed like a far away dream while sucking a stream of smoke into my lungs. My wallet had been carrying all of my R&R money, $260 dollars I'd taken out after the stand-down ceremony. I didn't know what I was going to do. I passed the pipe to George. *Something will turn up.*

Our entire platoon was crammed into one barrack, overflowing with sixteen bunkbeds stuffed into two tight rows. A desire for privacy had prompted our band to improvise a room by pushing two of the bunks apart and draping several poncho liners across the top to form a roof. Several more covered the sides and front to complete our quest for isolation. It worked great, serving its purpose by keeping out prying eyes if not the occasional catcall of the juicers ruling the remaining sectors of the barrack. It was good times; it was time to celebrate.

We were all there as the smoke thickened under the canopy. Hillbilly, sharing his wealth of backwoods philosophy. Ski and his endless banter. Soft-spoken Scott, my new best friend. George, spilling his heavy Brooklyn-accented jocularity. Mike Puccio, cooing his California repartee. Mocko Man's eternal smirk. Ross' easygoing smile and Pane's eternal optimism.

Well, not everyone. Mike's guitar strumming had faded in the wind. Pat's boyish grin was forever lost. Wad's cutting humor could not be found and Hippie no longer would share with us *his Frisco wisdom. ...*

✎ *...3:38 a.m., Tuesday, March 30, 1999, home...I stared into* the dark, Spock's words massaging my mind as I recalled the hypnotic words he had implanted into his comrades' heads. In my own mind his words began to fit together the remaining pieces of my life's puzzle.

"The bullets, are unreal, without body. They are illusions, only. Shadows, without substance. They will not, pass through your body, for they do not exist. They, are lies. Falsehoods. Specters without body. They are, to be ignored." *And the bullets could not cause any harm to their bodies!*

*What I have done over the years, is create another reality, a reality full of shadows, illusions, specters. And as I believe my false reality, so do I act, even though it is based on nothing but lies.* But, what I have never grasped was, my continued existence alone was enough to discredit these "bullets" that my adrenaline shot at me during a panic attack: the heart exploding in my chest, my mouth dry as sand, a mind feeling empty as Dorothy's scarecrow, the dizziness, the twitching, the breathlessness, the numbness and on and on and on and on. No way *would* I have survived, *should* I have survived if they, indeed, were real entities.

But they are not. They are mere manifestations caused by an unconscious trigger, an unconscious– *tripwire*– that I stumble over again and again. My subconscious has created this tripwire, a tripwire that, perhaps, my subconscious believes I *should* have run into so long ago in Dragon Valley– instead of Hippie.

But how can I avoid that tripwire? Or better yet, how can I disconnect the tripwire from its explosive charge– the white fear that shoots through me during a panic attack. But, I already *know* the warning signs before I trip the wire– just like Hillbilly walking point, checking for signs the VC left to mark a booby-trap. My tripwire leaves its marks, too. The breathing game it plays when I walk. The tenseness in my jaw and neck. The bumps and grinds clueing me it's about to begin. I've known it for years. I just didn't know that I...that I had the power to destroy it, to destroy it with the power of knowledge, of intellect and, yes, Spock...of logic.

To destroy it, then, I must learn to see it for what it is: a lie. I must learn to go on as if it never existed. Gradually, then, I will develop the ability to cut off the attacks with a prearranged word, thought, or even feeling. This will insert the "spoon" into the anxiety tripwire, just like that MA I used to set out, that little piece of plastic that prevented the claymore from going off. *Spock said, "I know the bullets are unreal, therefore they cannot harm me." I will become as sure as Spock, and, without the Vulcan mind meld. MY mind will be tuned...to a Higher Power....✐*

*...Hillbilly dug his* bowl into the large plastic bag, eyeing me with a squint and a nod. "What would *you* do with a rear job, Adams? Thinka all the fun you'd miss."

"Hey, if I get this you couldn't drag me outta there, man. A bed to sleep on every night, hot chow every–"

"I'm puttin' in for one-a-those rear fucking jobs," Pane broke in. "Ain't *even* gonna spend another day in the motherfucking bush."

"Maybe none of us will," Hillbilly predicted. "Seems ta me this whole fuck'n' shebang is winding down. As for me, I'm a look'n' at an early out."

"What about us new guys?" Scott broke in.

"Word is they'll be sending a bunch of ya up ta Da Nang ta pull perimeter guard. That'll be hot chow and a bed, too, doncha–"

"Hey, you fuck'n' potheads!" Retchin stuck a beer-flushed face between the ponchos. "What da fuck you doing in there?"

"Try'n' ta git away from *you* stink'n' juicers," Hillbilly replied. "Somebody git that man a mirror so he can see what a ugly fuck he is."

Wednesday, May 5, 1971, Day 196 / 169 to DEROS
—How ya gonna act—

Sergeant Major Thorn leaned back in his chair. "How many words per minute can you type?"

I tried to sound confident. "Fifty."

"That's good, Adams." –his swivel chair squeaked under his girth– "We'll see what we can do. Expect to hear from us in a few days." The fat sergeant, a dead ringer for Sergeant Garcia in the *Zorro* TV series, began rummaging through his paperwork. "That will be all."

"Thank you." *All right!* I thought as I jumped into the waiting jeep. *This is so sweet!* I sat straighter in my seat on the way back– things were starting to come together. After a brisk morning swim in a high sea, I'd learned that I, along with several others in my platoon, had been promoted to specialist four. It meant only a slight increase in pay, but the status of getting "private" out of your rank was a big plus. Now I was on my way.

A baby blue sky was fading to royal as I stepped into our barrack where a haze of candy-coated smoke was already filtering from under the blanket hootch.

"Well-hell," Ski chortled, "if it ain't the rear fucking echelon man."

"Not yet. But we'll see."

George passed me the roach. "Good stuff tonight, man."

"Should be," Hillbilly bantered. "Came fresh from the perimeter. So what did the *man* say?"

"Just that he'd let me know. Hafta wait and see."

"Well, good luck to ya, 'n' good luck ta *all of us*."...

✎*...11:33 a.m., Saturday, May 1, 1999, home...Shit! The mower* growls impatiently as I stop to consider if I should shut it down to let the wave pass. *No! I've come too far now to put up with this bullshit!* I throw the motor into gear and start another pass into the virgin crop, several weeks overdue for a trim.

My heart races beneath my shirt while my mind spins as quickly as the blade decapitating the overgrown rug. *...just the hormone, adrenaline, doing* *its thing, working through my system…not going to let it win this time…forty-eight years old, not going to fear it, it's now or never, no more waiting till next time, not going to run, going to be a victor, not a victim. Don't be afraid to breathe. Let it in. Transcend. Use my higher mind. I know better. It's going to stop, I know it can't hurt me, like those bullets, passing right through me, don't mean nothing, nothing at all!* My disputations flood my mind, making me lose track of time until I look up; the lower lawn is almost done. *Keep going!*

I move to the top section. My mind now ignores my heart and I relish the gorgeous day. I watch my daughter, Stef and my son, Craig, go one-on-one at the hoop while Lexi and Austin, two of my grandchildren, take turns on the swing. Sheryl is busy planting her spring crop of flowers, the rich soil begging for another chance to *create a miracle.…*✎

Thursday, May 6, 1971, Day 197 / 168 to DEROS
—man from Mars—

"Be there in a minute, Scott." I passed a twenty through the fence.

"You make numba one deal, GI." The boy handed me four plastic bags of the greenish-brown weed. He took a long drag on his American cigarette. "That bookoo good dew. You like."

"You bring more tomorrow? Someone will meet you here."

"No sweat, GI. I bring bookoo tomorrow. You see."

I stuffed the contraband into my fatigue jacket and hurried to join the detail crew, working on reinforcing the concertina wire on Chu Lai's southern perimeter.

"Ya get it?" Scott asked while helping George lift another roll of wire off the back of a deuce and a-half.

I lifted one of my pocket flaps enough to reveal a plastic bag. "Four of 'em."

\*        \*        \*

"So. Let me get this straight. You quit *school* to join the army?"

Scott caught himself as he stumbled on a piece of driftwood in the soft sand. "Sounds pretty dumb, huh? But it was something I had to do. Like it was my duty, you know."

"Pretty gutsy, man."

"What a night!" –Scott looked into the starlit sky– "This dew is good shit."

"Yeah. Beautiful." We walked in silence for a few minutes, our thoughts drifting with the hissing black surf.

"It won't be long now," I said.

"Waddya mean?"

"I mean, like, in a day or two…that'll be it. Just like at the RC. Like, we stand in formation and, they call out our names and…that's it. Gone. Over."

"Sucks."

"First Basic, then AIT. How many times does the Ar–"

Scott stops dead and grabs my arm. "Heyyyy…what's that?"

"What's what?"

Scott points into the blackness. "That."

A tinge of fear pricks the nap of my neck. "What? Where?"

"It's a…a…man. A little man."

"Where?"

"Right there, man. He's…green. You see 'im? He's right there."

I see nothing but shore brush swaying in the night breeze. I nod. "Yeaaah, no sweat, man. He ain't gonna hurt nothing. Maybe we should head back."

"You see 'im, doncha, Bob?"

"Yeah, man, but he ain't gonna hurt no one. He's looks like a pretty friendly guy to me."

"No he don't. Look at his eyes."

"Let's go, Scott." I pulled on his arm.

"Yeah, yeah, yeah. Let's get outta here. Let's run."

"Hey…" –I looked over my shoulder at the empty *beach*– "…*why not?*"…

✎…*7:11 p.m., Monday, May 8, 2000, home…I brushed the* dust from the tire. *90 p.s.i.* The small air compressor clattered as I studied the aging Spitfire Triumph 12 speed. Its chipped, scratched and faded red coat of paint had seen better days. Much better. Now yellow pollen from the silver maple coated most of the frame; dead leaves, dried mud and spider webs covered the rest. Buried in the garage, it had sat unused since the sweeter days before I had axed my Schwinn. *Maybe I should wipe it down first.* I capped the valve stem. *No. Let it be…it's just like me now.*

Turning the bike toward the road, I mounted the seat, took in a slow breath and coasted down the driveway. Turning left, I gingerly pcddled to the top of our hill, checking my breathing as I entered territory now abandoned for two years. *I'll just go a couple blocks and see how it goes, okay?* The road took me down and up another shallow hill, my mind controlling my breathing while I pumped up the far side. A level stretch lay ahead, three blocks of manicured homes typical of the river bluff neighborhood. Gigantic white oaks framed the avenue, now alive with the rebirth of spring, their emerging leaves blanketing the hill with velvet splendor. *God, it's been so long. I'd forgotten how beautiful the world is from the seat of a bike.* Soon the road gave way to a larger hill that bordered the water towers, the hill that had always marked the spot where my heart would kick in. *Turn around? Maybe I should. Make it simple this first time.* Several kids raced by me on their dirt bikes, passing me a bored glance. *No! I'm gonna keep going.* I glided down the hill, coasted through the saddle, then pumped up the far side. *Ain't so bad, ain't so bad.* Making the rise, the driveway of no return loomed ahead, but soon faded as my bike coasted by.

With each block my confidence increased. I made Seventh Street, passed my old safe spot by the power pole and headed into the neighborhoods. I peddled past homes and people my eyes had not seen for so long, catching glimpses of life: a man washing his car, two small girls racing their big wheels, several young boys jumping a plywood ramp on skateboards, a father and his young daughter jogging on the sidewalk, everyone unaware that what they were doing were the things I dreamed of– that made life worthwhile. *It's all so new! It's all so fantastic!* My mind grabbed a front row seat behind my eyes, craving to behold all before me as my body sucked in life like a vacuum cleaner, inebriated in the *experience of participation....*

✏ *...5:14 p.m., Friday, May 12, 2000, East Moline...I squeeze my* deflating back tire. *Shit! Shit! Shit!* Panic kicks my heart into high. *What am I gonna do? If I hurry, my heart might explode. If I don't, I'll be walking this thing home and then....* I start back fast as I dare, risking the faster pace than the unacceptable alternative of being stuck over a mile from my safe spot with a flat tire and no courage. *What happened? Monday I was doing so good, not a skipped beat or nothing! Now...?*

The road passes beneath me as I check my pulse and tire every minute, calculating what speed I have to maintain to beat the leaking tire home. *Did you plan this, God? What are you trying to do, kill me? Trick me to get out here, only to make me hurry back?*

A half-mile from home my panic deepens; the "HILL" looms ahead. *Okay, God* –the hill I had dreaded for ten years– *go ahead* –the hill I doubted I would make to the top alive– *take me out if you want!* I coast to the bottom, through the saddle and start up the far side. I force my legs to keep moving. *Make it* –I press harder– *hafta make it* –harder– *hafta...wha...?* The top comes and goes. My heart stops racing. Instead it downshifts into the string of ragged PVC's that signals recovery. *What...? I should be dead....*

✎ *...4:22 p.m., Monday, May 15, 2000, home...This is it.* I coasted down my drive with a fresh innertube in place. It would be so nice just to enjoy a pleasant, trouble-free ride. But Friday something had happened and I knew I had to put it to the test. I had always known it. But I never had the courage, the confidence, the stark raving mad lunacy to try it.

Down the shallow hill and up the other side. *Not bad...but, not bad enough.* Up the HILL, around the corner, across Seventh Street. *Not yet.* Along the avenue where the kids were jumping the ramps. *Almost ready. I feel it coming.* Past where the man had run with his daughter. *Come on, come on...Now!* and my heart falls into my trap, hitting *my* tripwire as it begins to race inside of me. *Good. That's good, heart. Now let's see what you're made of. Okay...mind-body-soul...let's go.*

I push faster. My heart speeds. I press faster, refusing to play the life and death game my mind throws at me. Why not? This is my last stand. There is no other way. This weekend had been like all the rest. Walking on thin ice, tiptoeing around my precious little heart and my delicate psyche. So why stop? Better to go down fighting than die like a scared rabbit.

I round the curve and continue another three blocks before turning into a cold wind that fights to impede my pilgrimage. *I'm not stopping! I'm not playing your goddamn game no more! Don't be afraid to breathe...just, let it go!*

My legs pump harder. I cross Thirtieth Avenue and speed through the neighborhoods to *Hardees*, my last safe spot. Coasting past the drive-through window, I eye Kennedy Drive and beyond, the GREAT BARRIER of the city limits.

*Do I keep going?*

*How much do I want it? Enough to forget the stress, forget the breathing, forget the stupid rules I've nailed myself down with for so long? Enough to let my body enjoy this beautiful day, the wind caressing this fantastic body God has blessed me with, to glean all the things in life I've been dying to experience for over ten years?*

*Or return to my prison?*

My heart races as I break through the invisible wall of the city limits, races from intense exercise as the fear and adrenaline melt away. *I've always known it would be like this.* "Well, *here it is!*" ...✎

Friday, May 7, 1971, Day 198 / 167 to DEROS
—party time—

My dusty boots fell with a thud beside my bunk. Reaching up to pull myself onto the bunk, I noticed a large manila envelope lying on top of my poncho liner.

"Back so soon?"  Yoss was reading one of his letters– "It's only eleven."

"Got done early. What's this?"

"Open it and see."

I pulled out an official looking document. "Air Medal award?"

"Yeah, Topp passed them out to most of us this morning."

"Cool," I said as I slid out a blue and gold ribbon. Attached below it and embossed in a circle of shiny brass was a soaring eagle gripping a golden bolt of lightning in its claws.

"Back so soon?" Ski said, coming through the front door. "Get the fence done?" he asked with a wink.

"All's well on the southern front," I answered, reaching into my pocket to reveal the top of a plastic bag. "Well, think I'm gonna crash. Wake me up when the fun begins, okay?"

"No sweat, your blanket's the roof anyway."

*        *        *

"Just about got it." –Scott held his head steady as I shaded in his wavy brown hair– "Okay," I said, turning the sketchpad around.

"Hey, man, that's really good. So I can send it to my girl?"

"Nope. I'm keeping this one. Tomorrow I'll do one you can keep."

"What about me?" George asked.

"What? Draw your ugly mug? I'm still gonna getcha for that stunt you pulled."

George crossed his eyes. "You mean this?"

382

"Hold it right there so I can sketch that."

"Send that to his mama," Puccio laughed, "She probably won't even notice."

Outside of our blanket hootch Retchin and Blondie were stomping up and down the aisle, shouting obscenities about having no ice to cool their brew.

"SHUT UP OUT THERE!" Hillbilly shouted as he stuck his head out of the poncho liner. "If ya ain't got eny gawdamn ice, why doncha go pull some outta Topp's ass."

Blondie stopped, swaying as he pondered the suggestion. "That's not a bad fucking idea, Hillbilly. Come on, Retchin, let's go pull some fucking ice outta Topp's ass."

### Saturday, May 8, 1971, Day 199 / 166 to DEROS
### —the band—

LT pushed the thumbtack into the cork on the small bulletin board by the front door. "Here it is, boys, today's work roster."

"For Christ sake, LT," Blondie complained, "they're working us to death, man. I just got off bunker guard an hour ago."

"Yeah," Hillbilly interjected, "had ta sleep on a cot 'stead of a bunk."

LT called out my name and handed me three letters, one of them with "*United States Army*" printed in the corner.

"I got it! Nelson. Yoss. I got it. I'll be working for 'HHC Band & Support Company', as a clerk typist."

"Band?" –Ski grabbed my letter– "You mean like horns and drums and shit? Says you're assigned to S-4. Whoa, that's the big boys."

Nelson held out his hand. "Congratulations, Bob. Good luck to ya."

"Party tonight?" George offered from his bunk. "We gotta celebrate this, man."

"Guess that depends on this fuck'n' roster." –Hillbilly scanned it– "Shit, Adams, ya got bunker guard tonight, starting at 2100."

"How ya gonna act?" Pane said. "The man can't even celebrate a rear job."

"*I'll* celebrate it for him," Mocko said. "I'll probably be getting a rear job in a few days, anyway."

Blondie paused while opening one of his letters. "The only rear job you'd ever get is peeling potatoes."

"Peel this," Mocko gestured.

It was a day in the clouds. Puccio, Scott, Ski and I spent the rest of the morning in the cool surf. George, hating the water as much as my old friend, Bill Andrews, opted to sunbathe on the long stretch of sand. After half-an-hour of diving into the surf, I swam to quieter waters to drift on the surface. *Could it be true?* A cloud passing in front of the sun was unable to fade the glow on my face. *My God, the letter says it is! No more bush, no more.... Just think...sleeping in a real bed every night, every single night...eating real food every single day!* I looked at Ski, floating near by with just his head and feet exposed. *What about these guys? Where they gonna go? We've been together a lifetime and now it's all going to end...just-like-that. The best friends I ever had....*

✎ *...9:43 a.m., Sunday, September 9, 2001, Julie's Restaurant, Albany, Illinois...A towboat chugged* up river, the dissipating heat from the massive triple stacks smudging the yellowing leaves beyond on Beaver Island. The aroma of thick country bacon turned my head toward a waitress bringing my breakfast of eggs, bacon, hash browns and wheat toast.

"Will there be anything else, sir?"

"Looks great, thanks."

I munched on a slice of bacon, returning my gaze to the autumn scene beyond the large picture window overlooking the Mississippi River. *Thank you, God*, I thought, recalling the last few weeks. *It's a dream come true...I'M RUNNING AGAIN! A few months ago I never woulda believed it! It's like my body has re-awakened, recalling the old ways, the breathing, the steady gate, keeping my hips level and everything going forward. Forward. Now I know everything IS going forward. Because it's over. I'm through it. Alas, I am through the dark years.*

I dug into my meal, savoring the restaurant's small-town atmosphere. Most of the patrons were locals, out for Sunday repast, to share both good and bad times to acquaintances around them.

*So what, no, WHY...why did it finally go away? Okay, let's take this one step at a time.* I paused to thank my waitress for refilling my coffee cup. *I think it started after getting back from the Hypack conference in New Orleans. Last January, yeah.* I stirred some cream into my coffee and took a sip. *That's good, that's good. That's when I decided to get back to my high school weight of 165. Somehow that started it all. Four months of Slim Fast and suffering! Two pounds a week, eight pounds a month, four months, that's 32 pounds, from 185 to 165 to 153. Then another five for a weigh-in of 148. Man, it feels good. Yep, that started it. By May I felt younger, more confident. Maybe it was because the dieting was something I could control...could see a tangible day-by-day change. Then there was this summer's trip to Yellowstone. Hiking up the side of that mountain, five hundred feet of switchbacks to Mystic Falls.*

*No...it's more than all of these. It's a combination of ALL of the events since I began fighting this thing and knocking it down, one peg at a time. Yes...it was a total life change. But, you know,* I speculated as I sipped my coffee, *if I had to pick one event that I could say finally destroyed it, it would have to be that day last month when I faced down my fear by gritting out my first run in more that a decade....*

✏ *...5:34 p.m., Sunday, August 12, 2001, Ben Butterworth Parkway, Moline, Illinois...The air chugged* though my lungs as I maintained a brisk walk, now passing the four mile mark. To my left, the Mississippi shimmered in the late afternoon sun, sending refreshing gusts across my bare chest as I reminisced the past few days. I had just returned from a trip with my parents and brother on our annual sojourn to Winfield, Missouri. It was good to visit old friends and relatives, especially a long visit with my best friend, Jim Dobson. He had taken us to St. Louis' Botanical Gardens, which my folks thoroughly enjoyed.

The shrill screams of two gulls fighting over a slice of bread divert my attention. *This walk feels so good. Why not...why not just...do it! My body will remember!* I veer toward a drinking fountain, my breathing free and easy. Downing a generous gulp, I throw water on my face and torso and begin a slow and steady jog. It is difficult. So different from the walking pace I had become accustomed to for more than ten years. The bouncing motion jars my body. I fight to breathe. By the time I cover a few hundred feet I am considering returning to a walk. *My body will remember, it's got to remember!* I cover another hundred feet. Thigh and calf muscles already ache from the unnatural gait. *This is no good, I don't think I can–*

"Hey, there, mind if I run with you?" A young lady who is standing alongside the walkway jumps in beside me. "You seem to be going just the right pace for me."

*I can't run with another person!* "Man, I'm barely moving."

"That's what I mean; I'm trying to get back in shape." –She keeps on– "Just got out of an *ugly* divorce and I need to drop twenty pounds. So I thought this'd be a good place to start."

*I don't know if I can do this!* I try to sound like I'm not out of breath. "I've lost forty-five pounds since January."

"Wow, how'd you do it?"

"Slim Fast…not eating…exercise…and torturous nights. Laying there with my stomach screaming in agony. It wasn't much fun."

"I bet. So you come here often?"

"'Bout every day this time."

"Maybe we can train together. I used to run track in college. Coach had us tape our thumbs to our thighs to keep us from swinging our arms. Arms shouldn't hardly move–"

"Mind if we walk for a minute. I need to catch my breath. This is my first attempt at running in more than ten years."

"Ten years? What was wrong?"

"Knees were shot," I say, slowing. My legs throb as I struggle for air through burning lungs. "So thought today would be a good day to start over."

"Me, too. By the way," –she extended her hand– "my name is Valerie."

"Bob," I say, taking her hand. "So, Valerie, are you from around here?"

"Moline. Work as a nurse at Trinity's emergency trauma unit."

"Wow. How do you stand working with trauma victims?"

"I love it. All the blood and guts…doesn't bother me a bit."

"You're kidding. You would've made a great combat nurse in Nam."

"No way. There's a big difference having to work on badly wounded soldiers." –she eyes me– "You ready to start again?"

We pick up the pace, my breathing sporadic, my legs shaking. *Please, please, whatever you do, do NOT die out here. This is so stupid. You can do this, man, you can DO THIS! You WILL do this!*

"So you were in Vietnam?"

I force myself to regain my composure. "Yeah." –I draw my first full breath, and my confidence increases– "I was a combat infantryman."

"I can't image how awful it must've been."

"I got through it. You know, Valerie, it makes you appreciate every second you're alive." –I smiled– "And I am so glad *to be alive!*"…✐

*     *     *

*...I leave the* Head's Last Stand and walk to the fringe of the beach to wait for my ride to bunker guard. The moon adds its sparkle to my shadow as I watch the gentle surf lap the shore, reminding me of the eternal Rock, solid and immutable. The faint rattle of laughter turns my head and my gaze rests on a yellow glow emanating through the barrack windows like the laughing eyes of a jack-o'-lantern. *I feel just like after my first mission.* I turn toward the fresh breeze grazing over the waters. *Shaving after that first wonderful shower, looking into the night, listening to the crickets chirp their song of life.* My gaze rise to the stars, hanging in the heavens like icicles in the moist night. *And now, here I am, through the wilderness, safe and sound.*

I hold my wrist to the moonlight. *Eight forty-five...jeep will be here soon.* I move to where the surf massages the sand hard and flat, face inland and stop. Tensing my body, I hold my arms in front of me. *This is for you...Hippie, for you...Moreno, for you...Pat, for you...Wad, my friend. And, this is for me...for a safe return home.* Crouching low, I spring into a perfect back flip.

# EPILOGUE

✎...*Sunday, December 07, 2005, Kofa National Wildlife Refuge, Arizona...The horizon stretches* in front of me forever. Ahead is my destination, Signal Peak, 4,877 feet of stony brilliance. Behind me I've left my Ford pickup camper in a small crook on the lee side of a boulder-strewn hill. The afternoon is warm for the middle of December, but that's okay. I'd been looking forward to this run all week to clear out the cobwebs and reflect on the last couple of weeks. Beneath my feet the rocky terrain crunches to my brisk gait as I bob between cracks and crannies lest a rattler or scorpion or other desert critter tries to take a chomp out of me. The desert floor is combed with dry washes falling from a nearby mesa that plunge me into sliding sprints down one side and clawing scrambles up the other before deciding whether to break left or break right to follow the relative flat top to the next wash. *God the colors! God the day!* I glance over my shoulder at the towering far away hump rising from the southern landscape. *Castle Dome Peak. To think I scaled that sucker, and then in July conquered twelve thousand plus Mount Charleston up by Vegas.* An abrupt skidding stop. Veer left to dodge a cholla. Check the next wash. Left? Right? Between the boulders, a rush to the bottom. *Wide and flat...follow this a spell.* Drop-off ahead, jump it and dash for the top.

*There!* Signal Peak springs from the horizon and grabs all of my senses. *Yeah! This is what it's all about!* A quick adjustment, a twist to the right, a sharp turn and a leap over a barrel cactus I race for the *far blue horizon...*✎

# MY LIFE IN A TATTOO

In February of 2005 I drove one of Chicago's premier tattoo parlors, "The Jade Dragon," and employed the awesome talent of an artist I only know as "Sam" to ink a design on my back that I had worked on for nearly six months. Below is its interpretation.

The sun: The 7th element of life; giver of all earthly things. My nirvana.

The 6 points leading to the sun:
➢ Element 1– my formative years, birth through the time that I was drafted into the Army at age 19.
➢ Element 2– my Vietnam tour of duty, which matured me into the man I am now.
➢ Element 3– post-Vietnam through age 30, a time of peace, laced with undercurrents of upcoming turmoil.
➢ Element 4– a period of tribulation, age 30 through 50, 20 years of struggling with my dragon, the focal point of my tattoo. The dragon rose from the ashes of my Vietnam experience, and it became a force of darkness that was determined to destroy me and all that I have become.
➢ Element 5– my current life. The dragon slain, it now lies submissive on my back, out of sight except when I choose to see it. I am at peace with myself and with all I see, want, or know.
➢ Element 6– this is still unclear to me, but I am sure that it is a period of distress, whether the time factor will be measured by years, months, or even days I do not know. But, with my learned presence of mind, I know I shall see it through.
➢ The 7th element, the nirvana, those last few moments when those fortunate enough may look back to view life in all of its splendor, and to the glory of what lies ahead, that final march into the sun.

Below my dragon is an array of lightening, extruding towards the zenith. These are those sudden events in life that comes as bolts of lightening: some good, some evil.

The eye of Ra, also known as the eye of Horus, takes its place as the tattoo's centerpiece. The right eye of Horus represents the sun, and is associated with the Sun God Ra. It was believed to have healing and protective power.

This brings me to the lower portion of the tattoo. At first glance it seems to be just a tribal design to fill in the lower back. Not so. It is my perception of the embodiment of fear, that *monster* that controlled me for 13 years, August of 1988 through August of 2001. This was the time in which the after-shocks of the Vietnam War shook my mind, body and soul to the core. Look closely, and you'll find that it consists of 13 separate parts, each representing a year in which I was plagued with PTSD. Imprisoned between the monster's horns is my heart, frozen with fear. It took all that I am and all that I have become to free myself from its powerful lies. *But I did it*, and now it, as the dragon, bends to *my* whims.

Robert Adams

# Glossary of Military Terms and Slang from the Vietnam War

**201 file**: a U.S. Army personnel file.

**AIT**: Advanced Individual Training. Specialized training taken after Basic Training, also referred to as Advanced Infantry Training.

**AK-47**: Soviet-manufactured Kalashnikov semi-automatic and fully automatic combat assault rifle, basic weapon of the Communist forces.

**AO**: Area of Operations.

**ARVN**: Army of the Republic of South Vietnam.

**banana clip**: crescent-shaped ammo magazine, capable of housing 30 rounds, standard on the AK-47 assault rifle, and later on the M-16.

**bandoleer**: cloth belt worn over the shoulder and across the chest, with pockets for carrying six M-16 magazines.

**battalion**: a military unit composed of a headquarters and two or more companies, batteries, or similar units.

**brigade**: During the Vietnam War, a division was organized into three brigades, with each brigade commanded by a colonel. A division consists of approximately 20,000 people. There were also separate infantry brigades functioning in the Vietnam War. The 11th, 196th, and 198th Infantry Brigades fought in the war until 1967, when they were brought together to reconstitute the Americal Division, or the 23rd Infantry.

**CA**: Combat Assault. The term is used to describe dropping troops from a helicopter into a LZ (Landing Zone).

**CE**: Combat Extraction. Removing troops by helicopter from a LZ.

**Chinook**: CH-47 cargo helicopter, nicknamed "shithook".

**CIB**: Combat Infantry Badge.

**CP**: Command Post. Either one of a company's four platoons that provides mortar support, or the platoon leader's hootch, located in the center of a NDP.

**CQ**: Charge of Quarters. An officer or enlisted personnel officially in charge of a unit headquarters.

**DET CORD**: Detonating Cord. An instantaneous fuse (transmitting at 25,000 feet per second) in the form of a long, thin, flexible tube loaded with explosive. Used to obtain the simultaneous explosion from widely-spaced demolitions, such as multiple claymores. Also used to fell trees by wrapping 3 turns per foot of tree diameter.

**dew**: marijuana.

**dust-off**: medical evacuation by helicopter.

**E-1**: private, **E-2**: private second class, **E-3**: private first class,

**E-4**: specialist, **E-6**: staff sergeant.

**Eleven Bravo** (11-B): the MOS (Military Occupational Specialty) of an infantryman.

**Freedom Bird**: the plane that took soldiers from Vietnam back to the World.

free-fire zone: the area designated in which the American army was allowed to fire first and ask questions later.

**Grunt**: combat infantryman.

**gunship**: armed helicopter.

**halozone tablet**: used to purify drinking water obtained from streams.

**HE**: High Explosives.

**Higher-Higher**: commanding officer(s) who ran the show in the bush from the safety of the rear.

**hot LZ**: a Landing Zone under enemy fire.

**Huey**: nickname for the Bell UH-1 series helicopters.

**in-country**: Vietnam.

**Ky Tra Valley**: (kee traw) Large mountainous area, located in the I Corps' southern AO.

**klick**: kilometer. 1,000 meters, or approximately 3,300 feet.

**Lima Charlie**: Loud and Clear. Term used during radio communications.

**LZ**: Landing Zone.

**M-16**: the standard U.S. military rifle used in Vietnam from 1966 on, successor to the M-14.

**M-60**: the standard lightweight machine gun used by U.S. forces in Vietnam.

**M-79**: single-barreled, break-action grenade launcher, which fired 40mm projectiles, nicknamed the "Blooper".

**mad minute**: a weapons free-fire practice and test session.

**marker round**: first round (smoke) fired by mortars or artillery, used to adjust the following rounds onto the target.

**medivac**: medical evacuation from the field by helicopter.

**mortar**: a muzzle-loading cannon with a short tube in relation to its caliber that throws projectiles with low muzzle velocity at high angles.

**MOS**: Military Occupational Specialty.

**MPC**: Military Payment Certificates. The military printed its own money, and, to prevent black marketeering the script was changed periodically without notice. MPC's were decorated with military themes, or perhaps images of Vietnamese peasants. During my tour in 1970-71 the "monopoly" money carried images of the American frontier, which led many villagers to believe that we still lived in the land of cowboys and Indians.

**napalm**: a jellied petroleum substance which burns fiercely, and is used as a weapon against personnel.

**number one**: the best.

**number ten**: the worst.

**NDP**: Night Defense Position.

**NVA**: North Vietnamese Army.

**over-under**: M-203, 40mm grenade launcher attached below an M-16. A lightweight, compact, breech loading, pump action, single shot launcher.

**P-38**: a tiny collapsible can opener.

**PFC**: Private First Class.

**PRC-25** (Prick 25): Portable Radio Communications. Model 25, a back-packed FM receiver-transmitter used for short-distance communications.

**Puff the Magic Dragon**: a large propeller-driven aircraft with a Minigun mounted in the door, capable of firing 6,000 rounds per minute. Also used to refer to gunship helicopters equipped with Miniguns.

**punji stakes**: sharpened bamboo sticks used in a primitive but effective pit trap; they were often smeared with excrement to cause infection.

**PX**: Post Exchange. Military store.

**R&R**: Rest & Recreation. Typically, a seven-day vacation taken during a one-year duty tour in Vietnam. Out-of-country R&R was in Bangkok, Hawaii, Tokyo, Australia, Hong Kong, Manila, Penang, Taipei, Kuala Lampur or Singapore. In-country R&R locations were at Vung Tau, Cam Rahn Bay or China Beach.

**RC**: Replacement Center. Where incoming troops were dispersed to their permanent duty stations.

**RS**: Re-Supply.

**RVN**: Republic of South Vietnam.

**S-3**: Operations.

**sit-rep**: situation report.

**six-by**: a large flat-bed truck usually with wooden slat sides enclosing the bed and sometimes with a canvas top, used for carrying men or supplies.

**skycrane**: huge double-engine helicopter (C-54) used for lifting and transporting heavy equipment.

**sky**: sky up, to go from one place to another, to flee or leave suddenly.

**TA-50**: individual soldier's standard issue of combat clothing and equipment.

**Topp**: a Top Sergeant (E-10 Master Sergeant).

**World**, the: America, home.

## Glossary of Vietnamese Terms and Slang

**bac-si**: doctor, also used to refer to medic in the U.S. Army.

**bac si de**: home-brewed rice whiskey.

**bic**: pronounced be-uk, Vietnamese term for "understand".

**bookoo**: bastardized French, from beaucoup, meaning "much" or "many".

**boom-boom**: "sex short time" with a prostitute, typical cost: $3-$5.

**caca dau**: pronounced "crocodile" by GI's, Vietnamese phrase for, "I'll kill you".

**didi** (didiing, didied): pronouced "dee-dee", a slang word for the Vietnamese word di, meaning "to leave" or "to go".

**didi mau**: pronounced "dee-dee ma-oh", Vietnamese slang for "go quickly".

**dinky dau**: pronounced "dinky-dow", a slang word for "to be crazy".

**du mi ami**: English approximation of the Vietnamese du ma, meaning literally "fuck mother".

**khong biet**: pronounced "no be-uk", Vietnamese for "I don't know" or "I don't understand".

**lai dai**: pronounced "lie die", meaning "Bring to me" or "Come to me".

**Tet**: Buddhist lunar New Year, Buddha's birthday.

**tee-tee**: pidgin for "very small".

Made in United States
Orlando, FL
30 September 2023

37455992R00245